The Taiwan Voter

The Taiwan Voter examines the critical role that ethnic and national identities play in politics, illustrated by the case of Taiwan. That country's elections often raise international tensions, and they have sometimes led to military demonstrations by China, as in the 1995–96 Taiwan Strait Crisis. Yet no scholarly books have examined the ways in which Taiwan's voters make their electoral choices in such a dangerous environment. Critiquing the conventional interpretation of politics as an ideological battle between liberals and conservatives, *The Taiwan Voter* demonstrates that in Taiwan the party system and the voters' response to it are instead shaped by one powerful determinant of national identity—the China factor. The book also takes up Taiwan's voter turnout, "pocketbook voting," and the effects of the new electoral system adopted in 2004.

Taiwan's electoral politics draws international scholarly interest because of the prominence of ethnic and national identification in its politics. Of course, identities matter almost everywhere. In most countries, though, the many tangled strands of competing identities present a daunting challenge for scholarly analysis. Taiwan, by contrast, is a country where the cleavages are both powerful and limited in number, so that the logic of the interrelationships among issues, partisanship, and identity are particularly clear. In this book, Christopher H. Achen and T. Y. Wang bring together experts on Taiwan to investigate the ways in which social identities, policy views, and partisan preferences intersect and influence each other. These novel findings have wide applicability to other countries, and thus they will be of interest to a broad range of social scientists interested in identity politics.

Christopher H. Achen is Professor of Politics and Roger Williams Straus Professor of Social Sciences at Princeton University.

T. Y. Wang is Professor of Politics and Government at Illinois State University.

NEW COMPARATIVE POLITICS

Series Editor	Michael Laver, New York University
Editorial Board	Ken Benoit, Trinity College, Dublin
	Gary Cox, Stanford University
	Simon Hix, London School of Economics
	John Huber, Columbia University
	Herbert Kitschelt, Duke University
	G. Bingham Powell, University of Rochester
	Kaare Strøm, University of California, San Diego
	George Tsebelis, University of Michigan
	Leonard Wantchekon, Princeton University

The New Comparative Politics series brings together cutting-edge work on social conflict, political economy, and institutional development. Whatever its substantive focus, each book in the series builds on solid theoretical foundations; uses rigorous empirical analysis; and deals with timely, politically relevant questions.

Curbing Bailouts: Bank Crises and Democratic Accountability in Comparative Perspective
  Guillermo Rosas

The Madisonian Turn: Political Parties and Parliamentary Democracy in Nordic Europe
  Edited by Torbjörn Bergman and Kaare Strøm

Political Survival of Small Parties in Europe
  Jae-Jae Spoon

Veto Power: Institutional Design in the European Union
  Jonathan B. Slapin

Democracy, Dictatorship, and Term Limits
  Alexander Baturo

Democracy, Electoral Systems, and Judicial Empowerment in Developing Countries
  Vineeta Yadav and Bumba Mukherjee

The Latin American Voter: Pursuing Representation and Accountability in Challenging Contexts
  Edited by Ryan E. Carlin, Matthew M. Singer, and Elizabeth J. Zechmeister

The European Union and the Rise of Regionalist Parties
  Seth K. Jolly

Gender Quotas and Democratic Participation: Recruiting Candidates for Elective Offices in Germany
  Louise K. Davidson-Schmich

Mixed-Member Electoral Systems in Constitutional Context: Taiwan, Japan, and Beyond
  Edited by Nathan F. Batto, Chi Huang, Alexander C. Tan, and Gary W. Cox

The Taiwan Voter
  Edited by Christopher H. Achen and T. Y. Wang

The Taiwan Voter

Christopher H. Achen
and T. Y. Wang, editors

University of Michigan Press
Ann Arbor

Published in the United States of America by the
University of Michigan Press
Manufactured in the United States of America
⊚ Printed on acid-free paper

2020   2019   2018   2017   4   3   2   1

A CIP catalog record for this book is available from the British Library.

Library of Congress Cataloging-in-Publication data has been applied for.

ISBN: 978-0-472-07353-5 (hardcover : alk paper)
ISBN: 978-0-472-05353-7 (paperback : alk paper)
ISBN: 978-0-472-12303-2 (ebook)
ISBN: 978-0-472-12303-2 (Open Access)

doi: http://dx.doi.org/10.3998/ mpub.9375036

The Open Access edition was funded by the Top University Project of National Chengchi University, made possible by a grant from Taiwan's Ministry of Education.

Contents

Preface

This book began at a conference in Taipei, Taiwan, on March 24, 2013. The Election Study Center of National Chengchi University hosted all the authors for an intense discussion of how a book about the Taiwan voter might be written. (A few contributors were "virtual attendees" via an Internet link.) Preliminary versions of chapters were presented and thoroughly discussed. After additional reviews and revisions, this book was accepted for publication by the University of Michigan Press.

The Election Study Center has provided extensive administrative and financial support to this project from the beginning. The book would have been impossible without the research excellence and professional colleagueship of the members of the Center. Their warm hospitality to each editor on multiple occasions has been a highlight of our professional lives.

A great many people and institutions also helped make *The Taiwan Voter* possible. T. Y. Wang's research sabbatical was funded by the Chiang Ching-kuo Foundation and Taiwan's National Science Council (now called the Ministry of Science and Technology). He also received a Summer Faculty Fellowship from Illinois State University to support this project. A grant to Wang from the Taiwan Foundation for Democracy paid for editing and other expenses of preparing the book for publication review. The Open Access edition was funded by the Top University Project of National Chengchi University, made possible by a grant from Taiwan's Ministry of Education. Princeton University's Politics Department and Illinois State University's Department of Politics and Government also helped with logistical support and research funding.

Larry Bartels, during his time as director of Princeton's Center for the Study of Democratic Politics, hosted a small conference that helped build a foundation for this book. Michele Epstein and Helene Wood provided the administrative support to make the conference successful. We thank all three of them.

Achen remembers with respect and gratitude his former colleague Tang Tsou of the University of Chicago Political Science Department, now deceased, who arranged a first visit to Taiwan. The trip was paid for by Taiwan's Government Information Office, which was then directed by Dr. Shao Yuming. That eye-opening initial encounter with the people of the island led to the professional relationships that have made possible Achen's participation in this project.

The anonymous reviewers for the University of Michigan Press gave us two rounds of thoughtful comments and criticism. The book is much better for their efforts. Gail Schmitt and Carissa L. Tudor provided editing assistance, and we are in their debt as well. We also thank our editors at the University of Michigan Press, Melody Herr and Mary Francis, supported by Danielle Coty, for their enthusiasm about our project and for their encouragement and guidance through the publication process. We have also very much appreciated the unwavering support of the series editor, Mic Laver.

To analyze Taiwan voters' political attitudes and electoral behavior, the contributors to this volume have utilized multiple waves of survey data, aggregate electoral data, and information gathered through focus group interviews, all collected on the island during the past two decades. Most of the data used in this book are taken from Taiwan's Election and Democratization Study (TEDS). This long-running series of representative national samples of Taiwan voters is the gold standard for academic election studies in Asia. The coordinator of the multiyear TEDS project is Chi Huang of the Election Study Center and the Political Science Department at National Chengchi University, Taipei, and the data are managed and distributed by the Election Study Center. More information is available on the TEDS website (http://www.tedsnet.org).

Other data sources for the book include the Taiwan National Security Survey (TNSS), sponsored by the Program in Asian Security Studies under the directorship of Emerson Niou of Duke University, and also a number of individual surveys conducted by the faculty of the Election Study Center, many of whom are contributors to this volume. Focus group interviews conducted by the faculty and staff of the Election Study Center also appear in subsequent chapters. Su-feng Cheng is the principal investigator for those projects.

The Taiwan Voter would have been impossible without all these data, and we very much appreciate the assistance that all these individuals have provided us.

We also owe thanks to a great many students and colleagues for advice and encouragement along the way. Achen is particularly grateful to the other members of the "Gang of Four dinner group," Da-chi Liao, Pei-shan Lee, and Vincent Wang, for their support and inspiration. Wang extends his gratitude to Ali Riaz for his encouragement and friendship through the years.

We are grateful to all those who have helped us. However, our interpretations of the TEDS, the TNSS, and other data are our own. Each author in this volume takes sole responsibility for the remaining errors and misjudgments in what he or she has written.

Most important, the editors thank our wives, Tena Achen and Christine Lee, for their patience with our overseas absences and their tolerance of our frequent lengthy work days while we finished editing this book. Our gratitude for their love goes beyond anything words can say.

CHAPTER I

The Taiwan Voter

An Introduction

Christopher H. Achen and T. Y. Wang

Taiwan's recent history is a remarkable saga. During the two decades from 1970 to 1990, Taiwan underwent dramatic economic change, as its gross domestic product grew at an average rate of 9 percent per year.[1] The economic success rapidly propelled Taiwan into the ranks of the newly industrialized countries. Democratization arrived in the late 1980s, too, with robust electoral competition between the two principal parties. The long-ruling, formerly authoritarian party was beaten at the polls in 2000 and handed over power peacefully, only to return in 2008 in an equally peaceful transition when its opponents lost. A third peaceful transition between parties took place in 2016. An impoverished Asian one-party authoritarian state had become in a few decades a prosperous, vibrant democracy.

The Taiwan success story has generated considerable scholarly interest. The initial studies focused on economic growth—the "Taiwan miracle" (e.g., Chan 1988; Clark 1987, 1989; Wang 2000). In the ensuing decades, scholarly research shifted its focus to Taiwan's political miracle, first the democratization and then the establishment of stable party competition (for example, the chapters collected in Tien 1996). As time has passed, however, Taiwan's domestic political economy has become a more typical example of the stresses, debates, and achievements of a rich democracy. Economic growth and employment, energy policy, the environment, public works, and many other familiar topics are frequent subjects of debate in Taiwan. However, those concerns are not unique to the island.

Taiwan's uniqueness lies elsewhere—in its relationship with China. No other topic or relationship plays so central a role in Taiwan's politics. It structures foreign policy; it structures the political party system; it structures much of how ordinary citizens orient themselves to politics. The fundamental role of "the China factor" will be explicitly or implicitly discussed in many chapters of this book.

In *The Taiwan Voter*, we focus on ordinary citizens' political preferences, attitudes, and choices since the onset of democratization. To study the causes of voting, we take up the conventional "big three"—party identification, issue orientation, and candidate evaluation—since there is a general consensus in political science literature that they exert influential effects on voting (Jacoby 2010). But to those three, we add a fourth—identity. In particular, we look closely at national identity, since it looms so large in Taiwan voting.

Though our concerns are primarily with citizens rather than with elites and institutions, we take note of institutional features of Taiwan democracy that shape the choices presented to its citizens. One chapter is specifically devoted to the recent change in the electoral rules that seems to have put Taiwan on its way to a classic two-party system.[2]

In this volume, we are reporting on one country, but our focus extends well beyond it. The study of Taiwan politics leads rapidly to interesting, sometimes difficult, theoretical puzzles. Why have citizen identities, usually taken as relatively fixed features of people's political lives, evolved so rapidly in Taiwan, while simultaneously one particular identity cleavage centered on "the China factor" has become increasingly consolidated as the most important political division in the country's politics? In the presence of this cleavage, how do Taiwan citizens[3] make their electoral decisions? We intend to go beyond the usual country study to ask questions like these. Implicitly, and sometimes explicitly, this book suggests comparisons with other countries that share one or another of these unusual features of Taiwan's politics, such as Japan, Canada, Ireland, and Israel. More generally, our findings have implications for every country in which national identities have large effects in electoral politics. Thus, we attempt to contribute not only to making sense of Taiwan, but more broadly to the theoretical understanding of democratic elections in general.

Using single-country studies to generate theoretical understanding has a long tradition in political science, and in electoral research in particular. The Columbia studies under Paul Lazarsfeld demonstrated the powerful role of group memberships and loyalties in American electoral decisions (Lazarsfeld, Berelson, and Gaudet 1948; Berelson, Lazarsfeld, and McPhee 1954). Angus Campbell and his Michigan colleagues' seminal work, *The American Voter*, showed how partisan identity shaped not only the vote but also the very way that citizens perceive the political world and form their political opinions (Campbell et al. 1960). David Butler and Donald Stokes's *Political Change in Britain* (1974) traced class conflict in politics, the parental transmission of partisanship, and the importance of local context in determining vote choices. A great many other articles and books, far too numerous to list here, have been devoted to such topics as voter turnout, economic voting, electoral institutions, and strategic voting in particular democratic systems around the world. No one would say of these contributions that they taught us only about the country in which they were carried out.

This point is particularly relevant in East and Southeast Asia, where electoral studies are few and our understanding is thin. It seems to us critically important to build a knowledge base for each democracy of the region. At present, no one could write a competent comparative volume called *The Asian Voter*: when the foundation stones are missing, no structure can be erected.

The problem of too little Asian country knowledge is also visible in some recent important contributions to comparative electoral behavior. For example, Thomassen (2005) compares what is known about electoral behavior across the European democracies. Evans and De Graaf (2013) study how class voting varies across Europe and the Anglo-Saxon countries. Carlin, Singer, and Zechmeister (2015) use the Latin American Public Opinion Project data at Vanderbilt University, among other sources, to show how partisanship, ideology, and economic factors have different force in different countries across Latin America. We are impressed by the depth of scholarship amassed by the many contributors to these edited volumes. But we are equally impressed by how often Taiwan fails to fit the conceptual frameworks they put forward. Of course, none of these three books deals with Asia; their agenda lies elsewhere. But even when Taiwan is explicitly included in the set of countries studied, as in Dalton and Anderson's (2011) comparative investigation of how the institutional and party-system features of each country create a context that shapes how citizens think and act in electoral politics, the fit is odd. Too often, Taiwan is assimilated conceptually to countries with a European-derived culture that it does not share. We go deeper into this topic in chapter 9 and in the concluding chapter 12. For the present, it suffices to say that we make no apologies for focusing on Taiwan. Getting each country right is a prerequisite to reliable comparisons, both within continents and regions and across them.

Thus we intend this volume to join the ranks of similar books on political behavior, such as *The Japanese Voter* (Flanagan et al. 1991) and *The Irish Voter* (Marsh et al. 2008). Like them, this book studies one country, but it does so as part of an international effort to understand electoral behavior in a variety of democratic systems. While we draw primarily on Taiwan's politics as observed in the multiyear nationwide surveys of the Taiwan's Election and Democratization Study (TEDS) and the Taiwan National Security Survey, we aim to speak to those interested in elections everywhere.

The Relationship to China

Taiwan at its closest point is only a little more than 100 miles from the Chinese mainland. Like any small polity next door to a powerful country, Taiwan necessarily pays careful, even obsessive attention to its neighbor. Indeed, Taiwan's politics revolves around the relationship with China. For Taiwan's citizens, the relationship to the mainland is multifaceted. China represents simultaneously a cultural heritage, a security threat, and an economic opportunity.

Cultural Heritage

Taiwan's cultural inheritance from the Chinese mainland is undeniable. Although its first settlers seem to have come from what is now the Philippines and Indonesia, Taiwan's modern history can be traced to the mid-seventeenth century, when residents from the coastal areas of China migrated to the island to escape from the war and devastation on the mainland. In that same period, the Portuguese arrived on the island, which they called "Formosa" ("beautiful"). The Dutch and Spanish also founded settlements. In the Tainan area, the oldest inhabited part of Taiwan, a temple still stands, dedicated to two gods with unmistakable white features. By 1684, however, China's Qing dynasty had driven out the Europeans and established a local government on the island. The Qing maintained at least a nominal administrative relationship with the island for the subsequent two-plus centuries. Like many dynasties before it, the Qing dynasty eventually collapsed under the weight of corruption and administrative failure. During the collapse, and in the wake of the First Sino-Japanese War, Taiwan's sovereignty was ceded to Japan in 1895, beginning another colonial experience, this one lasting half a century.

Although the initial stage of Japanese rule was marked by the island residents' armed resistance, insurrection was soon quelled by the colonial authority's adroit combination of repression, co-optation, and assimilation.

In some respects, the Japanese treated Taiwan as their own province, and they began its modernization. Certainly Taiwan was treated better than most other countries conquered by Japan just before and during World War II. During the colonial period, some Taiwan people adopted Japanese names and became naturalized Japanese citizens.[4] Many young people were drafted and served in the Japanese military during the war.

At the end of the war, Japan unconditionally surrendered to the Allied forces. Taiwan's sovereignty was returned to China, then led by the Nationalist (Kuomintang or KMT) government under Chiang Kai-shek. Chiang and two million of his mainland followers retreated to the island in 1949 after being defeated by the Communist troops on the Chinese mainland. To maintain their claim that they remained the sole legitimate rulers of the mainland, KMT leaders preached "recovering the Chinese mainland" as the sacred national mission. The eventual unification of Taiwan and China was taken as a given.

The Chiang regime also took a series of measures to "re-Sinicize" local residents in order to foster a Chinese identity. A China-centered curriculum was established in schools. Maps of the nation showed all of China, including the mainland, Taiwan, and all areas claimed by China, such as Tibet. Schoolchildren were taught in Mandarin, and their use of local dialects was punished. Ethnic television and radio programs were restricted as well. These measures, combined with the shared culture and languages stemming from the ancestral homeland, led many Taiwan citizens to view China as the principal source of their racial and cultural heritage. In some cases, they saw Taiwan and China as a political unity as well. In one or another sense, they identified as "Chinese" (Wang and Liu 2004). This ensemble of affective and historical ties continues for many Taiwan people to the present day, though increasingly in attenuated form.

Security Threat

The Chiang regime generally encountered a warm welcome from island residents after the KMT forces first arrived on Taiwan in 1945. But the initial enthusiasm of many local residents for returning to the ancestral "motherland" was substantially dampened when they saw the mainland troops sent to take control of the island. Impoverished and poorly educated, many of the soldiers were seen as beggars and thieves, less disciplined and capable than the Japanese they replaced. Nationalist officials in turn viewed the islanders with suspicion due to the half century of Japanese colonial rule. By 1947, the animosity between the KMT government and local residents culminated in the bloody crackdown against Taiwanese elites by Chiang's troops, a tragic event known as the "2–28 Incident" (Kerr 1965; Lai, Myers, and Wei 1991). This outbreak of hostility solidified the perception, especially in the older generation, of the KMT government as simply a new foreign regime and occupying force, this time from China rather than from Portugal or Japan.

While the Chiang regime actively advanced its claim to be the legitimate ruler of China, Beijing's leaders made the same claim, and they attempted to forcibly unify Taiwan with the Chinese mainland. During the 1950s and 1960s, several major battles were fought over Kinmen (also known as Quemoy) and Matsu, two small islands near the mainland but occupied by Taiwan. Although the 1970s saw a shift of Beijing's strategy away from a reliance on the "military liberation" of Taiwan to a wave of "peaceful initiatives," Chinese leaders have refused to renounce the use of force to resolve cross-Strait disputes. To force Taipei into acceptance of its unification formula, known as "one country, two systems," Beijing has isolated Taiwan internationally and has backed its claim to the island with the threat of military action.

As China increasingly won the diplomatic battle on the world stage, Taiwan went through a series of political changes toward democratization since the late 1980s. These included lifting martial law, legalizing political parties, ending restrictions on public assembly and freedom of speech, and the popular election of the president. The pace of democratic reform quickened after the pro-independence Democratic Progressive Party (DPP) was formed in 1986 and became the island's first major opposition party. An atmosphere of political tolerance emerged on the island as opinions different from the "one China" principle were permitted. Blaming President Lee Teng-hui for condoning a Taiwan independence movement on the island, Chinese leaders launched several missiles into the seas around Taiwan in an attempt to influence, first, the 1995 Legislative Yuan election, and then Taiwan's 1996 presidential election. The misguided effort backfired, with most Taiwan observers estimating that Lee's successful reelection effort was aided by the Chinese saber-rattling (Garver 1997; Cooper 1998, chap. 4).

During the 2000 presidential election campaign, Beijing leaders employed the tactic of a "paper missile," a White Paper on cross-Strait relations that promised military intervention if Taiwan moved toward independence. This attempt to disrupt the momentum of the pro-independence candidate, Chen Shui-bian of the DPP, probably backfired again. Contrary to China's expectations, these threats provided Chen with a late boost and a narrow margin of victory. Chen's election was a milestone in Taiwan's political development, and it illumined the sharp contrast with the mainland's political system, as political power was peacefully transferred from one political party to the other on the island for the first time and indeed on any territory where ethnic Chinese rule. While Beijing has subsequently moderated its unsophisticated and ineffective attempts at intimidating Taiwan voters (Tung 2005), especially after the China-friendly Ma Ying-jeou of the KMT was elected president in 2008, it has continued to aim more than a thousand short- and medium-range missiles at the island. As many in the older generation saw the authoritarian KMT as an illegitimate Chinese occupation force, younger generations now often see China under Communist Party rule as an authoritarian and less developed country with an aggressive military posture. In consequence, much of the Taiwan population views China as a threat to their economic prosperity and democratic way of life.

Economic Opportunity

Perhaps surprisingly, cross-Strait economic exchanges have flourished during the past two and a half decades despite tense political and sometime military relations between Beijing and Taipei. Since the ban on contacts between Taiwan and China was lifted by the Taipei government in 1987, economic exchanges between two sides of the Taiwan Strait have increased dramatically. Cross-Strait trade rose from $3.9 billion in 1989 to $31.2 billion in 2000, and further to $102.3 billion in 2007, despite the restrictive policies imposed by Taiwan's pro-independence Chen administration from 2000 to 2008. Taiwan investment in the Chinese mainland also increased, from $421 million in 1991–92, to $2.6 billion in 2000, and to about $10 billion in 2007.[5] Along with these investments, many Taiwanese investors have now relocated to the Chinese mainland.

The trade and investment flow seems unlikely to be slowed by political intervention in the near future. Reversing its predecessor, the Taipei administration under Ma relaxed trade restrictions. Since 2008, the Taipei government has reached more than a dozen accords with Beijing and has also signed the landmark trade deal known as the Economic Cooperation Framework Agreement (ECFA).[6] Nor is trade liberalization likely to be substantially slowed now that the opposition has again taken power in 2016. The pro-independence DPP has always had concerns about Taiwan's increasing economic integration with the Chinese mainland, worrying that expanding cross-Strait exchanges would increase the island's dependence on China and endanger its national security. Yet the DPP leadership increasingly recognizes the importance of the Chinese market to Taiwan's economic growth and prosperity, as demonstrated by the party's ambivalent campaign platform on cross-Strait relations during the 2012 and 2016 presidential elections and by the frequent visits to the Chinese mainland by key DPP politicians.[7] Even for the most anti-China politicians and citizens on Taiwan, the trade and investment opportunities across the Strait in the world's most populous country are too lucrative to ignore. Well-armed, sworn enemies can still do business.

Taiwan thus has a complex and ambivalent relationship with China that is characterized by cultural affinity, security menace, and opportunities for economic prosperity. Precisely because cross-Strait ties are close but unsettled, they have formed the basis of the key political cleavage on the island that has effects on every aspect of Taiwan's politics. In particular, this multifaceted relationship forces island citizens to decide whether they are Chinese, Taiwanese, or both. It also forces them to take a stand on Taiwan's future relations with China—the issue of "unification vs. independence"—also known as the *tongdu* issue. In turn, both these decisions are deeply implicated in voters' partisan identifications.

The Central Political Cleavage in Taiwan

Taiwan is an immigrant society within the Chinese diaspora. The shared language, culture, and ancestral homeland help shape the identities of Taiwan citizens. For a small number, the Chinese identity may preclude any national identification with Taiwan: they follow the KMT's traditional one-country view of China, of which Taiwan is a province. For these citizens, "I'm Chinese" means a great deal, including adherence to the position that there is only one China, that Taiwan is part of China, and that Chinese citizens are subject to the authority of the legitimate rulers of China (who are in Taipei). This view is essentially consistent with Beijing's official position, the sole disagreement being over the location of the legitimate all-China government.

At the other extreme, a Taiwan citizen may say, "I'm Chinese," meaning no more than an Irish-American does when she says proudly on St. Patrick's Day, "I'm Irish," even though her ancestors have been in North America for nearly 200 years and her sole national loyalty is to the United States. She would think it bizarre if Ireland claimed sovereignty over her. In short, among different citizens of immigrant lands like Taiwan or the United States, identification with the country of ancestral origin ranges from deep to superficial, and in some cases may be equivalent to outright rejection.

Indeed, the Allied war on the Axis powers in Europe during World War II was led by a German American, Dwight Eisenhower.

Identities may be central to personality, but even the deepest remain potentially malleable. Unexpected events or changes in an ancestral country's behavior can transform the complex of emotion and historical memory that constitutes national identity. The transformation can go in either direction, as Taiwan's history illustrates. A pan-Taiwanese identity first emerged after the Qing government ceded the island's sovereignty to Japan (Ching 2001). This development was soon impeded by the Japanese colonial authority's comprehensive assimilation policies (Brown 2004; Chu and Lin 2003). Then, after Taiwan's "glorious return" to Chinese rule might have provided an opportunity for the consolidation of a Chinese identity, instead the 2–28 Incident created a deep divide, particularly between the resident Minnan and the newly arrived mainlanders, often creating parallel differences in national and political identity.[8]

As chapter 3 explains, the Minnan/mainlander divide became increasingly blurry with the progression of time. Through politicians' conscious efforts, social contacts among various ethnic groups, interethnic marriages, and the spread of education, understanding, and respect among the various ethnic groups have been improved and ethnic conflict reduced. As a new generation of islanders has matured into adulthood, many have become relatively indifferent to the historical memories that had divided their communities in the past.

Simultaneously, many Taiwan citizens have been increasingly frustrated by the international isolation imposed by the Chinese government. Beijing's international application of its "one China principle" has significantly compressed the island country's international space. Chinese leaders persistently maintain that the Republic of China, the official name of Taiwan, has lost its legitimacy and that Taipei has no legal right to establish diplomatic relations with foreign governments or to participate in any international organizations with statehood as a membership requirement. The growing importance of China in international affairs has led many countries to break relations with Taipei as a prior condition for establishing official ties with Beijing. The number of nations having official relations with Taiwan dropped significantly in the 1970s and 1980s. Throughout the subsequent two decades, only about 30 countries, most of them small, diplomatically recognized Taiwan, and Taipei had membership in just a handful of international governmental organizations.

Taiwan's increasing diplomatic isolation coincided with a period of rapid economic growth and democratization on the island, leaving many in Taiwan with the sense that their lack of standing in the world community was discordant with their economic and political achievements. China was seen not only as a hypothetical military threat but also as a chronic irritant—an alien economic and political force opposed to their interests and self-respect. The Chinese missile tests during 1995–96 and military threats in 2000, both intended to intimidate Taiwan, raised the issue forcefully: Surely, Taiwan people said, no self-respecting country would treat its own citizens that way. Increasingly, the island's citizens began to question the Chinese aspect of their identities. Were they still Chinese, or had they now become just Taiwan people?

Taiwanese identity rose in parallel with sympathy for Taiwan independence. The two attitudes reinforced each other, with powerful implications for Taiwan's politics. The previously unquestionable "sacred mission" of unifying Taiwan with the Chinese mainland during the island's authoritarian era was now reconsidered in the minds of many island citizens. An increasing number of the island residents began to view Taiwan as a separate and independent political entity, not part of China (Wang and Liu 2004). The way was prepared for the pro-independence DPP to become what it had never been previously, a serious contender for political power. The precise causal relationships are not easily sorted out, but the association was clear and powerful: as Taiwan people increasingly abandoned their identity as Chinese, they became ever more likely to support the opposition DPP and the cause of Taiwan independence (Liu and Ho 1999). All these forces, combined with a more moderate DPP campaign platform and a split in the KMT, paved the way for Chen's victory in the 2000 presidential election (Rigger 2001, chaps. 8 and 9).

During the subsequent eight years, the pro-independence DPP government, like the Chiang regime before it, selectively endorsed some aspects of Taiwan's historical memories. To reinforce the idea that the island is a political entity separate from China, the "greater China nationalism" promoted by the KMT authoritarian regime came under severe attack during Chen's administration (Greene 2008). Chen's de-Sinicization measures, along with Beijing's tactics of diplomatic isolation, have had substantial effects on citizens' identity. By the time President Ma took office in 2008, more than half of the island residents were Taiwanese identifiers and very few of them subscribed to the Chinese identity alone. In total, 90 percent of the island residents considered themselves either purely Taiwanese or holders of a dual identity—regarding themselves as both Chinese and Taiwanese. In the view of some observers, the combination of Chinese threat and active governmental attempts to reinforce Taiwan consciousness has made inevitable "the ongoing consolidation of the Taiwanese nation" (Schubert 2008, 111).

The Taiwanese/Chinese divide has now gone beyond individuals' attachment to ethnic groups and has become embedded in different political communities at the national level. The contestation between the two identities is now more than the debate over Taiwan's sovereignty and has become the key political cleavage of the society, commonly known as the issue of "unification vs. independence." While this political cleavage involves the debate over Taiwan's ultimate sovereignty, it also structures opinions about how to interact with a rising China in the meantime. In all these ways, preferences about the island's relationship with the Chinese mainland have been and continue to be the most important issue of the society, while all other cleavages are distinctly secondary. Consequently, Taiwan can be characterized as *a single-issue society*, since the main cleavage affects almost all aspects of the island citizens' political attitudes and behaviors. Most notably, it is reflected in the voters' partisan identifications.

Indeed, Taiwan's political landscape has undergone significant change after the formation of the DPP in 1986. During the ensuing process of rapid democratization, the previous authoritarian system dominated by the KMT was transformed with the emergence of multiple minor political parties as spin-offs from the KMT. After Chen Shui-bian of the DPP was elected president in 2000, Taiwan's multiparty system increasingly moved into two distinctly separate and relatively equal political camps—the Pan-Blue Alliance and the Pan-Green Alliance, with the KMT and the DPP being the two leading parties in each, respectively. The Pan-Blue Alliance consists of the KMT, the People First Party (PFP), the New Party (NP) and the Nonpartisan Solidarity Union (NPSU), while the Pan-Green Alliance includes the currently ruling DPP and the Taiwan Solidarity Union (TSU). Even though none of the political parties advocates the island's immediate unification with China, Taiwan voters perceive the two political alliances as representing opposite positions on the issue of unification/independence. The Pan-Blue Alliance is perceived as adopting policies that move in a direction toward Taiwan's eventual unification with China, whereas the Pan-Green Alliance is seen as making plans that would lead to the island's ultimate independence. Thus, chapter 4 shows that citizens who hold a strong Taiwanese identity tend to espouse the island's de jure independence and provide electoral support for the Pan-Green Alliance, while those who continue to recognize the Chinese heritage as a part of their identity are more likely to back the Pan-Blue candidates.

As Lipset and Rokkan's (1967) "freezing hypothesis" famously claimed half a century ago, party systems become stabilized when they reflect preexisting cleavage structures in the society. Because Taiwan

citizens' partisan identifications notably reflect the most important political cleavage in the society, the island's political landscape has been
increasingly molded into two distinctly separate alliances that are led by
two major political parties. As chapter 10 explains, the 2005 electoral
reform that abandoned the single non-transferable vote (SNTV) electoral rules in favor of the mixed-member majoritarian system (MMM)
has further consolidated Taiwan's two-party system.

While the endogeneity of the key political cleavage and its effects on
Taiwan citizens' political life form a crucial part of our story, we will also
pay attention to the ways in which candidates' personal traits affect electoral
behavior. Chapter 8 shows that the importance of candidates' traits diminished as Taiwan democratized. Because political power was monopolized by
the KMT during the authoritarian era, most nominees for elected positions
shared the same party label and candidates' traits were voters' means of differentiation. As the issue of unification/independence became prominent in
a democratic Taiwan, partisan identification increasingly had major effects
on the island citizens' electoral decisions.

In sum, the central issue that dominates Taiwan politics is the debate
over the island's sovereignty and its long-term relationship with China. Individuals' stands on the unification/independence issue are closely related to
their national identities and deeply reflected in their partisan identification.
The cleavage is so deep that it has profound impacts on every aspect of the
island citizens' political life. All issues, including such minor policy questions as absentee voting or the adoption of an English translation system,
can become entangled in the main cleavage and be examined through a
partisan lens.[9]

Political Cleavage and Politics: Taiwan as a Test Case

Some countries are so consequential in the world that they have legions
of outside observers. The United States, China, Britain, France, Germany,
Japan, and Russia take up space in the sophisticated media of every country.
Political life in most small countries, however, is of interest only to their own
citizens. Taiwan is a small country, and its domestic politics typically makes
international news only as entertainment—when fistfights break out in the
parliament, known as the Legislative Yuan. Apart from specialists in East
Asian politics, no one outside Taiwan cares very much. Why should readers
with an interest in comparative electoral behavior want to read about Taiwan
in particular?

In our judgment, there are two good reasons to pay special attention to Taiwan. First, Taiwan is one of the best places to investigate the multifaceted effects of cleavage on politics. With cleavages defined as divisions that separate members of communities into groups (Rae and Taylor 1970), empirical research has variously linked political cleavages to conflict and partisan differences (Bonilla et al. 2011; Dahrendorf 1959; Dunning and Harrison 2010; Tilley, Evans and Mitchell 2008). Yet, cleavages are not all bad, as Lipset (1963, 78–79) argued half a century ago, because "[a] stable democracy requires relatively moderate tension among its contending political forces." However, if key differences in a society are allowed to accumulate and reinforce each other, cleavages may deepen, conflicts may grow intense, and extreme polarization may be manifested in voting and partisan divisions.

It is often argued that cross-cutting cleavages can mollify the intensity of conflict and reduce polarization. The overlapping cleavages make it difficult to build a coalition as few people are solely associated with any given cleavage. Conversely, this implies that conflict and political polarization are generally the most extreme when there is just one major cleavage in the society (Simmel 1908; Rae and Taylor 1970; Zuckerman 1975).

As we have noted, the current central axis of politics in Taiwan is the issue of unification vs. independence. Citizen's opinions on that issue are closely tied to their identity—Do they think of themselves as Chinese, as Taiwanese, or as both? Ethnic identity also plays a role: mainlanders are unlikely to define themselves as purely Taiwan citizens, while a majority of Minnan do so, and thus they have different positions on the unification/independence issue. Ethnic identity, national identity, and preferences over how to deal with a rising China are all interrelated and reinforce each other in Taiwan. Political parties on the island necessarily must define themselves in a way that makes sense in this context. They all have distinct and well-differentiated positions on the unification/independence axis, with two small parties (the NP and the TSU, respectively) holding down the extremes. This dominant issue structures party ideology and electoral strategies, while citizen's party identifications and vote choices map closely onto those issue positions.

The nexus of causal relationships for Taiwan citizens is thus theoretically complicated but empirically simple: ethnic identification, national identification, party identification, and political opinions connect closely to each other and reinforce each other. Each of them connects to vote choice. This set of relationship is relatively tight in Taiwan. To our knowledge, only Israel has a similarly close linkage among ethnic origins (Ashkenazic vs. Sephardic), concepts of the state (Israeli vs. Jewish), the central political dimension (relationship with the Palestinians), and party choice (Shamir and Arian 1999). Where relationships are strongest, causal patterns are most easily discerned. One can study Taiwan for the same reason Charles Darwin gathered scientific information on the Galapagos Islands: that is where the evidence is clearest.

The second reason for studying Taiwan is its strategic importance. Taiwan is a flashpoint in East Asia, one of the most likely places to set off a general Asian war. Domestic politics in China and Taiwan have perhaps been the central drivers of cross-Strait tensions. In Taiwan, the cross-Strait relationship is the key cleavage that profoundly shapes the interest structure of its electorate. If voting is a means for individuals to make collective decisions, it is crucial to know what Taiwan citizens are asking for and how these demands are manifested in their partisan support and vote choices. Thus, understanding Taiwan voters is important not only in its own right as a key mechanism of a young democratic polity but also for its impact at the collective level in preserving peace in East Asia. Until the last decade or so, even China did not pay close attention. The resulting misjudgments helped cause the missile crisis in 1996, with costly consequences for the mainland (Garver 1997; Cooper 1998, chap. 4).

In this volume, we make no pretense of sorting out the full set of causal relationships among the various kinds of identity and the resulting vote choices. Those relations necessarily differ among individuals: some will come to their partisanship because of their ethnicity, some because of their national identity, and some because of their policy views. Others will inherit a partisanship and let that determine their other identities, while still others will exhibit more complex patterns. We leave to others the full specification of all those causal paths—an important topic, but one that we must set aside.

Our perspective is rather that the key political cleavage is so powerful that it renders other differences among Taiwan voters secondary or unimportant. When any one component is inconsistent with another, there will be cognitive or psychological pressure to bring them into line. Therefore, the island citizens' portfolio of identities, their political opinions, and their vote choices are also "co-integrated" in the sense that time series analysts use the term.[10] That pressure may be strong or weak, it may be heeded quickly or slowly, it may be set aside, or it may be resisted. In any cross-section, some individuals may ignore their contradictory views or deliberately hold inconsistent views, and some may hold them for a lifetime. But for most individuals in a political system like Taiwan's, where one central, vivid issue dominates political life, where that issue is closely tied to important ethnic and national identities, and where the parties' stances reflect that issue, most individuals will show substantial consistency. We will not find many DPP supporters who have a Chinese identity and support Taiwan's unification with China, nor many mainlanders favoring immediate independence.

Demonstrating the power of a political cleavage manifested in many forms is a central feature of this book. Indeed, Taiwan is a perfect case for analyzing the effects of political cleavages and personal identities on politics. Many small countries are out of the international fray, and it matters little how their politics and policies evolve. Not Taiwan. Political identities are important in every political system, but often in such variegated or muted form that their effects are difficult to detect. Not in Taiwan. And institutions matter in every country, but changes in them are so rare and glacial that no one can be sure how much difference they make. Not in Taiwan. Succeeding chapters will demonstrate not just how interesting Taiwan politics is in its own right but how much Taiwan can teach us about how politics works in the many countries around the world where ethnic divisions and contested national identities are central to electoral politics.

Plan of the Book

This volume has 12 chapters. To make the volume accessible to both scholars and general audiences, contributors have intentionally avoided complicated statistical analysis. Not until the final chapter do we build a comprehensive statistical model based on the factors that previous chapters have identified.

After this introduction, the book proceeds to a chapter by Chia-hung Tsai, designed to introduce Taiwan electoral politics to those who may have little prior experience with the topic. It explores who Taiwan voters are and how they have voted in presidential elections since the rapid democratization began about two decades ago. Tsai finds that Taiwan's young democracy has increasingly consolidated into a competitive two-party system formed by the Pan-Blue and the Pan-Green Alliances, which are dominated by the KMT and the DPP, respectively. While the Pan-Blue Alliance has generally enjoyed the electoral advantage during most lower-level elections, the two parties have split the six presidential elections since democratization. The Pan-Green Alliance is increasingly competitive at all levels.

Tsai notes that a regional divide in Taiwan is clearly recognizable, validating the general view that the island consists of "a Blue North and a Green South" (the Pan-Blue Alliance dominates northern Taiwan and the Pan-Green Alliance dominates southern Taiwan.[11]) Due to the policies implemented by the KMT government during the authoritarian era, Taiwan voters who are mainlanders, well educated, more affluent, government employees, or in their 30s and 40s are more likely to support Pan-Blue candidates. The island citizens who belong to the Minnan ethnic group and who are less educated, less well-off, working in labor and agricultural sectors, or in their 20s tend to identify with the Pan-Green Alliance.

After this first chapter explores who Taiwan voters are, successive chapters take up the "big three"—party identification, issue orientation, and candidate evaluation—and how they affect the island citizens' political attitudes and behaviors. To these three, we add a fourth—identity, particularly national identity. As previously noted, the preference about Taiwan's future relationship with China presents a deep dividing line between the island's citizens. Precisely because the unification/independence issue is the key political cleavage, it closely intertwines with the island citizens' national identities, their partisan attachments, their issue preferences, and their views of the candidates.

In that spirit, in chapter 3 T. Y. Wang examines the development of political identity in Taiwan. The author shows that the "China factor" has been the essential component of the changing boundaries in group membership that shapes Taiwan voters' identities. Immediately after the KMT's retreat to the island, the ethnic divide between local citizens and mainlanders became salient. After democratization and other social changes, the ethnic cleavage was replaced by the contestation between Chinese and Taiwanese identities. As the majority of citizens now hold a Taiwanese identity and few are Chinese identifiers, the boundary of the Chinese/Taiwanese divide has gradually lost its political significance in domestic politics but has moved to a different level. Due to Beijing's forceful claim on Taiwan's sovereignty, the term "Taiwan" is no longer a purely geographic designation. Being "Taiwanese" increasingly implies an identity with Taiwan as an independent state. The shadows of both the ethnic cleavage and the Taiwanese/Chinese divide continue to be cast on the island citizens' partisan identifications.

Following the discussion of identity change on the island, in chapter 4 Ching-hsin Yu takes up the second of the "big four"—partisanship. He explores the trajectory of Taiwan voters' attachments to parties and how they are intertwined with their positions along the axis of unification/independence. The author traces the development of the island citizens' partisan identification and concludes that nonpartisan voters during the authoritarian era were not "independent" in its true sense. As the KMT monopolized political power and banned the formation of political parties, those who did not identify with the KMT were treated as "nonpartisan independents" lest they form a cohesive political force. Many of these citizens later became the loyal supporters of the newly established opposition DPP. Along with their junior partners, the KMT and the DPP later formed the Pan-Blue Alliance and the Pan-Green Alliance. Because each of the two political alliances has a distinctive position on the issue of Taiwan's future relations with China, which is the most important political cleavage on the island, Taiwan voters have developed a clear partisan attachment in the competitive two-party system. That said, a considerable number of citizens are nonpartisan and they behave differently according to their educational levels. Yu finds that highly educated independents are less interested in politics and less likely to vote but they are also more autonomous and politically moderate than their less educated counterparts.

The next three chapters turn attention to the third leg of the "big four"—citizens' issue orientation. Conventionally, political issues have been seen as crucial to the functioning of democracy. Political parties are expected to present policy options to electorates, allowing citizens to select those candidates who correspond most closely to their own ideological positions. The congruence of issue positions and ideology between citizens and political parties has thus become an important topic in electoral studies (e.g., Adams, Ezrow and Somer-Topcu 2011; Lachat 2011; Thomassen and Schmitt 1997; but, for a critique of this framework, see Achen and Bartels 2016).

Do issue preferences play a role in Taiwan citizens' voting calculus? If so, what are the important issues? How do they relate to the key political cleavage on the island? Chapter 5 by Shing-yuan Sheng and Hsiao-chuan Liao demonstrates the impact of the central political cleavage on Taiwan politics. Examining the evolution of four key political debates on the island, the authors show that reform vs. stability has become an issue of the past. The second issue, wealth distribution, fails to differentiate political parties because the partisan elites of various political affiliations have converged on the same ideological position and have attempted to outbid each other in order to win electoral support. Third, while environmental protection has the potential of becoming an important political issue after the disaster at the Fukushima nuclear plan in Japan, it is still an issue in the process of development in Taiwan. The most important political issue on the island, then, is and will continue to be Taiwan's future relationship with China, which is closely tied to the island citizens' identity as Chinese or Taiwanese.

The salience of Taiwan's relationship with China does not mean that such issues as the economy are unimportant. Empirical studies on the American presidency have long concluded that the state of the economy is an important contributing factor to electoral decisions. An abundance of literature has demonstrated the linkage between the electoral success of an incumbent government and its economic performance.[12] The logic is simple. When economic conditions are good, voters are likely to reward the incumbent with their vote. When the economy is bad, voters tend to switch their support to the challenger. Jimmy Carter's devastating defeat by Ronald Reagan in 1980 and George H. W. Bush's loss to Bill Clinton in 1992 are testimony to the conventional wisdom that "economics is the fate of politicians" (Norpoth 1985, 167).

Following this reward-punishment model, in chapter 6 Chia-hung Tsai explores the role of the economy in Taiwan citizens' voting calculus. The author finds mixed evidence for economic voting in the island country's presidential elections. While prospective economic evaluations are found to be an important determinant of Taiwan voters' electoral choices, the weight of the economy is overshadowed by, again, citizens' partisan affiliations. This finding shows that responses to the economy affect Taiwan voters' electoral calculus, but primarily through the colors of partisan lenses, which are closely aligned with their positions on the key political cleavage in the society.

Chapter 7 by Alexander Tan and Karl Ho examines the complex dynamics of cross-Straits relations, in particular the burgeoning economic exchanges with China after Ma Ying-jeou of the KMT was elected president in 2008. The authors find that island residents exhibit an ambivalent view of Taiwan's close and intensive interactions with the Chinese mainland since 2008. Following partisan lines, some of them feel that such ties are beneficial to the island's economy, while others express concerns about the security implications. In the aggregate, Taiwan voters recognize that isolation from China is not viable or even possible, yet getting too close to China also troubles them. This explains why the public changed its mind about the engagement policies of the Ma administration, initially favoring it after the DPP's isolationist policies during 2000–2008, but then coming to distrust close ties as they seemed to bring few benefits to most ordinary citizens. Thus, cross-Strait relations, or more broadly speaking "the China factor," affect not only how Taiwan voters see the future but also how they view the current administration.

Following these discussions of the impact of national identities, partisan attachments, and issue orientations on Taiwan voters' electoral decision, chapter 8 by Hung-chung Wang and Lu-huei Chen examines the last component of the "big four"—citizens' evaluation of candidates. Assessment of candidates for public office attracts considerable attention in each campaign season. Scholars and pundits analyze and dissect candidates' backgrounds and characters, and discuss how these personal traits affect voters' evaluation of candidates and their voting decisions. Citizens' evaluation of candidates is important because, it is argued, seeking for and digesting political information is costly. The assessment of candidates offers the public a useful shortcut as it seems to provide a clue as to how they will perform their duties once elected. In particular, given that the president occupies the principal position in the government, presidential traits and characters have important symbolic meaning, which set public standards for all political behaviors (Greene 2001; Kinder 1986; McCurley and Mondak 1995).

Following this line of research, Wang and Chen find that in Taiwan's presidential elections, KMT candidates tend to be viewed as more capable of dealing with cross-Strait relationships and economic development, while DPP nominees are associated with the issue of eliminating corruption and initiating political reforms. Perhaps surprisingly, the perception of candidates' personal traits has little effect on the island citizens' voting behavior. Taiwan voters' electoral decisions are largely determined by their partisan identifications, which, again, are closely in line with citizens' positions on the axis of unification/independence and their national identities. Thus, candidate issue ownership is applicable to Taiwan's parties, but voters' evaluation of candidates' personal characteristics and perceived competence are conditioned largely by their partisan affiliations.

In the context of Taiwan's electoral politics, it should occasion no wonder that Western notions of political "left" and "right" have little relevance in Taiwan, as Yi-ching Hsiao, Su-feng Cheng, and Christopher Achen explain in chapter 9. The left-right scale is irrelevant because the main cleavage in Taiwan is not the degree of government control of the economy, as previous chapters emphasize. Nor are "left" and "right" used to describe other aspects of political debates in Taiwan. Political elites make essentially no use of those words in Taiwan, and ordinary citizens are mystified by references to them. The confusions are exacerbated by particular connotations of "left" and "right" in both Mandarin and the Taiwanese dialect, as the authors explain.

While the "big four" are the most significant factors in voters' electoral calculus, they do not operate in a political vacuum. Institutional structures set a broad framework for the actions of both political parties and individuals. They set an approximate upper limit to the number of parties, configure the choice menu on the ballot, structure voters' electoral calculus, and provide incentives or disincentives for citizens to show up at the ballot boxes on election days (e.g., Cox 1997; 1999; Engstrom 2012). Thus chapter 10 by Chi Huang examines the effects of recent electoral system change on Taiwan's party system. As with the experience of Japan, which also adopted the mixed-member system a decade earlier, Taiwan has witnessed a dramatic change in its party system in the postreform era. The fast convergence toward two-party competition on the island is due in part to the interactions between the powerful presidency and political elites' ambition of synchronizing presidential and legislative elections. Because the issue of unification vs. independence is the single most important political cleavage on the island, as discussed in the previous chapters, it has played a hidden yet significant role in shaping the postreform party structure toward a "Pan-Blue vs. Pan-Green" system.

Chapter 11 by Chung-li Wu and Tzu-Ping Liu examines Taiwan citizens' political participation. Similar to the trend in many Western democracies, the path of turnout rates in the island country's presidential and legislative elections has gone downward since the early 1990s. Three particular factors affect individuals' turnout and other forms of political participation—age, party identification, and political knowledge. In general, older people, individuals identified with main political parties, and those equipped with more political knowledge tend to have a higher level of political participation. Because this more engaged group generally has higher socioeconomic status, these findings further confirm the conventional wisdom that citizens in the upper and middle classes tend to be more interested and involved in public affairs than individuals in the lower class. The chapter shows that the gap has widened in Taiwan in recent years.

Each of these chapters identifies one or more important aspects of Taiwan politics. The final chapter by Christopher Achen and T. Y. Wang brings together all of them to examine vote choice on the island. We have built a comprehensive statistical model based on the factors that previous chapters have identified and discuss their implications. The central finding is that one key dimension organizes Taiwan citizens' vote choices—the China factor. Should Taiwan accommodate itself to China's ever more powerful presence in Asia, or should it forcefully assert its status as a separate country and resist integration with the mainland? The answer to that question largely determines what Taiwan people think about related policy issues, which party they adhere to, and how they vote.

Thus, in contrast to left-right economic disputes, which dominate politics in many Western countries, politics in Taiwan is fundamentally about nationalism and the future of Taiwan's national identity. In that respect, Taiwan is one of many countries around the world in which similar issues shape domestic politics. In recent years, the world has seen a succession of crises and threats to peace in which national identity was the central issue— Bosnia, Kosovo, and the Ukraine, to list just three examples in which local wars have broken out and the major Western powers have taken an interest in restoring the peace. Taiwan, too, is an international hotspot with a potential for setting off a major international conflict. Thus far, democracy and peace have prevailed on the island. Hence, Taiwan has much to teach us, and we offer this book as a contribution to the international dialog about how differing conceptions of national identity can be managed peacefully.

Notes

1. National Statistics, Republic of China (Taiwan) at http://statdb.dgbas.gov.tw/pxweb/Dialog/Saveshow.asp (accessed March 15, 2015).

2. As in Japan, factional politics are prevalent in Taiwan. The island country's two major political parties have employed patron-client relationships for power distribution and voter mobilization. For a discussion of Taiwan's factional politics, see Batto and Huang (2016).

3. We use "Taiwan citizen" to mean any citizen of Taiwan because the term "Taiwanese" has various political connotations for different people. To some, "Taiwanese" refer to citizens living in the territory effectively governed by the Taiwan government, while to others the term means an ethnic designation opposed to "mainlander." Because the majority of support for the Pan-Green Alliance led by the Democratic Progressive Party comes from those who self-identify as "Taiwanese," a "Taiwanese" or a "Taiwanese citizen" thus may have a narrower and potentially partisan meaning in English.

4. One well-known example is former Taiwan president Lee Teng-hui, who freely admitted that he had become a Japanese citizen with a Japanese name during the colonial period. Throughout his life, his Japanese language skills were better than his Mandarin.

5. Retrieved from *Liang-An Jing-ji Tong-ji Yue-bao* (Monthly Report on Cross-Straits Economy) published by the Mainland Affairs Council, the Republic of China, at http://www.mac.gov.tw (accessed March 15, 2015).

6. For a complete list of cross-Strait agreements, see the Mainland Affairs Council website, the Republic of China, http://www.mac.gov.tw/ct.asp?xItem=67145&CtNode=5710&mp=1.

7. Greater Tainan mayor William Lai's visit to Shanghai is one of the most recent high-profile visits by DPP politician (Tsao and Chung 2014).

8. There are four major ethnic groups in Taiwan: Minnan, Hakka, mainlander, and aborigine. Minnan refers to island residents whose ancestors migrated to Taiwan from the Chinese mainland several hundred years ago. They are the largest ethnic group at 77% of the island's 23 million people. About 10% of Taiwan's total population is Hakka, descendants of immigrants who came to the island at roughly the same time as the Minnan from areas in central China. Both Minnan and Hakka are generally grouped together as "Taiwanese" even though they have different customs and habits and speak different dialects. Approximately 12% of the total population are mainlanders, those who arrived from the mainland in the late 1940s after the Chinese civil war, and their descendants. Aborigines, the original settlers, constitute less than 2% of the total population in Taiwan.

9. Taiwan has no system of absentee voting ("postal voting"). One of the main explanations often advanced is that China-based Taiwanese businesspeople and their family members rely on good relations with China and thus are potential KMT supporters. Hence, absentee voting is expected to increase the KMT's votes, and the DPP opposes it. Similarly, the Ma administration declared more than five years ago that Taiwan would start using the *pinyin* system for English translation, which is the phonetic system used in almost every part of the world, including the UN. Because the *pinyin* system was developed and adopted in the Chinese mainland, however, its usage was resisted by many DPP politicians (Economist 2014).

10. Some of the original applications were to currency exchange rates. Political scientists have studied arms races using the same ideas. In both instances, the complex causal details are much less important than showing that the system constantly attempts, in the midst of continual disturbances, to reach toward an equilibrium, even if it never attains it.

11. For a discussion of Taiwan's "Blue North and Green South" phenomenon, see Chou 2012.

12. For a concise review of the literature on economic voting, see Lewis-Beck and Stegmaier 2007.

References

Achen, Christopher H., and Larry M. Bartels. 2016. *Democracy for Realists*. Princeton: Princeton University Press.

Adams, James, Lawrence Ezrow, and Zeynep Somer-Topcu. 2011. "Is Anybody Listening? Evidence That Voters Do Not Respond to European Parties' Policy Statements during Elections." *American Journal of Political Science* 55 (2): 370–82.

Batto, Nathan, and F. Shin-at Huang. 2016. "Executive Competition, Electoral Rules, and Faction Systems in Taiwan." In *Elections in Taiwan and Japan under the Mixed-Member Majoritarian System*, ed. Nathan F. Batto, Chi Huang, Alexander Ç. Tan, and Gary Cox. Ann Arbor: University of Michigan Press.

Berelson, Bernard R., Paul F. Lazarsfeld, and William N. McPhee. 1954. *Voting: A Study of Opinion Formation in a Presidential Campaign*. Chicago: University of Chicago Press.

Bonilla, Claudio A., Ryan E. Carlin, Gregory J. Love and Ernesto Silva Méndez. 2011. "Social or Political Cleavages? A Spatial Analysis of the Party System in Post-Authoritarian Chile." *Public Choice* 146 (2): 9–21.

Brown, Melissa. 2004. *Is Taiwan Chinese? The Impact of Culture, Power, and Migration on Changing Identities*. Berkeley: University of California Press.

Butler, David, and Donald E. Stokes. 1974. *Political Change in Britain*. 2nd ed. London: Macmillan.

Campbell, Angus, Philip E. Converse, Warren E. Miller, and Donald E. Stokes. 1960. *The American Voter*. New York: John Wiley and Sons.

Carlin, Ryan E., Matthew M. Singer, and Elizabeth J. Zechmeister. 2015. *The Latin American Voter*. Ann Arbor: University of Michigan Press.

Chan, Steve. 1988. "Developing Strength from Weakness: The State in Taiwan." In *State and Development*, ed. Cal Clark, 38–51. New York: E. J. Brill.

Ching, T. S. Leo. 2001. *Becoming Japanese: Colonial Taiwan and the Politics of Identity Formation*. Berkeley: University of California Press.

Chou, Yin-lung. 2012. "A Study of the Pan-Green Political Landscape in Southern Taiwan" [in Chinese]. PhD diss., National Chengchi University, Taipei.

Chu, Yun-han, and Chia-lung Lin. 2003. "Consolidating Taiwan's New Democracy amid Competing National Identities." In *China Today: Economic Reforms, Social Cohesion and Collective Identities*, edited by Taciana Fisac and Leila Fernández-Stembridge, 240–67. London: Routledge Curzon.

Clark, Cal. 1987. "The Taiwan Exception: Implications for Contending Political Economy Paradigms." *International Studies Quarterly* 31:327–56.

Clark, Cal. 1989. *Taiwan's Development: Implications for Contending Political Economy Paradigms*. New York: Greenwood Press.

Cooper, John F. 1998. *Taiwan's Mid-1990s Elections*. Westport, CT: Praeger.

Cox, Gary W. 1997. *Making Votes Count: Strategic Coordination in the World's Electoral Systems*. Cambridge: Cambridge University Press.

Cox, Gary W. 1999. "Electoral Rules and the Calculus of Mobilization." *Legislative Studies Quarterly* 24 (3): 387–420.

Dahrendorf, Ralf. 1959. *Class and Class Conflict in Industrial Society*. Stanford, Calif., Stanford University Press,

Dalton, Russell J., and Christopher J. Anderson, eds. 2011. *Citizens, Context, and Choice*. Oxford: Oxford University Press.

Dunning, Thad, and Lauren Harrison. 2010. "Cross-cutting Cleavages and Ethnic Voting: An Experimental Study of Cousinage in Mali." *American Political Science Review* 104 (1): 21–39.

Economist. 2014. "Lost in Romanisation: Ideological Warfare over Spelling." June 7. http://www.economist.com/news/asia/21603500-ideological-warfare-over-spelling-lost-romanisation.

Engstrom, Erik. 2012. "The Rise and Decline of Turnout in Congressional Elections: Electoral Institutions, Competition, and Strategic Mobilization." *American Journal of Political Science* 56 (2): 373–86.

Evans, Geoffrey, and Nan Dirk De Graaf, eds. 2013. *Political Choice Matters*. Oxford: Oxford University Press.

Flanagan, Scott C., Shinsaku Kohei, Ichiro Miyake, Bradley M. Richardson, and Joji Watanuki, eds. 1991. *The Japanese Voter*. New Haven: Yale University Press.

Garver, John W. 1997. *Face Off: China, the United States, and Taiwan's Democratization*. Seattle: University of Washington Press.

Greene, J. Megan. 2008. "History, Identity, and Politics: The First Chen Shui-bian Administration's Efforts to Craft Taiwan's History." In *Presidential Politics in Taiwan: The Administration of Chen Shui-bian*, ed. Steven M. Goldstein and Julian Chang, 115–41. Norwalk, CT: EastBridge.

Greene, Steven. 2001. "The Role of Character Assessments in Presidential Approval." *American Politics Research* 29 (2): 196–210.

Jacoby, William. 2010. "The American Voter." In *The Oxford Handbook of American Elections and Political Behavior*, ed. Jan E. Leighley, 260–77. New York: Oxford University Press.

Kerr, George H. 1965. *Formosa Betrayed*. Boston: Houghton Mifflin.

Kinder, Donald. 1986. "Presidential Character Revisited." In *Political Cognition: the 19th Annual Carnegie Symposium on Cognition*, ed. Richard R. Lau and David O. Sears, 233–55. Hillsdale, NJ: L. Erlbaum Associates.

Lachat, Romain. 2011. "Electoral Competitiveness and Issue Voting." *Political Behavior* 33 (4): 645–63.

Lai, Tse-han, Ramon H. Myers, and Wei Wou. 1991. *A Tragic Beginning: The Taiwan Uprising of February 28, 1947*. Stanford: Stanford University Press.

Lazarsfeld, Paul F., Bernard Berelson, and Hazel Gaudet. 1948. *The People's Choice: How the Voter Makes Up His Mind in a Presidential Campaign*. 2nd ed. New York: Columbia University Press.

Lewis-Beck, Michael, and Mary Stegmaier. 2007. "Economic Models of Voting." In *The Oxford Handbook of Political Behavior*, ed. Russell Dalton and Hans-Dieter Klingemann, 518–37. Oxford: Oxford University Press.

Lipset, Seymour M., and Stein Rokkan. 1967. "Cleavage Structure, Party Systems, and Voter Alignments: An Introduction." In *Party Systems and Voter Alignments: Cross-National Perspectives*, ed. Seymour M. Lipset and Stein Rokkan, 1–64. New York: Free Press.

Lipset, Seymour Martin. 1963. *Political Man: The Social Bases of Politics*. Garden City NY: Doubleday.

Liu, I-chou, and Ho Szu-yin. 1999. "The Taiwanese/Chinese Identity of the Taiwan People." *Issues & Studies* 35 (3): 1–34.

Marsh, Michael, Richard Sinnott, John Garry, and Fiachra Kennedy. 2008. *The Irish Voter: The Nature of Electoral Competition in the Republic of Ireland*. New York: Manchester University Press.

McCurley, Carl, and Jeffery J. Mondak. 1995. "Inspected by #1184063113: The Influence of Incumbents' Competence and Integrity in U.S. House Elections." *American Journal of Political Science* 39 (4): 864–85.

Norpoth, Helmut. 1985. "Politics, Economics, and the Cycle of Presidential Popularity." In *Economic Conditions and Electoral Outcomes: The United States and Western Europe*, ed. Heinz Eulau and Michael S. Lewis-Beck, 167–86. New York: Agathon Press.

Rae, Douglas W., and Michael Taylor. 1970. *The Analysis of Political Cleavages*. New Haven: Yale University Press.

Rigger, Shelley. 2001. *From Opposition to Power: Taiwan's Democratic Progressive Party*. Boulder, CO: Lynne Rienner.

Schubert, Gunter. 2008. "Taiwan's Evolving National Identity since the DPP Take-over: From Civic to Ethnic?" In *Presidential Politics in Taiwan: The Administration of Chen Shui-bian*, ed. Steven M. Goldstein and Julian Chang, 185–213. Norwalk, CT: EastBridge.

Shamir, Michal, and Asher Arian. 1999. "Collective Identities and Electoral Competition in Israel." *American Political Science Review* 93: 265–78.

Simmel, Georg. (1908) 1964. *Conflict* and *The Web of Group Affiliations*. Glencoe, IL: Free Press.

Thomassen, Jacques, ed. 2005. *The European Voter*. Oxford: Oxford University Press.

Thomassen, Jacques, and Hermann Schmidt. 1997. "Policy Representation." *European Journal of Political Research* 32: 165–84.

Tien, Hung-mao. 1996. *Taiwan's Electoral Politics and Democratic Transition.* Armonk, NY: M. E. Sharpe.

Tilley, James, Geoffrey Evans, and Claire Mitchell. 2008. "Consociationalism and the Evolution of Political Cleavages in Northern Ireland, 1989–2004." *British Journal of Political Science* 38 (4): 699–717.

Tsao, Po-yen, and Jake Chung. 2014. "William Lai's Words Feed Online Feud." *Taipei Times,* June 9. http://www.taipeitimes.com/News/taiwan/archives/2014/06/09/2003592336 (accessed March 15, 2015).

Tung, Chen-yuan. 2005. "An Assessment of China's Taiwan Policy under the Third Generation Leadership." *Asian Survey* 45 (3): 343–61.

Wang, T. Y. 2000. "State Policy and Industrial Promotion in Taiwan: An Interrupted Time Series Analysis, 1956–1994." *International Journal of Public Administration* 23 (10): 1749–76.

Wang, T. Y., and I-Chou Liu. 2004. "Contending Identities in Taiwan: Implications for Cross-Strait Relations." *Asian Survey* 44 (4): 568–90.

Zuckerman, Alan. 1975. "Political Cleavage: A Conceptual and Theoretical Analysis." *British Journal of Political Science* 5 (2): 231–48.

CHAPTER 2

Who Is the Taiwan Voter?

Chia-hung Tsai

The purpose of this chapter is to provide an overview of recent Taiwan elections for readers who may not be familiar with them. The growing importance of the north-south divide in Taiwan's politics is emphasized. The chapter also explores how the supporters of the two party camps differ from each other. In particular, standard variables that are important for differentiating party supporters in many other countries, such as income and occupation, turn out to have only modest effects in Taiwan. Instead, ethnicity plays the most crucial role in shaping the voting and partisan identities of Taiwan citizens, just as the theoretical framework of this book suggests.

Recent Taiwan Presidential Elections

Chapter 1 has given a brief overview of Taiwan's history that highlights the island country's political development. In particular, it argued that the pivot of Taiwan politics is the citizens' political identities, which are both related to their ethnicity and manifested in their partisan affiliation with the Pan-Blue Alliance or the Pan-Green Alliance—the two major political camps that have formed since the late 1990s. Presuming that background, the present chapter begins with an exploration of Taiwan's general voting patterns as seen in election returns tabulated by the Central Election Commission. The scope of the analysis comprises the five presidential elections since 1996 when the island's president was first popularly elected, a time span of nearly two decades.[1] Since then, four more presidential elections have been held, with two peaceful transfers of power in 2000 and in 2008.

The rapid democratization on the island culminated in the 1996 presidential election, in which Taiwan voters exercised their political right to popularly elect their national leader for the first time. In the 1996 presidential election, two candidates—Lin Yang-kang and Chen Lu-an—were members of the KMT who only broke away from the party after they failed to secure its nomination. Chen ran as an independent and Lin was supported by the New Party—a KMT split-off strongly advocating Taiwan's unification with the Chinese mainland. Similarly, in the 2000 presidential election, James Soong left the KMT and ran as an independent against Lien Chan, the KMT nominee, and Chen Shui-bian, the DPP-affiliated candidate. Although Soong and Lien together polled nearly 60 percent of the votes, Chen won the election with merely 39.3 percent under the first-past-the-post voting system. After the election, Soong organized the People First Party and has since served as its chair.

Recognizing that a divided KMT would only benefit the opponents, Soong joined Lien as his running mate in the 2004 presidential election. However, a successful DPP campaign and an apparent assassination attempt on Chen's life 24 hours before the polls opened gave Chen the victory.[2] Then, in both the 2008 and 2012 elections, it was the KMT-affiliated Ma Ying-jeou who scored the victory. While the 2008 presidential election was a classic two-party race between the KMT and the DPP, the 2012 election was a three-party race with the PFP-affiliated Soong unsuccessfully attempting a comeback.

Thus, while there are multiple political parties on the island, even the smallest are either allies of the DPP or are KMT splinter groups. Hence the political landscape can generally be characterized by two political alliances—the "Pan-Blue" and the "Pan-Green"—led by the KMT and the DPP, respectively. The current chapter uses those terms for all the elections in the democratic era, even though the terms themselves did not appear until 2000. To simplify the analysis, vote shares of candidates in the five presidential elections are aggregated into those two blocs.

The Consolidation of Two-Party System

Figure 2.1 shows the electoral support enjoyed by the two party groups during the five presidential elections Taiwan has conducted since democratization, 1996–2012. A dominant electoral force in the mid-1990s, the Pan-Blue Alliance shrank rapidly during the subsequent decade, only to recover somewhat in the two most recent presidential contests. In recent years, the

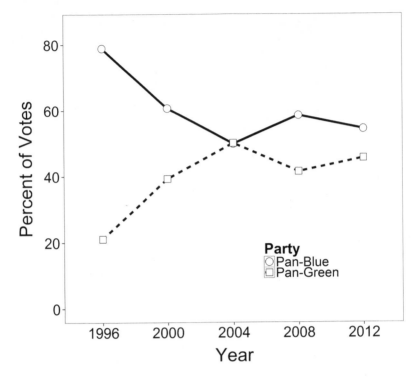

Fig. 2.1. Vote shares of the Pan-Blue and Pan-Green camps in the presidential elections, 1996–2012. *Data:* Election Study Center.

partisan divide on the island has been approximately 50–55 percent for the Pan-Blue Alliance and 40–45 percent for the Pan-Green Alliance, with the smaller parties of decreasing importance. It appears that Taiwan's political landscape has consolidated as a genuine two-party system dominated by the KMT and the DPP.

Many democracies in the world show strong regional differences in their voting patterns. Well-known historical examples include the late nineteenth and early twentieth-century "Solid South" in the United States (Archer and Taylor 1981; Tindall 1972), the traditional loyalty to the Labour Party in northern England and Scotland, the east vs. west divide in Korean and Ukrainian politics, and the strong support for the Liberal Party in Quebec, Canada, in the immediate postwar period. Taiwan also has a sharp regional division. Since 2000, the island country's electoral politics has increasingly displayed a strong north-south divide. In part due to the fact that the national government in Taipei has poured budget money into northern Tai-

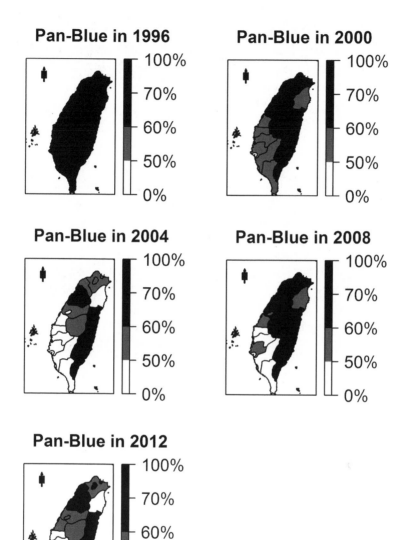

Fig. 2.2. Pan-Blue's vote shares in the presidential elections, 1996–2012. *Data:* Election Study Center.

wan, the disparity between the north and the rest of the country in development and living standard has grown. As cross-Strait relations become increasingly vital to Taiwan's economic development in the 2000s, voters in northern Taiwan, where high-tech industries, banking businesses, and the service industry gather, are more supportive of the KMT and its policies than those living in southern Taiwan.

The five choropleth maps in figure 2.2 set out the vote shares garnered by Pan-Blue presidential candidates during the five presidential elections. They show the emergence of the north-south divide. In the 1996 presidential election, running as the incumbent and the first native son to be Taiwan's national leader, the KMT's nominee, Lee Teng-hui, was widely popular. The Pan-Blue Alliance won at least 70 percent of the votes in every city and county on the island, in both urban and rural areas. In particular, voters in much of north-central Taiwan, including Taoyuan County, Hsinchu City and County, Miaoli County, and eastern Taiwan, were highly supportive of the three Pan-Blue candidates and in particular of Lee. The regional divide was not much in evidence.

As noted above, the 2000 presidential election was a three-way race among Chen Shui-bian, the DPP nominee; James Soong, the party switcher from the KMT to independent; and Lien Chan, the KMT nominee. Using the Jhuoshuei River as the traditional demarcation line between northern and southern Taiwan, figure 2.2 again shows that the regional disparity in electoral support for the two political alliances began to emerge in this election. The two Pan-Blue candidates received a combined vote share of 60 percent to 70 percent in many parts of northern Taiwan, especially in Taoyuan County and in Hsinchu City and County. The Pan-Green candidate Chen ran better in southern Taiwan but had little support in cities and counties in the north. Overall, Chen had less than 40 percent of the national vote. Had the Pan-Blue Alliance not been divided and thus split its electoral support, Chen would not have been able to win the 2000 presidential election.

The regional disparity in electoral support became even clearer in the 2004 election, as figure 2.2 shows. Pan-Blue candidates continued to garner large electoral support in northern Taiwan but were not able to receive more than 40 percent of votes in cities in the south, including Yunlin County, Chiayi City and County, Tainan City and County, Kaohisung City and County, and Pingtung County. Cities and counties in the central part of Taiwan, including Taichung City and Nantou County, Taichung County and Chunhwa County, became battleground areas as the Pan-Blue candidates barely secured a majority of votes.

The regional divide between a "Blue North" and a "Green South" appeared to become consolidated in the 2008 and 2012 presidential elections. In 2008, the Pan-Blue nominee, Ma Ying-jeou, won a landslide victory with a 58.5 percent to 41.5 percent victory. As figure 2 shows, however, while Ma was able to garner 60 percent to 70 percent of the vote in much of northern and eastern Taiwan, the electoral support for him was considerably weaker in southern cities and counties. Although Ma won his reelection bid in 2012, the regional disparity in electoral support continued. The Pan-Blue candidate continued to draw 60–70 percent of the vote in much of northern and eastern Taiwan, while southern Taiwan remained the stronghold of the Pan-Green Alliance.

Regional disparities in party support are due partly to purely regional factors. But northern and southern Taiwan also differ in ethnic composition, income, and occupations, which together account for some of the regional disparity. The remainder of the chapter takes up those forces accounting for the partisan divide.

Demographic Characteristics and Electoral Behavior

As we have seen, the Pan-Blue Alliance has enjoyed a 5–10 percentage point electoral advantage at the national level since 2000. This section will examine where that support comes from.

As chapter 1 pointed out, there are three major ethnic groups on the island—Minnan, Hakka, and the mainlanders. While they were all immigrants from the Chinese mainland, the Minnan and Hakka are the island residents whose ancestors migrated to Taiwan several hundred years ago. Mainlanders were originally largely composed of the followers of Chiang Kai-shek when the KMT government retreated to the island in 1949. Mainlanders now are primarily their descendants. Each ethnic group thus carries a distinct memory of Taiwan's modern history that may affect their partisan support. The ethnicity of Taiwan voters is closely related to their voting behavior (Wang 1998; Lin 1989; You 1996).

Figure 2.3 shows that mainlanders have been highly supportive of the Pan-Blue Alliance. Nearly 90 percent of mainlanders voted for its candidates in every election since 1996. By contrast, support for Pan-Blue candidates from the Minnan group has declined significantly since 1996 when the KMT nominee, Lee Teng-hui, received more than 80 percent of the votes from his fellow Minnan voters. In subsequent elections, the Minnan voters' electoral support for Pan-Blue candidates has fluctuated between 40 percent and 55 percent. Although the KMT-affiliated Ma won the election

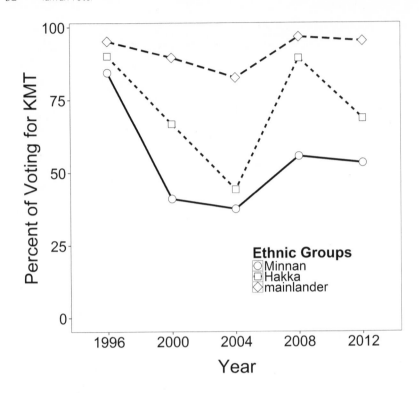

Fig. 2.3. Percentages of three ethnic groups voting for the Pan-Blue. *Data:* See Appendix 2.A3.

in 2012 with the majority support of the Minnan citizens, the gap between the mainlander and the Minnan voters for the Pan-Blue Alliance remains as large as 40 percentage points.

Last, the Hakka are more centrist. The majority of the Hakka group generally have provided their electoral support to Pan-Blue candidates. However, from 2000 to 2004, President Chen Shui-bian appointed many Hakka politicians as cabinet ministers in his first term. The ministry-level government agency, the Council for Hakka Affairs, and Hakka TV were also established in 2001 and 2003, respectively. Perhaps in consequence, Hakka voters swung to the DPP in 2004. However, the majority returned to the KMT in subsequent elections.

The evidence thus shows that the Pan-Blue Alliance generally has been able to garner majority support from the two minority ethnic groups on the island, the Hakka and the mainlanders, and that mainlanders are its most loyal supporters.[3] The majority group, the Minnan, leans to the Pan-Green. The Pan-Green alliance receives its electoral support primarily from the Minnan group, with very little backing from the mainlanders. Thus the ethnic cleavage between the mainlanders and the Minnan group is significant. Although mainlanders make up only about 12 percent of the island's population, their loyal support for the Pan-Blue Alliance and their high turnout rate, together with typically substantial Hakka backing for the KMT, suggest that the ethnic cleavage will continue to play an important role in Taiwan's politics.

In many countries, the parties are substantially based on income classes because that is a central cleavage in the political system. As we have already suggested in this book and as chapter 9 argues in detail, conventional left-right economic divisions do not describe Taiwan politics well. However, income might still matter to some degree. One of the legacies of the KMT's authoritarian rule has been Taiwan's successful economic development in the 1970s. The land reform and the Ten Major Construction Projects, for instance, helped bring rapid economic growth. While most Taiwan citizens have benefited from these economic policies, it has been argued that the well-off and the middle class have benefited most, and thus have generally been the most loyal supporters of the KMT (Winckler 1992). Figure 2.4 confirms this observation to some degree. Citizens of higher income appeared to support the Pan-Blue candidates more than those of lower income by roughly 10 percentage points in the last three presidential elections.

In addition, the figure shows a significant decline of support for the Pan-Blue Alliance by low-income citizens, from about 90 percent in the 1996 election to roughly 40 percent in 2004, and then stabilizing at about 55 percent. The changing partisan support by less affluent voters may appear exaggerated due to the "Lee Teng-hui Complex," referring to citizens' emotional attachment to the island country's first popularly elected president in 1996 (Hsu 1998, 2004). His broad popularity was not likely to be repeated when the KMT returned to mainlander candidates. Nonetheless, it is clear that in recent years, for whatever reasons, less affluent Taiwan voters tend to be less supportive of the Pan-Blue Alliance than their well-off countrymen. Yet as the graph shows, the impact of income is much smaller than that of ethnicity. Taiwan politics is simply not primarily about class conflict.

Another measure of class, closely associated with income, is respondents' education. Figure 2.5 shows that Taiwan voters with college or graduate school education tend to be more supportive of the Pan-Blue Alliance, while citizens with a lower level of education tend to back Pan-Green candidates. Note that the largest supporting gap among voters with different education

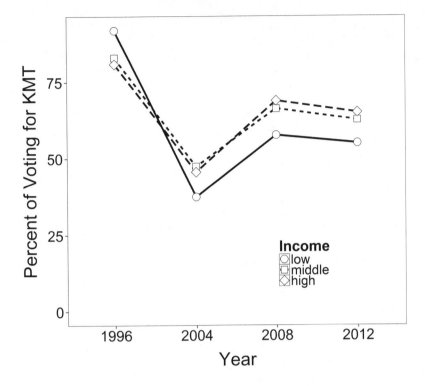

Fig. 2.4. Percentages of three income groups voting for the Pan-Blue. *Note:* The survey for the 2000 presidential election lacks the question on household income. See appendix 2.A1 for the categorization of income groups. *Data:* See appendix 2.A3.

levels appeared in 2004, while partisan support for the Pan-Blue Alliance nearly converged among educational groups in 2012. Again, the effects are very small compared to those of ethnicity, nearly disappearing in the most recent election.

Figure 2.6 gives social class one last chance. It displays vote shares for Pan-Blue candidates according to respondents' occupation. The differences in partisan support among different occupational groups appear to be rather consistent during the past five presidential elections. Specifically, Taiwan voters employed in the public sector, such as the military, governmental employees, and public school teachers, are highly supportive of the Pan-Blue Alliance, by roughly between 60 percent to 75 percent. This is followed by those in the private sector, with a Pan-Blue support rate between 50 to 60 percent. Citizens who earn their living by farming, fishing, and forestry

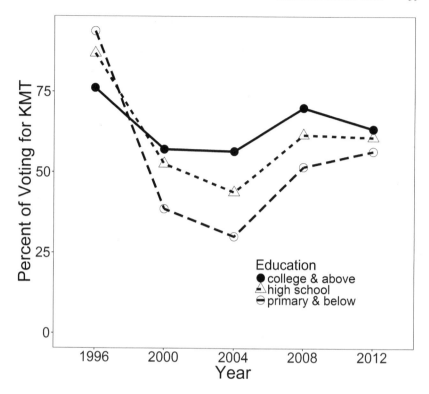

Fig. 2.5. Percentages of three education groups voting for the Pan-Blue. *Data:* See appendix 2.A3.

are least likely to support Pan-Blue candidates. The difference in support for the Pan-Blue Alliance between government employees and citizens in the agricultural sector are as high as 25 percentage points in the 2008 and 2012 elections. Since state employees are devoted supporters of the KMT, the Pan-Green Alliance relies on backing from voters in the agricultural and labor sectors. Thus there is clearly an occupational difference here, but it is tied in part to traditional mainlander dominance of government and to the reliance on fishing and farming in southern Taiwan, where the population is disproportionately Minnan. This raises the question of whether the effect of occupation is causal or merely correlational. Chapter 12 sorts out whether occupation itself has an impact on vote choice, or whether occupational differences simply proxy for other electoral forces, especially ethnicity and national identity.

Figure 2.7 raises the question of whether Taiwan politics is undergoing generational change. It shows the vote shares for Pan-Blue candidates based

Fig. 2.6. Percentages of five occupation groups voting for the Pan-Blue. *Data:* See appendix 2.A3.

on respondents' age. In general, the average vote and the over-time trends of all age groups are strikingly similar. Voters in their 30s and 40s tend to be a bit more supportive of the KMT and its political partners in recent years. However, it is noteworthy that the younger generation in its 20s became the age group least supportive of the Pan-Blue Alliance in 2012. While it remains to be seen whether this represents a trend, it may be indicative of a discontented younger generation that leaders of both the Pan-Blue and Pan-Green alliances need to cultivate. In any case, the differences are quite small and inconsistent in comparison with other factors examined in this chapter, and the evidence best fits the notion that Taiwan's electoral cleavages are relatively stable and generally reproducing themselves in younger generations thus far.

Lastly, one can ask how the ethnic cleavages seen in this chapter manifest themselves in partisanship. Party preferences are crucial: they structure not only presidential choices but also votes for lower-level offices. They

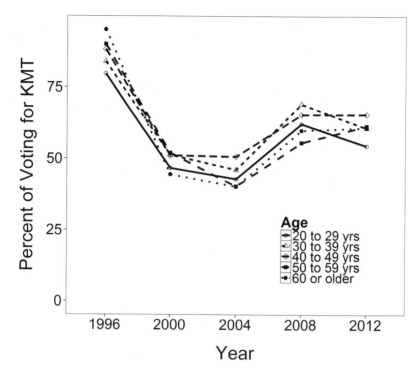

Fig. 2.7. Percentages of five age groups voting for the KMT. *Data:* See appendix 2.A3.

also determine how voters see the political world. Thus it is important to ask how different ethnic groups have evolved in their partisan attachments. For that purpose, annual data are available, not just information from presidential years.

Figure 2.8 show how KMT partisan loyalties of the three main ethnic groups have evolved since 1992. Remarkably, KMT identification is nearly constant among all three groups over a period of 30 years. And the differences among them are very large, amounting to more than 30 percentage points. It is clear that ethnicity is a key determinant of KMT partisanship.

Figure 2.9 gives the same information for DPP partisans. Prior to 2000, many citizens disguised their anti-KMT leanings by calling themselves "independents." But since Chen Shui-bian's first presidential race, DPP partisanship, too, has been very stable within each ethnic group. Apart from some disenchantment in the later years of the Chen presidency, the DPP has held the same share of partisans it attracted in its first successful presidential

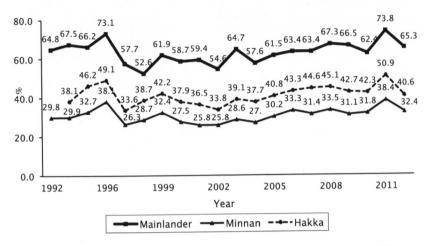

Fig. 2.8. Partisan identification with the Pan-Blue Alliance by ethnic groups, 1992–2012. *Data source: Core Political Attitudes among Taiwanese* (Election Study Center, NCCU).

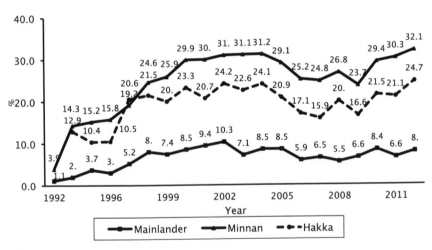

Fig. 2.9. Partisan identification with the Pan-Green Alliance by ethnic groups, 1992–2012. *Data source: Core Political Attitudes among Taiwanese* (Election Study Center, NCCU).

race. And, again, the differences between Minnan and mainlanders are very large, amounting to nearly 25 percentage points in recent years.

Thus in general, the evidence seems to suggest that Taiwan voters who are in their 30s and 40s, with higher level of education, who are relatively well-off, or are working in the public sector tend to be the most supportive of the Pan-Blue Alliance. Candidates of the Pan-Green Alliance are more appealing to citizens who are in their 20s, have low income, or are employed in the agricultural or labor sectors. None of these factors has effects nearly as large as ethnicity, which has by far the biggest impact on vote choices and on partisanship. However, as it will be shown in chapter 3, with Taiwan's democracy becoming increasingly consolidated the ethnic cleavage among its citizens has gradually been transformed and cloaked in their partisan attachments.

Conclusion

Drawing on survey data about Taiwan voters' electoral choices since 1996, this chapter has provided a general characterization of Taiwan voters. It has shown that the partisan preferences of citizens on the island are focused on the Pan-Blue and the Pan-Green alliances. As Taiwan's democracy has increasingly consolidated into a competitive two-party system, each alliance has become dominated by a single party, the KMT and the DPP, respectively.

The Pan-Blue Alliance has enjoyed a 5–10 percentage point electoral advantage during the past three presidential elections. This electoral gap is not constant across the island. For a variety of economic and historical reasons, Taiwan's political landscape is divided, with the Pan-Blue Alliance dominating the northern part of the island and the Pan-Green Alliance receiving strong support in the south.

The chapter has also shown that the two electoral alliances are based on different parts of the voting population. At the risk of oversimplification, one may say that citizens who are mainlanders, well-educated, more affluent, government employees, or in their 30s and 40s are more likely to provide electoral support for Pan-Blue candidates. On the other hand, voters who are less educated, less well-off, working in labor and agricultural sectors, or in their 20s tend to identify with the Pan-Green Alliance. But all these differences are dwarfed by the impact of ethnicity, which has very large impacts on both vote choices and on partisan identity.

This description of the support base of each party group raises a host of questions. Why are people in each of these sectors drawn disproportionately to one party rather than another? Are the differences primarily ideological, while demographic differences are merely incidental? Or do identity differences shape both opinions and partisan loyalties? Or does everything reduce to the economy and pocketbook voting? And why has popular support come to be focused on just two parties? Subsequent chapters take up these questions.

Appendix 2.A1

Wording and coding of demographic variables

Age. In what year were you born? 20–29 years old=1, 30–39 years old=2, 40–49 years old=3, 50–59 years old=4, 60 years old and above=5.

Education. What is the highest degree that you finished? Elementary school and below=1, high school=2, college/graduate school=3.

Occupation. What is your current occupation and position?

Income. What is your household's total income? See appendix 2.A2 for classification.

Ethnicity. What is your father's ethnicity? Minnan=1, Hakka=2, mainlander=3.

Region. Where do you live? Taipei City, Taipei County and Keelung City, Taoyuan County, Miaoli County, Hsinchu City, Hsinchu County Taichung City, Taichung County, Chunghwa County, Nantou City Tainan City, Tainan County, Kaohsiung City, Kaohsiung County, Pingtung County, Penghu County, Ilan County, Hwalien County and Taitung County.

Appendix 2.A2

Classification of Three Income Groups

According to the yearly family income data published by the Directorate-General of Budget, Accounting and Statistics, the monthly family income of the 20th percentile and 80th percentile is calculated. Based on these two numbers, respondent's income is categorized as low, middle, and high. For example, the 80th percentile of monthly family income was NTD 131,798 and the 20th percentile was NTD 24,680. Respondents who answered "no income," "below NTD 15,000," and "between NTD 15,000 and 30,000" fall into the low income group. Respondents who answered "between NTD 100,000 and NTD 200,000" and "more than 200,000" belong to the high income group. Respondents whose income is higher than NTD 30,000 but lower than NTD 100,000 are defined as the middle income group.

In 1998 and 2000, respondents were asked their personal income instead of their household income. Because it is difficult to translate between these two measures, we dropped those years from the tabulation.

Appendix 2.A3

List of Datasets

An Interdisciplinary Studies of Voting Behavior in the Presidential Election in 2000 (ESC 1996). Principal investigator: Yih-yen Chen.

An Interdisciplinary Study of Voting Behavior in the 1996 Presidential Election (ESC 2000). Principal investigator: John F. S. Hsieh.

Taiwan's Election and Democratization Study, 2002–2004 (III): The Presidential Election, 2004 (TEDS2004P). Principal investigator: Shiow-duan Hwang.

Taiwan's Election and Democratization Study, 2008 (TEDS2008P). Principal investigator: Ching-hsin Yu.

Taiwan's Election and Democratization Study, 2009–2012 (III): The Survey of the Presidential and Legislative Elections, 2012 (TEDS 2012). Principal investigator: Yun-han Chu.

Notes

1. Prior to 1996, Taiwan's president was indirectly elected by its now defunct National Assembly.

2. The reality of the assassination attempt is disputed between the parties.

3. Aboriginals also give the KMT majority support, so that the KMT is in many respects a coalition of minorities, while the DPP largely represents the majority sub-ethnic group. Many other countries have a similar party-bloc structure, including the United States, in which the Republicans get heavy support from the white majority while the Democrats are disproportionately a coalition of racial, ethnic, and religious minorities.

References

Archer, J. Clark, and Peter J. Taylor. 1981. *Section and Party: A Political Geography of American Presidential Elections from Andrew Jackson to Ronald Reagan.* New York: Research Studies Press.

Hsu, Huo-yan. 1998. "The Political Psychology of Lee Teng-hui Complex and Its Effects on Voting Behavior" [in Chinese]. *Xuan Ju Yan Jiu* [Journal of electoral studies] 5 (2): 35–71.

Hsu, Huo-yan. 2004. "Taiwan-China Complex and Taiwan-China Concern: Symbolic Politics in Taiwan's Elections" [in Chinese]. *Xuan Ju Yan Jiu* [Journal of electoral studies] 11 (2): 1–41.

Lin, Chia-lung. 1989. "Opposition Movement in Taiwan under an Authoritarian-Clientelist Regime: A Political Explanation for the Social Base of the DPP" [in Chinese]. *Taiwan She Hui Xue Ji Kan* [Taiwan: A radical quarterly in social studies] (Spring): 117–43.

Tindall, George B. 1972. *The Disruption of the Solid South.* Athens: University of Georgia Press.

Wang, Fu-chang. 1998. "Ethnic Consciousness, Nationalism, and Party Support: Taiwan's Ethnic Politics in the 1990s" [in Chinese]. *Taiwan She Hui Xue Kan* [Taiwanese sociological review] 2:1–45.

Winckler, Edwin A. 1992. "Taiwan Transition." In *Political Change in Taiwan,* ed. Tun-jen Cheng and Stephan Haggard, 221–59. Boulder, CO: Lynne Rienner.

You, Ying-lung. 1996. *Ming-yi yu Taiwan cheng-chi bien-chien [Public Opinion and Changing Taiwan Politics].* Taipei: Yue-Tan Press.

CHAPTER 3

Changing Boundaries

The Development of the Taiwan Voters' Identity

T. Y. Wang

The ubiquitous effect of identity in contemporary politics has been widely recognized in the scholarship of the social sciences. Political instability within societies or bitter conflicts between nations has frequently been attributed to differences in identity politics (Horowitz 2000; Isaacs 1975), and Taiwan is no exception to this pattern. Indeed, the issue of identity has important implications not only for the island country's domestic politics but also for its relationship with China; hence, Taiwan's identity politics may affect peace and stability in East Asia.

Taiwan voters' identities have undergone substantial changes since the Nationalist (Kuomintang) government led by Chiang Kai-shek retreated to Taiwan in 1949. Since then, the "China factor" has played an essential part in the formation and change of the island citizens' identities. The re-Sinicization efforts by the authoritarian KMT government, the infusion of two million of Chiang's followers, the rapid democratization in the ensuing decades, and the continuing rivalry between China and Taiwan have transformed the island residents' identity in form and in substance. This chapter aims to trace the trajectory of Taiwan voters' identity change. With the notion of "boundary" framed in the theoretical frameworks of primordialism and constructionism, this study employs quantitative survey data collected over two decades and qualitative information gathered by focus-group interviews and in-depth interviews.[1] It argues that the substance of identity is relational because it involves the distinction between what it is and what it is not. The comparison and reference to other groups thus establish the boundary, and hence the identity. As the boundary changes, identity evolves as a result. The political environment and the policies adopted by political elites on both sides of the Taiwan Strait since World War II provide the impetus to the formation and the change of Taiwan voters' identities. Specifically, the initial boundary along the ethnic line between Taiwan's local residents, known as "Taiwanese," and "mainlanders" during the authoritarian era, changed to the contestation between "Taiwanese consciousness" and "Chinese consciousness" as the island country entered the period of democratization. With China's forceful claim over the island, the Beijing government's hostility became one of the main driving forces in the growth of a distinct national identity. The boundary of identity politics on the island has thus shifted from the ethnic divide to the characterization of Taiwan as an independent state.

Boundary Change: The Development of Identity

Identity can be understood as a psychological attachment to a social/political category. The substance of identity is relational because it involves the distinction between what it is and what it is not (Abdelal et al. 2009; Barnett 1999). The comparisons and reference to other identities therefore sets up "boundaries" between groups of individuals that facilitate the formulation of the "we-group" and the "they-group." In this sense, the development of identity is dependent on individuals' interactions with others as well as the time and the place that the interaction occurs. As interactions and the context differ, the boundary changes and the content of identity may vary as a result. Even though a certain identity may bear the same label, its substance may be different as boundaries shift. Research on identity thus needs to examine the impetus to identity formation and change. Primordialism and constructionism,[2] the two most commonly invoked identity perspectives, provide the theoretical underpinning of the analysis.

In the discussion of the development of identity, proponents of primordialism maintain that identities are deeply rooted in primordial attachments, which, as Charles Cooley and Edward Shils conceptualized, are "not merely to the other family member as a person, but as a possessor of certain especially 'significant relations' qualities" (Shils 1957, 142). These qualities stem from "the givens . . . of social existence" that involve "immediate contiguity and kin connection mainly, but beyond them the givenness that stems from being born into a particular religious community, speaking a particular language, or even a dialect of a language, and following particular social practices" (Geertz 1994, 31). These primordial bonds, which are based on blood, speech, and custom, define human relations and establish boundaries among groups of people. These boundaries then have the power of generating psychological attachments to groups. Proponents of primordialism thus maintain that identities are deep-rooted in blood, culture, and language. Although the effects of such primordial ties may vary from individual to individual, their impacts are long lasting. As Geertz (1994) indicated, "for virtually every person, in every society, at almost all times, some attachments seem to flow more from a sense of natural—some would say spiritual—affinity than from social interaction" (31). As a result, identities rooted in blood, culture, and languages are assumed to be given and immutable.

The constructionist perspective refutes the primordialist view that identities are inherited and underivable (Gellner 2008; Laitin 1998). Constructionists maintain that identities can be fostered or intentionally constructed and that when social interactions change, identity can alter as a result. In this conception, boundaries can be artificially established. First, societies have various socialization mechanisms, such as education and family. Through these media, individuals are exposed to the customs and conventions of various groups, cultures, and norms of the society as well as to the historical memories of the nation. Feelings of distinctiveness from other groups of people are formed, and psychological attachments to these entities are created. Furthermore, most nations maintain an interpretative version of history that frequently emphasizes the oppression and exploitation of the people. To form a hostile "they-group" and unified "we-group," political elites frequently employ state institutions to exploit such unequal and exploitative historical memories. With the objective of mobilizing their fellow citizens, this collective group consciousness becomes an essential part of the public identity. Sometimes, in an attempt to change an existing identity or create a new identity, the state intentionally recognizes one or a few groups and ignores others. This is frequently done by subsidizing or celebrating the chosen groups' languages, cultures, or historical memories through education, propaganda, and other political means. As Gellner (2008, 54) succinctly points out in his discussion of national identity, "nationalism uses the pre-existing, historically inherited proliferation of cultures, or cultural wealth, though it uses them very selectively, and it most often transforms them radically. Dead languages can be revived, traditions invented, quite fictitious pristine purities restored." As a result, the celebrated group identity becomes the dominant one in the society, and a public identity is likely to be constructed through the engineering of the state. From the constructionist perspective, identities are more than the function of race and ethnicity, and they are not unchangeable and underivable. Because boundaries can be intentionally manipulated through policies and socialization media, identity can be constructed through deliberate efforts.

The China Factor and Taiwan's Changing Political Environment

The Boundary of Ethnicity

As noted in chapter 1, Taiwan's modern history has been closely linked to political development on the Chinese mainland. After the Qing dynasty established administrative control of the island in the seventeenth century, thousands of residents in coastal provinces migrated to Taiwan seeking a better life in the subsequent decade. Taiwan's sovereignty was later ceded to Japan by China's last imperial dynasty in 1895. Unlike the Chinese mainland, which was plagued by wars and chaos in the ensuing half century, Taiwan advanced to become a more modern society during the same period under the assimilation policy of the Japanese colonial authority. Although many Taiwan residents received a Japanese education, they still longed for their Chinese ancestral roots. The population was overjoyed when the island's sovereignty was returned to the Chinese government, which was controlled by the KMT at the end of World War II. The local residents' enthusiasm for returning to the "motherland" soon evaporated because the ruling authority dispatched to Taiwan in 1945 was corrupt and its policies discriminated against the local residents. As a result, many Taiwanese elites were filled with nostalgia for Japanese colonial rule, which was remembered as being efficient and honest. KMT officials in turn viewed the islanders with suspicion since they were under the influence of the Japanese Empire while the KMT government was fighting Japanese invaders on the mainland. The animosity between the KMT government and local residents, particularly the Minnan group, finally culminated in a bloody crackdown on the Taiwanese elites by KMT troops, a tragic event known as the 2–28 Incident of 1947. This outbreak of hostility solidified the local perception of the KMT government as simply a new foreign regime and occupying force (Lai, Myers, and Wou 1991).

The ethnic division on the island deepened further after the KMT government retreated to Taiwan after its humiliating military defeat on the mainland. Along with the government came two million of its followers, who were known as mainlanders. Insisting that the Republic of China (ROC) had the legitimate and sovereign claim over China, including both

Taiwan and the Chinese mainland, Taipei's ruling elites imposed harsh authoritarian rule. As it was stated in chapter 1, a series of prejudicial measures were implemented to "re-Sinicize" local residents to accept the view that Taiwan was part of a greater China and to foster their Chinese identity. By recognizing and celebrating China-centered historical memories, activities that might arouse local identities and promote Taiwan independence were censored and suppressed. Meanwhile, local residents' freedom of expression and association was substantially curtailed under martial law. Through interpretations of the constitution by the Grand Justice Court, clauses relevant to presidential term limits and regular parliamentary elections were suspended. Using all of China as the "imagined community,"[3] local residents' participation in legislative politics was restricted because Taiwan was deemed only one of the 36 provinces of the nation, and their representation in the parliament was treated as such (Wang 2008). The net effect of these authoritarian measures was that a small group of mainland elites effectively monopolized political power on the island, especially at the national level. The perception that mainlanders were the oppressor and local Taiwanese were the oppressed underlined the ethnic cleavage on the island. This ethnic divide thus became the first boundary among the island's residents in Taiwan's modern history. Many mainlanders believed that the only way to survive in this unfriendly environment was to support the KMT government. This rational calculation and their emotional affinity to the Chinese mainland strengthened the mainlanders' espousal of Chinese consciousness, which also turned into a partisan identification with the KMT.

Although the boundary between Taiwanese, particularly the Minnan group, and mainlanders continued to exist during the subsequent several decades, the ethnic division as a major social cleavage increasingly lost its political importance. First, constant social contacts among various ethnic groups in schools, workplaces, and other social settings help to narrow the differences between them. Most islanders' ability to speak the official language—Mandarin—and the ability to converse in local dialects by some mainlanders also enhanced mutual understanding among ethnic groups on the island. Interethnic marriages over the past several decades have blurred ethnic lines and produced a new generation that has been more accepting of different ideas from all ethnic groups. Most important, the rapid democratization on the island in the 1980s also contributed to weakening the significance of the ethnic divide. With the lifting of martial law, freedom of expression and association became constitutional rights protected by law. After Lee Teng-hui became the first native-born president in 1988, and later with the passage of constitutional amendments in the mid-1990s that stipulate popular elections of the presidency and a new parliament, mainlanders could no longer monopolize political power. Meanwhile, local politicians began to advocate such slogans as "collectivity of common fate" (*sheng-ming-gong-tong-ti*), "the rising new nation" (*xin-xing-min-zu*), and "the new Taiwanese" (*xin-Taiwanren*) in an attempt to ease the ethnic tension between Taiwanese and mainlanders and garner electoral support. As local residents' sense of relative deprivation in the power distribution dissipated, along with politicians' conscious efforts to allay ethnic tension, the antagonistic feeling between the mainlander and other ethnic groups gradually attenuated.

Empirical research employing interpretative approaches and quantitative analyses supports this conclusion (Chang 2006; Cheng 2009; Pao 2009; Wang 2008). Table 3.1 presents survey responses from the Minnan and Hakka groups on their views of Taiwan's ethnic relations. It shows that by 2006 about 40 percent of Minnan and Hakka respondents or their close relatives had intergroup marriages with mainlanders, and 67 percent of them felt they got along with mainlanders as equally well as with those of their own ethnic groups. About 69 percent believed that they had the same social status as mainlanders. As the boundary between local residents and mainlanders has become increasingly blurry, ethnic identity has lost its power of differentiation. That said, this does not mean that there is no political difference among Taiwan's major ethnic groups. As chapter 2 has shown, the

TABLE 3.1. Minnan and Hakka on Ethnic Tension

Are you or any of your close relatives married to a mainlander? (*N* = 934)	%
Yes	41.8
No	56.4
No response	1.7
Who do you get along with? (*N* = 1082)	**%**
Minnan and Hakka	24.1
Mainlander	2.7
Both about the same	67.0
No response	6.2
Do you feel those mainlanders you know have higher social status than you? (*N* = 934)	**%**
Better	14.2
About the same	69.1
Worse	2.8
No response	13.9

Source: Chen 2006.

ethnic cleavage among Taiwan citizens has gradually been transformed and cloaked in their partisan attachments. That is, the mainlanders as a group consistently have a disproportional partisan attachment to the Pan-Blue political alliance, whereas members of the Minnan group present the opposite pattern in their party identification with the Pan-Green camp. Alternatively, a new boundary between Taiwanese consciousness and Chinese consciousness has increasingly become prominent on the island.

The Boundary of Chinese/Taiwanese Consciousness

The contestation between Chinese consciousness (*zhong-guo-yi-shi*) and Taiwanese consciousness (*Taiwan-yi-shi*) concerns the interpretation of the relationship between Taiwan and the Chinese mainland.[4] In the conception of Chinese consciousness, "China" is a term that encompasses both cultural and political significance. To be Chinese implies belonging not only to a particular ethnic and cultural group but also to the political identity of the Chinese state known as *zhong-guo*, in which Taiwanese culture is a part of Chinese culture and the Taiwanese people are a part of the Chinese population. Since the island of Taiwan is an integral part of China, the eventual unification of Taiwan with the Chinese mainland is regarded as both natural and inevitable. Those who espouse Taiwanese consciousness, by contrast, challenge the idea that Taiwan is a part of China. They argue that the one-hundred-year separation of Taiwan from the Chinese mainland has created a Taiwanese culture distinct from that of the Chinese mainland. The ideas that Taiwan and China are one nation and that all Chinese must be ruled by a single government within the same state are thus rejected. Some even assert that "Taiwanese are not Chinese" and have opposed the assertion that Taiwan is a part of China in any sense (Shih 1992, quoted in Huang 1993, 49). While advocates of Chinese consciousness behold a China-centered interpretation of the island's relations with the Chinese mainland, proponents of Taiwanese consciousness take a Taiwan-centered view of the relationship.

As indicated earlier, during its authoritarian rule of the island, one of the major tasks of the KMT government was to foster Chinese consciousness and its accompanying Chinese identity so that local residents would accept the view that China was their motherland. Throughout the several decades after 1949, the leaders of the KMT upheld the principle of "one China," of which Taiwan was considered to be a part. Even after Lee Teng-hui became president, he was careful not to challenge the One China principle for fear of offending the party's old guard. Presiding over the newly established

National Unification Council, Lee promulgated the National Unification Guidelines in March 1991, symbolizing the commitment of his administration to Taiwan's eventual unification with the Chinese mainland. The rapid democratization that was set in motion in the late 1980s nevertheless later made the advocacy of Taiwan independence into a constitutional right protected by law. The previous China-centered school curriculum was also revised and shifted to a new emphasis on the island's history and culture (Wang 2001). In particular, local politicians' advocacy of such slogans as "the new Taiwanese" had the effect of fostering a new identity on the island. By the mid-1990s, Taiwanese consciousness has become the strongest alternative to Chinese consciousness.

The rivalry between the two perspectives rose to its zenith during the eight-year presidency of Chen Shui-bian, of the DPP, from 2000 to 2008. Chen has strong pro-independence credentials, and his affiliated DPP is the only major political party on the island that advocates the island's de jure independence. To raise the local population's Taiwanese consciousness and identity, the Taipei government under Chen's leadership launched a series of de-Sinicization initiatives on the island. As a result, Chinese consciousness and its related Chinese identity were under severe attack during Chen's presidency. Like the Chiang regime, the Chen administration selectively recognized a portion of Taiwan's historical memories, in particular those related to the 2–28 Incident. Other measures were adopted to promote an image that Taiwan is a separate political entity from China, including adding the phrase "Issued in Taiwan" to the island country's green passport cover and dropping the national emblem of the ROC as the official logo of Taiwan's overseas missions. With the revision of history textbooks, education has been used to change the collective memories of the Taiwan's citizens (Wang 2001; Wang and Chang 2005). The Chen administration's efforts to strengthen Taiwanese identity reached a climax when the Rectification Movement (*zheng-ming-yung-dong*) was launched in 2007 by replacing "China" in the names of all relevant government and state-run agencies with "Taiwan."[5] It also renamed the Chiang Kai-shek Memorial Hall and proposed a referendum for UN membership that was held during the 2008 presidential elections (Enav 2007; Mo and Shih 2007). All of these measures aimed to celebrate Taiwanese consciousness for its own sake and as a way of rejecting Chinese consciousness. As the contestation between the two perspectives became increasingly prominent on the island, the divide was manifested in the changing patterns of the island residents' self-identification as a Taiwanese or a Chinese.

During the period between 1992 and 2012, surveys conducted by the

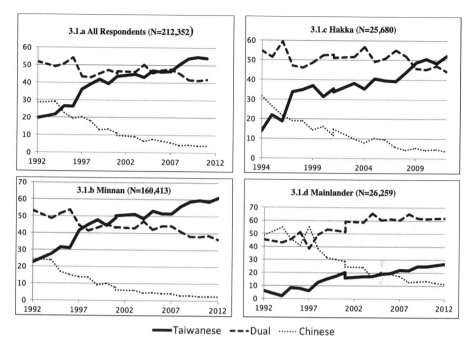

Fig. 3.1. Identity change by ethnicity, 1992–2012. *Data source: Core Political Attitudes among Taiwanese (Election Study Center, NCCU).*

Election Study Center, National Chengchi University, in Taiwan, asked respondents the following question:

> In our society, some people consider themselves Taiwanese, and others view themselves as Chinese, while still others see themselves as both Taiwanese and Chinese. What is your view on this matter?

Figure 3.1 shows that the island citizens' identity has undergone significant change over the course of past two decades, signifying the vicissitudes of Taiwanese consciousness and Chinese consciousness. Indeed, as figure 3.1.a demonstrates, the overall ratio of Taiwanese identifiers has increased substantially since 1992, from about 20 percent to 40 percent in 2000, and has continued rising. When President Ma Ying-jeou of the KMT was inaugurated in 2008, more than half of the island's citizens considered themselves Taiwanese. Four years later, the percentage of Taiwanese identifiers increased to 56 percent, an increase of more than 45 percent from two decades ago. During the same period, the proportion of Chinese identifiers on the island declined significantly, from close to 30 percent in 1992 to about 4 percent in 2012, a decline of about 25 percent. Interestingly, the percentage of dual identifiers on the island—those who see themselves as both Chinese and Taiwanese—has been quite steady, hovering around 45 percent since 2001, even though it also witnessed a slight decline by 2012.

The pattern of identity change appears to occur across ethnic lines for the three largest ethnic groups on the island. Figures 3.1.b and 3.1.c show that the changing patterns of both Minnan and Hakka groups resemble the overall trend in Taiwan, as increasing proportions of the two groups consider themselves Taiwanese while the number of Chinese identifiers has dropped significantly, to less than 5 percent by 2012. Currently, a substantial proportion of Minnan and Hakka, about 35 percent and 45 percent, respectively, hold dual identity, considering themselves both Chinese and Taiwanese. For the mainlanders, the ratio of Chinese identifiers also witnessed a significant decline during the same period, from about 50 percent in 1992 to around 10 percent in 2012, as figure 3.1.d shows. Like the Minnan and Hakka groups, the number of Taiwanese identifiers among mainlanders has increased during the same period, but substantially less so by comparison. Since 2004, more than 60 percent of them accepted that they are Chinese as well as Taiwanese.

Figure 3.2 also presents the distribution of identity change for the five political generations in Taiwan.[6] As with the overall trend, there was a steady increase of respondents holding Taiwanese identity and a continual decline of Chinese identifiers for each of the five generations. By 2012, more than half of all age groups were Taiwanese identifiers, while the proportions of Chinese identifiers fell to about 5 percent, except for respondents of the first generation, who were at least 81 years old and increasingly dying off. What is worth noting is that more than 60 percent of the fifth generation are holders of Taiwanese identity while very few of them are Chinese identifiers. That 40 percent to 50 percent of the third and the fourth generations are holders of dual identity probably is because these respondents received the China-centered education during their formative years under the KMT authoritarian rule.

What are the island citizens' views on the meaning of being Chinese/Taiwanese? An examination of the qualitative data from focus-group interviews conducted since 2000 shows that Taiwan voters tend to take a primordial view of being "Taiwanese." A recurrent statement made by all interviewees is that "I was born here, I grew up here, and therefore I am a Taiwanese," even though they do not reject their Chinese cultural origin. In response to questions on the definitions of Chinese and Taiwanese, a third-generation

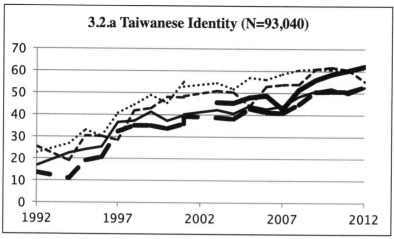

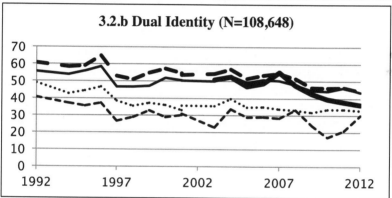

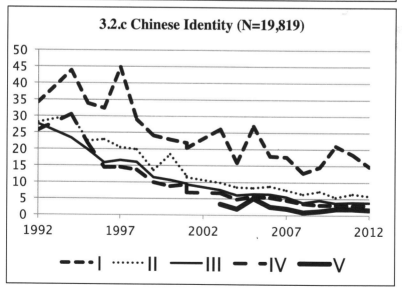

Fig. 3.2. Chinese/Taiwanese identity by generations, 1992–2012. *Data source: Core Political Attitudes among Taiwanese* (Election Study Center, NCCU).

interviewee stated in 2000 that "Taiwanese are those who live in Taiwan. We have the same customs . . . and we are 'made in Taiwan'" (2000SB05). For the fourth- and fifth-generation interviewees, the answer is more straightforward: "Chinese are those who were born in China and Taiwanese are those who were born in Taiwan" (2011TSQI06) and "those who were born in Taiwan are Taiwanese" (2011TSQI07).

Such a primordial conceptualization of Taiwanese identity appears to cross the ethnic line. Some mainlanders recognized that their immediate ancestors or even themselves were born on the Chinese mainland, but the very fact that they had been living in Taiwan for half a century led them to espouse Taiwanese identity. A first-generation mainlander contended in 2002 that "Taiwanese are those who live in Taiwan. Even though I came from the mainland, I am a Taiwanese as I have lived here for half a century" (2002–31). Another mainlander stated that "I am a Taiwanese. I was born here and grew up here. I drink Taiwan's water and eat Taiwan's rice. There is no mistake that I am a Taiwanese" (2011CUSQD06).

This primordial conceptualization also crosses the generational line, and in fact the tendency becomes stronger as interviewees get younger in age. For the fifth-generation respondents, to define who they are by birthplace is the most natural and straightforward approach. For instance, a 2011 fifth-generation interviewee defined "Taiwanese" in a blunt manner: "those who were born in Taiwan are Taiwanese" (2011TSQI07).

While there appears to be a consensus about the meaning of Taiwanese, respondents of different ethnic groups and generations have defined "Chinese" in two different but noncontradictory ways. Some conceptualize the term in a primordial sense, treating the association of culture and ethnicity as the defining characteristic of being Chinese. Since residents in Taiwan and on the Chinese mainland share many cultural and ethnic traits, "Taiwanese" is considered a subgroup of "Chinese," and thus logically "Taiwanese" is "Chinese," broadly defined. Others define the term with a political meaning by equating "Chinese" with "the citizens of the People's Republic of China (PRC)" and "China" with "the Chinese state" or "the PRC regime." In this conceptualization, they maintain that since Taiwanese are not citizens of the PRC, they are not "Chinese." Thus, in the mind of Taiwan voters, the term "Chinese" may have separate cultural and political connotations. Along with the quantitative survey data presented earlier, it appears that the vast majority of the island's citizens have employed the term of "Chinese" with a political meaning. This may explain why few of them are Chinese identifiers: they do not consider themselves citizens of the PRC. If they have emotional affinity with the country of China (*zhong-guo*), many respondents adopted

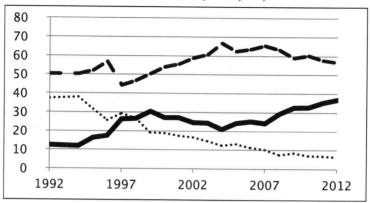

3.3.a Pan-Blue (N=82,469)

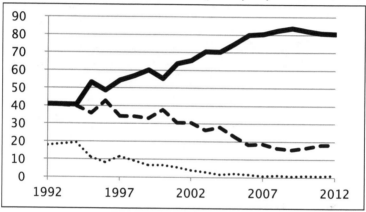

3.3.b Pan-Green (N=52,122)

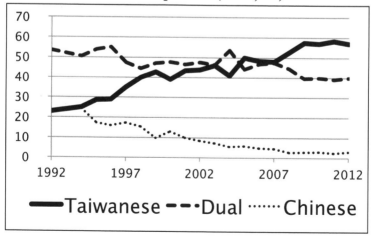

3.3.c Independent (N=85,685)

Fig. 3.3. Identity and partisan support, 1992–2012. *Data source: Core Political Attitudes among Taiwanese* (Election Study Center, NCCU).

dual identity, of which its Chinese element has a cultural meaning. In other words, when the term "Chinese" (*zhong-guo-ren*) is applied to Taiwan voters, it has less of the political designation that is traditionally associated with a Chinese polity and more of the cultural and ethnic connotations that should be more appropriately understood as "ethnic Chinese" (*hua-ren*).

Thus, the contestation between Taiwanese consciousness and Chinese consciousness has increasingly tilted toward the former as more and more citizens on the island become Taiwanese identifiers. Such a trend applies to all three major ethnic groups in Taiwan, including mainlanders, who traditionally espouse Chinese consciousness. While many mainlanders continue to view the word "China" as a term representing a culture, a nation, and a state and are holders of a dual identity, the majority of them have become indigenized to the point of accepting a part of their identity as being Taiwanese. However, like the ethnic divide on the island, Chinese/Taiwanese consciousness has also been cloaked by partisanship. Figure 3.3 shows that the island citizens holding Taiwanese identity tend to be supporters of the Pan-Green Alliance, led by the DPP, whereas those with Chinese identity and dual identity are more likely to develop a partisan attachment to the Pan-Blue Alliance, led by the KMT. Indeed, as subsequent chapters show, the KMT tends to be perceived by Taiwan voters as a party holding Chinese consciousness with a pro-unification stand, and the DPP as a party holding Taiwanese consciousness with a pro-independence position. Meanwhile, as the divide of Chinese/Taiwanese consciousness is increasingly cloaked by partisanship within a domestic context, the public discourse on the cleavage continues on the island but has shifted to a new boundary.[7]

The Boundary of National Identity

In addition to its domestic element, the rivalry between Chinese consciousness and Taiwanese consciousness also has an external dimension due to Beijing's forceful claim of the island. After being defeated by Communist troops in 1949, the KMT government, led by Chiang Kai-shek, retreated to Taiwan to continue what was perceived as the sacred mission of "recovering the mainland" from the Chinese Communists. By the late 1960s, the Chiang family's ambitious goal of national unification by the ROC, headquartered in Taipei, had become increasingly unlikely. The passage of UN Resolution 2758 in 1971, which recognized the Beijing government as "the only lawful representatives of China to the United Nations," symbolized the decisive victory of the PRC in the cross-Strait competition for international legitimacy. Since then, Beijing leaders have steadfastly applied their version of the One China principle in the international community: that "there is only one China in the world, Taiwan is a part of China and the government of the PRC is the sole legal government representing the whole of China" (TAO 2000). Refusing to recognize the legitimate existence of the ROC on Taiwan, Chinese leaders maintain that the island has no legal right to establish diplomatic relations with foreign countries or to participate in any international organizations requiring statehood as a condition of membership. Over the years, the increasing importance of China in international affairs has led many countries to break diplomatic relations with Taipei as a necessary condition for establishing formal ties with the Beijing government. The number of states recognizing the ROC dropped significantly in the 1970s and 1980s. To participate in international organizations, most of which are nongovernmental in nature, the Taipei government frequently had to compromise on its name, flag, and national anthem in order to meet Beijing's demands (Lee and Wang 2003; Wang, Lee, and Yu 2011). As of 2013, only twenty-three countries officially recognized the Republic of China, and Taipei was in just a handful of international governmental organizations. Beijing's tactic of diplomatic isolation is humiliating to Taiwanese citizens and seriously hurts their dignity because they believe that Taiwan is more qualified to enjoy the legitimacy as a state than such UN members as Nauru and the Marshall Islands.

Indeed, Taiwan witnessed significant economic growth and political development even as its international space was being squeezed by Beijing's tactic of diplomatic isolation. The island's manufacturing sector went through rapid expansion, with the country's GDP growing at about 9 percent per year during the two decades starting in 1970.[8] As one of the largest trading nations in the world and ranking among the top holders of foreign exchange reserves, Taiwan was considered one of the newly industrialized countries. In addition to its economic achievements, Taiwan also witnessed rapid democratization in the 1990s. With political power being peacefully transferred between political parties through regular elections since 2000, Taiwan has become a genuine democracy. The island country's lack of international standing simply does not match its political achievement and status as a world-class economy, and Taiwanese citizens blame Beijing for the country's lack of international legitimacy (Wang 2006).

Meanwhile, Beijing has also employed the tactic of military coercion. Refusing to renounce the use of military force to resolve the cross-Strait dispute, Chinese leaders have deployed more than 1,000 short-range ballistic missiles along China's coast area, targeting them at Taiwan. In order to weaken the

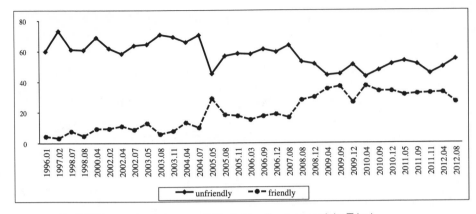

Fig. 3.4. Taiwan voters' views on Beijing's friendliness toward the Taipei government, 1996–2012. *Data source: Core Political Attitudes among Taiwanese.* (Election Study Center, NCCU).

island's defensive capability, Beijing has deliberately prevented any country from selling weapons to Taiwan. When Chinese leaders launched the eight-month-long missile test and military exercises in 1995–96 and issued saber-rattling threats in 2000, China became a genuine menace to the island citizens' democratic way of life and economic prosperity (Garver 1997; Wang 2001). Thus, Beijing's tactics of diplomatic isolation and military coercion have invited Taiwanese citizens' resentment. As a hostile "they-group" bearing the name "China" has formed in the mind of the island's citizens, the boundary of Chinese/Taiwanese consciousness that was largely confined to domestic politics has increasingly shifted to the level between a "Chinese state" and a "Taiwanese state."

Figure 3.4. shows that a large proportion of Taiwanese citizens have consistently sensed an "unfriendly" Chinese government since 1996. The feeling of Beijing's antagonism toward the Taipei government reached its zenith during the period 2000–2008, when President Chen was in office, as 60 percent to 70 percent of Taiwan voters perceived the animosity from across the Taiwan Strait. Data in table 3.2 demonstrate that there is a strong association between the island citizens' feeling of Beijing's enmity and their holding of Taiwanese identity. Qualitative data from focus-group interviews provide an interpretative understanding of this relation. In addition to the primordial ties mentioned in the last section, many focus-group respondents also justified their holding of Taiwanese identity by their frustration at Beijing's "suppression" (*da-ya*) of Taiwan in the international community. One of the respondents commented that "I was born here. . . . China continues bullying and suppressing us, which makes me feel that Taiwan is not like a country. When I travel abroad, I feel no country likes us [to be treated unfairly by Beijing]. . . . I am a Taiwanese. . . . I was born here. . . . I never feel that I am Chinese. . . . I am totally different from them" (2010S401). Some of them cited Taiwanese athletes' inability to carry the island country's national flag and to sing the national anthem in international sport competitions as examples of Beijing's "bullying practices" (*ya-ba*). As another respondent complained, "Because Chinese doesn't allow us to carry our national flag in international baseball games or Olympic competitions, . . . I feel they are always harassing us. . . . I feel they are bullying us. . . . [Interviewer: Do you think you are both Chinese and Taiwanese?] . . . No, I am just a Taiwanese!" (2010N403).

The resulting humiliation and resentment prevented Taiwan citizens from identifying with a hostile "China." At the same time, the loss of inter-

TABLE 3.2. Perceptions of Beijing's Friendliness and Chinese/Taiwanese Identity

	Friendly Beijing	Unfriendly Beijing	Total
Taiwanese identity	21.2	78.8	61.9
	13.1	48.8	(826)
Dual identity	49.9	50.1	34.4
	17.2	17.2	(459)
Chinese identity	64.0	36.0	3.7
	2.4	1.3	(50)
Total	100%	100%	100%
	(436)	(899)	(1335)

Source: Cheng 2013.
Note: Row percentages on top, total percentages underlined, and numbers of cases in parentheses.

TABLE 3.3. Identities and Views on Taiwan as an Independent State

	Taiwan and China are two independent states	Taiwan and the Chinese mainland are parts of China	Total
Taiwanese identity	80.2	19.8	58.8
	47.2	11.6	(637)
Dual identity	48.2	51.8	37.6
	18.1	19.5	(407)
Chinese identity	20.5	79.5	3.6
	0.7	2.9	(39)
Total	100%	100%	100%
	(715)	(368)	(1083)

Source: Cheng 2011.
Note: Row percentages on top, total percentages underlined, and numbers of cases in parentheses.

national legitimacy by the ROC has made the sense of belonging to "Taiwan" as a state the only distinction between them and citizens of China. The island residents' bitter feelings of Beijing's diplomatic "bullying" has thus hardened their identity with an independent Taiwan that is separate from China. As one respondent commented, "I feel I am a Taiwanese. . . . Because I was born here and grew up here . . . I feel that we really should tell people that [we are Taiwanese]. If we do not speak out, we would disappear . . . then when we go abroad, foreigners will not respect you and you will feel that you don't have a country any more" (2010N302). Another stated that "I will always emphasize that I am a Taiwanese when I go abroad" (2011TSQF04). Quantitative survey data in table 3.3 confirm that this sentiment is widespread, as about 80 percent of Taiwanese identifiers and 50 percent of dual identifiers now view Taiwan as an independent state. As the boundary between Taiwanese and Chinese gradually loses its power of differentiation within a domestic context, the external dimension of the boundary becomes increasingly prominent. The public discourse on the Chinese/Taiwanese distinction has shifted to the level of national identity.

Independence or Unification?

With a Taiwan-centered political identity becoming the overriding view on the island, one might conclude that Taiwan voters would lose their emotional attachment to China and support the island's de jure independence at all costs. Figure 3.5 presents the island residents' positions on the issue of independence versus unification. A quick glance at figure 3.5.a seems to confirm the above conclusion; that is, the overall support for a cross-Strait unification has declined precipitously. The declining support for unification is clearly visible across all generations, as figure 3.5.b shows, and there is little sign of it rebounding any time soon. While support for independence has been increasing since 2000, figures 3.5.a and 3.5.c indicate that its overall support has stabilized to about 20 percent between 2003 and 2012, although the fifth generation tends to be more supportive of independence. After the eight-year rule by the DPP, the only major political party on the island that has called for the establishment of a Republic of Taiwan, support for de jure independence has only increased slightly by comparison. It is important to note that, throughout the last two decades, 35 percent to 45 percent of respondents have remained undecided regarding their preferences over Taiwan's long-term status. Such a tendency is stronger for younger gen-

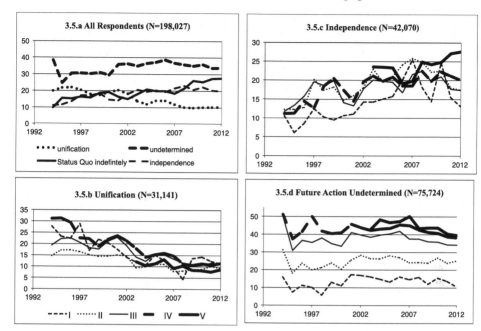

Fig. 3.5. Independence/unification by generations, 1994–2012. *Data source: Core Political Attitudes among Taiwanese.* (Election Study Center, NCCU).

erations, as figure 3.5.d shows, since 40 percent of the fourth and fifth generations have taken a wait-and-see position since 2008.

Previous analyses have shown that preferences for the island's future relations with China are conditioned by perceived costs (Hsieh and Niou 2005; Niou 2004; Wang 2005; Wu 1993). The majority of the respondents expressed a preference for independence if there would be no war with China, but they were not willing to if Beijing would respond violently. They rejected unification if there were great disparity between the two sides of the Taiwan Strait but were divided on the issue of unification if the social, economic, and political conditions of the two systems were relatively compatible. In particular, those respondents who took a wait-and-see position appear to be more sensitive to future circumstances than others (Wang 2009). Supporters of independence or unification are more likely to continue to back their respective positions even if the preferred positions are associated with high costs. The "undetermined" islanders, however, tend to switch their positions from one preference to the other when favorable conditions are present and thus serve as swing voters. Given their sizeable number, their decisions in either direction could form a majority that will determine Taipei's course of action regarding its future relations with Beijing. Overall, these findings show that Taiwan voters are pragmatic and risk averse on cross-Strait relations and that they are not willing to sacrifice their hard-won democratic way of life and economic prosperity for such radical political changes as declaring de jure independence or unification. Despite the rising Taiwanese identity on the island, Taiwan's future relations with China remain undetermined because the island citizens are pragmatic and risk averse.

Conclusions

As with many countries in the world, the formation and change of citizens' identities have played a major role in Taiwan's contemporary politics. To examine the trajectory of Taiwan voters' identity change, this study employs the notion of "boundary" framed in the theoretical frameworks of primordialism and constructionism. By analyzing quantitative survey data and qualitative information gathered through focus-group interviews over the course of two decades, it shows that the "China factor" has been the essential component of the changing boundaries that shape Taiwan voters' identities. Immediately after the KMT's retreat to the island, the identity boundary was set at the ethnic divide between local citizens and mainlanders because a small group of mainland elites monopolized political power. With the rapid democratization since the late 1980s, along with other social changes on the island, the ethnic divide has been replaced by the contestation of Chinese/Taiwanese consciousness manifested in the island citizens' holding of Taiwanese, Chinese, or dual identities. Because the majority of Taiwan voters have now adopted Taiwanese identity and few are holders of Chinese identity, the boundary of Chinese/Taiwanese consciousness has gradually lost its political significance within the domestic context. That said, the shadows of both ethnic cleavage and the Taiwanese/Chinese divide continue to be cast over Taiwan's politics because it is cloaked in the island citizens' partisan attachment. Meanwhile, due to Beijing's tactic of imposing diplomatic isolation on Taipei in the international community, a new boundary is increasingly apparent on the island. The term "Taiwan" is no longer a geographic designation, and "Taiwanese" now assumes the new meaning of an identity with Taiwan as an independent state.

These findings have both theoretical and policy implications. Theoretically, this study vindicates the constructionist argument that identity can be intentionally or unintentionally fostered through socialization media such as family and education. Both the KMT authoritarian regime ruled by the Chiang family and later the pro-independence DPP government led by Chen adopted a series of Sinicization and de-Sinicization measures, respectively, to promote the "desired" identities. However, the validity of constructionism does not reject the primordialist claim that identities are deep-rooted in blood, culture, and language and are assumed to be given and hard to change. The fact that a substantial proportion of mainlanders continue to hold Chinese identity, along with the justifications employed by members of the Minnan and Hakka groups for their holding of Taiwanese identity, demonstrates the power of primordial bonds in shaping individuals' identities. The empirical findings presented above suggest that both primordialism and constructionism are useful in understanding the development and the formation of identities.

This chapter also shows that identity is a relational concept that defines an individual psychological attachment. Because identity delineates what is and what is not, it sets boundaries and forms a "they-group" and a "we-group." When the boundaries change, the substance of the identity may be altered even though it may bear the same label. While the public discourse on Chinese/Taiwanese identity continues, the substance of Taiwan's identity politics has increasingly shifted to the relationship between a unified Taiwan and a hostile China. A new boundary of national identity has thus emerged on the island.

The empirical findings have important policy implications for cross-Strait relations. One of the major reasons for many island residents to switch their identities was Beijing's diplomatic isolation of Taiwan and military coercion of the island country. While successful in making Taiwan a pariah state in the international community, the Chinese leaders' forceful measures only invited resentment from Taiwan voters and hardened their identity with Taiwan as an independent state. The tendency also applies to mainlanders who have been strong holders of Chinese identity and supporters of cross-Strait unification. Since there is a strong association between holding Taiwanese identity and recognition of the island's independent and separate status from China, Beijing's forceful claim is counterproductive to its cause of unification. Given that the rising Taiwanese identity has yet to be translated into pursuit of the island's de jure independence, some creative thinking needs to take place by Beijing's new leadership in order to attract the active support of Taiwan voters so that cross-Strait disputes can be resolved peacefully.

Appendix 3.A1.

List of Data Sources

Survey Data:

1. *Core Political Attitudes among Taiwanese.* Election Study Center, National Chengchi University.
2. Lu-huei Chen. 2006. *The Origin and Political Effect of Taiwanese Identity.* Election Study Center, National Chengchi University.
3. Sufeng Cheng. 2011. *Taiwan Identity: Formation Typology and Its Political Consequences (II).* National Science Council Research Plan, NSC 99–2410-H-004–113.
4. Sufeng Cheng. 2013. *A Study of Presidential Popularity and Its Political Effects (II).* National Science Council Research Plan, NSC100–2410-H004–086-MY2.

Focus Group Interviews:

1. I-chou Liu. 2000. *A Study in Major Political Identification Concepts of Taiwan Public (I).* National Science Council Research Plan, NSC89–2414-H-004–022-SSS.
2. I-chou Liu. 2002. *A Study in Major Political Identification Concepts of Taiwan Public (II).* National Science Council Research Plan, NSC 89–2414-H-004–049.
3. Su-feng Cheng. 2010. *Taiwan Identity: Formation Typology and Its Political Consequences (I).* National Science Council Research Plan, NSC99–2410-H-004–113.
4. Su-feng Cheng. 2011. *Taiwan Identity: Formation Typology and Its Political Consequences (II).* National Science Council Research Plan, NSC99–2410-H-004–113.
5. Sufeng Cheng. 2013. *A Study of Presidential Popularity and Its Political Effects (II).* National Science Council Research Plan, NSC100-2410-H004-086-MY2.

Notes

1. A list of data sources is presented in the Appendix. The author would like to thank Professors Lu-huei Chen, Sufeng Cheng, I-chou Liu and the Election Study

Center, National Chengchi University in Taipei, for making the data available. All errors are my own.

2. Some scholars distinguish three theoretical approaches for identity research: primordialism, constructivism, and instrumentalism. Both constructivism and instrumentalism agree that identity is malleable by social linkages and not biological givens. Their difference lies in how these linkages are created. Thus, the instrumentalist approach is essentially "a variant of constructivism" (Dawisha 2002, 6).

3. For the meaning of "imagined communities," see Anderson 1991.

4. Group consciousness connotes identification with a group as well as an awareness of the relative position of the group in a society. Some scholars describe the rise of Taiwanese identity and its related awareness as the emergence of Taiwanese nationalism (e.g., Wu 2004). Because nationalism generally refers to a belief aiming to achieve and maintain national independence, it is frequently used for the analysis of colonial movements and ethnic conflicts that yearn to break free from domination (e.g., Fox 2004; Varshney 2003). As will be discussed below, this is not the case for Taiwan since the rise of Taiwan-centered awareness does not imply that the island's citizens are actively pursuing Taiwan's de jure independence and permanent separation from China. The island citizens' positions on the issues of independence and unification are more pragmatic and risk averse (see Hsieh and Niou 2005; Niou 2004; Wang 2005; and Wu 1993, 1996). Some Taiwanese scholars have thus preferred to use the term "consciousness" (e.g., Wang 2001; also see Rigger 2006). This study follows that reasoning.

5. For instance, the Chen administration renamed the state-run China Petroleum Corporation as CPC Corp, Taiwan. Other renamed agencies included the island country's shipbuilding corporation and its central bank (Bishop and Dickie 2007).

6. All respondents in the surveys are divided into five political generational groups based on the following four birth years as cutoff points: 1931, 1953, 1968, and 1982. The classification is based on the premise that respondents of each generation would be 18 years old when one of four significant political events occurred: (1) the retreat of the KMT government to Taiwan in 1949, (2) Taipei's withdrawal from the UN in 1971, (3) the establishment of the Democratic Progressive Party in 1986, and (4) the peaceful transfer of political power in 2000. Such a classification is based on the conceptualization that a political generation is a group of people who share common experiences and historical memories due to the fact that they are born in a same time period and live through the same social and economic environment (Mannheim 1952; Neumann 1965). For justifications on the significance of the four political events, see Chang and Wang (2005).

7. A private polling organization recently released a report that 60 percent of Taiwan citizens possess Chinese identity (*China Times*, March 5, 2013). The report generated some controversy on the island. It also invited concerns from foreign governments. Diplomats from the American Institute in Taiwan and Interchange Association, Japan, the "unofficial" representative offices of the United States and Japan, respectively, visited National Chengchi University's Election Study Center to discuss the findings.

8. National Statistics, Republic of China (Taiwan) at http://statdb.dgbas.gov.tw/pxweb/Dialog/Saveshow.asp (accessed March 15, 2015).

References

Abdelal, Rawi, Yoshiko Herrera, Alastair Iain Johnston, and Rose McDermott. 2009. "Identity as a Variable." In *Measuring Identity: A Guide for Social Scientists*, ed. Rawi Adbelal, Yoshiko Herrera, Alastair Iain Johnston, and Rose McDermott, 17–32. New York: Cambridge University Press.

Anderson, Benedict. 1991. *Imagined Communities: Reflections on the Origin and Spread of Nationalism*. New York: Verso.

Barnett, Michael. 1999. "Culture, Strategy, and Foreign Policy Change: Israel's Road to Oslo." *European Journal of International Relations* 5 (1): 5–36.

Bishop, Mac William, and Mure Dickie. 2007. "Taiwan Drops 'China' in Identity Move." *Financial Times*, February 12. www.ft.com/cms/s/581a6f9a-ba96-11db-bbf3-0000779e2340.html (accessed February 12, 2007).

Chang, Andy, and T. Y. Wang. 2005. "Taiwanese or Chinese? Independence or Unification? An Analysis of Generational Differences in Taiwan." *Journal of Asian and African Studies* 40 (1–2): 29–49.

Chang, Yu-Tzung, 2006. "Campaigning Events on Vote Choice: A Study of the 2004 Presidential Election in Taiwan." *Soochow Journal of Political Science* 22:121–59.

Cheng, Su-feng. 2009. "Ethnicity, Identity, and Vote Choice in Taiwan." *Journal of Electoral Studies* 16 (2): 23–49.

Dawisha, Adeed. 2002. "Nation and Nationalism: Historical Antecedents to Contemporary Debates." *International Studies Review* 4 (1): 3–22.

Enav, Peter. 2007. "Taiwan Leader Riles China, U.S." *Washington Post*, September 9. www.washingtonpost.com/wp-dyn/content/article/2007/09/09/AR2007090900579.html (accessed September 9, 2007).

Fox, Jonathan. 2004. "The Rise of Religious Nationalism and Conflict: Ethnic Conflict and Revolutionary Wars, 1945–2001." *Journal of Peace Research* 41 (6): 715–31.

Garver, John W. 1997. *Face Off: China, the United States, and Taiwan's Democratization*. Seattle: University of Washington Press.

Geertz, Clifford. 1994. "Primordial and Civic Ties." In *Nationalism*, ed. John Hutchinson and Anthony D. Smith, 29–34. New York: Oxford University Press.

Gellner, Ernest. 2008. *Nations and Nationalism*. 2nd ed. Ithaca, NY: Cornell University Press.

Horowitz, Donald L. 2000. *Ethnic Groups in Conflict*. 2nd ed. Berkeley: University of California Press.

Hsieh, John Fuh-sheng, and Emerson M. S. Niou. 2005. "Measuring Taiwanese Public Opinion on Taiwanese Independence." *China Quarterly* 181 (1): 158–68.

Huang, Zen-Jei. 1993. "Tai-du Yun-dong yu Tai-hai Liang-an Guo-jia Tung-yi Zheng-cezhi Yan-Jiu" [The Study of the Taiwanese independence movement and the reunification policies of both sides of the Taiwan Strait]. Master's thesis, East-Asia Institute, National Cheng-chi University, Taipei.

Isaacs, Harold R. 1975. *Idols of the Tribe: Group Identity and Political Change*. Cambridge: Harvard University Press.

Lai, Tse-han, Ramon H. Myers, and Wei Wou. 1991. *A Tragic Beginning: the Taiwan Uprising of February 28, 1947*. Stanford: Stanford University Press.

Laitin, David. 1998. *Identity in Formation: The Russian-Speaking Populations in the Near Abroad*. Ithaca, NY: Cornell University Press.

Lee, Wei-chin, and T. Y. Wang. 2003. *Sayonara to the Lee Teng-Hui Era: Politics in Taiwan, 1988–2000*. Lanham, MD: University Press of America.

Mannheim, Karl. 1952. *Essays on the Sociology of Knowledge*. Ed. Paul Kecskemeti. London: Routledge and Kegan Paul.

Mo, Yan-chih and Shih Hsiu-chuan. 2007. "Inscription Goes Up at Democracy Hall." *Taipei Times*, December 9 www.taipeitimes.com/News/front/archives/2007/12/09/2003391782 (accessed December 9, 2007).

Neumann, Sigmund. 1965. *Permanent Revolution: The Total State in a World at War*. 2nd ed. New York: Frederick A. Praeger.

Niou, Emerson M. S. 2004. "Understanding Taiwan Independence and its Policy Implications." *Asian Survey* 44 (4): 555–67.

Pao, Cheng-hao. 2009. "Party Identification and Vote Decision: An Over-Time Comparison for the 2000–2008 Presidential Elections." *Tamkang Journal of Humanities and Social Sciences* 40: 68–89.

Rigger, Shelley. 2006. *Taiwan's Rising Rationalism: Generations, Politics and "Taiwanese Nationalism."* Policy Studies 26. Washington: East West Center.

Shih, Ming. 1992. *Taiwan Bu-shi Zhong-guo de Yi-bu-fen* [Taiwan is not a part of China]. Taipei: Vanguard.

Shils, Edward. 1957. "Primordial, Personal, Sacred and Civil Ties." *British Journal of Sociology* 8 (2): 130–45.

Taiwan Affairs Office of the State Council of the PRC (TAO). 2000. "The One-China Principle and the Taiwan Issue." *People's Daily Online* [*Renmin Ribao*], February 21.

Varshney, Ashutosh. 2003. "Nationalism, Ethnic Conflict, and Rationality." *Perspectives on Politics* 1 (1): 85–99.

Wang, Fu-chang, 2001, "National Imagination, Ethnic Consciousness, and History: Content and Context Analyses of the 'Getting to Know Taiwan' Textbook Disputes." *Taiwan Historical Research* 8 (2): 145–208.

Wang, Fu-chang, 2008, "The Role of Ethnic Politics Issues in Taiwan's Democratization Transition." *Taiwan Democracy Quarterly* 5 (2): 89–140.

Wang, T. Y. 2001. "Cross-Strait Relations after the 2000 Election in Taiwan: Changing Tactics in a New Reality." *Asian Survey* 41 (5): 716–36.

Wang, T. Y. 2005. "The Perception of Threats and Pragmatic Policy Choice: A Survey of Public Opinion in Taiwan." *Issues & Studies* 41 (1): 87–111.

Wang, T. Y. 2006. "Taiwan's Bid for UN Membership." In *China's Rise, Taiwan's Dilemmas, and International Peace*, ed. Edward Friedman. New York: Routledge, 174–92.

Wang, T. Y. 2009. "Taiwan: Rising National Identity and the Challenges to Cross-Strait Relations." Presented at the Conference on State Secession and Separatism in Europe and Asia, Hong Kong Baptist University and University of Macau, December 7–9.

Wang, T. Y., and G. Andy Chang. 2005. "Ethnicity and Politics in Taiwan: An Analysis of Mainlanders' Identity and Policy Preference." *Issues & Studies* 41 (4): 35–66.

Wang, T. Y., Wei-chin Lee, and Ching-hsin Yu. 2011. "Taiwan's Expansion of International Space: Opportunities and Challenges." *Journal of Contemporary China* 20 (69): 249–67.

Wu, Naiteh. 1993. "National Identity and Party Support: The Social Basis of Party Competition in Taiwan." *Bulletin of the Institute of Ethnology* 74:33–61.

Wu, Naiteh. 1996. "Liberalism and Ethnic Identity: Searching for the Ideological Foundation of Taiwanese Nationalism." *Taiwanese Political Science Review* 1 (1): 5–40.

Wu, Yu-Shan. 2004. "Taiwanese Nationalism and Its Implications: Testing the Worst-Case Scenario." *Asian Survey* 44 (4): 614–25.

CHAPTER 4

Parties, Partisans, and Independents in Taiwan

Ching-hsin Yu

Taiwan is a new democracy in which elections have played a significant role in citizen political participation in the past decades. Mainstream electoral studies have paid much attention to voters' decision-making processes in elections. Factors that influence voters' electoral choices, such as partisanship, economic evaluation, candidate qualifications, and policy preferences, are often included in the discussions of voter behavior. Among those factors, citizen partisanship, or party identification, is often cited by scholars as the most consistent and influential one in Taiwan. However, the concept has met with confusing definitions and implications. On the one hand, Taiwan's political history has shaped a distinct developmental pathway of citizen partisanship. As Taiwan was undergoing a significant democratic transition in the mid-1980s, the party system evolved from a one-party hegemonic system to a two-party system, then to a multiparty system in the 1990s, followed by the formation of two major camps, the Pan-Blue and the Pan-Green, in the 2000s. Citizen partisanship also changed dramatically. On the other hand, as more research was devoted to the exploration of the behavior of partisan voters, political independents were of less concern. In addition to the differences between partisans and independents, there are various types of political independents, whose attitudes and behaviors are different from each other, so study of citizen partisanship in Taiwan calls for examination of these different kinds of independents.

This chapter intends to explore the evolution and distribution of citizen partisanship in Taiwan with a special interest in political independents. After a brief literature review, it will examine the historical origins of citizen partisanship and the evolution of the party system in Taiwan. It will then compare attributes and attitudes of different types of partisans and independents, such as political interest, preferences on the issues of unification and independence, support for democracy, voting, and vote choice. In conclusion, a reconsideration of the development of citizen partisanship and its impact in Taiwan is discussed.

Studies of Partisans and Independents

A system of voter identification was developed from the group theory since Campbell and his associates published their classical works on American voters (Campbell, Gruin, and Miller 1954; Campbell et al. 1960). It maintains that citizens tend to psychologically identify and behaviorally support a political group, or party, based on their personal experiences and preferences. The link to a given party will further shape citizens' political attitudes and issue positions. Party identification is not only a psychological attachment to a political party but also a cue for a citizen's political actions. Because citizens have different experiences with a political party their identification may have varying strength as a result. Some citizens may develop a strong party identification, others may have a weak attachment to a political party, and still others may possess a neutral feeling toward any groups. Therefore, American voters are typically categorized in one of five categories: Strong Democrat, Weak Democrat, Independent, Weak Republican, and Strong Republican; or in seven categories with the addition of Independent Democrat and Independent Republican (Weisberg 1993, 684).[1]

Regardless of its popularity, the concept of party identification has nevertheless suffered from the problems of dimensionality and transitivity (Converse 1966; Petrocik 1974; Weisberg 1980; Niemi, Wright, and Powell 1987; Bartle and Bellucci 2009). Generally speaking, the discussion of attitudes and behaviors of citizens with strong partisanship are less controversial. How to assess independents or citizens with weak partisanship raises a crucial issue so that they will not be treated as a residual category.

Political independents are generally characterized as having positive attributes like prudent judgment and adequate political involvement (Bryce 1929). However, the normative virtues of the political independents have been critically challenged by empirical studies (Campbell et al. 1960, 143). While the debate over what constitutes adequate qualifications of a nonpartisan voter will continue for a long period of time, the increasing popularity of survey data has enabled scholarly research to reexamine the nature of political independents (Burnham 1970; Dennis 1988; Keith et al. 1992; Magleby, Nelson, and Westlye 2011).

Studies of voters' party identification in Taiwan, beginning in the early 1970s, have primarily followed the research on American voters. As partisan attachment is widely recognized as one of the most influential factors affecting a voter's political decisions (Chen 1986, 1994; Chu 1996; Liu 1996, 1997), empirical studies have found that independents in Taiwan are largely female, less educated Minnans and Hakkas (in contrast to the mainlanders) with low socioeconomic status. They have less political interest and pay little attention to political affairs. More recent studies show that the number of independents had increased over time and the political attitudes and voting behaviors of less-educated independents differ from those of highly educated independents (Yeh 1994; Chu 2004; Wang 2010). The empirical evidence confirms the "revisionist" image of the political independent as characterized by the authors of *The American Voter*. It also demonstrates that a clear differentiation between pure independents and partisan leaners in Taiwan is sometimes difficult (Wang and Yu 2011).

Precisely because nonpartisan voters have varying degree of political attributes, their existence has crucial implications to a functioning party system and the health of democracy. Indeed, political independents frequently play a pivotal role in deciding the final outcome of a close election. They also function as a vital balance in an otherwise polarized society. This is especially important for a nascent democracy like Taiwan, where the party system has not yet stabilized. As the current research analyzes Taiwan voters' partisan identification, it will pay particular attention to political independents in Taiwan.

Partisanship before 1986

The development of citizen partisanship had a unique history in Taiwan in its early periods. The tragic incident that occurred on February 28, 1947 (the 2–28 Incident), created a deep antagonism between the incoming mainlanders and the Minnan. The latter learned from the incident that politics could be dangerous, and as a consequence, political apathy began to take root in their society. When the Kuomintang government moved to Taiwan, an authoritarian regime was quickly and firmly established. Constitutionally, the Temporary Provisions were implemented to establish martial law, to provide the president with tremendous discretionary power, and to prohibit the emergence of political opposition. No new political parties were allowed to be established under martial law. Any dissident opinions targeted at the government were also subject to repression. Intense political socialization aimed at enhancing citizen loyalty to the government, which was in reality loyalty to the ruling KMT, was widespread in the school curricula (Wilson 1970). With the assistance of state-controlled mass media, only selective information beneficial to the KMT regime was permitted to circulate. Equally important, the introduction of a political commissar further ensured the KMT's unchallenged status in regard to the military. A party-state run by the KMT, like that of many communist countries, became firmly established on the island. Under the authoritarian party-state structure, the KMT was therefore the only significant political party.[2] Citizens in Taiwan were either KMT members or not. No other political parties were able to compete for popular support against the KMT, so the situation was similar to that of the one-party hegemonic system as described by Sartori (1976).

Furthermore, under the name of Fa-tong (the sole legitimate government representing China), the KMT regime maintained an extensive political structure as it had done on the Chinese mainland. As "one China" was taken as given and Taiwan was regarded as one of China's 36 provinces, the political connection between the island and the Chinese mainland was emphasized by a Mainlander dominated regime. The political representation of Minnans and Hakkas was intentionally suppressed. As a result, a political division rooted in ethnicity emerged on the island (Wang 1993; Wachman 1994).

Despite the ethnic division, support of the KMT came from two sources. As indicated in chapter 3, the first group of supporters were the mainlanders who fled to Taiwan with the KMT government in the late 1940s. Because they followed the party leaders in the Sino-Japanese War and the Chinese Civil War, mainlanders have become the core supporters of the KMT (Wu 1995; Shyu, 1997). The second group of supporters has been the Minnan and Hakka through political indoctrination by the regime. After the disastrous defeat on the Chinese mainland, it was crucial for the KMT regime to establish strong local support in Taiwan. Unlike mainlanders who shared a similar history with the KMT leaders, Minnans and Hakkas were connected to the party by a mix of political, economic, and ideological incentives. Politically, a Minnan or Hakka with KMT membership had a better chance of being promoted in the government. Party membership was a proxy criterion for national loyalty and carried political expedience for the Minnan and Hakka who intended to have a career in the government. Economically, maintaining a close tie with the KMT would benefit businesses. By foregoing some prerogative interests, the regime effectively exchanged economic benefits for the political support of the Minnan and Hakka.

One noteworthy way the KMT regime built grassroots support was through the implementation of local elections. Since the early 1950s, local elections had been the KMT's main locus for recruiting local elites, distributing economic prerogatives, and marketing the regime's image of a "free and democratic China" in opposition to totalitarian Communist China. Of course, the outcomes of elections were managed by the KMT regime. Nonetheless, it is also reasonable to argue that local elections gave the Minnan and Hakka experience with party politics and the electoral process. Under the façade of a free and democratic China, the authoritarian KMT regime did provide a certain degree of pluralism in society. Non-KMT independent candidates found some room for political participation in elections. In spite of being outnumbered by the KMT candidates, the non-KMT candidates won seats in various local elections. The appearance and activities of these non-KMT candidates were typical symbols of electoral competition under the one-party hegemonic system. Indeed, there were some non-KMT candidates who consistently won elections in certain regions. The non-KMT elected politicians provided alternative choices for the Taiwan electorate, in particular, those Minnan and Hakka who had no partisan affiliation.

The non-KMT forces continued to grow during Taiwan's rapid economic and sociopolitical transition. The KMT regime found it more and more difficult to curb the expansion of the non-KMT forces in elections. Worse still for the KMT regime, diplomatic setbacks in the 1970s, such as losing its seat at the United Nations and the termination of formal relations with Japan and the United States, had facilitated further expansion of the electoral arena. The non-KMT candidates found more room for collective action in elections. For example, the group Dang-wai (meaning "outside the KMT"), which appeared in the early 1970s, unified the non-KMT candidates during elections. Members of Dang-wai were able to share common platforms and manifestos without being penalized by electoral regulations. Although Dang-wai members did not formally organize as a political party, they worked together in elections as if they were members of one. The Minnan/Hakka electorate was able to make a choice between the KMT candidates and the Dang-wai candidates in elections. Of course, although they competed against KMT candidates in elections, not all of the non-KMT candidates maintained similar political stances. Nor were all of the non-KMT candidates anti-KMT. Therefore, it would be premature to suggest that a quasi two-party system had taken shape in Taiwan. Nonetheless, the non-KMT forces did grow in one election after another. It was not until the Democratic Progressive Party was formally established in 1986 (although it was still illegal at that time) that a new party system with two meaningful political parties emerged in Taiwan (Cheng 1989; Lu 1992; Hsieh 2005).

The evolution of the party system before 1986 resulted in a peculiar pattern of citizen-party connectivity in Taiwan. First, a clear and stable partisanship between the mainlanders and the KMT had emerged in the early period when the KMT government moved to Taiwan. The mainlanders maintained a strong affiliation with the KMT due to their close dependence on the KMT in all respects. As the KMT regime made every effort to consolidate its control over the island, material enticements and purposive incentives provided by the KMT were used to facilitate its popularity among the Minnan and Hakka. For example, the KMT regime adopted several liberalization measures in the early 1970s, such as recruiting Minnan and Hakka elites into the party and gradually opening some electoral posts for public contestation, had effectively expanded its connection with the Minnan and Hakka. Together with the mainlanders, the more extensive connections between the KMT and Minnan and Hakka thus helped the KMT to maintain a consistent advantage in elections. However, except for those mainlanders and KMT-friendly Minnan and Hakka, a majority of the citizens in Taiwan were not registered KMT members.[3]

Second, the historical legacy had a significant effect on the development of citizen partisanship in Taiwan. Due to the unique sociopolitical development in the 1950s and 1960s, the label of "political party" acquired negative implications for some Taiwanese. The incident of February 28, 1947, the discriminatory political structure in place since the early 1950s, and the white-terror mentality prevented the Minnan and Hakka from embracing political affairs. Even though they had participated in local elections, their connection to the ruling KMT was weak. If they supported a KMT candidate in elections, it did not mean that they identified with the KMT. In fact, voters generally placed candidates above the party. It was the candidates, not the voters, who were directly connected to the KMT. Strong popular support for KMT candidates did not equate to strong support for the KMT. The candidate's personal image and connections generally were more important than the party label in elections (Chen 1986). Since the image of political parties was not that welcome, maintaining their stance as nonpartisan could be a good choice for many Minnan and Hakka voters. Also due to the fact that the non-KMT candidates were not allowed to engage in any organized campaign activities under martial law, the Taiwan electorate supporting non-KMT candidates was unable to form a normal partisanship, which KMT supporters could do.

Third, the Dang-wai represented a partially united front of non-KMT candidates in elections. At the beginning, the name of Dang-wai was merely an expedient way of differentiating non-KMT candidates from their KMT opponents. However, the term gradually acquired special political and organizational meanings. As the political system increasingly liberalized, members of the Dang-wai regularly engaged in island-wide electoral campaigns. Since martial law banned the formation of political parties, Dang-wai members used various names in different elections as common symbols to distinguish themselves. Consequently, the emergence of the Dang-wai provided Taiwan voters with a unique form of two-party competition.

The election of the Taiwan Provincial Assembly is a typical example that illustrates the development of political independents. The elections were implemented in 1951 and ended in 1994. Only two minor political parties, the Chinese Youth Party and the Democratic Socialist Party, which had been established in China during the Second World War, were allowed to present their candidates under party labels. However, as shown in table 4.1, the two minor parties were too weak to win a meaningful number of seats in the elections. Compared with those two parties, independent candidates performed much better. Even though the winning number varied from elections to elections due to a lack of organized campaigns, they managed to win from 15 percent to 27 percent of the electoral vote. They were thus a significant non-KMT force. The majority of Dang-wai independents unified under the DPP after 1986, which fared well in the elections of 1989 and 1994, garnering about 21 percent and 29 percent of the popular vote. The establishment of the DPP also suggested that there was a split among political independents. Those independents who did not join the DPP continued to run for election under a nonpartisan label. Popular support for non-DPP independents did not disappear, although it declined significantly.

The growth of political independents in local elections implies the existence of political space for non-KMT forces. The election results of the Provincial Assembly provide a larger picture in which the KMT was strongly

TABLE 4.1. Election Results: Taiwan Provincial Assembly (percentage of vote)

Year	1951	1954	1957	1960	1963	1968	1972	1977	1981	1985	1989	1994
KMT	78.18	84.21	80.30	79.45	82.43	84.51	79.45	72.73	76.62	76.62	70.13	60.08
DPP											20.78	29.11
New Party												2.53
Other parties	1.82		1.52		1.35					1.30		
Independent	20.00	15.79	18.18	20.55	16.22	15.49	20.55	27.27	23.38	22.08	9.09	7.59

Sources: Data are from the ROC Central Election Commission, the Taiwan Provincial Election Commission, and the Election Studies and Survey Data Archive of the Election Study Center of National Chengchi University.

dominant, although at the same time the number of political independents in Taiwan's political landscape was not insignificant. Unfortunately, other than these macro electoral results, there are little empirical data showing individual voters' partisanship. Micro studies of individuals' vote choices were not feasible until the mid-1980s, when academics began to introduce the concept of party identification and its relevance to Taiwan.

In a strict sense, there were only KMT partisans and it was difficult to identify the non-KMT supporters in elections. Although the non-KMT candidates often called themselves independents, their supporters were not exactly the same as "independent voters" according to definitions of party identification. They were voters who supported non-KMT candidates, regardless of how persistent their support would be. True partisan support did not develop until the establishment of the DPP in 1986, when the partisanship of Taiwan voters began to take on a different form than in previous decades. In particular, those who were non-KMT supporters before 1986 would not only support the individual candidates as they had before but also began to adjust to the new party label. Thus, it is difficult to provide a detailed portrait of non-KMT supporters because the fact that they were non-KMT supporters does not necessarily make them independents. Since there was a ban on the formation of political parties, supporters of non-KMT candidates (independent candidates) generally characterized themselves as independents (voters supporting independent candidates) even though they in fact were non-KMT supporters. Consequently, the concept of "independent" that is often cited as a counterpart of party identifiers carries a different connotation.

Equally important, the evolving party system consistently shaped citizens' partisanship differently than in the previous decades. In particular, Taiwan experienced a new political landscape after the KMT's disastrous defeat in the 2000 presidential election as some members left the party and organized the People First Party and the Taiwan Solidarity Union. Along with the New Party, a KMT split-off of 1994, they form a part of Taiwan's multiparty system. The island citizens' partisanship has become diversified as a result, which can be characterized as multipartisan including identification with the KMT, DPP, NP, PFP, and TSU.[4] Yet in addition to the increase in political parties, a significant characteristic of the party system after 2000 was the formation of the Pan-Blue and Pan-Green coalitions. The Pan-Blue includes the KMT, the NP, and the PFP, while the Pan-Green includes the DPP and the TSU. The key departure point of the Pan-Blue and Pan-Green mainly rests on their different stances with regard to cross-Strait policy. These alliances also have strong impacts on citizens' vote choice in elections. Hence, citizen's partisanship can be also understood in terms of their allegiance to the Pan-Blue Alliance or the Pan-Green Alliance, which presents a bipartisan structure.

Partisans and Independents since the 1990s

Thanks to the rapid advancement of electoral studies since the 1990s, more sophisticated findings about citizens' partisanship have appeared in Taiwan's academic community. This section will examine the attitudes and behaviors of partisans and independents in recent decades. Instead of using voter identification with an individual political party, it will use voter identification with the two major political camps mentioned above. Hence, following the prescriptions provided by *The American Voter* (Campbell et al. 1960), there will be seven categories of partisan: Strong Pan-Blue, Weak Pan-Blue, Leaning Pan-Blue, (pure) Independent, Leaning Pan-Green, Weak Pan-Green, and Strong Pan-Green. In order to provide a more concise meaning of "Independent," this chapter also uses education as a criterion to divide the Independents into three categories: low-educated, middle-educated, and high-educated. Consequently, there will be comparisons among party identifiers and political independents in terms of political interests, cross-Strait relations, support for democracy, voting, and vote choices. These variables are selected for comparison because they have been frequently identified as important aspects of the study of Taiwan voters. Through the application of these variables with cumulative survey data collected over the past two decades, it is expected that the analyses will contribute to the study of partisanship and the impacts of political independents in Taiwan. Descriptions and measurements of these variables can be found in appendix 4.A1.

General Distribution

The empirical findings regarding citizen partisanship shown in table 4.2 demonstrate certain consistencies and changes during the past two decades. In the early 1990s, when citizens started to experience contested elections between the KMT and the DPP, a majority of the voters identified themselves as nonpartisan. The number of independents was as high as 34 percent in 1992. Next in predominance were the Weak Pan-Blue and Strong Pan-Blue identifiers. As for the newly established DPP, its identifiers numbered far less than those of the Pan-Blue Alliance. This suggests that the KMT continued to enjoy a clear electoral advantage, as it had before. The number of independents declined in the legislative election of 1995 as only 22.5 percent of the electorate considered themselves as independents. Both the KMT and the DPP had more identifiers. In particular, around 32 percent of the electorate labeled themselves as Weak Pan-Blue. The presidential election of 1996 showed a similar pattern as in 1995 as the percentage of those identifying with the KMT and with the DPP rose. Only slightly less than one-quarter of the electorate identified themselves as nonpartisan. In particular, the KMT had enjoyed a strong surge of identifiers such that the combination of strong Pan-Blue, Weak Pan-Blue, and Leaning Pan-Blue comprised more than 50 percent of the electorate. The number of independents rose again in the elections for legislators in 1998. It seems that the surge of independents resulted from the decline of KMT identifiers. Meanwhile, the number of identifiers with the DPP, either Strong Pan-Green or the Weak Pan-Green, had increased slowly but steadily.

The independents reached their peak in the presidential election of 2000 and the legislative election of 2001. One key reason for the increase of independents had to do with the dramatic change in the party system at that time. On the one hand, the KMT suffered from an internal split before the presidential election, which led to a disastrous defeat in the presidential election and the DPP became the ruling party, 14 years after its establishment. On the other hand, new political parties, such as the PFP and the TSU, emerged in the 2001 legislative election. The unprecedented face of a multiparty system appeared in Taiwan. As political parties exhibited varying degree of quality, many citizens became reluctant to identify themselves as leaning toward a particular party. Thus, being an independent was the optimal choice for many voters. After 2001, the number of independents became somewhat variable in different elections, ranging from slightly more than one-third in the 2008 to about one-quarter in 2012.

One noticeable development was the gradual increase of partisan leaners since 2001. The percentages of both the Leaning Pan-Blue and Leaning Pan-Green categories, with some minor ups and downs, showed an increasing trend through 2012. The increase in partisan leaners resulted mainly from the emergence of coalitional electoral competition at that time; for example, members in the Pan-Blue camp (the KMT, the NP, and the PFP) cooperated in the presidential elections in order to defeat the Pan-Green candidates. However, in the legislative elections, each party in the Pan-Blue camp nominated its own candidates and competed against each other. The coexistence of cooperation and competition in these elections encouraged voters to swing their partisanship between pure independents and leaners.

Last, the percentages of strong party identifiers have been stable over the past two decades. The percentage of Strong Pan-Blue identifiers decreased when the KMT lost the presidential election in 2000, and the number continued to decline in 2001 and 2004 but then showed a slight surge from 2008 to 2012. As for the Pan-Green, winning the presidential election in 2000 did bring growth in the percentage of strong identifiers. The trend did not continue but maintained an average of between 4 percent and 6.5 percent from 2001 to 2012.

Political Interest

The general trend of partisan distribution for the past decades, as shown in table 4.2, is rather stable. However, unlike the partisans who have a clear political orientation, it would be imprudent to regard the political independent as a unified subset of the electorate. Many studies have provided a more detailed examination of the political independent, and, among the variables, educational level seems to be the most cited demographic criterion that differentiates subtypes of political independents. These studies argue that

TABLE 4.2 General Distribution of Partisanship

	1992	1995	1996	1998	2000	2001	2004.03	2004.12	2008.01	2008.03	2012
Strong Pan-Blue	15	13.4	15.3	10.4	8	4.5	5.2	5.1	8.6	7.1	7.9
Weak Pan-Blue	18.4	31.8	31.6	21.5	13.7	9	11.6	13.4	14.3	15.9	17
Leaning Pan-Blue	7.2	2.3	4.2	8.1	5.4	12.7	13	14.4	13.8	13.3	15.1
Independent	34	22.5	22.1	28.2	35.4	35.9	32.7	27.6	34.6	30.7	26.5
Leaning Pan-Green	3.2	1.2	1.9	5.5	4.4	13	11.5	13.5	10.5	11.8	11.2
Weak Pan-Green	6.9	12.2	11.2	13.6	15.9	13.1	13.6	13.7	8.7	11.1	11.3
Strong Pan-Green	3.2	3.2	3.7	7.2	8	5.7	5.8	5.9	4	5.2	6.5
NR	12.1	13.5	10	5.5	9.2	6.1	6.7	6.4	5.4	4.9	4.5

Sources: Data for 1996–2000 are from the Election Study Center at National Chengchi University, and data for 2001–12 are from the Taiwan's Election and Democratization Study Project (see List of Data Sources in appendix 4.A2).

Notes: 1: Numbers in the table are percentages of respondents in each election survey. 2: The elections in 1992, 1995, 1998, 2001, 2004.12 (December), 2008.01 (January), and 2012 are legislative elections. The elections in 1996, 2000, 2004.03 (March), 2008.03 (March), and 2012 are presidential elections. In 2012, the election for president and legislators were held at the same time.

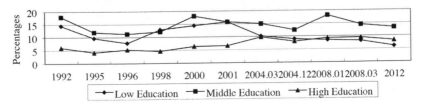

Fig. 4.1. Educational distribution among independents. *Data Sources and Notes:* Same as table 4.2.

differences in other demographic characteristics, such as gender, age, and career, do not reveal clear and consistent implications about the attitudes and behavior of the political independent, and the educational differences have continuously drawn researchers' attention in studies of the political independent. Therefore, this paper will also investigate the educational differences among political independents in Taiwan.

As indicated in figure 4.1, political independents in Taiwan have shown different patterns during the past two decades. In the early 1990s, trends in the percentages of political independents with low-level and middle-level educations were similar until early 2000s. Both categories also accounted for the majority of political independents at that time. Moreover, the percentage of moderately educated political independents has been the highest, while the numbers of least-educated political independents have decreased. By contrast, the highly educated political independent did not account for a very high percentage. Notably, the number of highly educated political independents increased after 2000 and exceeded that of the least-educated political independent. The different developments among the least, moderately, and highly educated political independents should enable researchers to get a more precise understanding about political attitudes and behavior.

The concept of political interest has been considered a driving force of political participation since the publication of *The People's Choice* (Lazarsfeld, Berelson, and Gaudet 1948). Those voters with a greater interest in politics would concurrently have more political information and would be more attentive to political activities than those less interested. The literature also suggests a close relationship between political interest and partisanship. Identifying with a political party would provide voters convenient and reliable cues for elections. Moreover, a political party continues to convey political messages to voters all the time. It is anticipated that citizens with a close relationship to a political party would have more political interest than those citizens who do not maintain such a party affiliation. The results in table

4.3 partially confirm these findings. The general pattern indicates, first, that independents have been the most uninterested in politics during the past two decades. Except for the presidential election in 2000 and the legislative election in 2004, independents were more likely to say that they do not have an interest in politics. Second, partisan voters, regardless of their strength of identification, did not have clear associations with political interest. Partisan leaners in the Pan-Blue camp were generally less interested in politics, yet even the stronger partisans in the Pan-Green camp showed an unanticipated low interest in politics. The overall trend suggests a moderate relationship between political interest and partisanship. Even though independents have shown a relative lack of interest in politics, the relationship between partisanship and political interest is not consistent.

Nonetheless, the relationship between independents and political interest has rather consistently and systematically followed educational differences. Figure 4.2 shows a different distribution of political interest among the three types of Independents. The least-educated independent has the lowest political interest compared to the other types of Independent. The percentage of lack of political interest in the least-educated independent exceeds 80 percent. By contrast, the highly educated independent consistently maintains a certain degree of political interest. The political interest of the moderately educated independent, as expected, lies in between. The graph clearly suggests that the least-educated independents have the least interest in politics.

TABLE 4.3 Distribution of Political Interest among Partisans

	1992	1995	1996	1998	2000	2001	2004.03	2004.12	2008.01	2008.03	2012
Strong Pan-Blue	31.4	38.1	25.4	42.1	13.5	42.4	38.9	10.8	53.3	38.9	34.5
Weak Pan-Blue	34.6	35.3	24.9	35.9	7.7	42.9	34.8	14.	56.5	39.5	34.1
Leaning Pan-Blue	34.9	38.2	29.8	48.4	13.1	46.4	37.4	10.1	63.3	37.7	34.6
Independent	46.7	50.8	40.7	58.8	22.3	66.3	54.2	23.7	72.5	52.3	48.5
Leaning Pan-Green	21.3	5.9	26.9	34.9	12	58	38.2	15.2	58.9	37.2	43.5
Weak Pan-Green	33	40	22.6	40.3	13.9	50.4	42.3	13.7	49.5	41.5	40.7
Strong Pan-Green	28.6	25.5	10	36.9	1.1	52.7	43.3	19.4	69.4	53.6	45.1

Source and Note: Same as table 4.2.

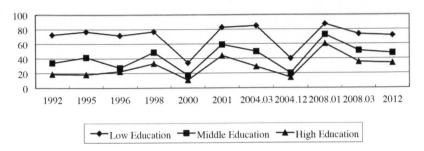

Fig. 4.2. Lack of political interest among independents with different educational levels. *Data Sources and Notes*: Same as table 4.2.

On Cross-Strait Relations

As mentioned above, the point of disagreement between the Pan-Blue and the Pan-Green camps has been their different positions on the issue of unification with China versus Taiwan independence. The choice is not an easy one for the majority of Taiwan citizens to make, and the preference of maintaining the status quo has become the more preferred alternative during the past decades. On average, up to 55 percent of Taiwan voters have chosen neither unification nor independence. This significant number has also implied that support for maintaining the status quo comes from all types of partisan citizen, and particularly from the independents. As indicated in table 4.4, the partisan difference of the two political camps is significant only between the strong party identifiers and the rest of the categories. Both

TABLE 4.4 Distribution of Support for Maintaining the Status Quo

	1992	1995	1996	1998	2000	2001	2004.03	2004.12	2008.01	2008.03	2012
Strong Pan-Blue	55	46	35.2	41.6	37.9	28.3	48.9	44.6	62.3	52.2	64.1
Weak Pan-Blue	60.9	52.5	51.1	44.4	46.6	54.6	60.4	68	67.4	67	66.9
Leaning Pan-Blue	68.6	62.9	57.6	56.1	53.1	50.2	65	56.9	73.7	71.3	69.9
Independent	51.2	48.5	51.3	54.3	51.2	55	57	58.6	55.9	64.4	66
Leaning Pan-Green	56.2	41.2	63	37.9	55.8	52.7	45	54.1	46.2	50.2	50.2
Weak Pan-Green	48.6	41.8	42.7	48.2	54.3	51.3	41.3	44.2	43.1	42.5	42.7
Strong Pan-Green	32.7	29.8	28.3	30.7	48.4	29.6	20	29.7	31.4	23.2	35.6

Data Sources and Notes: Same as table 4.2.

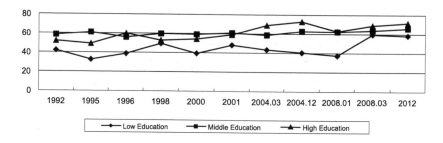

Fig. 4.3. Support among independents with different educational levels for maintaining the status quo. *Data Sources and Notes:* Same as table 4.2.

the Strong Pan-Blue identifiers and Strong Pan-Green identifiers (and relatively, the Weak Pan-Green identifiers) have lower support for maintaining the status quo. The Weak Pan-Blue, Leaning Pan-Blue, Independent, and Leaning Pan-Green, by contrast, are strong supporters of the status quo. In particular, Leaning Pan-Blue identifiers are the most likely to choose maintaining the status quo than all other types of partisans. While independents also choose maintaining the status quo, they do not present significant differences from party leaners.

If we take a closer look at independents' preferences on maintaining the status quo, figure 3 shows that there are noticeable differences among the three types. On the one hand, the highly educated independents have been very supportive of maintaining the status quo. The upward trend also suggests that the highly educated independents have become core supporters for maintaining the status quo. On the other hand, the least-educated independents have been less likely to support maintenance of the status quo. Yet the trend after early 2008 did show a strong increase up to 2012. As for the moderately educated Independents, their preference for maintaining the status quo resembles that of highly educated independents. Also, the attitudes of the moderately educated independents are also more stable than the other two types of independents.

Support for Democracy

As a member of the Third Wave democracies, Taiwan has made an admirably smooth and peaceful political transition over the past decades. However, those achievements in democratic transition did not automatically bring about good governance in Taiwan. Like many other Third Wave democracies, the challenges of political transition may not have been associated with the establishment of democratic institutions but, rather, with the new socio-economic issues occurring at the same time. In the past ten years, citizens in Taiwan have encountered sluggish economic development, repeated political corruption, and worsening social inequality. Consequently, the poor economic performance and ineffective governance could have disillusioned citizens about democracy and reminded them of the "good old days" in the authoritarian era (Chang, Chu, and Park 2007).

Fortunately, whether citizens lost their confidence in democracy under poorly performing governments is not clear. Table 4.5 shows that regardless of partisan differences, the majority of citizens have maintained rather strong support for democracy. Relatively speaking, citizens with stronger party identification are also more supportive of democracy. Pan-Green camp identifiers are more supportive of democracy than are Pan-Blue identifiers. The Strong Pan-Green identifiers, in particular, have been the most stable believers in democracy compared with other partisans. As for independents, their belief in democracy is not significantly different from the Leaning Pan-Blue identifiers but is slightly lower than for Leaning Pan-Green identifiers. Independents who are not supportive of democracy present a different picture when the level of education is taken into consideration. As figure 4.4 shows, support for democracy by independents displays a surge as well as a decline over the past decade. Independents' support for democracy increased significantly from 2000 to 2004, then dropped sharply from 2004 to 2012. Figure 4.4 further indicates that the highly educated independents have been slightly more supportive of democracy than both the moderately and least-educated independents. Yet the three types of independent have moved closer to each other in 2008 and 2012.

TABLE 4.5 Distribution of Support for Democracy

	2000	2001	2004.03	2004.12	2008.01	2008.03	2012
Strong Pan-Blue	51.8	81.7	72.9	88.3	54.7	44.5	59
Weak Pan-Blue	48.4	89.1	83.9	85.2	53.6	46.3	57.9
Leaning Pan-Blue	54.2	84.6	74.1	88.7	53.1	49.2	47
Independent	52	82.5	82.7	87.7	56.5	43.1	47.1
Leaning Pan-Green	53.3	89.7	89.3	93.6	54.5	48.8	60.6
Weak Pan-Green	61.2	92	93.1	91.4	61.2	59.4	63.7
Strong Pan-Green	70.2	90.9	89	94	81.6	75.8	73.9

Data Sources and Notes: Same as table 4.2.

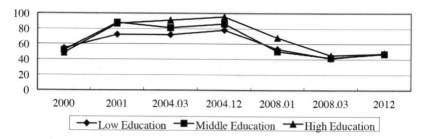

Fig. 4.4. Support for democracy among independents with different educational levels. *Data Sources and Notes:* Same as table 4.2.

Voting

One of the bedrock arguments made about party identification is the party's strong impact on citizen's voting. Citizens with stronger party identification are supposed to have stronger intentions of supporting the party with which they identify in elections. Partisan voters are therefore more likely to vote the way parties request. Table 4.6 presents the trends in not voting among different partisan voters. It shows, first, that stronger party identifiers are far more likely than others to cast their ballots in elections. Except for the Strong Pan-Green voters who had a higher percentage of not voting in 1996, 200412 and 200801, the number of those not voting in both the Strong Pan-Blue and Strong Pan-Green camps has been less than 10 percent. Table 4.6 also shows that weak party identifiers are less likely to vote than strong party identifiers. Both the Leaning Pan-Blue and Leaning Pan-Green identifiers are also less likely to vote than the weak party identifiers. Fourth, except for some elections, political independents tend to be the most unlikely to vote in elections. The general pattern of not voting and partisanship seems to reasonably confirm the conventional wisdom that partisanship does matter to a citizen's intention to vote or not.

Figure 4.5 provides additional information about different types of political independents and their intention to vote. In the early 1990s, there was no clear difference among the highly, moderately, and least-educated political independent in voting. Noticeably, this pattern changed in 1998, when highly educated political independents refrained from voting, as did the moderately educated political independent, though with a moderate change. This new pattern continued until early 2008. Also noticeably, the least-educated political independents were by no means absent from voting. They were more likely to vote than their more educated counterparts.

Vote Choice

Based on the perspectives of party identification, citizens with a certain partisanship would be expected to be more likely to support a given party in an election. In Taiwan, citizen partisanship is effectively associated with vote choice in elections. As indicated in table 4.7, different types of Pan-Blue identifiers revealed consistent support for their party candidate. Moreover, the strength of identification was also in agreement with the assumption of transitivity, in which stronger identifiers tend to vote for their partisan candidate more than weaker identifiers do. As for independents, in the 1996 election the Pan-Blue presidential candidate, Lee Teng-hui, dramatically outperformed his competitor, Peng Ming-min. More than 41 percent of Independents voted for Lee, while only 4 percent voted for Peng. This sharp difference also accounts for Lee's strong victory.

As discussed above, the KMT suffered a serious internal split during the presidential election in 2000. This internal split also led to a split among the Pan-Blue identifiers. Only 37.8 percent of Strong Pan-Blue identifiers and 34.8 percent of Weak Pan-Blue identifiers voted for their partisan candidate. The number was even smaller for those Leaning Pan-Blue identifiers. Independents were in favor of the Pan-Green candidate in 2000, which contributed to the electoral success of the DPP presidential candidate, Chen Shui-bian. As for the Pan-Green identifiers, they did not vote for the Pan-Blue candidate. Unlike the Pan-Blue identifier, the partisan boundary for the Pan-Green identifier was more consistent and predictable.

The presidential elections in 2004, 2008, and 2012 were typical Pan-

TABLE 4.6. Distribution of Not Voting

	1992	1995	1996	1998	2000	2001	2004.03	2004.12	2008.01	2008.03	2012
Strong Pan-Blue	3.1	6.5	6.1	6.3	4.3	9.8	2.2	9.2	8.5	3.7	4.2
Weak Pan-Blue	14.3	13.6	5.4	11.2	5.6	14.8	4.2	17.1	20.9	5.6	5.1
Leaning Pan-Blue	22	8.8	10.2	14.1	9.2	20.3	7.6	28.7	30.6	9.8	14.8
Independent	13.1	14.7	13	17.7	8.6	20.4	15.3	30.2	36.4	19.3	20.2
Leaning Pan-Green	14.6	5.6	7.4	28.4	7.5	22.5	10.5	29.8	25.4	16.4	12.2
Weak Pan-Green	9.5	11.6	6.3	12.7	8	14.8	4	15.7	18.5	9.4	11.2
Strong Pan-Green	4.2	4.3	11.5	8.1	2.1	7	0	10.8	12	2	2.5

Data Sources and Notes: Same as table 4.2.

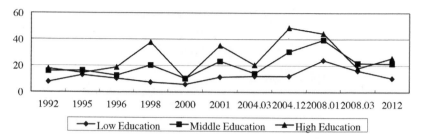

Fig. 4.5. Not Voting among Independents with Different Educational Levels. *Data Sources and Notes:* Same as table 4.2

Blue versus Pan-Green competitions, in which there were neither internal splits nor strong independent candidates. It is obvious that the impact of partisanship on elections became even stronger over time. Distribution of party identification in the three elections looked reasonable with no obvious deviations. Also, the strength of party identification was relatively consistent. Interestingly, unlike the 1996 and 2000 elections, in which independents one-sidedly favored either the Pan-Blue or the Pan-Green candidate, their vote choice seemed to be more divided. They had a higher tendency to support the Pan-Green candidate in 2004 but were more likely to back Pan-Blue candidates in the 2008 and 2012 elections. As the electoral competition between the two political camps became intense, the influence of independents has also increased. Interestingly, sizeable numbers of Taiwan voters continue to self-identify as independents, as table 4.7 shows. This could be due to the historical memories of one-party authoritarian rule that makes island citizens reluctant to report partisanship. It could also be the unsatisfactory performance of political parties as a whole, which leads to an

TABLE 4.7 Percentage of Votes for Pan-Blue Presidential Candidate

	1996	2000	2004.03	2008.03	2012
Strong Pan-Blue	87.6	37.8	87.4	94.9	95.1
Weak Pan-Blue	75.1	34.8	87.9	91.6	91.3
Leaning Pan-Blue	56.9	22.4	76.3	85.3	79
Independent	41.6/4.0	11.1/30.0	19.3/34.4	39.3/16.0	35.6/20.7
Leaning Pan-Green	28	7.8	4.2	9.3	10.8
Weak Pan-Green	29.5	8.2	0.8	5.2	3.4
Strong Pan-Green	21.2	4.3	0	1.9	1.7

Data Sources and Notes: Same as table 4.2.

Notes: (1) The two numbers for the Independent category represent the vote for the Pan-Blue candidate and the Pan-Green candidate, respectively. (2) Since the Pan-Blue and Pan-Green alliances were not formed until after 2000, vote shares of Pan-Blue candidates in 1996 and 2000 elections refer only to those of KMT candidates.

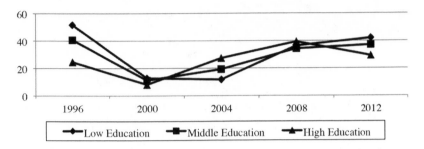

Fig. 4.6. Vote choice among independents with different educational levels. *Data Sources and Notes*: Same as table 4.2.

unwillingness of identifying with any party. For whatever reasons, political independents in Taiwan deserve further analysis in future research.

Figure 4.6 shows that highly educated independents were less likely to vote for the Pan-Blue candidate in the presidential election of 1996. In contrast, least-educated independents were strongly supportive of the Pan-Blue candidate. The support for the Pan-Blue candidate in the 2000 election declined concurrently among the three types of independents. The differences in vote choice among independents with different educational levels seen in 1996 disappeared. In 2004, highly educated independents were more willing to vote for the Pan-Blue candidate than their less educated counterparts. The election of 2008 was similar to that of 2000, with the three types of independents not showing much difference. Yet all the independents tended to show considerable support for the Pan-Blue candidate. The highly educated independents turned their backs on the Pan-Blue candidate in 2012. Both the moderately educated and least-educated independents had higher percentages of support for the Pan-Blue candidate. In addition to the changing patterns of vote choice among independents, figure 4.5 also reveals one significant feature: there is a correspondence between the elections that lead to power change and the convergence of vote choice among the three types of independents. The KMT's loss of power in the 2000 elections was accompanied by unified, declining support of independents. A similar instance occurred in 2008, when the Independents almost unanimously supported the Pan-Blue candidate who won the election.

Concluding Remarks

The evolution of the party system in Taiwan has been closely tied to the development of democracy. The development of citizen partisanship has taken a distinct route following the process of democratic opening. The long-standing KMT had monopolized the political marketplace early on, relegating citizen partisanship to nonpartisan status if they were not supporters of the KMT. Nevertheless, those nonpartisan citizens participated in elections, supported certain non-KMT candidates, and paved the way for alternative partisanship later on. The establishment of the DPP represents a watershed development in citizen partisanship, having made possible competing partisanship. Additionally, the development of a multiparty system and the formation of Pan-Blue and Pan-Green camps in the 2000s significantly transformed citizen partisanship. There have been both changes and continuity in the party system, as in citizen partisanship. Individually, each political party has certain social bases, yet those bases are somewhat shared by allied parties. That means a citizen might change his or her support from election to election. The difference on the policy of cross-Strait relations has separated the Pan-Blue and Pan-Green as well as supporters of each camp. Citizens seem to be in the situation of a two-party system, which has a distinct partisan boundary that is unable to be crossed. Therefore, a citizen in Taiwan could be either a supporter of the KMT, NP, and PFP, or a supporter of the DPP and TSU.

The distinct historical development of the political situation in Taiwan has also given birth to a considerable number of political independents. Repressive measures by the KMT in the early period generated a hostile political atmosphere for many Taiwanese, so maintaining a politically independent status was a naturally safe and expedient choice, and the implementation of local elections provided these non-KMT citizens channels of participation without committing to any partisanship. The existence of the independent thus went hand in hand with the development of the party system. The independent would later turn into a strong power base for the first meaningful opposition party, the DPP. As Taiwan entered a period of rapid political transition in the late 1980s, Taiwan citizens began to experience true two-party partisanship. This new situation soon transformed again as new political parties continued to emerge in the early 1990s and 2000s. Multipartisanship appeared following the establishment of the NP, the PFP, and the TSU. Nonetheless, the formation of multiple partisanship does not imply the eclipse of the independent, a considerable number of whom still exist in the political marketplace. Also notably, the multiparty system has been in fact more like two-party camps within which citizens are more likely to cast their ballots according to party coalition, especially in presidential elections.

Thus, citizen partisanship has been both continuous and changing. Strong partisan citizens are more consistently affiliated with a given party, but that is not the case for weak partisans and party leaners. The latter is obvious in the Pan-Blue camp. In contrast, the Pan-Green camp has enjoyed a more stable partisan affiliation with citizens. As for the independents, they generally resemble the conventional picture depicted in *The American Voter* (Campbell et al. 1960). Given the significant number of independents voting, they are certainly not to be ignored in elections, but they do behave differently according to their different educational levels. Though highly educated independents are less interested in politics and less likely to vote in elections, they do maintain a rather supportive attitude toward democracy and maintaining the status quo in cross-Strait relations. It is likely that these highly educated independents are comparably more autonomous and prudent than the least-educated independents, who are more likely to be mobilized in elections.

Modern democracy needs political parties. Even though the normative functions of the political party might change over times, the political party continues to be indispensable for democracy. More specifically, the formation and operation of the party system significantly affect the functioning of democracy. One of the core assumptions of party politics is a stable connection between citizens and political parties; the majority of the citizens in society are able to voice their preferences through political parties. Yet if a considerable number of citizens do not maintain a regular connection with a political party, it is therefore implied that the political party does not matter much in society. Worse still, a lack of partisan connection also implies a lack of important media transmitting citizens' political information. Citizens would drift around the political world without an anchor (Wattenberg 1986, 130). Given the evidence of a high degree of overlap in attributes between the pure independent and partisan leaners in Taiwan, a clear classification of leaners is important both theoretically and practically. If we treat leaners as extended partisan voters, then the number of independents is less significant. It also leads to the conclusion that a relative majority of the electorate is partisan and that political parties have penetrated the major part of society. The party system is then accordingly stable. On the other hand, if we treat leaners as equal to independents, then more than one-third of the electorate will be labeled as independents; thus there exists a strong segment of uncommitted nonpartisan voters in elections. The formation and essences of party competition would also be affected because more centrist party appeals, rather than purely partisan-oriented ones, would become dominant in elections. Therefore, the changing partisan alliances of these independents, somewhat including the leaners, continue to play a crucial role in Taiwan's electoral politics.

APPENDIX 4.A1. Measurements of Key Variables

Variable	Description and Measurements
Directions and strength of party identification	Before 2004, respondents were asked the following questions: i. Do think of yourself as close to any particular party? When respondents answer yes, then they are asked, (1a) Which party do you feel close to? and (1b) Do you feel very close to this party, somewhat close, or not very close?" (strong, weak). ii. When respondents answer no to question (i), then respondents are asked, "Do you feel yourself a little closer to one of the political parties than to the others?" If respondents answer yes, then they are asked (1a) again (leaners). iii. When respondents answer "no" to question (ii), then respondents are regarded as independents. After 2004, respondents were asked slightly different questions. i. Among the main political parties in our country, including the KMT, DPP, PFP, NP, and TSU, do you think of yourself as leaning toward any particular party? (yes, then ask (iii) and (iv); no, then ask (ii)). ii. Do you feel yourself leaning a little more to one of the political parties than the others? (yes, then ask (iii); no will be classified as independent) iii. Which party is that? iv. Do you lean very strongly, somewhat, or just a little to this party?
Pan-Blue and Pan-Green identifiers	Citizens who identify with the KMT, the NP, and the PFP are classified as Pan-Blue identifiers; citizens who identify with the DPP and the TSU are classified as Pan-Green identifiers.
Political interest	More generally, would you say that you are very, somewhat, not very, or not at all interested in politics? (not interested, very little/not much interested, somewhat interested, very interested)
Maintaining the status quo	Respondents are asked: "Concerning the relationship between Taiwan and mainland China, which of the following six positions do you agree with: (1) immediate unification; (2) immediate independence; (3) maintain the status quo, move toward unification in the future; (4) maintain the status quo, move toward independence in the future; (5) maintain the status quo and decide later; (6) maintain the status quo forever. (Items 1 and 3 are classified as pro-unification; items 2 and 4 are classified as pro-independence; items 5 and 6 are classified as maintaining the status quo.)
Support for democracy	Respondents are asked, "Some say that 'Democracy might have some problems, but it is still the best political institution.' Do you agree or disagree?" (strongly agree, agree, disagree, strongly disagree)

Appendix 4.A2.

List of Data Sources

Yih-Yen Chen. 1992. Electoral Behavior and Democratization in Taiwan: A Study of Legislative Election in 1992. National Science Council Research Plan, NSC 82-0301-H004-034.

Yih-Yen Chen. 1995. Electoral Behavior and Democratization in Taiwan (iv): A Study of Legislative Election in 1995. National Science Council Research Plan, NSC 84-2414-H-004-053 B2.

Hsieh, John Fu-sheng. 1995. An Interdisciplinary Study of Voting Behavior in the 1996 Presidential Election. National Science Council Research Plan, NSC 85-2414-H-004-017 Q3.

I-chou Liu. 1998. Constituency Characteristics and Voters' Behavior: An Integrative Study of Legislative Election in 1998. National Science Council Research Plan, NSC 88-2414-H-004-017.

Yih-Yen Chen. 1999. Integrative Study of Voting Behavior in the 2000 Presidential Election. National Science Council Research Plan, NSC89-2414-H-004-021-SSS.

Chi Huang. 2001. Taiwan's Election and Democratization Study, 2001 (TEDS 2001). National Science Council Research Plan, NSC 90-2420-H-194-001.

Shiow-duan Huang. 2004. Taiwan's Election and Democratization Study, 2002-2004(III): The Presidential Election, 2004 (TEDS 2004P). National Science Council Research Plan, NSC 92-2420-H-031-004.

I-chou Liu. 2004. Taiwan's Election and Democratization Study, 2002-2004 (1/4): The Legislative Election, 2004 (TEDS 2004L). National Science Council Research Plan, NSC 93-2420-H-004-005-SSS.

Yun-han Chu. 2008. Taiwan's Election and Democratization Study, 2005-2008(III): The Legislative Election, 2008 (TEDS2008L). National Science Council Research Plan, NSC 96-2420-H-002-025.

Ching-hsin Yu. 2008. Taiwan's Election and Democratization Study, 2008 (TEDS 2008P: Presidential Election). National Science Council Research Plan, NSC 96-2420-H-004-017.

Yun-han Chu. 2012. Taiwan's Election and Democratization Study, 2009-2012 (III): The Survey of the Presidential and Legislative Elections, 2012(TEDS2012). National Science Council Research Plan, NSC 100-2420-H-002-030.

Notes

1. Mainstream wisdom concerning party identification in the tradition of the Michigan school and American National Election Studies have postulated the concept as a long-term psychological attachment to a given group (a specific political party). For a party identifier, party identification is a sense of group identity or belonging. Also by definition, party identification should be stable, not having frequent fluctuations. Therefore, data collection begins with a nonspecific statement asking the respondent:

"Generally speaking, do you usually think of yourself as a Republican, a Democrat, an Independent, or what?" The wording of this question also probes the respondent's endurance of staying with a political party. Those respondents who answer with either "Republican" or "Democrat" are then asked, "Would you call yourself a strong Republican (or Democrat) or a not very strong Republican (or Democrat)?" This follow-up question allows the researcher to explore respondents' intensity of party identification. So, the two questions produce four types of party identifier: Strong Republican Identifier, Weak Republican Identifier, Weak Democrat Identifier, and Strong Democratic Identifier.

2. Although minor political parties, such as the Chinese Youth Party and the Democratic Socialist Party, came to Taiwan with the KMT government, they were merely window-dressing since the KMT monopolized all political resources (Tien 1989). Thus, both parties were too weak to challenge the KMT.

3. The actual number of registered KMT members has been in dispute. Some estimate that the party has more than 2.5 million members while others claim that it has had less than one million. The KMT has been reluctant to release its membership. The electoral defeat in the 2000 presidential election has led to a sharp decline in party membership. It is estimated that the KMT now has about 850,000 members (cited from Yu 2002).

4. There were other minor parties during this period. Because they either did not participate in any elections or failed to generate significant political impacts, this research excludes them from the discussion.

References

Bartle, John, and Paolo Bellucci, eds. 2009. *Political Parties and Partisanship: Social Identity and Individual Attitudes*. London: Routledge.

Bryce, James. 1929. *Modern Democracies*. London: Macmillan.

Burnham, W. D. 1970. *Critical Elections and the Mainsprings of American Politics*. New York: W. W. Norton.

Campbell, Angus, Philip E. Converse, Warren E. Miller, and Donald E. Stokes. 1960. *The American Voter*. Chicago: University of Chicago Press.

Campbell, Angus, Gerald Gruin, and Warren E. Miller. 1954. *The Voter Decides*. Evanston, IL: Row Peterson.

Chang, Yu-tzung, Yunhan Chu, and Chong-min Park. 2007. "Authoritarian Nostalgia in Asia." *Journal of Democracy* 18 (3): 66–80.

Chen, Yih-yan. 1986. "The Study of Voting Behavior in Taiwan: Reviews and Prospects" [in Chinese]. *Thought and Words* 23 (6): 557–85.

Chen, Yih-yan. 1994. "Predicting Voter's Choice in the 1992 Legislator Election: A Cluster Analysis" [in Chinese]. *Journal of Electoral Studies* 1 (1): 1–37.

Cheng, Tun-jen, 1989. "Democratizing the Quasi-Leninist Regime in Taiwan." *World Politics* 41 (4): 471–99.

Cheng, Tun-jen, and Stephan Haggard, eds. 1992. *Political Change in Taiwan*. Boulder, CO: Lynne Rienner.

Chu, Shiau-yu. 2004. "The Research of Independent Voters' Voting Behavior: Comparison and Analysis of the 2000 and 2004 Presidential Elections" [in Chinese]. Master's thesis, Ming Chuan University.

Chu, Yun-han. 1996. "The Partisan Factor in Electoral Choice: A Case Analysis of the 1991 National Assembly Election" [in Chinese]. *Journal of Electoral Studies* 3 (1): 17–48.

Converse, Philip E. 1966. "On the Possibility of Major Political Realignment in the South." In *Elections and Political Order*, ed. Angus Campbell, Philip E. Converse, Warren E. Miller, and Donald E. Stoke, 212–44. New York: Wiley.

Dennis, Jack. 1988. "Political Independence in America. Part I: On Being an Independent Partisan Supporter." *British Journal of Political Science* 18 (1): 77–109.

Hsieh, John Fuh-sheng. 2005. "Ethnicity, National Identity, and Domestic Politics in Taiwan." *Journal of Asian and African Studies* 40 (April): 13–28.

Keith, Bruce E., David B. Magleby, Candice J. Nelson, Elizabeth Orr, Mark C. Westlye, and Raymond E. Wolfinger. 1992. *The Myth of the Independent Voter*. Berkeley: University of California Press.

Lazarsfeld, Paul F., Bernard Berelson, and Hazel Gaudet. 1948. *The People's Choice: How the Voter Makes Up His Mind in a Presidential Campaign*. New York: Columbia University Press.

Liu, I-chou. 1996. "The Behavior of Taiwanese Voters in 1992: Consolidation of Partisan Ties." In *Taiwan's Electoral Politics and Democratic Transition: Riding the Third Wave*, ed. Hung-Mao Tien, 226–41. Armonk, NY: M. E. Sharpe.

Liu, I-chou. 1997. "Difficulties of Concept Measurement in Political Science: The Case of Party Identification" [in Chinese]. Presented at the Conference of Research Methods of Political Science, National Chengchi University, Taipei.

Lu, Alexander Ya-li, 1992. "Political Opposition in Taiwan: The Development of the Democratic Progressive Party." In *Political Change in Taiwan*, ed. Tun-jen Cheng and Stephan Haggard, 121–46. Boulder, CO: Lynne Rienner.

Magleby, David B., Candice J. Nelson, and Mark C. Westlye. 2011. "The Myth of the Independent Voter Revisited." In *Facing the Challenge of Democracy: Explorations in the Analysis of Public Opinion and Political Participation*, ed. Paul M. Sniderman and Benjamin Highton, 238–63. Princeton: Princeton University Press.

Niemi, Richard G., and Herbert F. Weisberg. 1993. *Classics in Voting Behavior*. Washington, DC: Congressional Quarterly.

Niemi, Richard G., Stephen Wright, and Lynda W. Powell. 1987. "Multiple Party Identifiers and the Measurement of Party Identification." *Journal of Politics* 49 (4): 1093–1103.

Petrocik, John R. 1974. "An Analysis of Intransitivities in the Index of Party Identification." *Political Methodology* 1:31–47.

Sartori, Giovanni. 1976. *Parties and Party Systems: A Framework for Analysis*. Cambridge: Cambridge University Press.

Shyu, Huo-yan. 1997. "Elections and Social Cleavages in Taiwan: Party Competition and Democratization" [in Chinese]. Paper presented at the conference "Elections on Both Sides of the Straits," Fairbank Center for East Asian Research at Harvard University, Cambridge, May 8–9.

Tien, Hung-mao. 1989. *The Great Transition: Political and Social Change in the Republic of China*. Stanford, CA: Hoover Institution Press.

Wachman, Alan M., 1994. "Competing Identities in Taiwan." In *The Other Taiwan: 1945 to the Present*, ed. Murray Rubinstein, 17–80. Armonk, NY: M. E. Sharpe.

Wang, Fu-chang. 1993. "Causes and Patterns of Ethnic Intermarriage Among the Hokkien, Hakka, and Mainlanders in Postwar Taiwan: A Preliminary Examination" [in Chinese]. *Bulletin of the Institute of Ethnology Academia Sinica* 76 (Autumn): 43–96.

Wang, Jong-tian. 2010. "The Types of Independent Voters and Their Voting Behavior: Some Observations from Taiwan's 2008 Presidential Election" [in Chinese]. *Journal of Electoral Studies* 17 (2): 35–70.

Wang, T. Y., and Ching-hsin Yu. 2011. "Independents and Voting Decisions: A Test of James Bryce's Hypothesis." Presented at the 2011 International Conference on Taiwan's Election and Democratization Study, National Chengchi University, Taipei.

Wattenberg, Martin P. 1986. *The Decline of American Political Parties, 1952–1984*. Cambridge: Harvard University Press.

Weisberg, Herbert F. 1980. "A Multidimensional Conceptualization of Party Identification." *Political Behavior* 2 (1): 33–60.

Weisberg, Herbert F. 1993. "Political Partisanship." In *Measurement of Political Attitudes*, ed. John P. Robinson, Phillip R. Shaver, and Lawrence S. Wrightsman, 681–736. San Diego, CA: Academic Press.

Wilson, Richard W. 1970. *Learning to Be Chinese: The Political Socialization of Children in Taiwan*. Cambridge, MA: MIT Press.

Wu, Nai-Teh, 1995. "Ethnic Consciousness, Political Support, and National Identity." *Taiwan Studies* 1 (2): 45–66.

Yeh, Ming-yan. 1994. "The Research of Independent Voters in Taiwan" [in Chinese]. Master's thesis, National Chengchi University.

Yu, Chilik. 2002. "New Issues in the Study of Public Administration in Taiwan: The Impact and Influence on the Civil Servant System by Alternation of Political Power" [in Chinese]. Presented at the Conference of Professor Chin-Chien Chang's Centennial Anniversary, Chinese Society for Public Administration, Taipei.

CHAPTER 5

Issues, Political Cleavages, and Party Competition in Taiwan

Shing-yuan Sheng and Hsiao-chuan (Mandy) Liao

Taiwan experienced rapid socioeconomic and political changes in the 1960s and 1970s and evolved from an authoritarian to a democratic political system beginning in the mid-1980s.[1] Since the early 1980s, many issues have emerged in Taiwan's political arena. Some of them quickly disappeared, some temporarily attracted the attention of Taiwan citizens but gradually declined in importance, and still others evolved into highly salient ones and have had deterministic impacts on party competition and, hence, party turnover. Unlike most industrial democracies, in which issues of wealth distribution and materialism/postmaterialism (or fundamentalism/postmodernism) create the most important political cleavages (Dalton 1988; Inglehart 1977, 1990, 1997; Lipset and Rokkan 1967; Moreno 1999), those issues have not evolved into prominent ones for party competition in Taiwan. Instead, during the 1980s, as Taiwan transitioned to democracy, parties competed on the issue of reform versus antireform (stability). The partisan elites of the Democratic Progressive Party framed the reform issues and attracted the attention of Taiwan voters. As a result, the DPP gradually transformed itself into a strong opposition party with the support of about 30 percent of the electorate at the beginning of the 1990s. After political reforms and the resolution of unfair political practices, the party faced the challenge of searching for a new issue to appeal to a larger share of the electorate. So, it shifted the battlefield and framed the independence/unification issue in order to connect with the enduring social cleavages—ethnicity and Chinese/Taiwanese identity. Soon, the issue not only dominated the political discussions of the elites and the public but it also shaped party competition and affected elections.

This chapter, which is based on observation of the period from 1996 to 2012, endeavors to answer the following question: Why have some issues evolved to create important political cleavages that have shaped party competition in Taiwan, whereas other issues have not? Four issues are discussed in this chapter: wealth distribution, environmental protection/economy, reform/stability, and independence/unification. We explore the answer to the research questions from the perspective of the elites and that of the public. From the viewpoint of the elites, we show how they frame and manipulate different issues in the political arena to attain their political goals. From the viewpoint of the public, we show how the voters' positions on issues coincide with manipulation by the partisan elites and how the voters perceive the importance of the issues.

Issues and Political Cleavages in Taiwan

The importance of issues in politics has long been recognized and emphasized by political scientists. Carmines and Stimson (1989, 3) describe it well in their classic book *Issue Evolution*: "To speak of politics is to speak of political issues." As they argue, there are many issues in a political system, but the majority of them lie dormant most of the time. Only a few issues occasionally "rise from partisan obscurity and become so contentious, so partisan, and so long lasting that they come to define the party system in which they arise, to transform the grounds of debate which were their origin" (Carmines and Stimson 1986, 901). According to Carmines and Stimson, which issues become salient and which remain dormant depend on the actions of partisan elites and the responses of the mass electorate. First, elites instinctively know that some issues may benefit them, and they work to clarify those issues and frame them in partisan terms. Second, the mass public must alter its cognitive perception of the parties with respect to new issues, care about the differences among parties, and even change its political attitude and vote choice according to its opinions about new issues. When a substantial part of the mass public starts to change its cognition, attitude, and behavior in this way, all parties in the political system are necessarily forced to take a position along the dimensions of the new issue. At this moment, the issue experiences an evolution and affects the agendas of parties, the discourses of the elites, and party identification and vote choice of the mass electorate. Carmines and Stimson illustrate an issue evolution in which the party elites grew increasingly polarized on civil rights in the 1960s and 1970s, leading the mass electorate to become similarly polarized on that issue.

Furthermore, Lipset and Rokkan (1967) argue that political cleavages reflect social cleavages, and social cleavages are determined dramatically by the historic conditions of national and socioeconomic development. Accordingly, specific national conditions lead to a variety of alliance patterns among leaders of various social groups. As a result, these cleavages define the potential social bases of political conflicts. Lipset and Rokkan's analysis offers a reasonable explanation for the rise of the party systems and voter alignments in advanced democracies. In most advanced democracies, the wealth distribution issue based on class is the most common factor and perhaps the most important political cleavage. However, approximately from the beginning of the 1970s, economic factors and traditional class-conflict models fail to explain contemporary political phenomena. Those who are materially better off protest the most, rather than those who are materially disadvantaged. Traditional political cleavage and theory of class conflict cannot explain this new political trend. Inglehart (1990, 1997) adds a new aspect—postmaterial or postmodern values based on noneconomic issues—to the formation of political cleavages. This new cleavage and the old wealth distribution cleavage are the most important issues in most advanced democracies (Moreno 1999).

Taiwan experienced rapid socioeconomic and political changes in 1960s and 1970s, and evolved from an authoritarian to a democratic political system beginning in the mid-1980s. A great deal of evidence suggests that from the mid-1980s to the beginning of the 1990s, when Taiwan experienced a transition to democracy, reform versus antireform (stability) was the most salient political issue (Cheng and Hsu 1996; Chu 1994; Shyu 1998; Wu 1993). As many new democracies in East Europe and Latin America, the democratic-authoritarian or reform-antireform is the most salient issue (Moreno 1999). Chu (1994) argued that the Taiwan public focused more on issues of political reform than on issues of economy and wealth distribution during this period because the Taiwan government's economic policies had successfully resolved the problems of wealth accumulation and distribution during the decades that economic development heated up. Hsieh and Niou (1996a) examined the 1992 legislative election and found that the reform/stability issue had the greatest impact on voters' evaluations of parties, followed by the wealth distribution and the independence/unification issues, with the environment/economy issue having the smallest impact. However, when Hsieh and Niou reviewed the 1993 local elections for county magistrates and city mayors, they found that the independence/unification issue and two valence issues—public work and anticorruption—had important impacts on voters' evaluations of the parties. Other positional issues such as wealth distribution, environment protection, and reform had limited impacts (Hsieh and Niou 1996b). Because the debate on independence versus unification was increasingly contested in the 1990s, when political scientists examined the 2001 legislative election, they found that independence/unification was the most influential issue and had considerable impact on voters' party evaluations and vote choice. The reform/stability issue had some impact and was the second most important political cleavage. The wealth distribution issue also had some impact and a significant effect on vote choice, but the environment/economy issue was still not influential in elections (Hsieh 2005; Sheng and Chen 2003).

Given the research results in previous literature, we may suspect that the impacts of different issues fluctuate in different elections. This chapter will systematically answer why and how some issues have created important cleavages that have shaped party competition in Taiwan while other issues have not. As noted, four issues are examined in this chapter: reform/stability, wealth distribution, environmental protection/economy, and independence/unification. We choose the four issues for two major reasons. First, the reform/stability issue and independence/unification issue have occupied Taiwan election platforms and have polarized Taiwan politics for a long time. The wealth distribution issue and the environmental protection/economy issue marked the old and new left-right issues that shape endurable political cleavages in advanced democracies although Taiwan is not such a case (Hsiao, Cheng, and Achen, chapter 9 of this book; Norris 2004). As parties and politicians in Taiwan raised these issues in elections and in the legislature frequently and sometimes caught the public's attention, these two issues did not form political cleavages.

The other reason for choosing these four issues is that they are position issues. A position issue is one on which the opinions among the electorate may easily be divided, such as the extent to which we should empower the government. On the contrary, issues such as economic development or anticorruption are valence issues—these are issues that are uniformly liked or disliked by the electorate (Fiorina 1981). Position issues are more likely to develop political cleavages and shape party competition than valence issues since parties can take opposing sides to mobilize the electorate (Stokes 1963). Valence issues have less potential to form a long-term political cleavage because they do not differentiate parties effectively.

Thus, this chapter will dissect the four issues in Taiwan and demonstrate their evolution from the perspectives of both the partisan elites and of the public. We selected the observation period from 1996 to 2012. Data are from two major databases: data on the elections of 1996, 1998, and 2000, which were collected by the Election Study Center at National Chengchi University, and data on the elections of 2001, 2004, 2008, and 2012, which were collected by the Taiwan Election and Democratization Study project. All of these data are from face-to-face interviews with individuals of the Taiwan public aged 20 and above and are based on probabilistic sampling.

In the following, we first focus on the partisan elites' role in issue evolution and discuss how partisan elites frame and manipulate the four issues in order to attain their political goals. We also demonstrate how Taiwan citizens perceive the elites' signals and update their positions on issues. Then, we discuss mass perception of the importance of issues. Last, we conclude with the issue evolution of the four focal issues in Taiwan.

The Framing and Manipulation of the Issues by the Partisan Elites

In the process of issue evolution, the elites of the Dang-wai (the non-KMT forces and the forerunner of the DPP before 1986; see chapter 4) and DPP play an important role, not only because the Dang-wai and DPP elites are strategic politicians but also because they are from the opposition forces when Taiwan endured a transitional period from authoritarian to democracy. They are ambitious to acquire governing power. Politicians of the opposition or minority parties naturally turn to new issues to improve their political situation, whereas politicians of the majority parties naturally seek to maintain the salience of the current agenda (Carmines and Stimson 1989, 12–13). The Dang-wai and DPP elites strategically search for issues that benefit their group's growth and strength. Furthermore, they frame and manipulate the issues to mobilize the mass public. From the beginning of the 1980s, the Dang-wai and DPP elites have capitalized on four major issues: political reform, social welfare, environmental protection, and Taiwan independence. The issues of political reform and Taiwan independence have been relatively more effective than the other two in terms of issue evolution. In the early 1980s, the Dang-wai and DPP elites used political reform issues to challenge the established authoritarian Kuomintang government and attract voters. After political reform was achieved, the DPP elites switched to the independence/unification issue and acted as an advocate of Taiwan independence from the beginning of 1990s. The success of manipulating issues to mobilize the mass public extended the support base of the DPP in the 1980s and 1990s and brought the DPP to the presidency in 2000 and 2004. However, once the DPP captured power, its room for manipulating issues became smaller for two reasons. First, once the DPP was in power, Taiwan voters were no longer satisfied with only rhetoric during elections; instead, they wanted to see the actual implementation of the DPP's campaign promises. Second, the DPP soon found that it was limited by fiscal difficulties; in particular, Taiwan has been in an economic downturn since 2000.

In the following, we will describe issue by issue how the elites have framed and manipulated them. We begin with the very first one that appeared in Taiwan politics—reform versus stability—and end with the most significant issue in Taiwan—independence versus unification.

The Reform/Stability Issue

Taiwan experienced rapid economic development from the beginning of the 1960s through the 1970s and 1980s. As a result, Taiwan society experienced dramatic socioeconomic change and transitioned from an underdeveloped country to an industrialized society in the 1980s. Accompanying this transformation, there emerged a new middle class with more education and sophisticated political skills. This new class and the politically suppressed Taiwanese, whose parents or grandparents had lived on the island before 1948, strongly pushed the dominant KMT government to undertake political reforms. However, the KMT government was reluctant to respond to the prodding. Utilizing a reform-oriented strategy, the Dang-wai gradually attracted the electoral support of Taiwan citizens. Eventually they got enough support to organize a formal party, the DPP, in 1986. Indeed, the Dang-wai got just 13.0 percent of all votes in the 1980 legislative election; however, the share of votes for the DPP (established in 1986) increased to nearly 30 percent by the end of the 1980s (see chapter 4 for details).

The reform/stability issue was the most salient one in the 1980s, during Taiwan's transition to democracy. Some Taiwan citizens were worried about instability because of the rapid and radical political reform. They tended to identify with the KMT, whereas those taking political reform more seriously tended to identify with the DPP (Sheng and Chen 2003). In a survey conducted in 1991 about the most significant problem in the country, 36.4 percent of respondents mentioned political structure, 14.2 percent mentioned national status and national identity, while only 9.3 percent mentioned wealth distribution (Wu 1993, 6).

The opposition forces made great efforts to promote political reform and earned a reputation for being reformist. There was a considerable number of issues on the reform agenda from the mid-1980s to the beginning of the 1990s, including the lifting of martial law in 1987, termination of the Temporary Provisions Effective During the Period of National Mobilization for Suppression of the Communist Rebellion, and with the return to a regular constitutional structure in 1991, full-scale elections of national representatives in 1992, a popular vote for the provincial governors and city mayors of Taipei City and Kaohsiung City in 1994, and direct elections for president in 1996. Even when the large and structural changes were achieved, the DPP continued its reformist role and turned its focus to social and economic reforms. These reforms include anticorruption, anticrime, constitutional reform, dealing with the KMT assets, and social welfare policies. In the process, the DPP legislators sometimes allied with members of the New Party, a newly established small party that sometimes collaborated with KMT legislators. The DPP might not be the owner of the particular reform issue as it was during the earlier period, but it was more active in this respect than the KMT (Sheng 2001).

A survey conducted by the Election Study Center in 1993 asked respondents about their impressions of the two major parties. The results showed that 35.8 percent of respondents perceived the DPP as a radical party, and 32.4 percent of respondents perceived it as a violent party. In contrast, 43.0 percent of respondents perceived the KMT as a conservative party (Liu 1994, 64). Even at the end of 2000 and the beginning of 2001, after the DPP had won the presidency and began to govern the country, the mass public's principal negative image of the DPP was still that it was violent and radical, whereas the principal positive image of the DPP was its contribution to democratic reform (Cheng 2004, 195–98). From figure 5.1, we can see that Taiwan voters on average located the DPP at 3.9 on the reform/stability issue dimension in 1996 and at 4.6 in 2001.[2] However, because of the fierce party competition in the legislature and in the elections, the DPP returned to the reform-oriented position that it had held in the past. The DPP government directed two financial reforms and held referendums on national issues in 2004. The slogan of President Chen's reelection in 2004 was "Taiwan first, Reform first." Not surprisingly, the public located the DPP at 3.9 in 2004. In contrast, the public perceived the KMT as taking stability more seriously and as being more conservative in regard to political reform. The public located the KMT at 6.9 in 1996 and did not shift much over the years, until 2008.

In mid-2006, President Chen Shui-bian and his family members were accused of improper trading of shares, misuse of government funds, and corruption.[3] In 2008, after leaving office, Chen Shui-bian was convicted of corruption and money-laundering, shocking the Taiwan public. When more evidence revealed that ex-president Chen had accepted money from

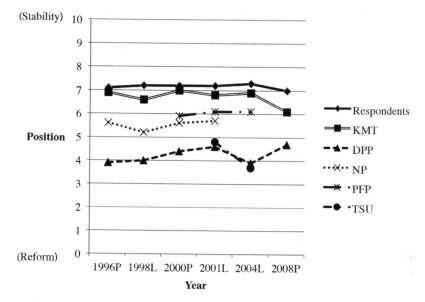

Fig. 5.1. Respondents' issue positions on reform/stability and their perceptions about the positions of the parties (1996–2008). *Source:* Appendix 5.A2. *Note:* On the horizontal axis, "P" indicates that surveys were conducted after the presidential election; "L" indicates that surveys were taken after the legislative election.

bankers during the second financial and banking reform, the public became even more disillusioned with both Chen Shui-bian and the DPP. In the 2008 election, the KMT presidential candidate, Ma Ying-jeou, took the opportunity to promote reforms in administrative ethics and social justice. He promised to initiate legislation on the criminal liability of illicit wealth of public servants and to comprehensively examine constitutional reform.[4] In contrast, as the governing party the DPP took social stability more seriously than when it was in opposition. The DPP candidate, Hsieh Chang-ting, stressed the importance of consensus on reform. The public's perception of the two parties' issue positions along the reform/stability spectrum reflects this situation. In 2008 the public perceived the DPP, which was rated at 4.7, as more centrist than in 2004, while the KMT, at 6.1, was seen as leaning more toward reform than it had been in 2004. Along with this development, both the KMT and DPP have taken a more centrist position since 2008. In such a case, there is less space for parties to manipulate this issue, which leaves the possibility of convergence of their issue position in the future.

The Wealth Distribution Issue

Unlike most advanced democracies, in which issues of wealth distribution are salient for party competition, issues of wealth distribution are relatively not so important in party competition in Taiwan. The evolution of this issue in Taiwan has gone through different phases. Before the mid-1980s, both the successful economic policy and the weak consciousness of the working class detracted from the attention given to wealth distribution issues (Chu 1994, 3). At the end of the 1980s and the beginning of the 1990s, social welfare issues became more prominent due to fierce party competition and the increasing gap between the rich and the poor; however, such issues have become less polarizing, since most parties strive to offer social welfare benefits and none of them want to be seen as opposing benefits. More important, the independence/unification issue has attracted most of the attention of the parties and the electorate. Last, after party turnover in the presidency in 2000, the differences between the parties' issue positions diminished while the DPP was in power and faced fiscal problems and the KMT stayed with a catch-all strategy on this issue. Later, we will discuss this issue according to its development over time and explain its ups and downs in Taiwan politics.

From the beginning of the 1980s, the parties and candidates emphasized wealth distribution issues more actively than before. This was connected to ethnicity, the most significant social cleavage in Taiwan.[5] When the KMT government was moved to Taiwan in 1949, many mainlanders who worked for the military, public sector, and education sector immigrated to Taiwan with the government; thus, a high proportion of public servants were mainlanders. So the KMT's social welfare policies in the early era focused more on these groups in order to consolidate its ruling apparatus. In 1987, the newly founded DPP set up a department whose purpose was forming an alliance with social-movement organizations in order to confront the KMT government. Responding to political reforms and to the challenge to its conservative welfare policies, and hoping to obtain widespread supports from the Taiwan voters, the KMT started a small-scale welfare program in the 1980s.

Before the 1980s, small-scale welfare programs did not arouse much discontent because class consciousness was weak. Taiwan's economy heavily relied on exports and small-scale enterprises, which created many outsourcing industries. When the big outsourcing factories could not accommodate all the contracts, they would farm out their contracts to small subcontractors. In 1986, 63.3 percent of workers in manufacturing industries worked in a factory with fewer than 10 employees (Hsieh 1989, 17).[6] Although these small-scale enterprises supported the economic development of Taiwan, they hindered the formation of working-class consciousness and stimulated mobility between classes (Chang 1987; Gates 1979; Hsieh 1989). The structure of these small enterprises created more possibilities for Taiwan workers to start their own businesses,[7] and from 1979 to 1987, 35 percent of Taiwan citizens chose to do so rather than be hired by others (Hsieh 1989, 12). Even among employees, 30 percent of them wanted to open their own business in the future (Stites 1985, 238). Moreover, the heads of the small enterprises, as well as society in general, also manipulated this desire for business ownership as a way to deal with unhappy workers (Hsieh 1989).[8] Because the working class in Taiwan prefers starting their own businesses to confronting their bosses, it has been rather difficult to form strong class consciousness among workers.

The issue of wealth distribution stirred up more controversy after the 1980s because the disparity between the rich and the poor grew as a result of the rapid economic development and social transformation. According to a survey on family income, the average income of the top 20 percent of richest families was as much as 4.1 times that of the bottom 20 percent of families in 1980. The ratio of the average income between the top 20 percent and the bottom 20 percent was 5.2 in 1992 (Directorate-General of Budget 2012). From the beginning of the 1990s, not only did the DPP promote wealth distribution legislation, it also actively searched for a new battleground in wealth distribution issues to attract voters. In the 1992 legislative election, one candidate campaigned on the promise of a pension for senior citizens and achieved a significant victory. Later in the 1993 elections for county magistrates and city mayors, many DPP candidates advocated pensions for the elderly (Wang 2003, 81–82). When the DPP candidates were elected, they kept their promise and granted NT3000 dollars to senior citizens. Even though these payments did not last long in many counties because of fiscal difficulties, the DPP acquired a reputation for caring about the social welfare of the average Taiwan citizen. In the DPP's 1999 survey on the question of a party's capability to design a fair and reasonable social welfare system, 32.9 percent of respondents considered the DPP qualified while 20.7 percent chose the KMT (Fell 2005, 39). It may be plausible that it was at that moment the DPP achieved ownership of the social welfare issue, especially that of care of the elderly.

However, the DPP's ownership of that issue did not last long, since the KMT was also competing for it. Worried that the DPP might take all of the credit for advocacy of legislation on social welfare, the KMT not only started to propose a national health insurance program but also struggled to propose its own version of policies on subsidies for seniors.[9] Eventually, the KMT cooperated with the DPP to pass legislation providing benefits to elderly farmers. Also, in 1995, the KMT government implemented the National Health Insurance program. Although the DPP initially gained the support of the electorate in part from promoting social welfare, both the DPP and KMT found their niches in the wealth distribution issue in the mid-1990s.

In other words, because of fierce electoral competition, a considerable number of social welfare issues became prominent in the Taiwan political arena. When a party or candidate advocates a policy that might benefit a specific group, political opponents may do likewise, or even advocate a more radical extension of the same policy aiming at the same target. Since most Taiwan parties and candidates attempted to take credit for welfare plans and avoid the blame for blocking such plans, the differences between the parties have gradually decreased (Chu 1994; Fell 2005; Sheng 2002; Sheng and Chen 2003). Furthermore, once the independence/unification issue appeared in the Taiwan political arena, it diverted much of the attention of the parties and the electorate from other issues. As Norris (2004, 119) claimed, "In Taiwan the parties were identified mainly by nationalist issues, about relationships with mainland China, rather than by left-right ideology."[10] Hence, the disparity of wealth distribution failed to form a strong political cleavage on the island.

Indeed, from 2000 to 2008, while the DPP was in power, the party became more concerned about the government's fiscal capacity and economic development and was not as active in promoting social welfare as it had been prior to that time. In September 2000, the newly elected DPP president, Chen Shui-bian, announced at a press conference, "Social welfare can be put off, but economic development can't be" (*United Daily News*, September 17, 2000, 1). Therefore, the differences on the social welfare issue between the parties became smaller. As figure 5.2 shows, in 2000 Taiwan voters on average rated the DPP's position on the wealth-distribution issue dimension at 6.5, while the KMT on average was at 4.8 on the same issue dimension (questionnaire shown in a2 of appendix 5.A1). However, in 2004, after the DPP had been in power for four years, the rating was 6.0, compared to 5.6 for the KMT. In 2012, the DPP was at 5.4, while the KMT was at 5.1 along the spectrum of wealth distribution; thus, the issue positions of the two major parties in promoting wealth distribution had converged.

Figure 5.2 also demonstrates that the DPP became more centrist on wealth distribution in the perception of Taiwan public. Thus, it is not surprising that many Taiwan voters felt that the DPP had become closer to

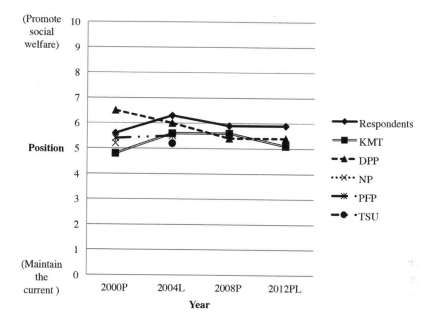

Fig. 5.2. Respondents' issue positions on social welfare/tax raises and their perceptions about the parties' positions (2000–2012). *Source:* Appendix 5.A2. *Note:* On the horizontal axis, "P" indicates that surveys were conducted after the presidential election; "L" indicates that surveys were taken after the legislative election. In 2012 the presidential election and the legislative election were held at the same time.

business interests and played money politics soon after it was elected (Liu 2003). According to a survey conducted in 2002, two years after Chen Shui-bian became president, 42 percent of the respondents perceived that the DPP was too close to big business and to consortiums and spoke for the wealthy (*United Daily News*, July 29, 2002, 3).

The small differences between the issue positions of the two major parties has constrained the DPP's advantage on the wealth distribution issue. A political cleavage due to opposition positions in the wealth distribution issue has been difficult to develop. Take regulations on subsidies for senior citizens as an example. In 2002 the KMT, together with the People First Party, first proposed and passed a regulation to provide subsidies to the elderly except for those with retirement pensions. Instead of discussion on whether the subsidies were affordable for the government and were fair to other minority groups, legislators from different parties competed to propose their own versions of subsidies. Some proposed to broaden the qualifications, while others proposed to raise the amount of the allowance. Even though a less disputable revision of the legislation was made on June 2003, the parties continued to propose revisions to the qualifications and the amount of the allowance. In total, there were 30 legislative proposals from different parties and legislators in the Fifth Legislative Yuan (Sheng 2005a). From the perception of the public, all of the parties seemed to converge at a neutral place on the wealth distribution issue. Thus, it becomes more difficult for the electorate to differentiate parties on the basis of the wealth distribution issue.

More important, in order to maintain its overwhelming dominance in Taiwan politics, the KMT has adopted a catch-all strategy, not a one-sided one. It will not give up the votes of laborers or farmers even though it may stand closer to public servants and capitalists due to its historical background. It may give wealth distribution issues less priority but will not oppose improving wealth distribution. On the contrary, the DPP, which was established through the strong support of disadvantaged and dissatisfied groups, focuses on social welfare programs to gain votes; however, the KMT's strategy makes it difficult for the DPP to create confrontational situations effectively.

Overall, although the wealth distribution issue has been a point of contention in elections for a long period of time, it did not emerge as a significant political cleavage in the society. The disparity between the rich and the poor has widened in recent years, however, due to the economic downturn and money politics in Taiwan (Sheng 2013). According to a survey on family income, the average income of the top 20 percent of richest families was as much as 6.2 times that of the bottom 20 percent of families in 2010 (Directorate-General of Budget 2012). If we limit the observations to the top 5 percent of richest families and the bottom 5 percent of families, the ratio in income between them is even greater. It was 32.7 in 1998, 55.1 in 2005, and 93.9 in 2012 (Ministry of Finance 2013). Because of the worsening imbalance in wealth distribution, social welfare issues have become more salient (as evidence will show in the next section), and the parties have used this issue as a means to gain the support of disadvantaged voters. Indeed, in the 2012 election, voters concerned more about social welfare were more likely to vote for the DPP (Sheng 2013). After the election, persisting disputes on wealth distribution issues, such as minimum wage and maximum hours, labor pensions, and pensions of retired public servants, have made the rising gap in wealth a prominent issue in the Taiwan society. From the experience of advanced democracies, wealth distribution becomes a salient issue when there are a large-scale changes or economic depressions, or both

(Dalton 1996; Lipset and Rokkan 1967). Will the rising gap in wealth in the Taiwan society polarize elites and voters and become an important political cleavage in the future? In our view, the issue of wealth distribution may not be able to single-handedly form a significant political cleavage due to the similar stands of political parties in Taiwan. However, if it aligns with the identity issue, the scenario may be different, a point that we will discuss in the conclusion.

The Environmental Protection/Economy Issue

Since the beginning of the 1980s, the Taiwan public has started to notice the environmental deterioration resulting from rapid economic development. However, the ruling KMT emphasized development, in which economic growth was the top priority, at the expense of environmental protection (Tang and Tang 1997). Protesting the KMT's promotion and endorsement of heavily polluting industries, several environmental protection groups were organized to confront the KMT government. The DPP played an important role in the protests. In 1986, Lukang residents were mobilized to oppose a DuPont investment that had been endorsed by the KMT government. This protest made DuPont withdraw its project of establishing chemical factories in Lukang. This incident prompted many antipollution protests in the following years. In 1991, when the KMT government decided to build a fourth nuclear power plant in Kongliao, many Kongliao villagers were mobilized to oppose this policy by demonstrations and sit-ins at the proposed nuclear power plant's location. A violent clash with the police occurred, and a policeman's death brought the incident to nationwide attention. From then on, demonstrations accompanied the building project of the fourth nuclear power plant. The growing polarization of the proenvironment and pronuclear groups brought the former into closer alignment with the DPP (Ho 2005a, 405–7), which energized its base of support by mobilizing people who cared about environmental protection.

As shown in figure 5.3, when respondents were asked to locate the position of the parties on the environmental protection/economy issue dimension (with higher scores indicating economic development and lower scores as environmental protection), the DPP was rated at 5.0 in 1998 while the KMT had a score of 7.3 (questionnaire shown in a3 of the appendix 5.A1). However, after the DPP became the ruling party, its desire to stimulate economic recovery led it, like the KMT, to favor more developmentalist policies. When it faced a trade-off between the environment and the economy, most of the time the DPP favored the latter over the former, frustrating many Taiwan voters who cared about environmental issues (Ho 2005b).

Take the construction of the fourth nuclear power plant as an example. After President Chen Shui-bian came in power in 2000, he issued an executive order to halt the construction of the plant in October. This decision brought about severe political battles and resulted in a serious political crisis between Chen, the Executive Yuan, and the Legislative Yuan.[11] Later, the Council of Grand Justices issued the Interpretation No. 520, which stated that the Executive Yuan's actions had a "procedural flaw" for not reporting to the Legislative Yuan before making the decision to halt the construction. The value of stock market went down at least 2.5 percent as a result. In the end, the Executive Yuan and the Legislative Yuan reached a compromise to restart the construction with a consensus that a "nuclear free homeland" was the objective in the long run. The political compromise appeased the opposition parties, but frustrated people who stood for environment protection and expected the DPP would have made a difference. Although a few DPP leaders continued their fight against the use of nuclear energy and proposed to hold a nationwide referendum on the fate of the fourth nuclear plant, Chen did not endorse their proposal and chose promoting economic development rather than environmental protection as his top priority (Fell 2012, 187–88). The data in figure 5.3 demonstrate that the public has gradually changed its view of the DPP on environmental issues.

In contrast, the KMT was rather stable at around 7.2 on the issue spectrum of environmental protection/economy until 2008. In the 2008 presidential campaign, Ma Ying-jeou promised to initiate land restoration and reductions in carbon emissions. His platform also included the imposition of an energy tax and establishment of green traffic networks and buildings. As for controversial public works, such as the highway between Su-ao and Hua-lien, he promised to respect the results of environmental reports. When Ma Ying-jeou repeated his promises for legislation and policy at the National NGO Environmental Forum (Green Party Taiwan 2009), environmental groups had great hope that he would fulfill them.[12] The perception of the electorate with regard to the KMT's position on environmental issues was at 6.8 in 2008, which reflected this expectation to some degree. Meanwhile, Hsieh Chang-ting, the DPP presidential candidate in 2008, held to the DPP's traditional policy, which included ceasing the construction of the highway, and the party was perceived at 5.4 on the issue spectrum of environmental protection/economy.

Although antinuclear protests continued to occur in Taiwan after the

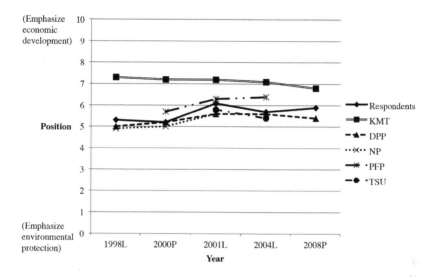

Fig. 5.3. Respondents' issue positions on environmental protection/economy and their perceptions about the parties' positions (1998–2008). *Source:* Appendix 5.A2. *Note:* On the horizontal axis, "P" indicates that surveys were conducted after the presidential election; "L" indicates that surveys were taken after the legislative election.

fiasco of halting the construction of the fourth nuclear power plant, this issue failed to catch the public's attention as it did in 2000/2001. As both the KMT and the DPP are generally in favor of developmental policies, it was not until the Fukushima nuclear incident of 2011 that the safety of nuclear energy became politically significant again. The Fukushima incident, which occurred in Japan on March 11, 2011,[13] turned the public's attention to environmental protection. When the KMT government requested a budget increase in 2012 to fund the ongoing project of building the fourth nuclear plant, the public loudly and clearly voiced their serious concerns about the safety of nuclear energy. Several environmental groups instituted protests again. A TEDS survey conducted in 2013 showed that 60.1 percent of respondents believed the government should halt constructing the plant, while only 27.3 percent supported the project (Sheng 2014). The DPP seized the opportunity to put forward the proposition of a nuclear-free homeland. The party's elites also joined in the 309 NO NUKE Parade with environmental groups. To defuse the crisis, the KMT government announced in 2013 that a referendum on the fate of the power plant would be held later. Under the growing pressure, the KMT government finally announced in April 2014 that the construction of the fourth nuclear power plant would be moth-balled for three years.[14] It is worth noting that this move did not represent a KMT position shift because it keeps the option of restarting the construction in the future.

If the KMT continues to emphasize the economy while the DPP stands for environmental protection, this issue may provide a political environment in which to start discussions and debates. However, since the Taiwan public is much more concerned about economic prosperity than environmental protection (as evidence will show in the next section) and the ruling party cares more about economic growth, which is the case for both the KMT and the DPP, the environmental protection issue has difficulty in evolving to become a significant political cleavage (Sheng and Chen 2003). Further, as Inglehart (1990) noted, the new political cleavages of postmaterialism (such as environmental protection) do not necessarily attract votes because the supporters of those new issues are more active on issue agendas rather than being passively dominated by partisan elites. In other words, it is more difficult for partisan elites to manipulate the environmental protection issue. Thus, even when the issue of environmental protection becomes more salient in the Taiwan political area, its influence on party competition and elections may still be less than that of existing political cleavages.

The Independence/Unification Issue

After the achievement of political reforms and the reorganization of unfair political structures, the DPP, with 30.0 percent support of the electorate at the beginning of the 1990s, faced the challenge of finding a new issue to continue its political life. Which issue was the DPP able to maneuver most effectively to attract Taiwan voters in the next stage? Two major issues gradually drew attention from the DPP elites at the beginning of the 1990s. One was the pursuit of Taiwan independence, and the other was the pursuit of a welfare state (as discussed above). When the issue of Taiwan independence was raised in the political arena, it was connected to Taiwan's most important social cleavages, those of ethnicity and Chinese/Taiwanese identity, so that it was easily perceived by voters and aroused the emotions of substantial portions of the Taiwan public.

Even though the DPP is pro-independence, its position on the independence/unification spectrum has shifted at different times to attain its political goals. In 1991, when it was eager to claim a position for Taiwan independence, the DPP passed the Taiwan Independence Clause just two months before the National Assembly election. The DPP headquarters issued several full-page and article-style ads on why it advocated a sovereign and independent Republic of Taiwan (Fell 2005, 99). However, it received only 23.6 percent of the vote in the 1991 election, worse than its usual outcome. In the following legislative election in 1992, taking into account that Taiwan voters were not so comfortable with a radical stand on Taiwan independence, the DPP packaged Taiwan independence into a more diluted form and deemphasized the issue. The term "Republic of Taiwan" vanished from its ads and the more moderate "diluted Taiwan independence" replaced "pure Taiwan independence" (Fell 2005, 100).

In 1996, an independence-oriented DPP presidential candidate, Peng Ming-min, made "Want Independence, Oppose Unification, Love Peace" his campaign slogan. Again, this pledge moved the DPP to a more radical independence-seeking position. The public perceived the DPP as an extreme party in this regard and placed it at 2.0 on the independence/unification spectrum in 1996, whereas the public perceived the KMT at 6.1, and the average position of the public's own view was at 5.2 (figure 5.4, questionnaire shown in a4 of appendix 5.A1). The DPP garnered only 23.1 percent of all votes in 1996. This serious defeat continued in the 1998 legislative election. While the public stood at 5.0 on the independence/unification spectrum, the DPP was perceived at 2.3, far from the public's average position. The DPP received 29.6 percent of the vote, less than what an ambitious and energetic party would expect.

The continuous electoral defeats prompted the DPP to reconsider its position on the independence/unification issue. Before the 2000 presidential election, the DPP tried to take a centrist stance on the independence issue and to convince Taiwan voters that it had the ability to handle cross-Strait relations. First, the DPP passed the Resolution on Taiwan's Future, which returned to its original principle of Taiwan self-determination. The second step was Chen Shui-bian's speech "The New Central Way," which referred to a vague middle way on the independence/unification issue (Fell 2005, 106). In the 2000 presidential election, Chen Shui-bian was elected with 39.3 percent of the vote. Another key factor that contributed to this victory was that two candidates—Lien Chan and James Soong—ran on the pro-unification side and split the vote.

Chen Shui-bian knew well that he would not be so lucky in the next election. To compete in a single plural electoral system with two parties, the median position might be a better position strategically. From then until the 2001 legislative election, Chen hewed to a centrist position on the independence/unification issue. The first move in this direction was his

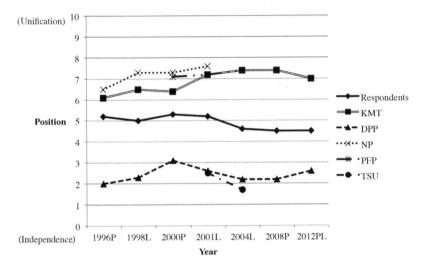

Fig. 5.4. Respondents' issue positions on independence/unification and their perceptions about the positions of the parties (1996–2012). *Source:* Appendix 5.A2. *Note:* On the horizontal axis, "P" indicates that surveys were conducted after the presidential election; "L" indicates that surveys were taken after the legislative election.

inaugural speech, in which Chen declared the Four Noes plus One Without pledge,[15] emphasizing that the new government would take a centrist position on the issue. Taiwan voters did receive this signal and thus revised their image of the DPP. As shown in figure 5.4, the Taiwan public on average located the DPP at 3.1 in this issue dimension. It was the first time that the Taiwan public placed the DPP at this moderate position on the independence/unification issue.

After Chen was in power, he still faced an opposition-controlled legislature. Although some legislators left the KMT and followed James Soong to a new party, the PFP, together the KMT and PFP still held more than half of the seats in the legislature. The situation for Chen's government was worse since the KMT legislators were much more cohesive than usual because of the serious partisan conflict during the elections and a divided government created after the elections (Hawang 2003; Sheng 2003, 2008). In the meantime, the PFP legislators cooperated with the KMT legislators on most substantial legislation because they shared the same supporting groups (Yu 2005). On the other hand, the DPP faced a challenge from a newly founded party, the Taiwan Solidarity Union, a party more extreme than the DPP on the independence/unification issue dimension. As a result, Chen's government faced a political dilemma.

In hoping to win a majority in the legislature to implement Chen's campaign promises, the DPP adopted two campaign strategies in the 2001 legislative election. The first was to run a national campaign. Normally, candidates running under a multimember district with a single nontransferable vote electoral system try to distinguish themselves from other candidates of the same party because they target the same bloc of party supporters. Thus, they have incentives to run independent and local campaigns; that is, to focus on serving constituents and bringing pork-barrel projects to their constituency, rather than concentrating on national issues (Sheng 2005b). However, in 2001 the DPP ran its campaign by promoting national campaign ads, and it prohibited its candidates from running independent campaigns. Expecting a coattail effect from the national star, Chen Shui-bian, the DDP candidates followed this policy.

The DPP's second electoral strategy was to declare publicly that it intended to be a government for all people; that is, the government would work for all Taiwan citizens, not only for DPP voters. Therefore, it took a centrist position on the independence/unification issue and did not emphasize either the independence/unification issue or the Taiwanese/Chinese identity issue (Fell 2005, 140–41). Instead, the party emphasized other issues, such as social welfare and the political corruption of the era of the old KMT government. In the 2001 legislative election, the only party emphasizing independence was the TSU. The TSU won 7.8 percent of the vote and 13 seats. The only party emphasizing unification was NP, which nearly disappeared, getting only 2.6 percent of the vote and one seat in 2001.

By pursuing these strategies, the DPP won 33.4 percent of the vote and 38.7 percent of all seats in the legislature. Although the DPP increased its number of seats and became the largest party in the legislature, the 38.7 percent of seats was still not enough to control the legislature. Even if it could get support from the TSU on most important legislative roll-call votes, the total fraction of seats in the Pan-Green bloc (44.5% of the total) still would be outvoted by the opposition coalition, the Pan-Blue bloc, formed by the KMT, PFP, and NP. After the DPP failed to win support from a majority of the voters, it faced a severe fight with the Pan-Blue bloc in the legislature. Consequently, the DPP government was able to accomplish little and could not implement its campaign promises.

Soon after the 2001 legislative election, the DPP found that the TSU had attracted voters who favored an extreme position on Taiwan independence. Several substantial moves showed the TSU's aggressiveness and steadfast position. For example, the TSU initiated a proposal to revise the President and Vice-President Election and Recall Law to limit the qualification of a presidential candidate: only those born in Taiwan would have the right to be a presidential candidate. Another obvious example was the firm position TSU legislators took, while the Plebiscite Law was under debate, in favor of having substantive issues such as Taiwan independence decided by plebiscite. Also, when creating Regulations for Managing the Relations between Citizens of the PRC and Taiwan, the TSU always stood for very strict restrictions on people from China. Compared to the TSU's firm stand on the independence issue, the DPP appeared ambiguous and hesitant on the issue.

Fearing that they would lose the electoral support of pro-independence voters to the TSU, the DPP started to shift to a more pro-independence stance after the 2001 legislative election. Constrained by its ruling position, the DPP did not declare for Taiwan de jure independence. Rather, it played a safe game; namely, to consolidate its original voter base by resorting to Taiwan self-determination and Taiwan nationalism. The 228 Hand-in-Hand Rally before the 2004 presidential election was designed to present the DPP as the party that loved Taiwan. Further, the DPP advocated Rectify the Name of Nation and Drafting the New Constitution in the later legislative elections. All of these actions contributed to the party's position shift to an extreme pro-independence stance in 2004. The Taiwan public discerned this shift and placed the DPP at 2.2, almost the same as its position in 1996 (figure 5.4).

The DPP continued its pro-independence strategy even as President Chen's second presidential term was almost over. In the cover letter of application for membership in the United Nations, Chen requested the admission of Taiwan (Office of the President, July 20, 2007), which was different from the earlier request, "Readmission of the Republic of China." The DPP further proposed a referendum that requested the government to continue to apply for membership in the United Nations under the name of Taiwan. The DPP presidential candidate for the 2008 election, Hsieh Chang-ting, supported this referendum despite the opposition of the United States and China. The United States and China worried that the next step of the DPP would be an independence referendum. When Hsieh visited the United States during the election, he stated that an independence referendum would not be necessary since Taiwan was already substantially independent. He claimed that the "cross-Strait common market" policy of his KMT opponent, Ma Ying-jeou, was a preliminary step to unification with China. As a result, the Taiwan public rated the DPP's position at 2.2 and the KMT's at 7.4 in 2008 (figure 5.4).

The DPP lost the 2008 election. This defeat led the party to reconsider its claims on the issue of independence/unification. Hsieh had linked an open economic policy with Taiwan nationalism but failed to provide a better substitute policy for Taiwan's economic recession. This strengthened the public's impression about the DPP's lack of ability to deal with both economic and cross-Strait issues. Over half of the Taiwan public (54.3%) thought that the KMT performed better on cross-Strait issues in 2008 (Sheng 2013). Some moderate DPP elites, such as Tuan Yi-kang, claimed that the mass public was tired of the DPP's dogmatic views on the issue of independence/unification. Furthermore, after 2001 the public in general placed themselves at 4.5–4.6 along the spectrum of independence/unification. According to Downsian median voter theorem, it is expected that parties will seek a more centrist position when most of the public stands at the middle. During the 2012 election, the DPP presidential candidate, Tsai Ing-wen, adopted a moderate strategy on the issue of independence/unification. She claimed that she would unconditionally carry on the existing cross-Strait policies if she won the election. She also admitted the importance of an open economic policy and trade with China and committed herself to dealing pragmatically with the relationship with China. However, she denied the "1992 consensus"[16] and made a vague assertion of "Taiwan consensus." The mass public still perceived the DPP at 2.6 on the spectrum of independence/unification, even though this was the second closest placement to the center for the DPP since 1996.

In contrast, the Taiwan public perceives the KMT as a pro-unification party. This perception is based on the KMT's long-standing political declaration in support of eventual unification with China. In 1990, the KMT government set up the National Unification Council. In 1991, the council drafted "Guidelines for National Unification," which called for a phased approach toward unification. However, Lee Teng-hui, the KMT's president who held office from 1988 to 2000, maintained a vague position on the independence/unification issue. Early in 1991 and 1992, when the DPP passed the "Taiwan Independence Clause" and advocated a radical Republic of Taiwan pledge in elections, Lee was lenient toward the DPP. His blurred and ambivalent attitude on unification with China made the New KMT Alliance, a hard-line faction on the unification position, accuse Lee of being a supporter of gradual independence. Lee's attitude toward independence/unification contributed to the departure of the New KMT Alliance from the KMT and its formation of the NP in 1993.

During the campaign for the 1996 presidential election, when facing Lin Yan-kang and Chen Lu-an, two candidates who were strongly pro-unification, Lee Teng-hui was still vague about his position on independence/unification. A survey conducted by the Election Study Center in 1996 asked respondents about Lee's position on that issue. The results showed that 23 percent of the respondents considered Lee as favoring unification, 22.1 percent considered him as favoring independence, 23.0 percent thought he favored the status quo, and 31.9 percent were not aware of Lee's position at all (Sheng 2002). This explained why Taiwan voters located the KMT at 6.1 on the independence/unification dimension in 1996.

From 1996 to 2000, when Lee was still the KMT's leader, Taiwan voters considered the KMT as a party inclined to the right of center on the independence/unification issue. This perception changed when Lee left the KMT and became the spiritual leader of the TSU. The KMT reserved the option of unification with China and strongly stood for an open economy with China. After 2000, Taiwan citizens located the KMT at around 7.0 on the unification side of the dimension. In 2008 the KMT presidential candidate, Ma Ying-jeou, announced the No Unification, No Independence, and No Use of Force pledge on the independence/unification issue. Also, in his inaugural speech, he promised to foster more direct exchanges in cross-Strait relations and draft a peace pact with China. After Ma took office, he encouraged friendlier and more peaceful relations with China, such as frequent Chiang-Chen talks,[17] opening direct investment in China, and allowing Chinese tourists and students to visit Taiwan. He also advocated signing the Cross-Strait Financial Supervision and Cooperation Memorandum and the Cross-Strait Economic Cooperation Framework Agreement to strengthen economic relations across the straits. Although the No Unification pledge seemed to make him a little more centrist, his economic and cultural policies, which encouraged closer relations with China, contributed to his pro-unification position in the public's perception. The public rated the KMT's position at 7.4 along the independence/unification spectrum.

Furthermore, the concurrence between the issue position of the KMT's and DPP's identifiers and the issue position that those identifiers perceive their party to have is noteworthy, as figure 5.5 demonstrates. The issue position of KMT identifiers and their perception of the KMT's issue position correspond to each other. This situation is more apparent when we compare the issue position of DPP identifiers with their perception of the DPP's issue position. The concurrence may not be coincidental. Brody and Page (1972) argue that a voter may be persuaded by a candidate's position and thereby consider that position to be his own. The public's perception on issues will be "distorted" by "pre-existing partisan attitudes." In order to maintain cognitive consonance, party identifiers will selectively absorb information and form their issue position close to their preferable partisan position (RePass 1971). Research on American voters has shown this possibility. For example, Page and Jones (1979), Markus and Converse (1979), and Markus (1982) specify their models with reciprocal causal relationships among party, issue, and candidate factors by a simultaneous-equation statistical method. The concurrence in figure 5.5 implies that partisan elites have influenced Taiwan citizens in shaping their issue position.

Specifically speaking, elites try very hard to attract Taiwan citizens to their side. They frame and develop the issues. They persuade and convince the Taiwan public that certain issues are important and that their position benefits the public the most. The ups and downs of the issue positions of party identifiers show that they recognize the shift of their party's issue position and that they will shift their issue position accordingly. The DPP identifiers are more likely to be persuaded by the DPP elites, while the Pan-Blue identifiers are less likely to be persuaded by the DPP elites. And the KMT identifiers are more likely to be persuaded by the KMT elites, while the Pan-Green identifiers are less likely to be persuaded by the KMT elites. In other words, when voters pick up the signal of political elites' rhetoric or action on the issues, or both, they are selectively persuaded. In such a case, we should be able to find that an individual's party preference affects his issue position so that a concurrence between his position and his perception of his preferable party's issue position appears, as in figure 5.5.[18]

For example, the DPP identifiers perceived the DPP's issue position as more centrist (3.2) on the issue spectrum in 2000, when Chen Shui-bian offered the New Central Way policy. At the same time, the DPP identifiers also moved to a more centrist position (4.3) in 2000. Another example occurred in 2008. When the DPP strongly catalyzed the birth of the Admission of Taiwan to the United Nations referendum and Hsieh Chang-ting claimed that he would not propose an independence referendum because Taiwan was substantially independent, the DPP identifiers placed the DPP's issue position at 2.0, the most pro-independence stance that they have ever considered for the DPP. Meanwhile, they rated themselves at 2.9, also the most pro-independence placement that they have ever had.

Another interesting phenomenon in figure 5.5 is the trend in the issue position of KMT and DPP identifiers. Compared to their perception of the parties, Taiwan voters tend to be more centrist than their preferred parties,

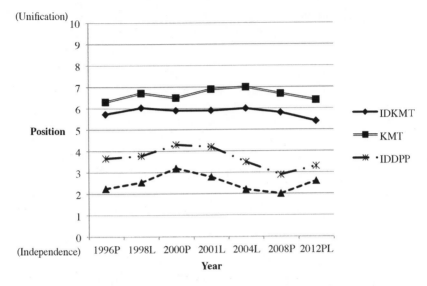

Fig. 5.5. Party identifiers' issue positions on independence/unification and their perceptions about the positions of the parties (1996–2012). *Source:* Appendix 5.A3. *Notes:* 1. IDKMT = KMT identifiers. IDDPP = DPP identifiers. Here the placements of the KMT and DPP are the average perception of KMT identifiers and DPP identifiers, respectively; that is, KMT=KMT as perceived by KMT identifiers; DPP=DPP as perceived by DPP identifiers. 2. On the horizontal axis, "P" indicates that surveys were conducted after the presidential election; "L" indicates that surveys were taken after the legislative election.

even though their positions generally fluctuate with those of their parties. This may imply that Taiwan citizens, although standing close to the position of their preferred party, do not consider themselves as extreme as their parties on this issue. In other words, the issue position of party identifiers seems not to deviate from that of independent voters too much on average. Furthermore, not only their perceptions on parties' issue positions but also their issue positions were prone to be centrist in 2012. Indeed, DPP identifiers perceived themselves at 3.3 on the issue spectrum in 2012 (2.9 in 2008), while KMT identifiers placed themselves at 5.4 in 2012 (5.8 in 2008). Fell argues that the fluctuations of party position were determined by intraparty struggle in the two main parties after 2008 and suggests that the new generation of leaders have sought "more consensual politics" (2011, 93). Convergence to a more centrist stance on the issue of independence/unification for both the DPP identifiers and KMT identifiers may be possible in the future unless political parties on the island become extreme.

The Most Important Problem Facing Taiwan

In this section, we discuss how the public perceives the most important problem the country is facing and whether the public's perspective responds to the elites' issue agenda. Survey data were collected after presidential and legislative elections from 1996 to 2012 (questionnaire wordings are in a5 of the appendix 5.A1). Since this is an open-ended question, there are divergent responses. However, we managed to subdivide respondents' answers into eight categories: economic prosperity, independence/unification/cross-Strait affairs, wealth distribution/social welfare, party/politician's ability and corruption, social order and national security, political/social reform/stability, environmental protection, and others. Table 5.1 shows the results.

Based on data from the table, we find that the Taiwan public was extremely concerned about economic prosperity, especially in 2001 and 2008, when Taiwan's economy was in a downturn. Also, the public was concerned about social order and national security, especially in 1996 and 2004, when tensions with China occurred in the Taiwan Strait. Sometimes, the public takes the party or politician's characteristics (e.g., ability, integrity, and corruption) more seriously. However, economic prosperity, social order, and national security, as well as the party's and politician's ability or corruption,

TABLE 5.1. The Most Important Problem Facing Taiwan in Elections

Issue	1996P	2001L	2004P	2004L	2008P	2008L	2012PL
Independence/unification/cross-Strait affairs	32	7	26	25	27	9	22
Political or social reform/ stability	0	0	3	3	2	3	2
Wealth distribution /social welfare	0	1	3	6	0	6	6
Environmental protection	0	0	1	2	0	0	0
Economic prosperity	23	55	35	21	15	63	38
Social order and national security	32	7	7	19	10	10	2
Party or politician ability/ corruption	0	4	5	10	7	0	4
Others	3	13	3	4	10	1	5
Don't know	9	12	16	9	28	8	20
Refuse to answer	1	1	1	1	1	0	1
Total	100.0%	100.0%	100.0%	100.0%	100.0%	100.0%	100.0%

Sources: Data for 1996 are from the Election Study Center at National Chengchi University, and data for 2001 and after are from the Taiwan's Election and Democratization Study Project.

Note: After the year, "P" indicates that surveys were conducted after the presidential election; "L" indicates that surveys were taken after the legislative election.

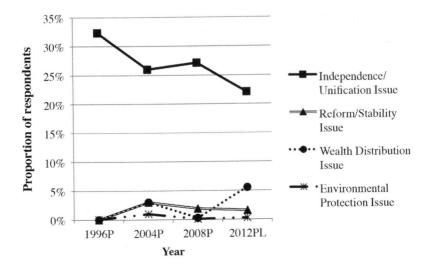

Fig. 5.6. The proportion of voters defining the most important position issue in the presidential elections. *Source:* Table 5.1. *Note:* Data is not available for 2000. On the horizontal axis, "P" indicates that surveys were conducted after the presidential election; "L" indicates that surveys were taken after the legislative election.

are valence issues, in which there is near-universal agreement on the ends of policy (Fiorina 1981, 18). Since most partisan elites (and the public) take the same side on the valence issues, those issues have little potential to develop into a long-term political cleavages.[19]

Figures 5.6 and 5.7 illustrate only the importance of position issues—specifically, the four focal issues of this chapter—in the perception of the public. Figure 5.6 presents the public's perspective on those issues in the presidential elections, and figure 5.7 shows the situation for the legislative elections. Several points are noteworthy.

First, from the public's perspective, the independence/unification issue has been the most important position issue across years both in the presidential and legislative elections. The proportion of respondents who consider this issue most important is much greater than the proportion for other issues (figures 5.6 and 5.7). As previously discussed, politicians have manipulated this issue most of the time. When the Taiwan independence issue was raised in the political arena, it was connected to Taiwan's most important cleavages, that of ethnicity and Chinese/Taiwanese identity, so that it was easily perceived by voters and aroused the affections and disaffections of substantial portions of the Taiwan public. Also, the independence/unifica-

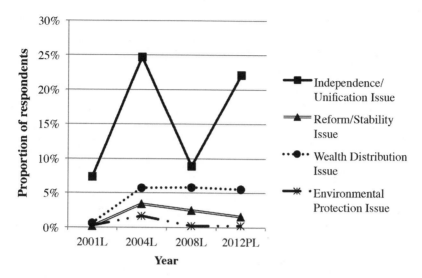

Fig. 5.7. The proportion of voters defining the most important position issue in the legislative elections. *Source:* Table 5.1. *Note:* On the horizontal axis, "P" indicates that surveys were conducted after the presidential election; "L" indicates that surveys were taken after the legislative election.

tion issue is connected to relations with China, so that it is also related to national security and economic prosperity. This makes the independence/unification issue even more important.

Second, the independence/unification issue is of more importance in the presidential elections than in the legislative elections. Presidential candidates' election platforms target national voters, whereas legislative candidates target their own constituents. In order to attract voters, it is possible that issues involved in presidential elections tend to be national and important affairs, while issues involved in legislative elections are diverse—from national to local affairs. Even in the same year, the proportion of the respondents considering the independence/unification issue the most important was only 9.0 percent in the legislative election held in January 2008; however, it was 27.0 percent in the presidential election held in March of the same year (table 5.1).

Moreover, the importance of the independence/unification issue fluctuates more in the legislative elections than in the presidential elections. More than 25.0 percent of the respondents perceived the issue as the most important position issue in almost all presidential elections. However, in the legislative elections, only 7.0 percent and 9.0 percent of the respondents perceived it as the most important position issue in 2001 and 2008 whereas 25.0 percent did in the 2004.[20] In 2003, the TSU initiated the Campaign for Rectifying the Name of Taiwan and invited the former president, Lee Teng-hui, to be its spiritual leader. Later they sponsored the Call Taiwan Taiwan parade. Afraid of losing too many pro-independence voters, the DPP and Chen Shui-bian expressed their support for this campaign both explicitly and implicitly (*New Taiwan Weekly News*, September 12, 2003).[21] Chen Shui-bian also requested national enterprises to change "China" to "Taiwan" in their names. The independence/unification issue had occupied the spotlight in the 2004 legislative election. This further demonstrates that the public gets cues from the parties and politicians in order to shape its perspective on politics. As in the United States, Democrats mention prodemocratic issues more, whereas Republicans uphold conservative values and issues (RePass 1971, 395). Elites' emphasizing or deemphasizing of a certain issue may affect the public's perspective on the issue agenda (Chihibber and Torcal 1997, 31).

Last, issues other than independence/unification are not as important from the public's perspective, but the importance differs across issues. More people consider the wealth distribution issue more salient in the legislative elections than in the presidential elections. Also, as the economic situation has declined, the economically disadvantaged strongly felt relatively exploited; thus, more people paid attention to the wealth distribution issue. So from 2004, a number of respondents (6.0%) considered wealth distribution the most important problem facing Taiwan (figure 5.7). As for the political reform issue, few voters took it as the most important issue in either the presidential elections or legislative elections, although reform/stability had been the top issue in the 1980s and early 1990s (Hsieh and Niou 1996b). The DPP elites promoted many reform programs, whereas the KMT stressed stability. Political stability occupied the top 10 advertisements of the KMT during elections until the party turnover (Fell 2005, 26). However, the importance of the reform/stability issue faded after Taiwan's transition to democracy.

The environmental protection issue has the least respondents who perceive it as an important problem. Candidates' campaign platforms emphasizing economic growth usually get more attention than those emphasizing environmental protection. Furthermore, the ruling party tends to stress economic growth rather than environmental protection. An example is that even though for a long time the DPP claimed to protect the environment, it compromised in favor of economic development when it was in power (Ho 2005b). Thus, it is not surprising that relatively few politicians emphasize the environmental protection issue. As a result, few respondents consider environmental protection to be an important problem compared to other issues.

Overall, partisan elites' manipulation of the issues, such as developing an issue, shifting the issue position, and emphasizing one issue while deemphasizing another, has an impact on how Taiwan citizens perceive the issues.

Conclusions

This chapter has examined four issues: reform/stability, wealth distribution, environmental protection/economy, and independence/unification. We have shown how partisan elites frame and manipulate these issues to attain their political goals and how Taiwan voters respond. Research findings show that for all of the four issues, Taiwan voters are able to perceive the parties' issue positions, shape their own issue position, and make political judgments based on the issues. This shows that issue politics has gradually evolved in Taiwan politics, although the impacts across issues differ.

In the process of issue evolution in Taiwan, the Dang-wai and DPP elites played an important role. They strategically searched for issues that benefited the party's growth and strength, then clarified and manipulated the issues to mobilize the mass public. Having emerged in the authoritarian era, the DPP emphasized the political reform issues first. After accomplishing political reform, it moved to the issue of Taiwan independence. The DPP elites were successful in raising this issue, so that the party grew gradually in the 1980s and 1990s and won the presidency in 2000 and 2004. However, it lost the 2008 and 2012 presidential elections, and it has not broken through the bottleneck of seat shares (40.0%) in legislative elections. One of the major reasons is that the DPP cannot achieve a breakthrough on issue games.

Following Taiwan's gradual democratization and political reform in the 1980s and 1990s, it has become more difficult for the DPP to identify new and attractive reform issues. The DPP has tried raising several such issues after 2000, such as the return of the KMT assets obtained in the authoritarian era, revision of the 18 percent preferential interest rates for the pensions of retired public servants, the reform of the constitution, and the restructure of the legislature. The DPP has attained its goal on some issues, but it cannot take all of the credit because several parties were involved in the regulation-making process. Some reform issues, such as preferential treatment for retired civil servants, are still controversial and might only help to consolidate the DPP's original base of support but not broaden its voter base.

Regarding the environmental protection/economy issue, the debate on whether to continue the construction of a fourth nuclear plant has stirred up mass attention recently. The disaster at the Fukushima nuclear plant in Japan has further stimulated the public's concern about the safety of nuclear energy. If the KMT government had not been able to defuse the issue, the DPP could have taken advantage of it to attract the electorate. However, the KMT government decided to mothball the construction of the fourth nuclear power plant for fear of losing electoral support even though the option to use nuclear energy was kept open. In addition, as a result of the economic downturn since 2000, the Taiwan public is more concerned about economic prosperity, and the governing party has always considered economic growth as the top priority in its agenda. Without polarizing elites and voters, the environmental protection/economy issue has little chance of evolving into a salient political cleavage.

Thus, the independence/unification issue remains the most influential issue in Taiwan politics because all major parties have clear and polarized positions on it and it is connected to enduring social cleavages—ethnicity and Chinese/Taiwanese identity. As it was demonstrated in figure 5.4, the positions of the parties, in particular those of the KMT and the DPP, are obviously separated more than those in figures 5.1, 5.2, and 5.3. This situation provides partisan elites with opportunities to manipulate the issue in order to attract voters. The Taiwan public in turn responds to the elites, shapes its issue position, and perceives the importance of the issues accordingly. Among position issues, these types of interactions between partisan elites and the mass public is especially effective with the independence/unification issue. Moreover, this issue is relatively important also because Taiwan voters make political decisions based on it (Cheng and Hsu 1996; Fell 2005, 2012; Hsieh and Niou 1996a, 1996b; Shyu 1998; Sheng 2002, 2013; Sheng and Chen 2003). From 2000 to 2008, party positions on the independence/unification issue became more polarized. The Pan-Green's position on the issue dimension was moving toward a more pro-independence stance. In the meantime, the Pan-Blue's position was becoming more pro-unification. In 2012, although both the KMT and the DPP were perceived as a little prone to being centrist (the KMT moved from 7.4 to 7.0 on the scale, while the DPP moved from 2.2 to 2.6), the difference between the two parties was still very large. The continuing polarization between the two parties has made the independence/unification issue more salient and has had decisive impacts on the political attitudes and behavior of Taiwan voters. It is quite possible that all parties will keep focusing most of their efforts on framing and manipulating this issue.

Last, the wealth distribution issue in Taiwan has not become as salient as it has been in other advanced democracies even though the disparity between the rich and the poor has become more severe in recent years. Political parties and candidates have frequently manipulated the issue of wealth inequality to gain electoral support from disadvantaged voters. Since they generally attempt to take credit for welfare programs, they tend to outbid each other. The differences between the positions of political parties on wealth distribution are thus small. Indeed, all major parties in Taiwan have little differences on this issue and have difficulty in distinguishing themselves from one another. As a result, the wealth distribution issue has not been polarized to the extent of becoming a significant political cleavage.

Will this issue become an important political cleavage in the future? There are two possible scenarios. The first one is that the welfare distribution issue is absorbed into the dominant cleavage of independence/unification and polarizes political elites and voters. There is evidence that elites of major parties took a ride on the independence/unification issue to evoke the public's consciousness of wealth inequality in Taiwan. In 2008 and 2012 elections, the KMT fielded the argument that Taiwan's economic misfortune was related to cross-Strait tension and campaigned on expanding economic relations with China, such as signing the Economic Cooperation Framework Agreement. Entrepreneurs of big businesses welcome this proposal and nearly unanimously endorsed the KMT presidential candidate, Ma Ying-jeou. In contrast, the DPP opposed the proposal and advertised ECFA's negative effects with a dialect limerick popular among disadvantaged groups: "Female cannot find good husbands, male cannot find good jobs, and sons have to find a job in Heilongjiang."[22] Evidence shows that working class and self-employed citizens tend to oppose the ECFA, while business owners and people with managerial responsibilities generally support the accord (Lin and Hu 2011). It is also worth noting that Taiwan voters' positions on cross-Strait economic exchange are reflected in their partisan identification. Supporters of the Pan-Blue Alliance generally consider the ECFA beneficial to Taiwan's economy, while the Pan-Green identifiers tend to view the accord negatively. If this situation continues, the welfare distribution issue may be absorbed into the dominant cleavage of independence/unification in such a way that economically disadvantaged citizens are more pro-independence while the advantaged publics are more pro-unification. In such a case, class politics may emerge and wealth distribution may become more salient in Taiwan through the strength of identity issue. Independence and unification cleavage along with class conflicts may aggravate polarization in the Taiwan society.

However, another scenario is also possible that may not contradict the first one. That is, the KMT will slow down its pace with China for fear of losing electoral support due to its contentious nature, while the DPP will be unwilling to sacrifice economic prosperity and will moderate its pro-independence position. The DPP presidential candidate Tsai Ing-wen announced in the 2012 election that she would accept all cross-Strait agreements signed between the KMT government and Beijing if she were elected. This shows that the DPP cannot stand against the wishes of big businesses when it is in power. In that case, the elites of both parties may stand close to the centrist position on the major issue dimension and bring a less polarized society to Taiwan.

Appendix 5.A1

Questionnaire Wording

a1: On the reform/stability issue
Looking at Taiwan's overall development, some people believe that large scale reform is the most important thing, even if it means sacrificing some social stability. Other people believe that stability is the most important and that reform should not be allowed to affect social stability. On this card, the position that large-scale reform is the most important thing is at 0 on a scale from 0 to 10, and the position that social stability is most important is at 10. About where on this scale does your own view lie? As you understand it, about where on this scale does the position of the KMT lie? About where on this scale does the position of the DPP lie? About where on this scale does the position of the PFP lie? About where on this scale does the position of the TSU lie?

a2: On the wealth distribution issue
Regarding the question of social welfare, some people believe that the government should merely maintain the current system in order not to increase people's taxes. Other people believe that the government should promote social welfare, even though it will lead to tax increases. On this card, the position that maintaining the current system is the most important thing is at 0 on a scale from 0 to 10, and the position that promoting social welfare is most important is at 10. About where on this scale does your own view lie? As you understand it, about where on this scale does the position of the KMT lie? About where on this scale does the position of the DPP lie? About where on this scale does the position of the PFP lie? About where on this scale does the position of the TSU lie?

a3: On the environmental protection/economy issue

Regarding the question of economic development versus environmental protection, some people in society emphasize environmental protection while others emphasize economic development. On this card, the position that emphasizes environmental protection is at 0 on a scale from 0 to 10, and the position that emphasizes economic development is at 10. About where on this scale does your own view lie? As you understand it, about where on this scale does the position of the KMT lie? About where on this scale does the position of the DPP lie? About where on this scale does the position of the PFP lie? About where on this scale does the position of the TSU lie?

a4: On the independence/unification issue

In our society people often talk about the question of Taiwan independence from or unification with China. Some people say that Taiwan should declare independence right away. Other people say that Taiwan and China should unify right away. Yet other people have opinions between these two positions. On this card, the position that Taiwan should immediately declare independence is at 0 on a scale from 0 to 10, and the position that Taiwan should immediately unify with the mainland is at 10. About where on this scale does your own view lie? As you understand it, about where on this scale does the position of the KMT lie? About where on this scale does the position of the DPP lie? About where on this scale does the position of the PFP lie? About where on this scale does the position of the TSU lie? The questionnaire wordings are identical in most years, except for 1996P and 2000P. However, the survey results of the two years with slightly different wordings did not deviate from common expectation much; thus, the authors kept them in the discussion.

a5: The most important problem facing Taiwan

During the presidential (legislative) election campaign, many different problems faced by our country were raised. What do you think is the most important political problem facing Taiwan today? (Open-ended question)

Note: The wording of this question might be slightly different on cross surveys, but the core element of the question is the same: that is, in the respondent's perspective, what is the most important political problem facing Taiwan today?

APPENDIX 5.A2. Respondents' Issue Positions and Their Perceptions about the Positions of Parties (1996–2012)

Issue Election	Respondents	KMT	DPP	NP	PFP	TSU
Reform/stability						
1996P	7.1	6.9	3.9	5.6		
1998L	7.2	6.6	4.0	5.2		
2000P	7.2	7.0	4.4	5.6	5.9	
2001L	7.2	6.8	3.6	5.7	6.1	4.8
2004L	7.3	6.8	3.9		6.1	3.7
2008P	7.0	6.1	4.7			
Wealth distribution						
2000P	5.6	4.8	6.5	5.2	5.4	
2004L	6.3	5.6	6.0		5.5	5.2
2008P	5.9	5.6	5.4			
2012PL	5.9	5.1	5.4			
Environment/economy						
1998L	5.3	7.3	5.0	4.9		
2000P	5.2	7.2	5.2	5.0	5.4	
2001L	6.1	7.2	5.6	5.6	6.3	5.8
2004L	5.7	7.1	5.6		6.4	5.4
2008P	5.9	6.8	5.4			
Independence/unification						
1996P	5.2	6.1	2.0	6.5		
1998L	5.0	6.5	2.3	7.3		
2000P	5.3	6.4	3.1	7.3	7.1	
2001L	5.2	7.2	2.6	7.6	7.2	2.5
2004L	4.6	7.4	2.2		7.4	1.7
2008P	4.5	7.4	2.2			
2012PL	4.5	7.0	2.6			

Source: Data for 1996–2000 are from the Election Study Center at National Chengchi University, and data for 2001–12 are from the Taiwan's Election and Democratization Study Project.

Note: Entries are respondents' means on a scale of 0 to 10. After the year, P" indicates that surveys were conducted after the presidential election; "L" indicates that surveys were taken after the legislative election.

APPENDIX 5.A3. Party Identifiers' Issue Positions and Their Perceptions about the Positions of Parties on Independence/Unification (1996–2012)

Election	KMT Identifiers	KMT (as perceived by KMT identifiers)	DPP Identifiers	DPP (as perceived by DPP identifiers)
1996P	5.7	6.3	3.7	2.3
1998L	6.0	6.7	3.8	2.5
2000P	5.9	6.5	4.3	3.2
2001L	5.9	6.9	4.2	2.8
2004L	6.0	7.0	3.5	2.2
2008P	5.8	6.7	2.9	2.0
2012PL	5.4	6.4	3.3	2.6

Source: Data for 1996–2000 are from the Election Study Center at National Chengchi University, and data for 2001–12 are from the Taiwan's Election and Democratization Study Project.

Note: After the year, "P" indicates that surveys were conducted after the presidential election; "L" indicates that surveys were taken after the legislative election.

Notes

1. The authors thank the Election Study Center at National Chengchi University for providing the data from the 1996, 1998, 2000 elections, and the Taiwan Election and Democratization Studies Project for providing data from the 2001 to 2012 elections. The coordinator of multiyear project TEDS is Professor Chi Huang (National Chengchi University). The authors are alone responsible for views expressed herein.

2. The measurement of respondents' positions on the reform/stability issue and their perceived positions of the parties are based on the questionnaire shown in a1 of the appendix 5.A1.

3. Shih Ming-te, a former colleague of Chen, initiated the "Million Voices against Corruption, President Chen Must Go" campaign and appealed to Chen to resign from office. Shih and his followers, all in red shirts, sat outside the presidential office from September until the prosecutors charged Chen and his family with corruption; however, the court did not process the case against Chen in 2006. The reason is that the president has immunity from criminal accusations when he is president, according to the constitution.

4. Liou Hsiao-Hsia, "Ma versus Hsieh: Comparison of Their Pork Barrels," *United Daily News*, March 15, 2008, http://mag.udn.com/mag/vote2007–08/storypage. jsp?f_MAIN_ID=357&f_SUB_ID=2361&f_ART_ID=73230 (accessed May 8, 2013; in Chinese).

5. For more discussion on the ethnic cleavage, see chapter 3 of this book.

6. Even in 2011, in all industries, 78.6 percent of employees worked in companies with fewer than 5 workers while 90.9 percent worked in companies with fewer than 10 workers (Directorate-General of Budget 2012).

7. Since the subcontractors, who usually had worked for the big outsourcing factories, still relied on contracts from the original factories, the owners of small factories

did not consider themselves to be "capitalists" or even "bosses" (Hsieh 1989). Their relations with their employees, who usually had been their former colleagues from the big factories, were more like partnerships, not the confrontational relationships between capitalists and labor.

8. A legislator from a business district once appealed to his electorate in the working class that he had "many well-achieved friends in business. They all used to work as apprentices or workers. They all claimed they have been in difficulty with their bosses when they were hired. However, they all opened their own business later with the assistance of their original bosses. So, workers do not always work for others; someday you will become employers" (Chang 1987, 21; in Chinese).

9. The KMT leaders did not plan full-scale subsidies to the elderly from the beginning. However, via hearings, media attention, and direct petition to President Lee Teng-hui and Premier Lien Chan some legislators from the agricultural districts, such as Chen Chih-ping, Lin His-shan, and Wong Chung-chun, appealed to the KMT leaders to support subsidies for elderly farmers (Sheng 2001, 90–91).

10. One of the reasons for parties to hold onto the independence/unification issue, rather than left-right ideology, may be the failure of the Taiwan public to distinguish between the left and the right. Chen (2003) found out that only half of Taiwan citizens can identify their position along the left-right spectrum, a rather low rate compared to citizens in most democracies. Hsiao, Cheng, and Achen also find that the Taiwan public misunderstands the meanings of "left" and "right" (see chapter 6).

11. The KMT, PFP, and NP united and proposed to impeach the newly elected president. BBC News, "Taiwan's Suspension of NUKE4 Causes Political Crises," October 30, 2000, http://news.bbc.co.uk/hi/chinese/news/newsid_998000/9987432.stm (accessed October 8, 2015).

12. Green Party Taiwan, "Ma Ying-jeou Do Not Forget Your Promise of Carbon Tax on Earth Day," December 18, 2009. http://www.greenparty.org.tw/index.php/discuss/comment/233–2009–12–18–04–29–18 (accessed May 8, 2013; in Chinese).

13. An earthquake and the following tsunami severely damaged the Fukushima nuclear plant. The radiation leak endangered the neighborhood, causing the Japanese government to order the evacuation of residents in the area. For months, people were suspicious of food and water from the area because of possible radioactive contamination. Even now, Fukushima residents still cannot return to their homes.

14. Central News Agency, "Mothballed Nuclear Power Plant Can Be Activated Anytime: President," July 31, 2015. http://focustaiwan.tw/news/aipl/201507030027.aspx (accessed October 9, 2015).

15. The Four Noes and One Without pledge is essentially that as long as China does not have an intention to use military force against Taiwan, Chen Shui-bian would not declare independence, change the name of the nation, push for the inclusion of the so-called state-to-state description in the constitution, or promote a referendum on the issue of independence versus unification.

16. The 1992 consensus refers to a memorandum of a meeting between the semiofficial representatives of China and Taiwan in 1992. It stated that both sides recognized the principle of one China. More specifically, China and Taiwan belong to one China but the definition of one China is based on their own interpretation. However, the DPP denied the existence of 1992 consensus.

17. The Straits Exchange Foundation (the chairman, Chiang Pin-kung, represents Taiwan) and the Association for Relations across the Taiwan Straits (the chairman, Chen Yunlin, represents the PRC) are in charge of most communication and negotiation on nonpolitical issues.

18. To the contrary, a number of studies of Taiwan voters also have shown that individuals' issue positions may affect their party preferences and party identification (Hsieh and Niou 1996a, 1996b; Hsieh 2005; Sheng and Chen 2003). We do not disagree with this argument and accept the possibility of the reciprocal relationship between issue position and party preference.

19. For a discussion on various issues in Taiwan, readers may refer to the following chapters of this book: chapter 6 on economic issue, chapter 7 on cross-Strait relations, and chapter 9 on wealth distribution.

20. In 2012, the presidential election and the legislative election were held together so that the proportion of the independence/unification issue rose.

21. Tien Yu-bin, Hsu Gu-cheng, and Chang Kim-Guo, 2003, "Support for Rectifying the Name of Taiwan, the Public Is the Evidence," *New Taiwan Weekly News*, September 12, no. 390 (in Chinese).

22. Heilongjiang is located in northeastern China and has frigid weather in the winter.

References

BBC News. 2000. "Taiwan's Suspension of NUKE4 Causes Political Crises," October 30. http://news.bbc.co.uk/hi/chinese/news/newsid_998000/9987432.stm. Accessed October 8, 2015.

Brody, R., and B. Page. 1972. "The Assessment of Policy Voting." *American Political Science Review* 66:450–58.

Carmines, Edward G., and James A. Stimson. 1986. "On the Structure and Sequence of Issue Evolution." *American Political Science Review* 80:902–21.

Carmines, Edward G., and James A. Stimson. 1989. *Issue Evolution: Race and the Transformation of American Politics* Princeton: Princeton University Press.

Central News Agency. 2015. "Mothballed Nuclear Power Plant Can Be Activated Anytime: President." July 31. http://focustaiwan.tw/news/aipl/201507030027.aspx. Accessed October 9, 2015.

Chang, Pen-tsao. 1987. "How to Improve Harmony between the Labor and the Capitalists after Lifting Martial Law." *Industrial Fortnight* 181:19–21.

Chen, Luhu, Keng Su, Tu Ping-Lan, and Huang Quan-Po. 2009. "Rational Self-interest or Emotional identity? An Analysis on Factors Which Influence the Positions of Taiwanese Public in Cross-Strait Economic and Trade Relations." *Soochow Journal of Political Science* 27 (2): 87–125.

Chen, Wen-chun. 2003. "The Blue and the Green: The Political Ideologies of the Mass Public in the 2000 Taiwan Presidential Election" [in Chinese]. *Journal of Electoral Studies* 10 (1): 41–80.

Cheng, Su-feng. 2004. "Party Image in Taiwan—an Application of Focus Group." *Journal of Electoral Studies* 11 (2): 185–216.

Cheng, Tun-jen, and Hsu Yung-ming. 1996. "Issue Structure, the DPP's Factionalism, and Party Realignment." In *Taiwan's Electoral Politics and Democratic Transition: Riding the Third Wave*, ed. Tien Hung-Mao, 137–73. Armonk, NY: M. E. Sharpe.

Chihibber, Pradeep, and Mariano Torcal. 1997. "Elite Strategy, Social Cleavages, and Party Systems in a New Democracy Spain." *Comparative Political Studies* 30 (1): 27–54.

Chu, Yun-Han. 1994. "Party Competition, Conflict Structure, and Democratic Consolidation." Paper presented at the conference on Democratization and Party Politics and Elections, Taipei, July 8, 1994.

Cox, Gary. 1990. "Centripetal and Centrifugal Incentives in Electoral Systems." *American Journal of Political Science* 34: 903–35.

Dalton, Russell J. 1988. *Citizen Politics in Western Democracies*. Chatham, NJ: Chatham House.

Dalton, Russell J. 1996. "Political Cleavage, Issues, and Electoral Change." In *Comparing Democracies*, ed. Lawrence LeDuc, Richard G. Niemi, and Pippa Norris, 319–42. London: Sage Publications.

Directorate-General of Budget. 2012. *Statistical Yearbook of National Economics: The Republic of China 2005*. Taipei: Accounting and Statistics, Executive Yuan, Republic of China.

Fell, Dafydd. 2005. *Party Politics in Taiwan: Party Change and the Democratic Evolution of Taiwan*. London: Routledge.

Fell, Dafydd. 2011. "The Polarization of Taiwan's Party Competition in the DPP Era." In *Taiwan's Democracy: Economic and Political Challenges*, ed. Robert Ash, John W. Carver, and Penelope B. Prime, 75–98. London: Routledge.

Fell, Dafydd. 2012. *Government and Politics in Taiwan*. London: Routledge.

Fiorina, Morris P. 1981. *Retrospective Voting in American National Elections*. New Haven: Yale University Press.

Gates, Hill. 1979. "Dependency and Part-Time Proletariat in Taiwan." *Modern China* 5 (3): 381–408.

Green Party Taiwan. 2009. "Ma Ying-jeou Do Not Forget Your Promise of Carbon Tax on Earth Day." December 18. http://www.greenparty.org.tw/index.php/discuss/comment/233–2009–12–18–04–29–18.

Hawang, Shiow-duan. 2003. "The Predicament of Minority Government in the Legislative Yuan." *Taiwanese Political Science Review* 7 (2): 3–49.

Ho, Ming-sho. 2005a. "Taiwan's State and Social Movements under the DPP Government, 2002–2004." *Journal of East Asian Studies* 5: 401–25.

Ho, Ming-sho. 2005b. "Weakened State and Social Movement: The Paradox of Taiwanese Environmental Politics after the Power Transfer." *Journal of Contemporary China* 14 (43): 339–52.

Hsieh, John Fuh-sheng. 2005. "Ethnicity, National Identity, and Domestic Politics in Taiwan." *Journal of Asian and African Studies* 40 (1–2): 13–28.

Hsieh, John Fuh-sheng, and Emerson M. S. Niou. 1996a. "Issue Voting in the Republic of China on Taiwan's 1992 Legislative Yuan Election." *International Political Science Review* 17:13–27.

Hsieh, John Fuh-sheng, and Emerson M. S. Niou. 1996b. "Salient Issues in Taiwan's Electoral Politics." *Electoral Studies* 15: 219–35.

Hsieh, Kuo-hsiung. 1989. "Workers Become Bosses: Class Mobility in Taiwan Manufacturing Industry." *Taiwan: A Radical Quarterly in Social Studies* 2 (2): 11–54.

Inglehart, Ronald. 1977. *The Silent Revolution: Changing Values and Political Styles among Western Publics.* Princeton: Princeton University Press.

Inglehart, Ronald. 1990. *Cultural Shift in Advanced Industrial Society.* Princeton: Princeton University Press.

Inglehart, Ronald. 1997. *Modernization and Postmodernization: Cultural, Economic and Political Change in 43 Societies.* Princeton: Princeton University Press.

Lipset, Seymour Martin. 1981. *Political Man: The Social Bases of Politics.* Baltimore: Johns Hopkins University Press.

Lipset, Seymour Martin, and Stein Rokkan. 1967. "Cleavage Structure, Party Systems, and Voter Alignments." In *Consensus and Conflict: Essays in Political Sociology,* ed. Seymour Martin Lipset, 113–85. New York: Transaction Books.

Lin, Thung-Hong, and Alfred Ko-We Hu. 2011. "Cross-Strait Trade and Class Politics in Taiwan." *Thought and Words* 49 (3): 95–134.

Liu, Aron. 2003. "The Political-Business Relationship in Taiwan: Since the 1990s." *Journal of Culture and Society* 16: 97–126.

Liu, I-chou. 1994. "Generational Difference of Party Image among Taiwanese Voters." *Journal of Electoral Studies* 1 (1): 53–73.

Markus, Gregory B. 1982. "Political Attitudes during an Election Year: A Report on the 1980 NES Panel Study." *American Political Science Review* 76:538–60.

Markus, Gregory B., and Philip E. Converse. 1979. "The Dynamic Simultaneous Equation Model of Electoral Choice." *American Political Science Review* 73:1055–70.

Moreno, Alejandro. 1999. *Political Cleavages: Issues, Parties, and the Consolidation of Democracy.* Boulder, CO: Westview Press.

Norris, Pippa. 2004. *Electoral Engineering: Voting Rules and Political Behavior.* Cambridge: Cambridge University Press.

Page, Benjamin I., and Calvin C. Jones. 1979. "Reciprocal Effects of Policy Preferences, Party Loyalties, and the Vote." *American Political Science Review* 73: 1071–90.

RePass, David E. 1971. "Issue Salience and Party Choice." *American Political Science Review* 65: 389–400.

Sheng, Shing-yuan. 2001. "An Exploratory Study on Formal and Informal Legislative Participation: The Case of the Third Legislative Yuan." *Issues and Studies* (Chinese edition) 40 (5): 81–104.

Sheng, Shing-yuan. 2002. "The Issue Taiwan Independence vs. Unification with the Mainland and Voting Behavior in Taiwan: An Analysis in the 1990s." *Journal of Electoral Studies* 9 (1): 41–80.

Sheng, Shing-yuan. 2003. "The Influence of the Legislative Branch and the Executive Branch in the Process of Lawmaking: A Comparison of the Unified and Divided Governments." *Taiwanese Political Science Review* 7 (2): 51–105.

Sheng, Shing-yuan. 2005a. "Legislative Proposals of Legislators: Analyses of the 5th Legislative Yuan." Presented at the Annual Conference of the Taiwan Politics Association, Taipei.

Sheng, Shing-yuan. 2005b. "Constituency Representative and Collective Representative: The Representative Roles of Taiwanese Legislators." *Soochow Journal of Political Science* 21: 1–40.

Sheng, Shing-yuan. 2008. "Party Leadership and Cohesion in the Legislative Yuan: Before and after the First Party Turnover in the Executive Branch." *Taiwan Democracy Quarterly* 5 (4): 1–46.

Sheng, Shing-yuan. 2013. "Issues, Party Performance and Voters' Voting Behavior." In *2012 Presidential and Legislative Elections: Changes and Continuation*, ed. Chen Lu-huei, 203–27. Taiwan: Wunan Press.

Sheng, Shing-yuan. 2014. "Why Do They Oppose to Continue Constructing the Fourth Nuclear Power Plant?" Presented at the international conference on "The Maturing of Taiwan Democracy: Findings and Insights from the 2012 *TEDS* Survey," National Chengchi University, Taipei, March 22–23.

Sheng, Shing-yuan, and Chen Yih-yan. 2003. "Political Cleavage and Party Competition: An Analysis of the 2001 Legislative Yuan Election." *Journal of Electoral Studies* 10 (1): 7–37.

Shyu, Huo-yan. 1998. "Taiwan Election and Social Cleavage: Party Competition and Democratization." In *Cross-Straits Local Elections and Political and Social Changes*, ed. Chen Ming-tong and Cheng Yuan-nien, 127–68. Taiwan: Yuedan Press.

Stites, Richard. 1985. "Industrial Work as an Entrepreneurial Strategy." *Modern China* 11 (2): 227–46.

Stokes, Donald. 1963. "Spatial Models of Party Competition." *American Political Science Review* 57 (2): 368–77.

Tang, Shui-yan, and Tang Ching-ping. 1997. "Democratization and Environmental Politics in Taiwan." *Asian Survey* 37 (3): 281–94.

Wang, Shu-twu. 2003. "The Wealth Distribution Policy under the Party Turnover: An Analysis of the Senior Citizens' Life Allowance of Middle-to-Low Income Households." *Journal of Taiwan Wealth Distribution* 4:79–105.

Wu, Nai-teh. 1993. "Social Cleavage and Party Competition." Paper presented at the Democratization and Party Competition Conference, Academia Sinica, Taipei, June 11, 1993.

Yu, Ching-hsin. 2005. "The Evolving Party System in Taiwan, 1995–2004." *Journal of Asian and African Studies* 40 (1–2): 105–23.

CHAPTER 6

Economic Voting in Taiwan

Micro- and Macro-Level Analysis

Chia-hung Tsai

In chapter 5, Sheng and Liao find that the Taiwan voters consider economic prosperity as the most important problem facing the country, especially when Taiwan's economy was in a downturn. It is, therefore, important to examine the Taiwan voter in this light. Economic voting theory posits that voters tend to cast their votes in elections based on their assessment of government performance in regard to the economy. That is, if voters perceive that the current government is doing a good job in handling the economy, they are likely to vote for the incumbent party (or candidate) in order to have it remain in office. But if voters are dissatisfied with their economic conditions, they may affect a party turnover by voting against the incumbent party (or candidate). The foregoing can be regarded as the basic rationale of economic voting at the micro level.

This chapter has found mixed evidence of economic voting in the 2008 and 2012 Taiwan presidential elections. On the one hand, partisanship overshadows retrospective economic assessment, but on the other, prospective economic evaluation is a major determinant of voting behavior. Our aggregate-level analysis, however, suggests that disposable income per capita (DIPC) explains the incumbent party's vote shares. But the standard error on DIPC is larger than the .05 significance level. It is argued here that people tend to make their choices based on what the government will do in the near future, while macro economic conditions affect election outcomes.

Economic Voting Theory

In the 1970s, Kramer (1971) argued that a party's vote share represents the sum of three parts: party identification, past economic performance, and incumbent advantage. He found that changes in real personal income during the election year explained more than half of the variation in the vote. Since then, political scientists have developed a great number of models explaining, or even predicting, electoral outcomes (Abramowitz 1996; Erikson 1989; Fair 1978; Hibbing and Alford 1981; Lewis-Beck and Rice 1992; Rosenstone 1983). Tufte (1978) provided an engaging analysis of the impact of economic factors on congressional voting. His analysis shows that presidential popularity, along with yearly change in real income per capita, fit the election results from 1948 to 1976 very well. MacKuen, Erikson, and Stimson (1989) regressed presidential approval on political events and consumer sentiment and concluded that approval is a function of economic evaluation. Prior research on economic voting also implied that the president is largely held accountable for the national economy; thus, voters who are not satisfied with the national economy will send a signal targeting the president's performance (Erikson 1989).

Individual-level analysis of economic voting clarifies the mechanism by which the economic situation can affect political behavior. Key (1966) emphasized that voters look at the past records of the incumbent, and Downs (1957) argued that voters will base their preference on candidates' past performance when considering candidates' promises. Kinder and Kiewiet (1981) provided a theoretical foundation for pocketbook and sociotropic voting. They argued that personal finances may provide a shortcut to information but that sociotropic voting does not place higher informational demands on voters. They claimed that "[r]ather, voters must only develop rough evaluations of national economic conditions, and then credit or blame the incumbent party accordingly" (132). Feldman (1982) maintained that pocketbook voting occurs only among people who hold on to economic individualism. Fiorina (1978), however, endorsed the retrospective voting theory that the vote for the incumbent president's party is a function of individual personal income. Markus (1988) pooled survey data from the National Election Studies from 1956 to 1984 and found that both the aggregate-level economic indicators and personal finances are significant predictors of presidential voting choices. Nadeau and Lewis-Beck (2001) emphasized the influence of incumbency in the election: people choose retrospective pocketbook voting when the incumbent president is running in the election.

At the aggregate and individual levels, the logic of *retrospective* voting is straightforward: voters opt to support the incumbent who has improved economic conditions. The *prospective* voting theory instead assumes that people would choose the candidate who holds out a better prospect. Lanoue (1994) found that the effects of retrospective economic judgment are more consistent than prospective ones, whereas Lockerbie (1992) found that better prospects are more important than backward judgments. One of the underlying differences between the prospective and retrospective frameworks concerns the amount of information needed to make the forward or backward judgment. Considering that the modern economic situation involves many aspects, including employment, housing, food prices, and so on, voters' memory and understanding of past economic records may be challenging. Moreover, retrospective judgments can be subject to partisan framing: the incumbent may stimulate prosperity, but the opposition may paint it in dismal colors, for example, as causing less equality and greater inflation. Finally, the incumbent can hardly claim credit or be blamed for short-term economic fluctuations. Therefore, I assume that the reward model of economic voting is less effective than the prospective framework.

The other dimension of economic voting studies is whether personal finances or the national economy has more influence on voting. Duch and Stevenson's content analysis (2008) showed that citizens do indeed possess information regarding the macro economy. Gomez and Wilson (2006) found empirical evidence that sociotropic voting is common among less sophisticated people because they consider the national economy to be the president's sole responsibility. Economic voting, therefore, does not require sophistication. Understanding national economic situations may not demand too much information because voters can make a rough evaluation of the national economy.

Finally, there is the question about whether micro- or macro-level data analysis is superior regarding economic voting. The problem of endogeneity in cross-sectional data can be avoided with aggregate-level data analysis; however, aggregate data have fewer observations. Being aware of the trade-off, I analyze both types of data in this chapter.

The Case of Taiwan

It is not a coincidence that Taiwan voters embrace the value of economic growth, due to a shortage of natural resources. As in Japan and other East Asian countries, politics is geared to economic growth (Lumley 1976). When the Kuomintang government moved from Nanjing to Taipei in 1949, its priority was land reform, and land reform, economic planning, and shrinking the financial gap between the rich and the poor were the KMT's primary accomplishments.[1] In the 1950s and 1960s, the KMT government focused on economic growth (Chang 1965). According to Tien (1989, 26), the average GNP growth rate during the decade of 1953–62 was 7.5 percent. In the next decade, the number increased to 10.8 percent. By 1991, exports accounted for 47.1 percent of GDP (Wu 1995, 59). Unfortunately, Taiwan's economy has faltered since the 1990s. Not only did the growth of national income flatten, but disposable household income also declined. Labor shortages, inadequate infrastructure, and concerns over the environment slowed down the rate of growth. Although the KMT has been credited with economic development, the issue of social inequality and a power struggle cost the KMT the 2000 presidential election.

Although the KMT lost the 2000 and 2004 presidential elections, it called for improving cross-Strait relations, arguing that the future of Taiwan's economy could hinge on economic cooperation with China. Tan and Ho in chapter 7 show the rapid increase in the amount of Taiwan's investments in China after 2000. While more and more capital and technical expertise flows to China in exchange for cheap labor, land, and low environmental regulation, the resulting closer tie between Taiwan and China indeed stimulated Taiwan's economy, a result credited to the KMT even though it was not in power at the time. In contrast, the Democratic Progressive Party government discouraged the growing economic ties to the mainland, citing the concern for national security. The quest for economic growth shaped the 2008 presidential election, and the KMT returned to power.

Scholars have found evidence of economic voting in Taiwan, but their findings are not conclusive. Hsieh, Lacy, and Niou (1998) supports prospective sociotropic voting in Taiwan's first popular presidential election, but Sheng (2009) suggested that both prospective and retrospective economic perceptions were important in the 2008 presidential election. Hsiao (2013) also stressed the strength of prospective economic perception. Wu and Lin's (2013) analysis showed no effect of economic evaluation but found that voter perception of cross-Strait relations is a powerful predictor. More important, Wu and Lin (2012) discussed the validity of retrospective and prospective economic evaluations. Because the 2008 presidential election was held in March and the postelection survey is conducted in July and August due to the availability of student interviewers, they argued that responses to these questions might be endogenous to voting choice. They suggested that prospective economic views are more likely to predict voting behavior if the election result is known before the survey is in the field. Their theory conforms to the findings of the American literature, yet they stop short of testing it with aggregate-level data.

In chapter 7, Tan and Ho find that the Taiwan voters' evaluations of the national economy and their own personal economic situations are not independent from partisan identification and preference on the independence/unification issue. More precisely, those who preferred unification or the status quo were more likely to evaluate the state of the economy positively, while pro-independence respondents had a more negative view. If the confounding effect of party support on economic evaluations indeed exists, it is hard to verify economic voting.

To confirm that economic outcome matters in mass political decisions, I will attempt to analyze both macro- and micro-level data. Since the Ma administration signed the Economic Cooperation Framework Agreement with Beijing in 2010, which is expected to increase Taiwan's trade with the Chinese mainland, I will focus on the public's assessment of the national economy. Indeed, previous research has shown that the sociotropic consideration, not pocketbook concerns, correlates with voting decisions (Kinder and Kiewiet 1979; Erikson 1989). Our hypotheses are thus:

1. Prospective economic evaluation is a significant predictor of voting behavior when partisan predisposition is controlled for.
2. The partial effect of retrospective economic evaluation on voting behavior is significant when partisan predisposition is controlled for.
3. The percentage change in disposable income per capita is associated with an incumbent's vote share, all other things being equal.

Findings

Survey Data Analysis: The 2004, 2008, and 2012 Presidential Elections

The national postelection survey data conducted by Taiwan's Election and Democratization Studies was chosen for this analysis. These three surveys use a stratified sampling frame that covers all of the cities and counties except two surrounding islands, Kin-men and Mat-zu.

Each survey asks respondents' retrospective economic evaluation: "Would you say that over the past year, the state of the economy of Taiwan has gotten better, stayed about the same, or gotten worse?" For the prospective evaluation, the wording is "Would you say that in the forthcoming year, the state of the economy of Taiwan will get better, stay about the same, or get worse?" For both the retrospective and prospective economic evaluations, I code the response of "worse" as 1, "about the same" as 2, and "better" as 3.

To increase the predictive power of our economic voting models, I code self-identification as with either the Pan-Blue or Pan-Green camp. If respondents identified themselves with either the KMT, the People First Party, or the New Party, they are categorized as in the Pan-Blue camp. If respondents identified with the DPP or the Taiwan Solidarity Union, they are considered Pan-Green supporters. More than 30 percent of respondents, however, responded that they identified with neither camp. Therefore, I created two dummy variables representing support for the Pan-Blue and Pan-Green camps. Table 6.1 shows the wording of the questions and the coding schemes.

Economic Evaluations, Economic Records, and Incumbent's Vote

Tables 6.2 and 6.3 present the distribution of retrospective and prospective evaluations of national economic conditions in three elections. In 2004, only one-third of respondents said that the economic situation had become

TABLE 6.1. Individual-Level Variables

Variables	Questions	Coding of Response
Retrospective evaluation	"Would you say that over the past year, the state of the economy of Taiwan has gotten better, stayed about the same, or gotten worse?"	"worse" = 1 "about the same" = 2 "better" = 3
Prospective evaluation	"Would you say that in the forthcoming year, the state of the economy of Taiwan will get better, stay about the same, or get worse?"	"worse" = 1 "about the same" = 2 "better" = 3
Pan-Green identification	"Of the following five political parties, which party do you support the most?"	DPP, TSU = 1
Pan-Blue identification	"Of the following five political parties, which party do you support the most?"	KMT, PFP, New Party = 1

worse than it had been one year before (table 6.2). But in 2008, the percentage had almost doubled. Although the KMT government tried to address the economic problems by building closer ties with China, in 2012 more than 40 percent of those polled said that the economy was worse than before. As for the prospective economic evaluation, the three elections have differing distributions. In 2004 and 2012, a plurality of the respondents said that economic conditions would be the same in the future. In 2008, however, the proportion of respondents who said that economic conditions would become worse is a little higher than that of people who said economic conditions would remain the same.

Before estimating the effects of national economic evaluation on vote choice, the bivariate relationship between economic evaluations and vote choice is assessed. Table 6.3 shows the strong association between retrospective evaluation and incumbent voting in 2004. About 70 percent of people who felt that the economic situation had improved voted for the incumbent party, the DPP. On the other hand, nearly 75 percent of those who that that economic times were bad supported the challenger.

Table 6.3 also shows that in 2008 approximately 65 percent of people answered that the economic situation had gotten worse, and half of them voted for the challenger, the KMT. People who said that the economy had

TABLE 6.2. Retrospective and Prospective Evaluation of National Economy

		2004	2008	2012
Retrospective	Worse	34.89	66.67	43.82
	Same	38.51	30.27	38.58
	Better	26.61	3.07	17.60
Prospective	Worse	25.07	38.29	30.00
	Same	47.58	36.85	48.24
	Better	27.35	24.87	21.76

Note: Column percentages are in cells.

TABLE 6.3. Retrospective Evaluation of National Economic Condition and Vote Choice, 2004–2012

		Nonincumbent	%	Incumbent	%	Total
2004	Worse	251	70.51	105	29.49	356
	Same	171	43.29	224	56.71	395
	Better	82	25.55	239	74.45	321
2008	Worse	393	50.13	391	49.87	784
	Same	309	83.29	62	16.71	371
	Better	33	84.62	6	15.38	39
2012	Worse	322	64.40	178	35.60	500
	Same	152	32.14	321	67.86	473
	Better	35	14.23	211	85.77	246

stayed the same overwhelmingly supported the challenger. Fewer than 50 percent of respondents considered that the economic situation was getting better and they clearly voted for the KMT. As for 2012, most respondents who thought that the economy had gotten worse voted for the challenger, but most respondents who answered "stayed the same" and "better" voted for the incumbent party. In other words, retrospective economic voting occurred in 2012.

The first panel of table 6.4 shows that most people who said that the future economy would become worse voted for the challenger in 2004, and that 85 percent of people who thought that the economy would improve voted for the incumbent party. This result confirms the prospective economic voting theory.

However, the second panel of table 6.4 suggests the reverse pattern in 2008; more than 90 percent of people who felt that the economy would get better voted for the nonincumbent party, whereas more than 60 percent of the people who were pessimistic about the future economy voted for the incumbent. Wu and Lin's (2012) theory applies here in that voters may use the election outcomes to justify their economic responses. In 2008, it is the winning challenger rather than the losing incumbent who benefits from a good economic prospect—a prospect judged after the election.

As for 2012, an election won by the incumbent, table 6.4 shows that more than 80 percent of people who were optimistic about the future economy voted for the incumbent in 2012 and that more than 60 percent who thought the opposite voted for the challenger. This result suggests that voter perceptions of the economic future have an impact on voting.

These contingency tables suggest that voting is conditional on both prospective and retrospective concern about the national economy. To estimate the partial effect of retrospective and prospective economic evaluation in

TABLE 6.4. Prospective Evaluation of National Economic Condition and Voting for the Incumbent, 2004–2012

		Nonincumbent	%	Incumbent	%	Total
2004	Worse	207	78.41	57	21.59	264
	Same	249	50.30	246	49.70	495
	Better	48	15.34	265	84.66	313
2008	Worse	156	34.14	301	65.86	457
	Same	283	67.38	137	32.62	420
	Better	296	93.38	21	6.62	317
2012	Worse	240	66.67	120	33.33	360
	Same	233	40.59	341	59.41	574
	Better	36	12.63	249	87.37	285

2004, 2008, and 2012, our economic voting model is set up as follows:

Pr(Y) = β0 + β1 × Retrospective evaluation + β2 × Prospective evaluation + β3 × Pan-Green + β4 × Pan-Blue + u

Where Y = 1 when voting for the incumbent party and 0 otherwise.

I ran three logistic regression models for each of the three years so that I could assess the consistency of the estimates. The outcome variable was whether voters chose the incumbent party or not. Notice that the DPP was the incumbent party in 2004 and 2008, and the KMT was running the government in 2012. Independent variables include evaluation of the economy and party identification. Retrospective and prospective evaluations of the national economy are estimated respectively and jointly for each election. Considering that the proportion of people who identified themselves as independents was constantly around 40 percent, I classified individual partisanship as Pan-Green, Pan-Blue, and independents. Tan and Ho's chapter also suggests that the partisans of both incumbent and opposition parties have different views on the economy. Therefore, two dummy variables, representing Pan-Green and Pan-Blue, have been included in the models.

Table 6.5 partially confirms the hypotheses. Either retrospective or prospective economic assessment alone would increase the probability of voting for the incumbent in 2004 and 2012 when both Pan-Green and Pan-Blue identification is controlled for. When both retrospective and prospective evaluations are included in the full models of 2004 and 2012, retrospective economic evaluation has no influence on voting behavior in 2004 and 2012. Comparing the measure of model fit by AIC and BIC, I find that the retrospective voting model has a larger value (worse fit) than the prospective voting model and the full model in each year. The retrospective model also does poorly if goodness of fit is also measured by -2×ln(likelihood), where again, the larger the value, the worse the model fits the data.

The signs of the coefficients for both retrospective and prospective evaluations in the full model were negative in 2008. As in tables 6.3 and 6.4, people who felt that the economy would get better and people who felt that the economy had become worse voted for the nonincumbent party. It seems that the electorate deserted the DPP because of poor economic conditions in addition to the KMT's economic promise, including the "six-three-three" slogan.[2]

Our survey data analysis suggests that people tend to use the future economic situation as the yardstick for voting. If the incumbent has failed to bring about a better economic situation, he will lose many votes even though

TABLE 6.5. Logistic Regression Models of Voting for the Incumbent Party, 2004-2012

	2004 DPP			2008 DPP			2012 KMT		
	Retrospective	Prospective	Full	Retrospective	Prospective	Full	Retrospective	Prospective	Full
Intercept	-0.293	-1.336***	-1.313***	0.524†	0.430	1.161**	-0.725*	-1.414***	-1.610***
	(0.308)	(0.368)	(0.394)	(0.312)	(0.292)	(0.364)	(0.283)	(0.318)	(0.352)
Pro-Green	3.388***	3.294***	3.301***	3.413***	3.301***	3.299***	-3.129***	-3.156***	-3.116***
	(0.365)	(0.365)	(0.368)	(0.244)	(0.243)	(0.246)	(0.278)	(0.281)	(0.282)
Pro-Blue	-3.860***	-3.771***	-3.774***	-3.249***	-3.011***	-3.036***	2.840***	2.849***	2.794***
	(0.334)	(0.336)	(0.337)	(0.383)	(0.386)	(0.388)	(0.251)	(0.252)	(0.255)
Retrospective	0.332*		-0.028	-1.062***		-0.805***	0.536***		0.221
	(0.149)		(0.173)	(0.221)		(0.237)	(0.150)		(0.167)
Prospective		0.839***	0.854***		-0.762***	-0.569***		0.863***	0.768***
		(0.174)	(0.198)		(0.157)	(0.165)		(0.157)	(0.172)
AIC	513.585	494.065	496.038	584.124	583.463	573.917	650.530	631.597	631.841
BIC	533.494	513.974	520.925	604.464	603.804	599.342	670.953	652.021	657.370
Log likelihood	-252.792	-243.032	-243.019	-288.062	-287.732	-281.958	-321.265	-311.799	-310.921
Deviance	505.585	486.065	486.038	576.124	575.463	563.917	642.530	623.597	621.841
Number of observations	1,072	1,072	1,072	1,194	1,194	1,194	1,219	1,219	1,219

Notes: *** $p < 0.001$, ** $p < 0.01$, * $p < 0.05$. Standard errors are in parentheses.

his performance in office was good. Nevertheless, people may not track the incumbent's past record if they find the economic prospect appealing.

Why do people tend to use their perceptions of future economic situation as the basis for voting? The first possible explanation is that people may link the current economic conditions with partisan squabbling. In 2004 and 2008, the DPP cited the KMT's obstructive legislature and China's threat for their mediocre performance. In 2012, the KMT argued that they had inherited the economic problems caused by the DPP's policy of "self-isolation" from China and the world. The second explanation is that the incumbent government has the resources to set up the agenda (Page and Shapiro 1992); the incumbent government may either stimulate the economy in the election year or divert people's attention from economic conditions to national security or inequality. For instance, the DPP proposed an unprecedented national referendum in the 2004 presidential election. In consequence, the economic record did not stand out as a clear-cut issue.[3]

If retrospective economic voting does not take place, how can the *future* national economy drive voting behavior, especially in 2012? One of the possible explanations is that the Taiwan voters responded to the notion of "peace dividend" proposed by the Ma administration. Ma personally has repeatedly emphasized the benefits of closer ties with China, including more trade surpluses, faster integration with the East Asian economy, and stronger national security. The prospect of a better economy pictured by the Ma administration thus may explain the prospective economic voting in Taiwan.

Across the nine models, an individual's attachment to either the pan-Blue or pan-Green camp is a major predictor of incumbent voting. In 2004 and 2008, people who identified themselves as Pan-Green supporters voted for the incumbent party, but Pan-Blue supporters did not do so. In contrast, Pan-Blue supporters tended to choose the KMT in 2012, but Pan-Green supporters voted the other way. While economic voting does occur, the partisan variables are consistently much more powerful.

Although survey data analysis supports prospective sociotropic voting, it relies on voter perceptions and self-reporting. Aggregate-level studies of economic voting instead focus almost completely on the effect of macroeconomic performance on elections. To predict an election outcome, there are a great number of economic indicators to choose from. Erikson (1989) followed Hibbs's (1987) and Tufte's (1978) investigations of macroeconomic conditions and the presidential elections, arguing that the relative growth of per capita income change has largely determined the election outcomes. Tsai (2000) also found that real personal income per capita explains presidential popularity well, in addition to political events and war. Therefore,

I calculated the percentage change of disposal income per capita from the previous year. In addition, I include the percentage change in the year before the election year.

Because there is a perfect correlation between the DIPC in 2002 and 2003, the change in DIPC has no impact on the vote shares. Therefore, our analysis drops the 2004 presidential election. The DPP was the incumbent in 2008, so its vote share is regressed on Chen Shui-bian's vote share in 2004. Likewise, Ma's vote share in 2012 is regressed on his vote share in 2008 as he challenged the DPP's ticket. Our aggregate-level economic voting model is:

$$Y_t = \gamma0 + \gamma1 \times (\text{DIPC change})_{t-1} + \gamma2 \times (\text{DIPC change})_{t-2} + \gamma3 \times (\text{Incumbent's vote share})_{t-4} + u$$

The dependent variable is the raw percentage of votes won by the DPP and KMT in each city/county respectively; I divided the number of votes for each party by the number of valid votes. The first predictor variable is the percentage change in the DIPC from the previous year. Because the presidential election is held in March, people judge the president's performance by the change in their income during the year between the two years before the election to the year before it. For the 2008 election, the first percentage change in DIPC was determined as (DIPC2007 − DIPC2006)/DIPC2006, and for the 2012 election, as (DIPC2011 − DIPC2010)/DIPC2010.

To capture the possible influence from the economic situation two years prior to the two elections, I used (DIPC2006 − DIPC2005)/DIPC2005 for the 2008 model, and for the 2012 model, (DIPC2010 − DIPC2009)/DIPC2009. Finally, I included as a covariate the DPP or KMT vote shares in the city/county four years earlier.

The personal income data came from the Directorate General of Budget, Accounting and Statistics (DGBAS) of the Executive Yuan.[4] The vote-share data comes from the Election Study Center, National Chengchi University (http://esc.nccu.edu.tw). It was jointly collected by the center and the Central Election Committee.

Our data are from 23 cities and counties for the 2008 election and from 20 for the 2012 election. That is because Taichung County, Tainan County, and Kaohsiung County were merged with Taichung City, Tainan City, and Kaohsiung City, respectively, in 2010. Fortunately, DGBAS provides the DIPC of the three counties *as if* they had been merged back to 2000. Therefore, I am able to calculate the percentage change in the DIPC for those three metropolitan areas for the 2012 election model.

Before estimating the effects of personal income factors, I plotted the change in the vote from 2004 to 2008 against the percentage change in

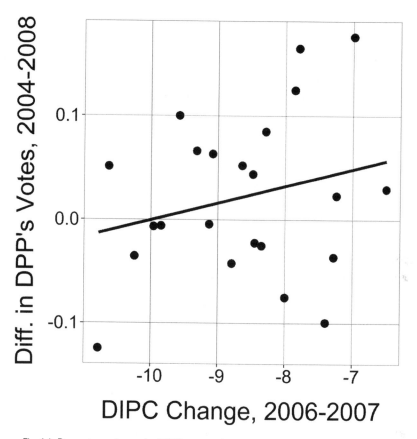

Fig. 6.1. Percentage change in DIPC versus change in incumbent's (DPP) vote share, 2008

DIPC from 2006 to 2007 for the DPP (fig. 6.1), and I constructed a similar scatter plot for the KMT in the 2012 election (fig. 6.2). The prediction line in figure 6.1 rises as the change in DIPC increases, and the R-squared is 0.06. This plot implies that the DPP lost votes everywhere but they gained votes in the cities or counties where the average income increased. Figure 6.2 shows a flat line, which suggests that the KMT lost votes even in the cities or counties where income per capita increased. Both plots suggest that the aggregate economic indicator may not be able to predict the variation in incumbent's vote share very well.

Table 6.6 shows four models. The first model presents the effects of the DPP's vote share in 2004 and percentage changes in DIPC from 2007 and 2006 on the variation of DPP's vote share. The second model drops the change in DIPC from 2006. The third model demonstrates the effects of

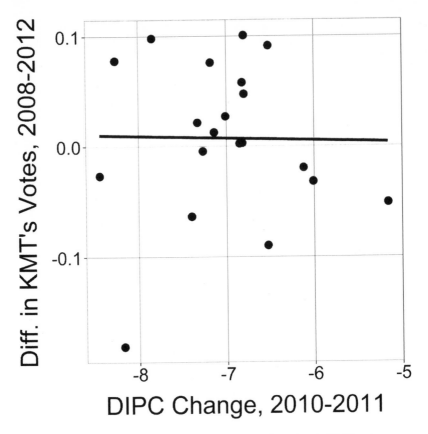

Fig. 6.2. Percentage change in DIPC versus change in incumbent's (KMT) vote share, 2012

the KMT's vote share in 2008 and percentage changes in the DIPC in 2011 and 2010. Finally, the fourth model drops the second lagged DIPC variable.

The first column shows that a 1 percentage point increase in disposable income per capita in the preceding year produces about a 2 percentage point gain in Chen's vote share in 2008. When the second lag variable is dropped, the coefficient increases to 3.76. As for the 2012 election, the third column shows that Ma's vote share would increase by 2 percentage points with a one unit change of disposable income per capita. The fourth column displays a similar result as the two-year lag variable is dropped. Because the variation in disposable income per capita across 20 or 23 cities is small, the effect of change between one year before the election and the preceding year is not significant, but it is substantial. Bartels and Zaller (2001) similarly found that the contribution of economic growth (GDP or real disposable income, RDI) to an incumbent's vote share is about 2 percent. However, the relatively large standard errors here limit our ability to tell exactly how an incumbent's vote share reflects the economic conditions in cities and counties.

To improve the standard errors, the 2008 and 2012 data are combined as a dataset with 43 observations. In addition to the coefficients on the lagged vote and on the change in DIPC, a dummy variable indicating the 2012 election is estimated. Table 6.7 shows that the finding in table 6.6 still holds; the coefficient and its standard error of change in DIPC both shrink as the number of observations double. Therefore, the t-ratio remains small.

The conclusion is that the Taiwan voters continue to vote for the incumbent regardless of their disposable income one or two years prior. This result seems to validate the effect of partisan identification shown in chapter 5. Both incumbents' vote shares in 2004 and in 2008 predict the outcome variables very well, which means that voters who voted for a party tended to vote for it again, regardless of which party was in office. The coefficient of the incumbent's vote share in the second model is smaller than that in the third model, which suggests that some Pan-Blue voters switched to the PFP in 2012.

Survey data analysis implies that some people participated in "negative" retrospective voting in 2008: people who thought that the economy had

TABLE 6.6. Models of the Incumbent Party's Vote Share in 2008 and 2012

	2008	2008	2012	2012
(Intercept)	−8.45***	−8.96***	−5.58***	−5.39***
	(1.49)	(1.36)	(1.17)	(1.15)
Chen's vote share in 2004	1.00***	1.00***		
	(0.03)	(0.03)		
Percentage change in DIPC from 2007	2.48	3.76		
	(3.60)	(3.28)		
Percentage change in DIPC from 2006	−3.73			
	(4.19)			
Ma's vote share in 2008			0.97***	0.97***
			(0.02)	(0.02)
Percentage change in DIPC from 2011			2.61	2.32
			(2.62)	(2.59)
Percentage change in DIPC from 2010			−2.86	
			(3.15)	
R-squared	0.99	0.99	0.99	0.99
Adj. *R*-squared	0.98	0.98	0.99	0.99
N	23	23	20	20

Note: ***$p < 0.001$, two-tailed test. Standard errors are in parentheses.

become worse may have voted for the challenger (i.e., the KMT). Table 6.6 and 6.7, however, show that there is a positive association between the DPP's vote shares and income growth. The gap between the individual- and aggregate-level data analysis needs more examination.

Conclusion

In this paper, I examined evidence of economic voting in the 2004, 2008, and 2012 presidential elections. On the one hand, I found that partisanship is a better predictor of outcome than retrospective economic assessment. On the other, prospective economic evaluation is a major determinant of voting behavior when controlling for partisanship. Notice that in 2008, prospective evaluation of the economy may reflect people's judgment on the newly elected government's handling of the economy rather than a true preelection prospective judgment.

Our aggregate-level analysis suggests that economic conditions may not explain the incumbent party's election results. Instead, only the previous election outcome is a good predictor. Our economic indicator, DIPC of one and two years, could involve measurement errors because some people hide portions of their real income, such as rent and stocks. More work is needed to devise a good macroeconomic voting model.

One of our findings is that the electorate does not punish incumbents for their performance in the first term. This is interesting because it implies

TABLE 6.7. Model of Combined Incumbent Party's Vote Share in 2008 and 2012

	Incumbent's vote share
(Intercept)	−8.03***
	(0.86)
2012 presidential election	1.78***
	(0. 36)
Incumbent's vote share in the last election	0.99***
	(0.02)
Percentage change in the previous year	2.10
	(2.14)
R-squared	0.99
Adj. R-squared	0.99
N	43

Note: ***$p < 0.001$, two-tailed test. Standard errors are in parentheses.

that the incumbent has the advantage. A possible cultural explanation is that people in Taiwan dislike sudden change. Instead, they tend to wait before throwing the incumbent out. Certainly, I need more election results to test this hypothesis.

To be sure, as both macro- and micro-level data analysis show, retrospective or prospective economic voting is shadowed by party identification and the underlying national identity. From the normative perspective, it may impede political accountability; politicians can play identity cards instead of handling the economy well. However, economic growth will remain one of the main sources of legitimacy. As a new generation arises, new parties are emerging, and independents are increasing (see chapter 4), socioeconomic voting may become as important as national identity.

Notes

1. In Taiwan, economic development in the 1960s and 1970s had not widened income inequality as it had in other developing countries (Ferdinand 1996). By the 1980s, Taiwan's disparity between the rich and the poor was one of the lowest in the world (Roy 2003).

2. "Six-three-three" means a 6% economic growth rate, under 3% unemployment rate, and raising income per capita to USD $30,000.

3. In January 2004, President Chen initiated the defensive referendum under Article 17 of the Referendum Act. Because the DPP's party platform states that "any change of Taiwan's independence status quo should be decided via referendum," the international community harshly rebuked DPP's referendum proposal (Lin 2004). The Pan-Blue camp blasted the DPP for holding the referendum and presidential election on the same day, asking voters to boycott the referendum. Tsai, Hsu, and Huang (2007) argued that the two political camps polarized on the referendum issue more than on the independence/unification issue.

4. Regarding statistics by county or city, please look at this link http://statdb.dgbas. gov.tw/pxweb/Dialog/statfile9.asp. Dozens of indicators by city and by year can be assessed through this interactive web page. Unfortunately, it is only in Chinese. On the English version of the DGBAS's website (http://eng.stat.gov.tw/mp.asp?mp=5), there is no such web page.

References

Abramowitz, Alan I. 1996. "Bill and Al's Excellent Adventure: Forecasting the 1996 Presidential Election." *American Politics Research* 24 (4): 434–42.

Bartels, Larry M., and John Zaller. 2001. "Presidential Vote Models: A Recount." *PS: Political Science & Politics* 34 (1): 9–20.

Chang, David W. 1965. "U.S. Aid and Economic Progress in Taiwan." *Asian Survey* 5 (3): 152–60.

Downs, Anthony. 1957. *An Economic Theory of Democracy.* New York: Harper and Row.

Duch, Raymond M., and Randolph T. Stevenson. 2008. *The Economic Vote: How Political and Economic Institutions Condition Election Results*. Cambridge: Cambridge University Press.

Erikson, Robert S. 1989. "Economic Conditions and the Presidential Vote." *American Political Science Review* 83 (2): 567–73.

Fair, Ray C. 1978. "The Effect of Economic Events on Votes for the President." *Review of Economics and Statistics* 60 (2): 159–73.

Feldman, Stanley. 1982. "Economic Self-Interest and Political Behavior." *American Journal of Political Science* 26 (3): 446–66.

Ferdinand, Peter. 1996. "The Taiwanese Economy." In *Take-off for Taiwan?*, ed. Peter Ferdinand, 37–65. London: Royal Institute of International Affairs.

Fiorina, Morris P. 1978. "Economic Retrospective Voting in American National Elections: A Micro-Analysis." *American Journal of Political Science* 22 (1): 426–43.

Gomez, Brad T., and J. Matthew Wilson. 2006. "Cognitive Heterogeneity and Economic Voting: A Comparative Analysis of Four Democratic Electorates." *American Journal of Political Science* 50 (1): 127–45.

Hibbing, John R., and John R. Alford. 1981. "The Electoral Impact of Economic Conditions: Who Is Held Responsible?" *American Journal of Political Science* 25 (3): 423–39.

Hibbs, Douglas A., Jr. 1987. *The American Political Economy: Macroeconomics and Electoral Politics in the United States*. Cambridge: Harvard University Press.

Hsiao, Yi-ching. 2013. "Economic Accountability and Voting Choice: An Analysis of the 2012 Presidential Election" [in Chinese]. In *2008 nian zong tong yu li fa wei yuan xuan ju: Bian qian yu yan xu* [The 2012 presidential and legislative election: Continuity and change], ed. Lu-huei Chen. Taipei: Wunan.

Hsieh, John Fu-sheng, Dean Lacy, and Emerson M. S. Niou. 1998. "Retrospective and Prospective Voting in a One-Party-Dominant Democracy: Taiwan's 1996 Presidential Election." *Public Choice* 97:383–99.

Key, V. O., Jr. 1966. *The Responsible Electorate: Rationality in Presidential Voting*. Cambridge: Belknap Press of Harvard University Press.

Kinder, Donald, and D. Roderick Kiewiet. 1979. "Economic Discontent and Political Behavior: The Role of Personal Grievances and Collective Economic Judgments in Congressional Voting." *American Journal of Political Science* 23 (3): 495–527.

Kinder, Donald, and D. Roderick Kiewiet. 1981. "Sociotropic Politics: The American Case." *British Journal of Political Science* 11 (1): 129–61.

Kramer, Gerald. 1971. "Short-Term Fluctuations in U.S. Voting Behavior, 1896–1964." *American Political Science Review* 65 (1): 131–43.

Lanoue, David J. 1994. "Retrospective and Prospective Voting in Presidential-Year Elections." *Political Research Quarterly* 47 (1): 193–205.

Lewis-Beck, Michael S., and Tom W. Rice. 1992. "Presidential Popularity and Presidential Vote." *Public Opinion Quarterly* 46 (4): 534–37.

Lin, Jih-wen. 2004. "Taiwan's Referendum Act and the Stability of the Status Quo." *Issues and Studies* 40 (2): 119–53.

Lockerbie, Brad. 1992. "Prospective Voting in Presidential Elections, 1956–1988." *American Politics Research* 20 (3): 308–25.

Lumley, L. A. 1976. *The Republic of China under Chiang Kai-shek*. London: Barrie and Jenkins.

MacKuen, Michael B., Robert S. Erikson, and James A. Stimson. 1989. "Macropartnership. 83 (4): 1125–42.

Markus, Gregory B. 1988. "The Impact of Personal and National Economic Conditions on the Presidential Vote: A Pooled Cross-Sectional Analysis." *American Journal of Political Science* 32 (1): 137–54.

Nadeau, Richard, and Michael Lewis-Beck. 2001. "National Economic Voting in U. S. Presidential Elections." *Journal of Politics* 63 (1): 159–81.

Page, Benjamin, and Robert Shapiro. 1992. *The Rational Public*. Chicago: University of Chicago Press.

Rosenstone, Steven J. 1983. *Forecasting Presidential Elections*. New Haven: Yale University Press.

Roy, Denny. 2003. *Taiwan: A Political History*. Ithaca: Cornell University Press.

Sheng, Shin-yuan. 2009. "The Impacts of Economic and Welfare Issues on Voting Behavior: An Inquiry into the 2008 Presidential Election" [in Chinese]. *2008 nian zong tong xuan ju: Lun er ci zheng dang lun ti zhi guan jian xuan ju* [The 2008 presidential election: The critical election of the second party turnover], ed. Lu-huei Chen, Ching-hsin Yu, and Chi Huang. Taipei: Wunan.

Tien, Hung-mao. 1989. *The Great Transition: Political and Social Change in the Republic of China*. Stanford, CA: Hoover Institution Press.

Tsai, Chia-hung. 2000. "American Voter Responses to International Political Events and Economic Conditions: 1920–1996." *EurAmerica* 30 (3): 143–91.

Tsai, Chia-hung, Yung-ming Hsu, and Hsiu-tin Huang. 2007. "Bi-Polarizing Politics: Explaining the 2004 Presidential Election in Taiwan" [in Chinese]. *Xuan Ju Yan Jiu* [Journal of Electoral Studies] 14 (1): 1–31.

Tufte, Edward R. 1978. *Political Control of the Economy*. Princeton: Princeton University Press.

Wu, Chin-en, and Yi-tze Lin. 2012. "Economic Voting and Presidential Elections: An Assessment of Validity and Endogeneity" [in Chinese]. *Taiwan Zheng Zhi Xue Kan* [Taiwan Political Science Review] 16 (2): 175–232.

Wu, Chin-en, and Yi-tze Lin. 2013. "Cross-Strait Economic Openness, Identity, and Vote Choice: An Analysis of the 2008 and 2012 Presidential Elections" [in Chinese]. *Xuan Ju Yan Ji* [Journal of Electoral Studies] 20 (2): 1–36.

Wu, Jaushieh Joseph. 1995. *Taiwan's Democratization: Forces behind the New Momentum*. New York: Oxford University Press.

CHAPTER 7

Cross-Strait Relations and the Taiwan Voter

Alexander C. Tan and Karl Ho

The saying "politics stop at the water's edge" probably is not applicable to the case of Taiwan because "high" international politics and "low" domestic politics converge at the island state. The most prominent of the factors is Taiwan's relations with China, which seem to penetrate to the core of Taiwan's domestic politics and especially its electoral politics. While elsewhere, electoral politics tend to be defined by the prominence of national or domestic concerns, we learn from earlier chapters, chapter 3 in particular, that the China factor (as an external factor) affects Taiwan's perception of its security, both political and economic, and influences citizens' identity formation and political preferences. A complete picture requires us to examine the role of cross-Strait relations in defining voter identity.

We will begin by briefly examining Taiwan's economic relations with China and suggesting that despite greater interaction, the perceptions of Taiwan voters have not significantly changed in favor of China. In fact, we suggest that empirical evidence shows that Taiwan voters are ambivalent about the increasing cross-Strait economic interaction. In the following section, we examine how this ambivalence and vulnerability has politicized Taiwan society and how this politicization helps paint a picture of who the Taiwan voter is.

Cross-Strait Relations, the Economy, and Security

One of the features of Taiwan's economy after 1990 has been increasing economic relations with China, which brought risks along with the profits.

The obvious benefit was the relatively benign impact of the 2008 global financial crisis on the Taiwan economy as the growth in demand from China following the crisis alleviated the decline in orders from Europe and the United States. The increase in cross-Strait economic ties predates Taiwan's inauguration of democracy, which began in the late 1980s. Although it was not officially sanctioned at the time, Taiwan companies and businesses had been trading and investing in China through third parties (mostly in Hong Kong). The surge in economic interactions was brought about by the convergence of several factors such as the relative political relaxation in Taiwan, but more noteworthy was the complementary change occurring in the industrial structures of the two economies, in which Taiwan's industrial restructuring saw the manufacturing industries move to China. As these sunset (and generally more labor-intensive) factories migrated to China for production, they in fact established and created integrated production networks, further accelerating economic integration. How important is China to Taiwan's economy? How integrated are the two economies? To answer these questions, two economic indicators are important—trade and investments. Figure 7.1 shows Taiwan's exports and imports with China as a percentage of total exports and imports, while figure 7.2 shows the amount of Taiwan's annual investments in China.

As figure 7.1 shows, exports to and imports from China have increased substantially in the last 20 years. Since the first handover of executive office from the Kuomintang to the Democratic Progressive Party in 2000, the annual increase in the China trade as a proportion of total Taiwan trade has steeply increased. Beginning at 2.9 percent of total exports in 2000, China became a major trade partner of Taiwan in the span of a decade, and by 2013 it accounted for 26.8 percent of Taiwan's total exports. Although the import figures are significantly smaller, by 2010 imports from China accounted for about 15.8 percent of total Taiwan imports. Masked under these two statistics is the more important statistic—the huge trade surplus in favor of Taiwan. Since 1990, the trade surplus has favored Taiwan such that by 2013 it amounted to about US$39 billion. To simply state that numerous Taiwan businesses and companies are profiting hugely from the China trade is an understatement.

As with the surge in trade with China, Taiwan's investments in China have also increased rapidly. Figure 7.2 shows the amount of investment in China on an annual basis. Although these figures were approved officially, they were very likely underreported. What is unmistakable is the rapid increase in the amount of Taiwan's investments in China, which grew from US$2.6 billion in 2000 to more than US$14 billion in 2010 and US$9.2

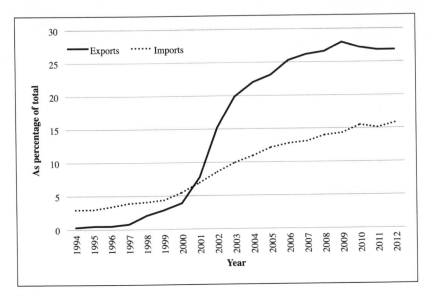

Fig. 7.1. Taiwan's trade with China. *Source:* Cross-Straits Economic Monthly Report, Mainland Affairs Council, http://www.mac.gov.tw (accessed April 19, 2014).

billion in 2013. As mentioned earlier, the surge in investment is partly a consequence of Taiwan's industrial restructuring, as labor-intensive industries looked to reduce their production costs, which increased due to rising business costs in Taiwan. However, as Taiwan businesses and the economy benefit from the China trade, the rapid increase of Taiwan investment in China has constantly raised the specter of industrial hollowing-out, whereby manufacturing industries move out of Taiwan en masse, leaving only administrative or design facilities.

Besides the perils of industrial migration, the increasing trade and investments in China also means that Taiwan businesses are exposed to risk without any legal protection, because the two governments do not recognize each other or have any bilateral framework to address economic disputes. There is the fear within Taiwan that, beyond the China economic factor, Taiwan's constrained international status is limiting Taiwan's ability to be part of any burgeoning regional economic integration groups and thereby affecting Taiwan's future economic performance. In this sense, the Ma administration's push for the signing of the Economic Cooperation Framework Agreement with China is perceived as a way to provide a legal framework for cross-Strait trade and investments, as well as to allow Taiwan to be included in future re-

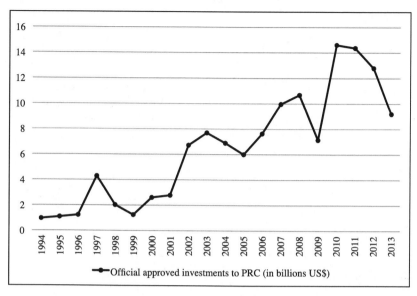

Fig. 7.2. Officially approved investments by Taiwan in China. *Source:* Cross-Straits Economic Monthly Report, Mainland Affairs Council, http://www.mac.gov.tw (accessed April 19, 2014).

gional economic integration. The ECFA, in one sense, can be seen as simply a de jure recognition of what is a de facto burgeoning cross-Strait economic tie that has been going on for decades.

If we follow the neoliberal perspective in international relations that increasing economic interdependence and functional relations will lead to greater trust and to peaceful relations between interdependent states, it provides us with only an incomplete picture of Taiwan's perception of cross-Strait ties, because the politics of the ECFA also signals Taiwan's own insecurity and sense of vulnerability.

When asked to rate the People's Republic of China (PRC) government's attitude toward the Taiwan government and people, more than 40 percent of Taiwan respondents believe that the PRC government is unfriendly to the Taiwan people, and over half believe that China is unfriendly to the Taiwan government (except for a dip in 2011; see earlier chapter). The height of this hostility, from the Taiwan point of view, was greatest in the second-term campaign of independence-minded President Chen Shui-bian in 2004, where 79.4 percent of respondents believed that China is hostile to the Taiwan government. Juxtaposing the trade and investment statistics from 2000 to 2010 with the perceived hostility data is quite revealing. Contrary to the expectations of neoliberal and interdependence theory at a time when trade and investments are trending upward, the Taiwan people's perception of hostility has stayed stubbornly high and has not declined in any appreciable way.

The growing economic integration between China and Taiwan creates a threat to Taipei, due to China's sovereignty claims over the island, and makes Taiwan vulnerable, due to its increasing economic dependence on China. There are concerns within Taiwan society about whether this dynamic represents a risk or an opportunity for Taiwan. This vulnerability affects Taiwan citizen's perceptions of national security, driving a wedge among the elites—which is also reflected among Taiwan voters—and directly shapes contending strategies of how to best handle cross-Strait relations. The contentious politics took center stage during the negotiations and eventual signing of the ECFA. There is a very clear political divide, which is reflected in the positions of the two major parties. The KMT believes that expanding these ties is important for Taiwan's continued economic dynamism, while the DPP argues that increasing economic ties with China threatens national sovereignty and security (Gold 2009).

This heightened sense of vulnerability and the divided outlook on how best to approach the cross-Strait economic policy is also reflected by citizens' views on the pace of cross-Strait interactions. At the height of President Chen's administration, a fairly large group of respondents believed that the pace of cross-Strait interactions was too slow (see 2004 and 2006 in table 7.1) with more than one in four stating so. By 2008, the Three Direct Links, which began in November 2008, and then the broader ECFA in June 2010 triggered a significant swing to the "too fast" category, with more than one in three worried about the fast pace. This segmentation at the voter level is largely reflected in the divided discourse of party politicians, with the resultant political polarization at the elite and voter levels being duly noted by numerous political observers (Clark and Tan 2012b; Huang 2008; Liao and Yu 2008). It is fair, then, to infer that cross-Strait economic relations have become highly politicized (Clark and Tan 2012b), a point that we will return to in the following section.

Cross-Strait Economic Relations and the Voters

In the previous section, we pointed out the highly politicized nature of cross-Strait economic relations (specifically the policy-making process in Taiwan) resulting from the drastically contrasting visions of the proper strategy to deal with cross-Strait ties. So how have cross-Strait economic relations become highly politicized? How does the Taiwan voter reflect the politicization of cross-Strait economic policy making?

The contradictory claims to sovereignty of the PRC and the ROC had underlain the conflicting relationship between these two polities since the end of the Chinese Civil War and the establishment of the PRC. Yet in the mid-1980s and the mid-1990s, a seeming détente existed between the two states until the missile crisis in 1995–96, during Lee Teng-hui's presidency. The détente broke down as a result of different and contradictory perceptions of territorial sovereignty despite the growing social and economic ties between the two countries. China calculated that growing ties would rein in separatism in Taiwan, while Taiwan's democratization and growing economic wealth stimulated the growth of a Taiwanese identity separate from China (Clark and Tan 2012a, 2012b). Indeed, it is not an exaggeration to

TABLE 7.1. Views on the Pace of Cross-Straits Interactions, 2001–2008

	Just right	Too fast	Too slow	Don't know	N
Mar-01	38.6	17.8	22.0	21.6	1,077
Jul-01	35.5	17.3	20.3	26.8	1,100
Feb-02	37.7	15.8	17.8	28.7	1,081
Apr-02	36.5	13.1	17.5	32.9	1,091
Jul-02	30.7	16.4	18.4	34.5	1,091
Dec-02	29.6	15.4	19.6	35.5	1,076
May-03	30.7	23.4	20.2	25.7	1,082
Aug-03	30.6	20.5	19.5	29.4	1,149
Nov-03	32.1	17.0	17.5	33.4	1,100
Apr-04	39.9	15.1	20.2	24.7	1,083
Jul-04	36.6	14.2	20.8	28.4	1,153
Dec-04	35.8	19.1	25.2	19.9	1,067
May-05	40.2	25.7	18.9	15.1	1,084
Aug-05	34.1	25.1	25.0	15.7	1,096
Nov-05	33.6	22.4	30.6	13.4	1,102
Apr-06	30.6	19.9	34.5	15.0	1,088
Sep-06	36.2	26.2	25.1	12.5	1,068
Dec-06	35.6	19.6	29.6	15.2	1,073
Apr-07	34.5	22.5	30.2	12.7	1,072
Aug-07	36.1	21.0	28.7	14.2	1,095
Dec-07	40.7	18.6	32.2	8.5	1,067
Mar-08	40.8	18.9	35.2	5.1	1,068
Aug-08	40.6	29.5	17.5	12.4	1,094
Oct-08	38.6	30.1	20.5	10.8	1,081
Dec-08	47.5	37.2	14.5	0.8	1,068

Source: Mainland Affairs Council, ROC, http://www.mac.gov.tw/ (accessed April 19, 2014).

state that Taiwan's policies toward cross-Strait relations over the last two decades constitute a game in which domestic and foreign policy are closely intertwined as relations with China dominate the domestic political discourse
and form the main political and social cleavage separating the two major
parties—the KMT and DPP (Clark and Tan 2012a, 2012b).

In the last section, we noted that the growing economic linkages have not
lessened the feeling of hostility to China and vulnerability among Taiwan
citizens, as shown by public opinion surveys. In fact, as mentioned earlier,
Taiwan's growing wealth and its democratization have stimulated Taiwanese
identity formation and consciousness despite the growing economic links
with China over the last two decades.

Do these preferences color the Taiwan voters' perception of cross-Strait
economic relations and the benefits and costs that it entails? In other words,
how politicized is the cross-Strait linkage, and how does it reflect who the
Taiwan voter is? To answer these questions, let us look at how the evaluation
of the economy, as well as the benefits of the ECFA, is affected by the preference for independence or unification and by party identification.

Table 7.2 shows the distribution of how citizens evaluate the benefits of
the ECFA based on their preferred position on the issue of independence/
unification. Ignoring the middle categories of "status quo and decide later"
and "status quo forever," it is evident from the statistics shown in the table
that preferences on the issue of independence/unification are highly correlated with respondents' evaluations of the benefits of the ECFA. Citizens

TABLE 7.2. Evaluations of ECFA on the Economy by Independence/Unification Preference and Partisan
Identification

	Worse	Same	Better	N
Unify now	3.7%	44.4%	51.9%	1,569
Maintain status quo, unification later	6.3%	32.8%	60.9%	1,569
Maintain status quo and decide later	8.5%	41.1%	50.4%	1,569
Maintain status quo forever	12.8%	43.0%	44.2%	1,569
Maintain status quo, independence later	20.6%	55.2%	24.2%	1,569
Independence now	38.8%	53.1%	8.2%	1,569
Nonresponse	25.0%	61.1%	13.9%	1,569
	Worse	Same	Better	
Kuomintang	3.5%	27.4%	69.1%	1,570
Democratic Progressive Party	27.0%	58.1%	14.9%	1,570
New Party	0.0%	50.0%	50.0%	1,570
People First Party	5.3%	42.1%	52.6%	1,570
Taiwan Solidarity Union	14.3%	78.6%	7.1%	1,570

Source: TEDS 2012, Election Study Center, National Cheng-chi University.

who have a preference for unification are less likely to claim that the ECFA is bad for Taiwan, whereas citizens who prefer independence are more likely to point out the costs to Taiwan's economy by evaluating the country as worse off as a result of the ECFA. It is not difficult to infer from these numbers that evaluation of the ECFA is very much influenced by the citizens' views on the independence/unification issue rather than the objective criteria of whether the economy is actually growing or not.

Another way to view the politicization of Taiwan's cross-Strait economic interaction is how different partisan identifiers evaluate the impact of the ECFA on the economy in general. Ignoring identifiers of the minor parties (regardless of whether they are Pan-Blue or Pan-Green), it is clear from the data in table 7.2 that the respondents' identification with the KMT or the DPP colors their views of the impact of the ECFA on the state of Taiwan's economy. About 85 percent of DPP supporters claim that the ECFA has made Taiwan's economy worse or kept it the same as before, while more than 69 percent of KMT supporters give a positive evaluation to the ECFA. Yet again, it is not too huge a leap to infer that the voters' evaluations of cross-Strait economic relations are more probably based on their partisanship rather than on objective measures of general economic performance and health.

The impact of partisan identification and preference on the independence/unification issue goes beyond just the evaluation of cross-Strait economic relations as symbolized by the ECFA; it also permeates and colors the Taiwan voters' evaluations of the state of the general economy as well as their evaluations of their own personal economic situations. Table 7.3 shows how different respondents divided along their independence/unification preferences evaluate the state of Taiwan's general economy. These figures correlate well with the evidence presented in table 7.3 regarding the ECFA's impact on Taiwan's economy. In general, voters who preferred independence for

TABLE 7.3. Evaluations of the Economy by Independence/Unification Preference

	Worse	Same	Better	*N*
Unify now	41.4%	27.6%	31.0%	1,783
Maintain status quo, unification later	34.6%	42.6%	22.9%	1,783
Maintain status quo and decide later	37.8%	43.9%	18.2%	1,783
Maintain status quo forever	43.3%	37.0%	19.6%	1,783
Maintain status quo, independence later	51.5%	34.0%	14.6%	1,783
Independence now	69.9%	25.7%	4.4%	1,783
Nonresponse	47.4%	47.4%	5.1%	1,783

Source: TEDS 2012, Election Study Center, National Cheng-chi University.

Taiwan were more likely to evaluate the state of the economy poorly, while unifiers and status quo respondents had a generally more positive view.

When approaching the voting booth, however, Taiwan voters take on the China factor in a more subtle manner. While the evaluations of the ECFA can be filtered through their stance for unification or independence in the future—hence, generating favorable or unfavorable views on the economic pact, respectively—a closer look at the data in table 7.4 reveals more about the intricacy of the electoral calculus. For those who rated the ECFA as beneficial for personal economy, three-quarters, or a majority, of respondents reported voting for the pro-unification KMT candidates Ma Ying-jeou and Wu Den-yih. Of those who viewed the ECFA negatively, only slightly half chose the DPP candidates Tsai Ing-wen and Su Jia-chyuan. The deciding voter group comprised those who believed that the economy is not affected either way by the ECFA. In this group, the KMT solicited much stronger support (46.7% versus 30.5% for the DPP). Even when including those who refused to respond, the opposition DPP was clearly unable to mount enough support by opposing the agreement (see chapter 6 on more analyses of ECFA and economic voting in Taiwan).

The evaluation of economy and cross-Strait economic ties cannot be totally separated from the preference regarding national status as well as from the partisan identification that points to the obvious politicization and polarization along this dimension. When using objective economic indicators, such as economic growth and trade statistics, the current statistics show that cross-Strait economic linkage is a boon for the Taiwan economy; for example, the huge trade surplus in favor of Taiwan that translates to huge capital inflows for Taiwan companies and to increasing foreign exchange reserves for Taiwan. It is also evident that Taiwan businesses benefit from investments in China, because the increasing amount of investment can be

TABLE 7.4. Evaluations of ECFA on the Personal Economy by Presidential Vote Decisions

	Worse	Same	Better	N
TSAI Ing-wen and SU Jia-chyuan	50.8%	30.5%	5.4%	1,569
MA Ying-jeou and WU Den-yih	18.1%	46.7%	75.0%	1,569
James SOONG and LIN Ruey-shiung	4.0%	1.8%	1.8%	1,569
Nonresponse	2.3%	1.1%	0.0%	1,569
Refused to answer	11.9%	8.0%	5.4%	1,569
Nonvoter	13.0%	11.9%	12.5%	1,569
	100.0%	100.0%	100.0%	

Source: TEDS 2012, Election Study Center, National Cheng-chi University.

interpreted to mean that there is still profit to be made despite some stories of failed investments and corporate bankruptcies.

Is Taiwan's economy more vulnerable and less secure as interaction with China increases? Since politics is an interplay of subjective and objective realities, the Taiwan voters' responses to this question largely depend on the ideological and partisan lenses they wear—where the voter stands depends on where they sit regarding their partisan identification.

Some Concluding Thoughts

This chapter explores the complex dynamics behind the relationship between cross-Strait economic ties and elections in Taiwan. Specifically, we examine how the burgeoning cross-Strait economic transactions affect the perceptions of the Taiwan voters on how they perceive the vulnerability and security of Taiwan, as well as the perils and profits of this economic interaction for Taiwan's destiny (and for their own economic welfare).

When addressing the question whether foreign policy has only negligible impact on voting decisions, Aldrich and his associates emphasize the accessibility of attitudes toward such policy and very importantly the distinct positions between parties and candidates (Aldrich, Sullivan, and Borgida 1989; Aldrich et al. 2006). Indeed, Taiwan voters are clearly concerned with the cross-Strait relations (and relatedly the economic interactions) between the two sides. The attitude toward this important factor is readily accessible to voters not only in how they view their future but also how they choose their government. That subtle calculus is reflected in party identification and perceptions of the national economy. From the empirical evidence we present in this chapter, we demonstrate that the connections between the issues of economic development and fostering cross-Strait relations, and subsequently how the voters cast their ballots, are convoluted. With the status quo option available, for instance, voters evade directly factoring in the choice of unification or independence (at least not immediately) when choosing the government but instead are inclined to resort to a party that can negotiate a fine balance as far as dealing with the Chinese government is concerned. For the Taiwan voters, being economically and politically isolated are clearly not good for the economy, yet getting too close to China could be inviting trouble. This view explains the shift in public opinion after the pro-unification KMT returned to power in 2008. Since then, more and more voters have come to believe that the pace of cross-Strait interactions has been too fast and that the government should put a brake on unification (see chapter 3). This is quite an about-face compared to the DPP administration in the 2000–2008 period.

In the course of our exploration, the evidence (at least in the current and short term) points to the ambivalence and seeming bifurcation of the Taiwan voters with respect to their assessment of the current state of cross-Strait economic ties and the strategies to deal with continuing engagement with China. These views are most definitely colored by how the voters place themselves in the dominant political and social cleavages in Taiwan as expressed by partisan identification and ideological positions. Consequently, as Clark and Tan (2012a, 102) suggest, questions can be raised about the long-term stability of closer economic relations while the views on sovereignty remain incompatible, thereby creating the paradox that the existing stability in cross-Strait relations may well be a portent of future tensions and instability.

References

Aldrich, John, Christopher Gelpi, Peter Feaver, Jason Reifler, and Kristin Thompson Sharp. 2006. "Foreign Policy and the Electoral Connection." *Annual Review of Political Science* 9:477–502.

Aldrich, John H., John L. Sullivan, and Eugene Borgida. 1989. "Foreign Affairs and Issue Voting: Do Presidential Candidates "Waltz before a Blind Audience?" *American Political Science Review* 83 (1): 123–41.

Clark, Cal, and Alexander C. Tan. 2011. *Taiwan's Political Economy: Meeting Challenges, Pursuing Progress.* Boulder, CO: Lynne Rienner.

Clark, Cal, and Alexander C. Tan. 2012a. "The Paradoxes in Taiwan's 'Two-Level Game' concerning Cross-Strait Relations." *American Journal of Chinese Studies* 19:89–104.

Clark, Cal, and Alexander C. Tan. 2012b. "Taiwan's Increasingly Boxed-in Economy: Economic Performance and Democratization." *Korea Observer* 43 (1): 113–43.

Gold, Thomas. 2009. "Taiwan in 2009: Eroding Landslide." *Asian Survey* 50: 65–75.

Huang, Minhua. 2008. "Polarized Politics, Divided Perceptions, and the Political Consequences in Taiwan." Paper presented at the International Conference on Polarized Politics in a Comparative Perspective—America, South Korea, and Taiwan, Taipei, January 26.

Liao, Dachi, and Eric Chen-hua Yu. 2008. "Are Taiwanese Politics Polarized? An Overview since 2000." Paper presented at the International Conference on Polarized Politics in a Comparative Perspective—America, South Korea, and Taiwan, Taipei, January 26.

Niou, Emerson. 2011. "The China Factor in Taiwan's Domestic Politics." Paper presented at the Conference on Democracy and Diplomacy in East Asia, University of Tokyo, Tokyo, September 16.

Wang, T. Y. 2005. "The Perception of Threats and Pragmatic Policy Choice: A Survey of Public Opinion in Taiwan." *Issues & Studies* 41 (1): 87–111.

Wang, T. Y., Lu-huei Chen, and Shu Keng. 2010. "Symbolic Politics, Self-Interests and Threat Perceptions: An Analysis of Taiwan Citizens' Views on Cross-Strait Economic Exchanges." In *Taiwan's Politics in the 21st Century: Changes and Challenges*, ed. Wei-chin Lee, 159–84. Singapore: World Scientific.

CHAPTER 8

Evaluation of Presidential Candidates' Personal Traits

Hung-chung Wang and Lu-huei Chen

In the study of political behavior, which factors affect an individual's voting behavior attract the most scholarly attention, and political scientists have expended much effort searching for the answer. Using a sociopsychological approach, the authors of *The American Voter* proposed a model called the funnel of causality to explain American voters' decision making. That model makes a distinction between the short-term factors—issue and candidate—and the long-term factor—party identification—on voting. The authors concluded that among all determinants, voters' party identification plays the most important role in determining vote choice (Campbell et al. 1960).

Although Campbell and his colleagues also suggested the importance of candidate evaluation on the vote, they did not put much emphasis on it. The candidate, in their model, is treated as an idiosyncratic and short-term factor and is dominated by the more enduring factors of party identification and issue. Nevertheless, their model is criticized for giving little credit to the importance of the candidate, since the stability of party identification and its impact on election results have diminished. Scholars have argued that candidate evaluation needs to be viewed as more meaningful than had been thought (Miller and Shanks 1996; Niemi and Weisberg 2001; Wattenberg 1991).

In Taiwan, the candidate has played a very important role because multiparty politics did not emerge until the 1980s. In one-party politics, the electorate can choose only individual candidates from the same party, so one must focus on the candidate rather than on the party. And much research suggests that even after Taiwan switched its party system from a one-party system to a multiparty system in the late 1980s, the candidate was still a critical factor in Taiwan's elections and significantly affected electoral outcomes at both the central and local levels (Cheng, Chen, and Liu 2005; Hawang 1996; Liang 1994; Shyu 1995; Yu 2003).

Nevertheless, that research did not systematically analyze the candidate factor to determine which factors influence the formation of people's candidate evaluations, whether the candidate factor still plays an important role in people's vote choice when party identification is also included in the analysis, and whether party competition affects individuals' political behavior. To correct this deficiency, in this chapter we will address these questions and attempt to provide answers.

We begin by reviewing how individuals form their candidate evaluation and introduce the criteria used for measuring candidates' qualities. Then we explain the sources of the data and the measurement of candidate qualities employed in this research, and then look at Taiwan voters' evaluations of the presidential candidates in the 1996, 2004, and 2012 elections. We then analyze the relationship between the people's perception of candidates' personal traits and their party identification, and whether candidate evaluation matters in vote choice.

The Formation of Candidate Evaluation and the Measurement of Candidates' Personal Qualities

How do citizens form their candidate evaluations? This issue has attracted substantial scholarly attention and two information-processing models are widely employed to explain it. The first one is the online model, which is impression-driven and contends that an individual's opinion is composed of evaluations formed as information is encountered. This opinion is then updated as new information arrives (Kim and Garrett 2012; Lodge, McGraw, and Stroh 1989; Zaller 1992). The second model is memory-based and maintains that individuals form their own opinion when a judgment is needed. Individuals then retrieve the relevant information from their long-term memory, forming a judgment based on what comes to mind (Kim and Garrett 2012; Lodge, McGraw, and Stroh 1989; Zaller 1992). Both models are considered valid, but there is no consensus on which model is more powerful in explaining an individual's evaluation formation. However, scholars generally agree that the assessment of candidates' professional and personal qualities has a significant impact on voters' final voting decision (Flanigan and Zingale 1998; Niemi and Weisberg 1993; Rahn et al. 1990).

To be more precise, as suggested by Miller and Shanks, "evaluations of a candidate concerning a specific personal quality presumably represent the accumulation of many impressions, both positive and negative, of a candidate" (1996, 417). In other words, candidate evaluation is a collection of an individual's perceptions of a candidate's personal traits. This evaluation may be affected by various influential sources and general attributions derived from individuals' own partisanship. In addition, candidate trait may be more salient under certain conditions, such as in times of crisis like facing a terrorist threat (Merolla and Zechmeister 2009).

Which personal traits are adopted by voters to evaluate a candidate? Previous studies of U.S. voters may offer some ideas on this issue for the case of Taiwan. The authors of *The American Voter* examined citizens' evaluations of candidates in the 1952 and 1956 U.S. presidential elections based on three types of personal traits: record and experience, abilities, and personal characteristics (Campbell et al. 1960). These measurements were also employed by Lewis-Beck et al. (2008) to test peoples' perception of the candidates running in the 2000 and 2004 U.S. presidential elections. Kinder and his colleagues categorized respondents' answers to the question about the best definition of an ideal president into two kinds of "abstract qualities." The first quality is personality: citizens' "judgments about what an ideal president should and should not be like as a person." The second kind is performance: "what an ideal president should do or should avoid doing while in office" (1980, 317). Their research findings demonstrate that competence and trust are the most important qualities for an ideal president. Furthermore, the well-educated respondents considered that an ideal president is competent, and they expected a president to be an "exemplary manager," whereas citizens with lower educational levels claimed that "likeability and personal morality" are the most important qualities that an ideal president should possess, and they expect a good president to be an "exemplary friend" (Kinder et al. 1980, 320).

Miller, Wattenberg, and Malanchuk (1986) proposed five generic dimensions for candidate evaluation: competence, integrity, reliability, charisma, and personal attributes. Their research suggests that these five dimensions influence individuals' candidate evaluation, and among them, competence plays the largest role. In addition, Miller and Shanks (1996, 420–25) employed nine survey questions to investigate U.S. voters' perceptions of the two candidates, George H. W. Bush and Bill Clinton, in the 1992 presidential election. These survey questions examined respondents' evaluations of the following candidate qualities: "cares about people like me," "inspiring," "compassionate," "gets things done," "intelligent," "a leader," "knowledgeable," "honest," and "moral." However, according to their analysis of the election, Americans' vote choice was not strongly determined by their perception of the candidates' personal traits. Evaluation of candidate qualities made only a small contribution to Clinton's victory (Miller and Shanks 1996).

Although scholars may use different personal traits to measure citizens' candidate evaluation, we consider that the measurement proposed by Kinder et al. (1980) is a very reasonable one due to its generality. As noted earlier, Kinder et al. simply divided the candidates' personal traits into two types: personality and performance. This abstract classification can include in the analysis personal traits used by other scholars and is easier for conducting further research. Therefore, by following the measurement established by Kinder et al., we used these two personal qualities—personality and performance—as the major dimensions with which to investigate the Taiwan public's evaluation of candidates in the 1996, 2004, and 2012 presidential elections.

Data and Measurement for Taiwan's Presidential Candidates

As mentioned earlier, the candidate factor has, for a long time, been considered to be a crucial variable influencing Taiwan citizens' voting behavior. Compared to party identification and issue, systematic study of the candidate factor has been rare in Taiwan. Moreover, previous research on candidate factors focused on single elections (Cheng, Chen, and Liu 2005; Hawang 2005; Yu 2003). It does not offer us an overall picture of candidate evaluation in Taiwan. Nor does this literature suggest a pattern for how the island's citizens evaluate their candidates. Because Taiwan citizens generally pay more attention to candidate traits in presidential elections, candidate-oriented voting tends to be more significant, a political phenomenon echoing the observation of Tverdova (2011). Therefore, instead of using the results of a single election, we will focus on the candidates who ran for Taiwan's presidency in 1996, 2004, and 2012, and especially on the winners of these three elections—Lee Teng-hui, Chen Shui-bian, and Ma Ying-jeou—observing the change and continuity in candidate evaluation after Taiwan's democratization.[1]

To achieve this goal, we used data from surveys conducted for the three elections mentioned above.[2] Nevertheless, we found that no survey question dealing with candidate evaluation was employed consistently in public opinion polls in Taiwan, so making a comparative study via identical survey questions was impracticable. As a consequence, we decided to adopt the measurement established by Kinder and his colleagues (1980) to investigate citizen perceptions of candidates' personal traits. We simply divided a candidate's traits into two groups—personal character and competence—and used them to determine how individuals form their candidate evaluation. Furthermore, some scholars have suggested that citizens' candidate evaluation is conditioned by their party identification (Baker, Lawrence, and Tavits 2006; Campbell et al. 1960; Miller and Shanks 1996), so we investigated the relationship between individuals' perceptions of a candidate's personal traits and their partisanship to see whether that was true in this case. Furthermore, we also examined whether this perception was significantly associated with people's vote choice in the presidential elections. The survey questions employed from the 1996, 2004, and 2012 public opinion polls can be found in appendix 8.A1. We employed these survey questions to determine which candidate had an advantage in certain personal traits.

Candidate Evaluation in the 1996, 2004, and 2012 Presidential Elections

The 1996 presidential election represents a very important milestone in Taiwan's process of democratization because it was the first direct election for the national leader. The leading candidate in this election was the incumbent president, Lee Teng-hui. He ran for president in 1996, after having held office for eight and a half years, and chose Lien Chan, who was the premier during that time, as his running mate.[3] That Taiwan citizens could directly choose their chief executive came about because Lee had decided to adopt direct elections as the new electoral system for selecting the president.

Lee was born in Taiwan in 1923 and grew up while Taiwan was ruled by Japan (1895–1945). He was educated in Japanese schools and was thus strongly influenced by Japanese culture. He then studied in the United States, receiving his master's degree from Iowa State University in 1953 and his PhD from Cornell University in 1968, both in agricultural economics. While Lee was an economist with the Joint Commission on Rural Reconstruction in 1971, he was recommended to President Chiang Ching-kuo for a position in the cabinet and became its youngest member at that time. He then achieved remarkable success in his political career, being appointed to several important positions, including mayor of Taipei City in 1978 and governor of Taiwan Province in 1981. Most important, President Chiang nominated Lee to be his vice president in 1984.

Lee is a unique political figure. After Chiang died in January 1988, Lee succeeded him as president of Republic of China (Taiwan) and chairman of the ruling party, the Kuomintang. Undoubtedly, Lee was an excellent political strategist. He was low-key while serving as the governor of Taiwan Province and as Chiang's vice president, but as president Lee displayed his skill at statecraft by gradually expelling his opponents—the nonmainstream faction of the KMT—from certain important positions in the central government, army, and ruling party, thus consolidating his power.

While Taiwan citizens possess various ethnic identities and have different partisan affiliation, as chapter 3 points out, they commonly have had a unique psychological connection with Lee. Members of the Minnan and Hakka groups liked and felt close to Lee because he was the first president who had been born in Taiwan. Mainlanders also supported him early in his term because he was promoted by Chiang. This unique psychological attachment was commonly known as the Lee Teng-hui Complex (Shyu 1995, 1998).

However, Lee's promotion of Taiwanization provoked some segments of the KMT who believe that Taiwan should maintain a close relationship with China. Angered by Lee's localization policy, these politicians left the KMT and formed the New Party. In order to confront this nonmainstream faction, Lee needed help from central government outsiders. He thus recruited certain local politicians to fill the vacancies in the executive and legislative branches of the central government; however, many of these local politicians were corrupt. As a result, even though Lee was called the father of Taiwan democracy, he was criticized for spreading "black and gold" politics in Taiwan.

In 1996, Lee was the official nominee of the KMT. Failing to secure the support of the KMT, the former president of the Judicial Yuan, Lin Yang-kang,[4] and the former president of the Control Yuan, Chen Lu-an, both decided to leave the party and run as independents in Taiwan's first direct presidential election. The Democratic Progressive Party, the first major opposition party in Taiwan, nominated Peng Ming-min, an exile who had been an opponent of the authoritarian regime of Chiang Kai-shek. Although Lee had to compete with these very well known and capable opponents, he defeated them by a huge margin.[5] Indeed, Lee was the only presidential candidate in Taiwan's democratic history who was able to garner electoral support from voters of different partisan affiliations and ethnic backgrounds. A survey shows that, in 1996 presidential election, Lee received 70.6 percent of the votes from members of the Minnan group and also won the majority support of the mainlander (51.2%) and the Hakka (79.4%) voters (Hsieh 1995). While 94 percent of the KMT identifiers supported Lee, close to 30 percent of the DPP supporters also voted for him in Taiwan's first democratic election.

How did the Taiwan public evaluate the candidates running for the president in 1996? As shown in table 8.1, candidates' personal character was measured on the basis of the respondents' perceptions of the following: affinity with the people, leadership, integrity, trustworthiness, and understanding the needs of the people. The measures of competence were the candidates' ability to deal with economic development, ethnic harmony, law and order, and peaceful development of cross-Strait relations. Respondents were asked to judge which candidate had the advantage over the other opponents with regard to these characteristics. Table 8.1 shows that then incumbent president Lee received the most positive evaluation, both in terms of personal character and competence, than the other candidates. Specifically, 66.2 percent of the respondents believed that Lee was the candidate who had the strongest leadership qualities. In addition, Lee also received higher ratings for trustworthiness, affinity with the people, and understanding the needs of the people. The only exception was the item of integrity because only 10.7 percent of respondents felt that Lee had a better record than the other candidates. However, it is worth noting that most respondents (50.5%) thought there was no difference among candidates regarding their level of integrity.

Lee's advantage was also demonstrated by respondents' perception of candidates' competence. Among the measurements of competence, 63.9 percent of respondents said Lee was the candidate who knew how to promote Tai-

TABLE 8.1. Candidate Evaluation in the 1996 Presidential Election

Personal Character	Chen	Lee	Peng	Lin	ND*	Total	N
Affinity with the people	24.2%	40.6	3.7	8.2	23.2	100.0	1,396
Leadership	1.5%	66.2	6.8	3.1	22.4	100.0	1,396
Integrity	24.9%	10.7	9.6	4.3	50.5	100.0	1,396
Trustworthiness	10.9%	43.6	6.7	5.7	33.2	100.0	1,396
Understands the needs of the people	13.2%	35.5	9.0	5.3	36.9	100.0	1,396

Competence	Chen	Lee	Peng	Lin	ND	Total	N
Economic development	1.6%	63.9	3.9	3.3	27.4	100.0	1,396
Ethnic harmony	14.8%	39.6	5.7	6.8	33.2	100.0	1,396
Law and order	6.4%	41.4	4.8	10.9	36.5	100.0	1,396
Peaceful development in cross-Strait relations	7.4%	45.3	2.8|	8.0|	36.5	100.0	1,396

Source: Hsieh 1995.

Notes: 1. Entries are row percentages. 2. ND = no difference. 3. Chen = Chen Lu-an; Lee = Le Teng-hui; Peng = Peng Ming-min; Lin = Lin Yang-kang.

wan's economic development. Moreover, Lee was also considered the candidate who could deal with peaceful development of cross-Strait relations, law and order, and ethnic harmony better than the other candidates. In short, among the candidates campaigning for the 1996 presidential election, Lee Teng-hui had a much higher positive evaluation than his opponents.

Taiwan's first party turnover took place in 2000 after the DPP candidate, Chen Shui-bian, won the 2000 presidential election. Chen was born in 1950 to a poor farming family in southern Taiwan. Although lacking family financial support during his youth, Chen did very well at school and entered the law school at National Taiwan University in 1970. He passed the bar examinations even before completing the law school program and became the youngest lawyer in Taiwan's history. Chen had a very successful career as a lawyer, and his first connection with politics was defending the participants in the Formosa Incident in 1980.[6] Afterward, he turned to politics professionally, winning a seat on the Taipei City Council in 1981 and then becoming a member of Taiwan's parliament, the Legislative Yuan, in 1989. His victory in the first mayoral election in the capital city, Taipei, in 1994 was a critical achievement for Chen and the DPP because he was the first non-KMT mayor since 1972.

Chen was an extremely popular politician. He had the courage to do things that traditional politicians had not dared to do. For instance, he appointed young people as government officials and improved the administration of the Taipei city government. In addition, he was also the first politician to dress up as such characters as Superman and Santa Claus to show his affinity with the people on certain occasions. In short, Chen was a new type of politician and was regarded as the symbol of the opposition party, even though he was also criticized by his opponents for his bold actions.

Although Chen was a quite popular mayor and his job approval rating exceeded 70 percent in his first term, he was defeated by Ma Ying-jeou in the 1998 mayoral election. Chen then decided to run for president as the DPP candidate in the 2000 election, defeating Hsu Hsin-liang, the former DPP chairman, in the primary. Chen eventually took advantage of the split in the KMT in the 2000 election, becoming the first non-KMT president in history.[7] Chen, however, garnered a low approval rating in his first term as a result of the economic downturn, the increasing tension between Taiwan and China, and the partisan antagonism between the Pan-Blue and the Pan-Green camps. Moreover, his opponents in the 2000 presidential election, Lien Chan and James Soong, who were leaders of the Pan-Blue Alliance, formed a formidable alliance as running mates in the 2004 presidential election. As a result, it was a general belief that Chen would lose his reelection bid.

However, a mysterious assassination attempt against Chen's life occurred 19 hours before the polls opened, giving him a needed boost, and Chen was reelected by a historically small margin of 0.2 percent of the total votes. Supporter of the Pan-Blue Alliance suspected that the assassination attempt was faked by Chen's followers in order to gain sympathy votes. Thus, Lien and Soong refused to concede. Instead, they challenged the electoral outcome in court.

To assess citizens' candidate evaluation in the 2004 presidential election, five questions in the TEDS2004P survey were used: getting things done, integrity, sincerity and trustworthiness, understanding the needs of people, and affinity with the people. In addition, 10 traits served as measurements of candidate competence: ethnic harmony, political stability, economic development, eliminating black and gold politics, Taiwan's international status, democratic reform, law and order, peaceful development of cross-Strait relations, the unemployment problem, and education reform.

Table 8.2 shows how the Taiwan public evaluated the candidates running for president in 2004. The incumbent president, Chen, received more positive evaluations than Lien in terms of personal character except for sincerity and trustworthiness. Among these indicators, Chen had a significant advan-

TABLE 8.2. Candidate Evaluation in the 2004 Presidential Election

Personal Character	Chen	Lien	ND*	Total	N
Gets things done	48.4%	11.3	40.3	100.0	1823
Integrity	23.6%	14.0	62.5	100.0	1823
Sincerity and trustworthiness	21.0%	23.3	55.7	100.0	1823
Understands the needs of people	31.4%	12.7	55.9	100.0	1823
Affinity with the people	46.9%	9.8	43.3	100.0	1823

Competence	Chen	Lien	ND	Total	N
Ethnic harmony	21.2%	28.6	50.3	100.0	1823
Political stability	19.5%	25.5	55.0	100.0	1823
Economic development	13.2%	32.6	54.2	100.0	1823
Eliminate black and gold politics	41.3%	8.0	50.7	100.0	1823
Taiwan's international status	20.3%	21.8	57.9	100.0	1823
Democratic reform	31.2%	11.3	5.2	100.0	1823
Law and order	17.9%	16.4	65.7	100.0	1823
Peaceful development in cross-Strait relations	9.4%	39.5	51.1	100.0	1823
Unemployment problem	11.4%	25.4	63.2	100.0	1823
Education reform	9.8%	24.6	65.6	100.0	1823

Source: Hawang 2003.

Notes: 1. Entries are row percentages. 2. ND = no difference. 3. Chen = Chen Shui-bian; Lien = Lien Chan.

tage over Lien for getting things done and for affinity with the people. The results are different when we look at respondents' perceptions of Chen's and Lien's competence. Respondents tended to give Lien a more positive evaluation than Chen, whose only advantages were in eliminating black and gold politics, democratic reform, and law and order. Among these measurements, respondents significantly agreed that compared with Chen, Lien was more likely to promote peaceful development of cross-Strait relations, since they knew that the DPP government had failed to maintain harmonious relations with mainland China.

The DPP's eight-year dominance of the central government began with Chen Shui-bian's victory in 2000 and ended with the election of Ma Ying-jeou in 2008. Ma was born in Hong Kong in 1950 and then moved to Taiwan. Both of his parents were officials of the KMT and public servants in the central government. Ma is a superstar of the Pan-Blue camp and has several advantages over most Taiwan politicians. First, Ma has had much experience as a civil servant. Immediately after receiving his SJD from Harvard Law School in 1981, Ma returned to Taiwan and served as deputy director of the First Bureau of the Presidential Office and as President Chiang Ching-kuo's English interpreter. In 1988 Ma was appointed to the chair of the Research, Development and Evaluation Commission, becoming the youngest cabinet member in the ROC government. He then was named to be deputy minister of the Mainland Affairs Council, the institute in charge of cross-Strait relations, and minister of justice. In 1998, he was elected mayor of Taipei City in his first election, in which he defeated the incumbent, Chen Shui-bian, which was an indication of Ma's popularity. Second, like John F. Kennedy, Ma is a good-looking man and also is an alumnus of Harvard University. His civility has won him the middle class's support, particularly that of women. However, Ma was accused of being a spy for the KMT government while he was studying in the United States, a charge he firmly denied, and has also been criticized by opposition parties for his conservative political stance.

Although Ma was questioned for his status as a U.S. permanent resident during the campaign period, he easily defeated the DPP candidate, Frank Hsieh, in the 2008 presidential election. Ma's landslide victory brought the KMT back to power.[8] However, he faced the same problem that had plagued Chen Shui-bian in Chen's first term: Taiwan's economic downturn. Although cross-Strait relations became more peaceful after Ma took office, that achievement did not help his approval rating. In 2012, he was challenged by two opposition-party chairpersons, Tsai Ing-wen of the DPP and James Soong of the People First Party.

Table 8.3 shows the Taiwan public's evaluation of candidates in the 2012 presidential election. In the TEDS2012 survey data, the measurements of a candidate's personal character included the respondents' perceptions of whether the candidate "understands the needs of people," "ever made you feel angry," "ever made you feel afraid," and "ever made you feel hopeful." As for candidate competence, we examined how respondents evaluated candidates' capability, whether they are "able to protect Taiwan's interests," and whether they can "maintain cross-Strait peace."

As data in table 8.3 shows, respondents are more likely to see Ma as a politician who knows citizens' needs, acts in a way to not make citizens' worry, and presents the country with a hopeful future. While similar assessments in these respects are also applied to Tsai, Ma had a significant advantage over Tsai in terms of perceived competence. In particular, about 60 percent of the respondents believed that Ma could better handle the issue related to cross-Strait relations.

Even though most citizens were not satisfied with his performance as the country's president, Ma was able to defeat his opponents in the 2012 presidential election, Tsai and Soong. If candidate evaluation does influence individuals' vote choice, we may make the inference that Ma's advantage in dealing with the relationship between Taiwan and China was the determining factor leading to his victory in 2012.[9]

Perceptions of Candidate Personal Traits versus Party Identification

After examining how Taiwan citizens evaluated the candidates running for the 1996, 2004, and 2012 presidential elections, we went further and inves-

TABLE 8.3. Candidate Evaluation in the 2012 Presidential Election

Personal Character		Ma	Tsai	ND*	Total	N
Understands the needs of people	%	36.9	32.4	30.8	100.0	1,826
Not make you feel unhappy	%	22.6	**33.8**	43.6	100.0	1,826
Not make you worry	%	34.0	26.8	39.2	100.0	1,826
Makes you feel hopeful for the future	%	16.9	**26.3**	56.8	100.0	1,826
Competence		Ma	Tsai	ND	Total	N
Capability	%	40.4	31.5	28.0	100.0	1,826
Protect Taiwan's interests	%	40.7	31.2	28.1	100.0	1,826
Maintain cross-Strait peace	%	**59.4**	13.2	27.4	100.0	1,826

Source: Chu 2011.

Notes: 1. Entries are row percentages. 2. ND = no difference. 3. Ma = Ma Ying-jeou; Tsai = Tsai Ing-wen.

tigated the relationship between the perception of the candidates' personal traits and respondents' party identification since the latter is treated as the most crucial factor affecting people's political behavior.

Petrocik (1996) proposed the theory of issue ownership, suggesting that each political party has its own advantages in handling certain issues. For example, the Republican Party is positively identified with issues associated with taxes, whereas the Democratic Party has a good reputation in dealing with issues related to social welfare. According to Petrocik, candidates focus their campaign efforts on these issues to win voter support, and voters will vote for the candidate if they think the party's issues are important to them.

Based on Petrocik's theory, Hayes (2005) then developed the theory of trait ownership to explain the origins of candidate trait perception, examining the connection between candidate traits, party issues, and strategic candidate behavior. Hayes pointed out that American voters tend to connect the issues owned by a political party with their evaluation of the candidates' personal traits, suggesting that the evaluation of candidate's personal trait is conditioned by party label. For example, the Democrats tend to be regarded as more compassionate and empathetic than their counterparts, whereas GOP candidates are expected to be strong leaders with high moral standards. Thus, the winning strategy for a candidate is to trespass on his or her opponents' trait territory (Hayes 2005). Although research shows that partisan identifiers tend to evaluate candidates of their own party more favorably (Campbell et al. 1960), Hayes's study reminds us that some candidates may be viewed as superior or inferior in certain personal traits because of their party labels. In short, perceptions of candidate personal traits can be partisan.

Indeed, scholarly research has demonstrated that the theory of issue ownership can be equally applied to the case of Taiwan because major parties on the island have divergent positions on a number of important issues. For example, because the KMT and the DPP have opposite views on the issue of cross-Strait relations the KMT is generally perceived as a pro-unification party and the DPP a party for Taiwan independence (Hsieh and Niou 1996; Lin, Chu, and Hinich 1996). Similarly, the public tends to view the KMT as a pro-stability party and the DPP as a party associated with political reform (Hsieh and Niou 1996; Sheng 2007; and Wang 2012). In general, Taiwan citizens tend to view the KMT as superior in managing issues related to the economy, education, and cross-Strait relations. Alternatively, gender equality, social welfare, and governance at the local level are the winning issues for the DPP (Chang 2010). Interestingly, even though Taiwan citizens experienced economic hardship during Ma's first term, they still consider the KMT as competent to manage Taiwan's economy (Sheng 2013).

Why do the KMT and the DPP own these particular issues? In the case of the economy, Taiwan enjoyed its longest economic boom when the KMT presidents, Chiang and Lee, held office, but the country suffered an economic downturn when the DPP was in power. As a result, the public tends to think that the KMT is more competent to manage the national economy. On cross-Strait relations, the DPP views China as the main threat to Taiwan's sovereignty and national security while Beijing leaders also strongly oppose the DPP's pro-independence stance. Cross-Strait relations were tense as a result during the 2000–2008 period when the DPP was in power. Because the KMT's official position is for unification and the Ma administration adopted a policy of rapprochement toward China, the relationship between Taipei and Beijing was peaceful during Ma's presidency. As a result, the KMT is considered as more competent to handle Taiwan's relationship with China. Regarding the reform issue, the KMT, as a long-term ruling party, has an extensive record of corruption. The DPP politicians, especially in their early stage of career as city mayors or county magistrates, were known for their rectitude and determination for reform. Hence, political reform is a DPP-owned issue.

Therefore, we would like to investigate whether the theory of trait ownership is also applicable in the case of Taiwan. We not only examine whether all respondents, no matter their party affiliations, agree that certain candidates are superior in some personal characteristics, but we also assess whether there is a direct link between the parties' issue ownership and the Taiwan citizens' perceptions of candidates' personal traits.

As noted above, Lee Teng-hui overwhelmed his opponents in the 1996 competition in all respondents' evaluations of personal traits, both personal character and competence. Among these personal character evaluations, some of them are worthy of further analysis. Figure 8.1 illustrates how respondents affiliated with different parties evaluated the candidates' leadership in 1996. Regardless of their party affiliation, all respondents thought that Lee had the strongest leadership compared to the other candidates. It is not a surprise that the KMT supporters (88.8%) endorsed their chairman's leadership, but even non-KMT supporters acknowledged that Lee was superior as a national leader: 49.0 percent of the DPP and 47.5 percent of the NP respondents had a positive view of Lee's leadership. This result demonstrates the advantage that the incumbent chief executive has.

Respondents' perceptions of the 1996 presidential candidates' capability in handling economic development are presented in figure 8.2. The pattern is very similar to that for leadership. Lee's capability in dealing with economic issues was also approved by respondents from different parties. A

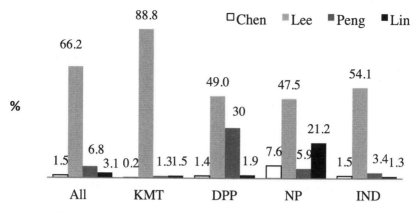

Fig. 8.1. Trait: Leadership in 1996. *Source:* Hsieh 1995.

majority of the DPP (54.8%) and the NP (50.0%) supporters also thought that Lee was the best candidate to handle the national economy, suggesting that the KMT candidate, Lee, had the advantage on this issue. Lee also had the advantage in regard to the issue of cross-Strait relations. According to figure 8.3, the majority of the Taiwan public agreed that Lee was more likely to manage the relationship between Taiwan and China well. Among all partisans, the KMT and the DPP supporters and the independents reported that Lee would be better able to manage peaceful cross-Strait relations than his opponents. The NP partisans were the only exception: they claimed that Lin was the candidate who would be more competent in this respect. The only personal trait for which Lee did not have an advantage was integrity (figure 8.4). Chen won more endorsements among all citizens in integrity. In the Taiwan public's mind, Lee was not the most incorruptible candidate. Furthermore, more KMT party members gave Chen credit for this personal trait instead of Lee (21.4% vs. 19.2%), showing that respondents seemed to have a strong impression that Lee was connected to black and gold politics while in office.

According to the above analysis, the 1996 presidential election displayed Lee's dominant advantage in the Taiwan public's perception of the candidates' personal traits. However, the 2004 election is another story. Only two candidates represented two party coalitions in the run for the presidency, and those two candidates had their own advantages with regard to personal traits, as we already mentioned above. As figure 8.5 shows, Chen had the advantage for the trait "getting things done." Regardless of their party identification, respondents reported that Chen was more likely than Lien to get

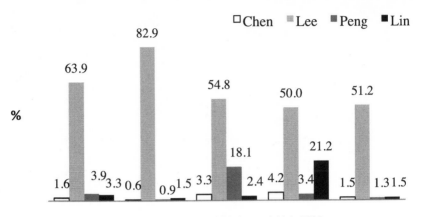

Fig. 8.2. Trait: Economic development in 1996. *Source:* Hsieh 1995.

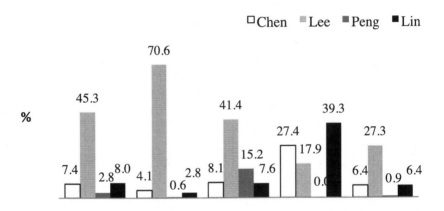

Fig. 8.3. Trait: Peaceful development in cross-Strait relations in 1996. *Source:* Hsieh 1995.

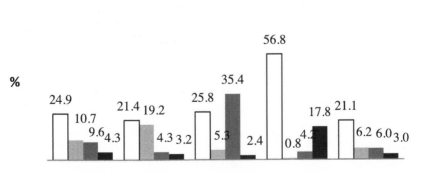

Fig. 8.4. Trait: Integrity in 1996. *Source:* Hsieh 1995.

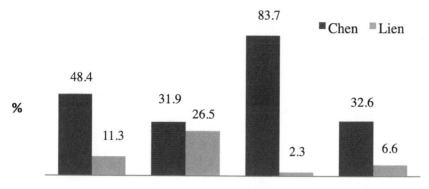

Fig. 8.5. Trait: Get things done in 2004. *Source:* Hawang 2003.

things done. Most important, the percentage of Pan-Blue supporters who thought that Chen was more likely to fulfill the president's duty was higher than that of those who thought that Lien was (31.9% vs. 26.5%).

Differential public assessment of economic development is reflected in figure 8.6, which shows that the Pan-Blue and the Pan-Green supporters gave their candidates a more positive assessment on this issue (67.0% and 31.6%). Independents gave Lien a higher rating than Chen (22.8% vs. 7.2%). In other words, Lien was considered to be more capable of handling the issues associated with the national economy. Respondents may have formed this perception because Lien had been the premier of the Executive Yuan under Lee Teng-hui and had served as the country's vice president. Lien's term of office also coincided with the period during which Taiwan experienced a booming economy. As a result, Lien had the advantage on this issue. Figure 8.7 illustrates the respondents' perception of the candidates' ability to deal with cross-Strait relations, showing a pattern quite similar to that of figure 8.6. With the exception of the Pan-Green identifiers, the Taiwan public all agreed that Lien owned this trait. Actually, among the Pan-Green supporters, the proportion of those who endorsed Chen only slightly exceeded that who endorsed Lien (22.7% vs. 21.5%). Obviously, this issue was a weak point for Chen, and citizens did not believe he was capable of handling this issue.

The DPP candidate's advantage shows up in matters of the elimination of black and gold politics and democratic reform. According to figures 8.8 and 7.9, respondents generally thought that Chen was more capable than Lien in dealing with these two issues (41.3% vs. 8.0% in elimination of black and gold politics and 31.2% vs.11.3 % in democratic reform). Particularly among the Pan-Blue supporters, the proportion of those who endorsed Chen as being capable of eliminating black and gold politics is almost the

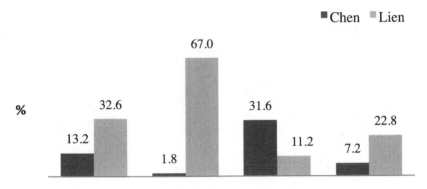

Fig. 8.6. Trait: Economic development in 2004. *Source:* Hawang 2003.

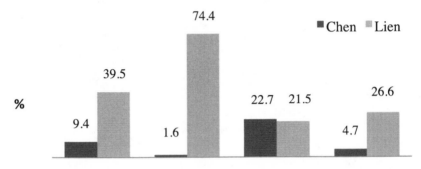

Fig. 8.7. Trait: Peaceful development in cross-Strait relations in 2004. *Source:* Hawang 2003.

same as that of those who thought Lien was, suggesting that the KMT candidate's weakness was associated with the issue of corruption. The KMT candidate's predominance on the cross-Strait relations issue is also shown in figure 8.10. In addition to Ma winning all respondents' endorsements, both the KMT partisans and independents agreed that he was more capable than Tsai of handling peaceful relations between Taiwan and China. Tsai did not have an advantage on this issue even among her supporters.

On the basis of the figures presented above, we find that party's issue ownership is highly associated with voters' perceptions of candidate personal traits. Respondents generally reported that the KMT candidates—Lee, Lien, and Ma—were more capable of dealing with the KMT-owned issues—economic development and cross-Strait relations—than their opponents. On the other hand, DPP candidates have an advantage on the issue of reform, including democratic reform and elimination of black and gold politics. In short, our research findings suggest that on certain issues some

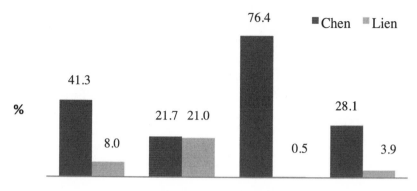

Fig. 8.8. Trait: Eliminate black and gold politics in 2004. *Source:* Hawang 2003.

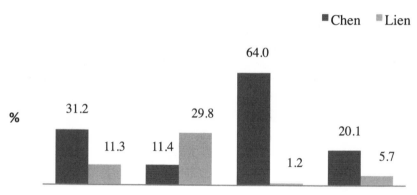

Fig. 8.9. Trait: Democratic Reform in 2004. *Source:* Hawang (2003).

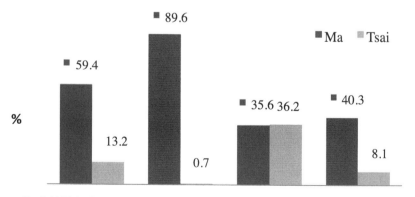

Fig. 8.10. Trait: Cross-Strait peace in 2012. *Source:* Chu 2011.

candidates are superior to their opponents because of their party's ownership of the issues.

Perceptions of Candidate Personal Traits vs. Vote Choice

Since the candidate factor is viewed as one of the three most critical factors affecting people's voting behavior, we next focus on whether these perceptions of candidate personal traits have a significant impact on the Taiwan public's vote choice. Tables 8.4, 8.5, and 8.6 show the relationship between vote choices and citizens' perceptions of a candidate's capability of handling peaceful development of cross-Strait relations, which is the main political cleavage in Taiwan. Data in these tables suggest that the perception of candidates' personal traits did not significantly correspond to vote choice in the 1996, 2004, and 2012 presidential election. For example, among the DPP supporters in table 8.4, a majority (50.0%) of those who considered Lee to be the best one to handle the issue still voted for the DPP candidate, Peng. The vast majority of KMT identifiers, no matter which candidate won their endorsement, decided to support Lee in the 1996 election. The only exception was for partisan independents: they were the only group whose vote choice corresponded highly with their evaluations of a candidate's capacity to handle issues related to cross-Strait relations. Respondents of the 2004 and 2012 survey behaved in a similar way, as data in tables 8.5 and 8.6 show as the vast majority of KMT and DPP supporters made their electoral decisions based on partisan affiliations. The results appear to show that party identification still played a more important role than candidate evaluation in affecting vote choice. In fact, the relationship between vote choice and such candidate traits as boosting economic development, eliminating black and gold politics, and promoting democratic reform are very similar. The empirical findings are not shown here due to space limitation.

Moreover, as tables 8.5 and 8.6 show, Pan-Green supporters are more likely to be split on the question of which candidate is most competent in dealing with cross-Strait relationships than Pan-Blue identifiers. This can be explained by the theory of issue ownership, which suggests that each political party has advantages on certain issues. Since the KMT is perceived as being more competent to handle Taiwan's economic development and relationship with China, it is not surprising that Pan-Green supporters are more divided in this regard. However, they still make their vote choices based on partisan affiliations even though they credit Pan-Blue candidates with a stronger ability to deal with cross-Strait relationships.

Overall, the empirical evidence from the 1996, 2004, and 2012 presidential elections allows us to draw the following conclusion: the effect of candidate evaluation on vote choice is not as significant as that of party identification. Taiwan citizens' electoral decisions are mainly guided by partisan affiliation rather than by evaluation of candidate personal traits.

Conclusion

This chapter has explored how the Taiwan public evaluates candidate quality. We focused on candidates running in the 1996, 2004, and 2012 presidential elections, investigating people's perception of the candidates' personal traits.

TABLE 8.4. Perception of Peaceful Development in Cross-Strait Relations versus Vote Choice in 1996

KMT		Vote choice				
		Chen	Lee	Peng	Lin	Total
Personal	Chen	4 (20.0%)	15 (75.0)	0 (0.0)	1 (5.0)	20 (100.0)
trait	Lee	3 (0.9)	311 (95.7)	3 (0.9)	8 (2.5)	325 (100.0)
preference|	Peng	0 (0.0)	1 (100.0)	0 (0.0)	0 (0.0)	1 (100.0)
	Lin	0 (0.0)	8 (80.0)	0 (0.0)	2 (20.0)	10 (100.0)

DPP		Vote choice				
		Chen	Lee	Peng	Lin	Total
Personal	Chen	3 (18.8)	5 (31.3)	8 (50.0)	0 (0.0)	16 (100.0)
trait	Lee	2 (3.1)	26 (40.6)	32 (50.0)	4 (6.3)	64 (100.0)
preference	Peng	0 (0.0)	2 (6.3)	30 (93.8)	0 (0.0)	32 (100.0)
	Lin	0 (0.0)	3 (25.0)	8 (66.7)	1 (8.3)	12 (100.0)

NP		Vote choice				
		Chen	Lee	Peng	Lin	Total
Personal	Chen	11 (40.7)	4 (14.8)	0 (0.0)	12 (44.4)	27 (100.0)
trait	Lee	3 (18.8)	4 (25.0)	1 (6.3)	8 (50.0)	16 (100.0)
preference	Peng	0 (0.0)	0 (0.0)	0 (0.0)	0 (0.0)	0 (0.0)
	Lin	3 (8.8)	1 (2.9)	0 (0.0)	30 (88.2)	34 (100.0)

IND		Vote choice				
		Chen	Lee	Peng	Lin	Total
Personal	Chen	10 (43.5)	10 (43.5)	1 (4.3)	2 (8.7)	23 (100.0)
trait	Lee	7 (7.4)	78 (82.1)	9 (9.5)	1 (1.1)	95 (100.0)
preference	Peng	0 (0.0)	0 (0.0)	0 (0.0)	1 (100.0)	1 (100.0)
	Lin	3 (18.8)	2 (12.5)	3 (18.8)	8 (50.0)	16 (100.0)

Source: Hsieh 1995.

Notes: 1. Chen = Chen Lu-an; Lee = Le Teng-hui; Peng = Peng Ming-min; Lin = Lin Yang-kang. 2. KMT = Kuomintang; DPP = Democratic Progressive Party; NP = New Party; IND = partisan independent.

TABLE 8.5 Perception of Peaceful Development of Cross-Strait Relations versus Vote Choice in 2004

Pan-Blue PID		Vote choice		
Personal		**Chen**	**Lien**	**Total**
trait	**Chen**	2 (28.6)	5 (71.4)	7 (100.0)
preference	**Lien**	5 (1.4)	358 (98.6)	363 (100.0)
Pan-Green PID		*Vote choice*		
Personal		**Chen**	**Lien**	**Total**
trait	**Chen**	123 (99.2)	1 (0.8)	124 (100.0)
preference	**Lien**	97 (94.2)	6 (5.8)	103 (100.0)
IND		*Vote choice*		
Personal		**Chen**	**Lien**	**Total**
trait	**Chen**	21 (100.0)	0 (0.0)	21 (100.0)
preference	**Lien**	32 (34.8)	60 (65.2)	92 (100.0)

Source: Hawang 2003.
Notes: 1. Chen = Chen Shui-bian; Lien = Lien Chan. 2. IND = partisan independent.

TABLE 8.6. Perception of Cross-Strait Peace versus Vote Choice in 2012

Pan-Blue PID		Vote choice		
Personal		**Ma**	**Tsai**	**Total**
trait	**Ma**	591 (98.3)	10 (1.7)	601 (100.0)
preference	**Tsai**	2 (66.7)	1 (33.3)	3 (100.0)
Pan-Green PID		*Vote choice*		
Personal		**Ma**	**Tsai**	**Total**
trait	**Ma**	16 (10.1)	143 (89.9)	159 (100.0)
preference	**Tsai**	2 (1.2)	168 (98.8)	170 (100.0)
IND		*Vote choice*		
Personal		**Ma**	**Tsai**	**Total**
trait	**Ma**	100 (72.5)	38 (27.5)	138 (100.0)
preference	**Tsai**	2 (7.7)	24 (92.3)	26 (100.0)

Source: Chu 2011.
Notes: 1. Ma = Ma Ying-jeou; Tsai = Tsai Ing-wen. 2. IND = partisan independent.

Following previous research, candidate personal traits were divided into two types: personal character and competence. Our empirical results reveal some interesting trends.

First, candidate evaluation appears to be highly associated with electoral outcome. Lee Teng-hui's overwhelming advantage in citizens' perceptions of candidate personal traits matches his landslide victory in the 1996 election. However, that overwhelming advantage was not reproduced by the candidates running in the 2004 election. Neither Chen Shui-bian nor Lien Chan was able to win respondents' endorsements in all personal traits. Instead, as noted above, Chen had the advantage in personal character and Lien had the advantage in competence. The intense competition between Chen and Lien in citizens' perceptions of candidate quality reflects the historically small winning margin in the 2004 presidential election.

Second, our research confirms that the theory of candidate trait ownership is also applicable in Taiwan's case. Although candidate evaluation is conditioned by party identification, in that people are more likely to give their own party's candidate a higher evaluation, candidates representing different parties do own certain personal traits that are highly correlated with the political issues owned by their parties. In Taiwan, KMT candidates, in respondents' perceptions, are more likely to manage economic development and cross-Strait relations well, whereas DPP candidates are considered a better choice to deal with reform issues, such as elimination of black and gold politics.

However, our analysis shows that citizens' vote choices do not necessarily match their evaluations of candidate personal traits. Supporters of the two major parties in general still vote for their party's candidate even though they think that their party's nominee does not have the advantage in certain personal traits. Party identification still plays a critical role in the Taiwan public's vote choice. Partisan independents were the only group whose candidate evaluation matched their vote choice. This result does not mean that independents' candidate evaluation single-handedly determine their electoral decisions, which is arguably decided by many determinants.

In the funnel of causality model proposed by Michigan scholars, candidate, issue, and party identification are three major factors determining vote choice. We, in this chapter, begin with the analysis of how respondents evaluate their presidential candidates' personal traits and then include political issues and party identification into our research. Our findings demonstrate that party identification, due to parties' issue ownership, conditions how respondents evaluate candidates. In short, the result confirms that party identification is the most important factor in Taiwan citizens' voting behavior.

Do these results demonstrate that candidate evaluation has no impact on the Taiwan public's voting decisions? In our opinion, it may be inappropriate to draw such a conclusion because here we have examined only the relationship between citizens' evaluations of single candidate's personal traits and vote choice, whereas citizens' voting decisions may be determined by a comprehensive evaluation of candidate quality. Unfortunately, the existing survey data do not allow us to investigate the effect of comprehensive candidate evaluation on vote choice. Furthermore, here we analyzed only individuals' candidate evaluation in presidential elections.

The results may be different if we focus on the effect of candidate evaluation at the local level.

Last but not least, we believe that candidate evaluation is valuable in analyzing the Taiwan citizens' voting behavior, but data on this topic that is both more concise and accurate awaits further research. For example, attempts can be made to investigate which type of candidate trait, among personal character and competence, is more likely to play the larger role in determining people's vote choice. Moreover, the relationship between citizens' party identification and evaluation of candidate personal traits should also receive more attention from Taiwan scholars. Which candidate trait is more important than others? Is there an evaluation gap between the two major parties' supporters? For instance, KMT supporters may place more weight on a candidate's competence, whereas DPP partisans may consider personal character to be more important. There is still a need for more research on this subject.

Appendix 8.A1. Survey Questions Employed as the Measurements of Candidate Evaluation

1996 Presidential Election

Personal Character

- Which candidate do you think has the most **affinity with the people**?
- Which candidate do you think has the strongest **leadership**?
- Which one is the most **incorruptible**?
- Which one is the most **trustworthy**?
- Which one has the best **understanding of people's needs**?

Competence

- Which one is more likely to have the ability to promote **economic development**?
- Which one is more likely to have the ability to promote **ethnic harmony**?
- Which one is more likely to have the ability to improve **law and order**?
- Which one is more likely to have the ability to promote **peaceful developments in cross-Strait relations**?

2004 Presidential Election

Personal Character

- First, let's look at **getting things done.** How good is Chen Shui-bian (Lien Chan) at getting things done?
- Concerning **incorruptness,** how incorrupt do you think Chen Shui-bian (Lien Chan) is?
- Concerning **sincerity and trustworthiness,** how sincere and trustworthy do you think Chen Shui-bian (Lien Chan) is?
- Concerning **understanding the needs of the people,** how well do you think Chen Shui-bian (Lien Chan) understands the needs of the people?
- Concerning affinity with the people, how much do you think Chen Shui-bian (Lien Chan) has **affinity with the people?**

Competence

- Do you think the candidates on the Chen Shui-bian (Lien Chan) ticket have the ability to promote **ethnic harmony?**
- Do you think the candidates on the Chen Shui-bian (Lien Chan) ticket have the ability to **maintain political stability?**
- Do you think the candidates on the Chen Shui-bian (Lien Chan) ticket have the ability to promote **economic development?**
- Do you think the candidates on the Chen Shui-bian (Lien Chan) ticket have the ability to eliminate **black and gold politics (gangster and money politics)?**
- Do you think the candidates on the Chen Shui-bian (Lien Chan) ticket have the ability to raise **Taiwan's international status?**
- Do you think the candidates on the Chen Shui-bian (Lien Chan) ticket have the ability to promote **democratic reforms?**
- Do you think the candidates on the Chen Shui-bian (Lien Chan) ticket have the ability to improve **law and order?**
- Do you think the candidates on the Chen Shui-bian (Lien Chan) ticket have the ability to promote **peaceful developments in cross-Strait relations?**
- Do you think the candidates on the Chen Shui-bian (Lien Chan) ticket have the ability to resolve **the unemployment problem?**
- Do you think the candidates on the Chen Shui-bian (Lien Chan) ticket have the ability to handle **educational reform?**

2012 Presidential Election

Personal Character

- How would you rate Tsai Ing-wen (Ma Ying-jeou; James Soong) using a 0 to 10 scale, if 0 means that you think the candidate does not understand at all the needs of ordinary people and 10 means that a candidate completely **understands the needs of ordinary people?**
- Has Tsai Ing-wen (Ma Ying-jeou; James Soong), because of the kind of person she is or because of something she has done, ever **made you feel unhappy?**
- Has Tsai Ing-wen (Ma Ying-jeou; James Soong), because of the kind of person she is or because of something she has done, ever **made you worry?**
- Has Tsai Ing-wen (Ma Ying-jeou; James Soong), because of the kind of person she is or because of something she has done, ever **made you feel hopeful for the future?**

Competence

- I'd like to ask you to evaluate the **capability** of three presidential candidates, how would you rate Tsai Ing-wen (Ma Ying-jeou; James Soong) using a 0 to 10 scale?
- How would you rate Tsai Ing-wen (Ma Ying-jeou; James Soong) using a 0 to 10 scale, if 0 means candidates are completely incapable of protecting Taiwan's interests, and 10 means that candidates are completely able to **protect Taiwan's interests?**
- How would you rate Tsai Ing-wen (Ma Ying-jeou; James Soong) using a 0 to 10 scale, if 0 means candidates are completely incapable of maintaining cross-Strait peace, and 10 means that candidates are completely able to **maintain cross-Strait peace?**

Notes

1. Regarding candidate evaluation, we focus here on people's perception of two candidates' personal traits: personal character and competence. However, no question was included in the 2000 and 2008 surveys that examined respondents' evaluation of these two dimensions. Since the three waves of survey data we used already included all winners in the direct presidential elections, we decided not to include the 2000 and 2008 data in our analysis.

2. The first dataset analyzed in this chapter is from "An Interdisciplinary Study of

Voting Behavior in the 1996 Presidential Election." That research project was conducted by the Election Study Center, National Chenchi University, Taiwan, and the principal investigator was Professor John Fu-sheng Hsieh. The second dataset is from "Taiwan's Election and Democratization Study, 2002–2004 (III): The Presidential Election, 2004 (TEDS 2004P)." The principal investigator was Professor Shiow-duan Hawang for TEDS 2004P. The third dataset is from "Taiwan's Election and Democratization Study, 2009–2012 (III): The Survey of the Presidential and Legislative Elections, 2012 (TEDS2012)." The principal investigator was Professor Yun-han Chu for TEDS 2012. The coordinator of the multiyear-project TEDS is Professor Chi Huang (National Chenchi University). More information is available on the TEDS website (http://www.tedsnet.org). These survey data provide information about the Taiwan citizens' evaluation of presidential candidates.

3. Before 1996, instead of being selected by direct election, presidents of the Republic of China were elected by the members of the National Assembly. Lee served as president in this way from 1990 to 1996. Lee originally considered that the selection of the national leader was the duty of the National Assembly, but he then changed his mind to promote direction elections for the presidency.

4. Although Lin ran as an independent, he and his running mate, Hau Pei-tsun, the former premier, were strongly endorsed by the New Party in the 1996 presidential election. Hence, Chen, in fact, was the only candidate running for the election independently.

5. Lee won 54.0% of popular votes in the 1996 presidential elections; Peng, Lin, and Chen received 21.1%, 14.9%, and 10.0%, respectively.

6. *Formosa Magazine* was a magazine created by certain anti-KMT individuals. On December 10, 1979, a prodemocracy demonstration led by members of *Formosa Magazine* took place in Kaohsiung and demanded democracy in Taiwan. However, the demonstration was prohibited by the KMT's authoritarian regime and was suppressed by the police. The leaders of the demonstration were arrested and accused of treason. The Formosa Incident is regarded as a very important event in the history of Taiwan's democratization because of its huge impact on Taiwan society.

7. In the 2000 presidential election, Chen won 39.3% of popular vote. His opponents, Soong and Lien, received 36.8% and 23.1%, respectively.

8. In the 2008 Taiwan presidential election, Ma won 58.4% of popular vote whereas Hsieh received only 41.6%. Corruption in the Chen administration and the economic recession were considered the main factors contributing to Ma's landslide victory.

9. Ma won 51.6% of popular vote, whereas Tsai and Soong received only 45.6% and 2.8%, respectively.

References

Baker, David C., Adam B. Lawrence, and Margit Tavits. 2006. "Partisanship and the Dynamics of Candidate Centered Politics in American Presidential Nominations." *Electoral Studies* 25: 599–610.

Campbell, Angus, Philip E. Converse, Warren E. Miller, and Donald Stokes. 1960. *The American Voter*. New York: Wiley.

Chang, Ching-ching. 2010. "Political Advertising in Taiwan's Elections and Perception of Issue/Trait Ownership" [in Chinese]. *Chuanbo yu Shehui Xuekan* [Communication and Society] 11: 31–69.

Cheng, Su-feng, Lu-huei Chen, and Jia-wei Liu. 2005. "The Candidate Factor in Taiwan's 2004 Presidential Election" [in Chinese]. *Taiwan Minzhu Jikan*□[Taiwan Democracy Quarterly] 2 (2): 31–70.

Chu, Yun-han. 2011. "Taiwan's Election and Democratization Study, 2009–2012 (III): The Survey of the Presidential and Legislative Elections, 2012 (TEDS2012)." NSC 100–2420-H-002–030. Taipei: National Science Council.

Flanigan, William H., and Nancy H. Zingale. 1998. *Political Behavior of the American Electorate*. Washington, DC: CQ Press.

Hawang, Shiow-duan. 1996. "The Importance of Candidate Images and Capabilities in Presidential Election" [in Chinese]. *Xuanju Yanjiu* [Journal of Electoral Studies] 3 (1): 103–35.

Hawang, Shiow-duan. 2003. "Taiwan's Election and Democratization Study 2002–2004 (III): The Presidential Election, 2004 (TEDS 2004P)." NSC 92-2420-H-031–004. Taipei: National Science Council.

Hawang, Shiow-duan. 2005. "Candidate Image, Feeling Thermometer, and Presidential Voting Behavior" [in Chinese]. *Taiwan Minzhu Jikan* [Taiwan Democracy Quarterly] 2 (4): 1–30.

Hayes, Danny. 2005. "Candidate Qualities through a Partisan Lens: A Theory of Trait Ownership." *American Journal of Political Science* 49 (4): 908–23.

Hsieh, John Fu-sheng. 1995. *An Interdisciplinary Study of Voting Behavior in the 1996 Presidential Election*. Taipei: National Science Council.

Hsieh, John Fu-sheng, and Emerson M. S. Niou. 1996. "Salient Issues in Taiwan's Electoral Politics." *Electoral Studies* 15 (2): 219–35.

Kim, Young-mie, and Kelly Garrett. 2012. "On-Line and Memory-Based: Revisiting the Relationship between Candidate Evaluation Processing Models." *Political Behavior* 34 (2): 345–68.

Kinder, R. Donald, Mark D. Peters, Robert P. Abelson, and Susan T. Fiske. 1980. "Presidential Prototypes." *Political Behavior* 2 (4): 315–36.

Lewis-Back, Michael S., William G. Jacoby, Helmut Norpoth, and Herbert F. Weisberg. 2008. *The American Voter Revisited*. Ann Arbor: University of Michigan Press.

Liang, Shin-wu. 1994. "Research on the 1994 Taipei Mayor Election: The Testing of the Predictive Model-Candidate's Image Indicators" [in Chinese]. *Xuanju Yanjiu* [Journal of Electoral Studies] 1 (2): 97–130.

Lin, Tse-min, Yun-han Chu, and Melvin J. Hinich. 1996. "Conflict Displacement and Regime Transition in Taiwan: A Spatial Analysis." *World Politics* 48 (4): 453–81.

Lodge, Milton, Kathleen M. McGraw, and Patrick Stroh. 1989. "An Impression-Driven Model of Candidate Evaluation." *American Political Science Review* 83 (2): 399–419.

Merolla, Jennifer L., and Elizabeth J. Zechmeister. 2009. "Terrorist Threat, Leadership, and the Vote: Evidence from Three Experiments." *Political Behavior* 31 (4): 575–601.

Miller, Arthur H., Martin P. Wattenberg, and Oksana Malanchuk. 1986. "Schematic Assessments of Presidential Candidates." *American Political Science Review* 80 (2): 521–40.

Miller, Warren E., and J. Merrill Shanks. 1996. *The New American Voter*. Cambridge: Harvard University Press.

Niemi, Richard G., and Herbert F. Weisberg. 1993. *Classics in Voting Behavior*. Washington, DC: CQ Press.

Niemi, Richard G., and Herbert F. Weisberg. 2001. *Controversies in Voting Behavior*. Washington, DC: CQ Press.

Petrocik, John R. 1996. "Issue Ownership in Presidential Elections, with a 1980 Case Study." *American Journal of Political Science* 40 (3): 825–50.

Rahn, Wendy M., John H. Aldrich, John L. Sullivan, and Eugene Borgida. 1990. "A Social-Cognitive Model of Political Candidate Appraisal." In *Information and Democratic Processes*, ed. John Ferejohn and James Kuklinski, 136–59. Urbana: University of Illinois Press.

Sheng, Shing-yuan. 2007. "Issue, Political Cleavage and Party Competition in Taiwan: From the Angles of the Elites and the Public." Presented at the Annual Meeting of the American Political Science Association, Chicago, August 30–September 2.

Sheng, Shing-yuan. 2013. "Issues, Party Performance and Voters' Voting Behavior" [in Chinese]. In *2012 nian zongtong yu lifaweiyuan xuanju: Bianqian yu yanxu*[2012 presidential and legislative elections: Changes and continuation], ed. Lu-huei Chen, 203–27. Taiwan: Wunan Press.

Shyu, Huo-yan. 1995. "'Lee Teng-hui Complex' and Voting Behavior: A Psycho-political Analysis of Vote Choice in the 1994 Taiwan's Gubernatorial and Taipei Mayoral Elections" [in Chinese]. *Xuanju Yanjiu* [Journal of Electoral Studies] 2 (2): 1–36.

Shyu, Huo-yan. 1998. "The Political Psychology of Lee Teng-hui Complex and Its Effects on Voting Behavior" [in Chinese]. *Xuanju Yanjiu* [Journal of Electoral Studies] 5 (2): 35–71.

Tverdova, Yulia V. 2011. "Follow the Party or Follow the Leaders? Candidate Evaluations, Party Evaluation, and Macropolitical Context." In *Citizens, Context, and Choice: How Context Shapes Citizens' Electoral Choices*. ed. Russell J. Dalton and Christopher J. Anderson. New York: Oxford University Press, 126–48.

Wang, Hung-chung. 2012. "The Impact of Political Awareness and Elite Discourse on Taiwanese Issue Positions: A Simple Test of Zaller's Mainstream Effect and Polarization Effect" [in Chinese]. *Taiwan Minzhu Jikan* [Taiwan Democracy Quarterly] 9 (2): 71–124.

Wattenberg, Martin P. 1991. *The Rise of Candidate-Centered Politics: Presidential Elections of the 1980s*. Cambridge: Harvard University Press.

Yu, Ching-hsin. 2003. "Exploring the Electorate's Ideal Candidate: The Case of the 2000 Presidential Election in Taiwan" [in Chinese]. *Dongwu Zhengzhi Xuebao* [Soochow Journal of Political Science] 17: 93–120

Zaller, John R. 1992. *The Nature and Origins of Mass Opinion*. New York: Cambridge University Press.

CHAPTER 9

Political Left and Right in Taiwan

Yi-ching Hsiao, Su-feng Cheng,
and Christopher H. Achen

The left-right ideological dimension is an important conceptual tool for understanding most European democratic countries and their former colonies, such as those in North and South America. Party competition, the electorate's voting decisions, and governmental policy making can all be described in that framework (for example, Barnes 1971; Bartle 1998; Dalton 2008; Dalton and Tanaka 2007; Erikson, Wright, and McIver 1993; Norris 2004, 97–125; Potrafke 2009).[1] In its mathematical form, the "spatial model" of left-right voting has been a favorite of theorists since Hotelling (1929) and before. Of course, citizens in Western countries vary in how well they understand the dimension (Stokes 1962; Converse 1964; Converse and Pierce 1986, 127–29; Fuchs and Klingemann 1989; Inglehart 1990; Lewis-Beck and Chlarson 2002). Nevertheless, political elites, scholars, and journalists make ready use of it to describe their national politics.

The ubiquity of "left" and "right" in the elite discourse of their countries has led some Western scholars to imagine that, in some form or another, those terms must be meaningful political concepts in virtually every country. Thus Sigelman and Yough (1978, 356) write that "party systems throughout the world can meaningfully be profiled in terms of polarization along the left-right continuum." Similarly, Converse and Pierce (1986, 112) say, "This currency of 'left,' 'center,' and 'right' has of course been widely exported, and is a commonplace for politically sophisticated observers around the world."

This same logic is embedded in the Comparative Study of Electoral Systems (CSES) international surveys, in which every participating country is required to ask the following question:[2]

In politics people sometimes talk of left and right. Where would you place yourself on a scale from 0 to 10, where 0 means the left and 10 means the right?

In Taiwan, however, left-right language is simply not used to describe the current party system—not by ordinary people, not by journalists, not by politicians, and not by Taiwan scholars. Asking them about it is like asking them about sharia law or dancing the flamenco—cultural concepts that are prominent elsewhere but not in Taiwan.

Since they lack the appropriate political context, how do Taiwan citizens answer the CSES question? What do they understand by political "left" and "right"? Scholars have occasionally remarked on anomalies in the use of left-right language in Taiwan (for example, Chen 2003), but no one has focused explicitly and in detail on how Taiwan citizens perceive "left" and "right" in politics. The purpose of this chapter is to do so. We begin by reviewing the use of left-right language in Western democracies. Then we proceed to the Taiwan case.

The Concept of a Left-Right Dimension

The political concepts of left and right originated during the French Revolution two centuries ago, when the more radical supporters of the Revolution sat on the left in the Estates General, with their ideological opponents on the right. Thus, from its beginnings the left-right distinction in the West reflected ideological divisions over tradition and hierarchy in society. "By left we shall mean advocating social change in the direction of greater equality—political, economic, or social; by right we shall mean supporting a traditional more or less hierarchical social order, and opposing change toward greater equality" (Lipset et al. 1954, 1135).

In the modern era, the left-right dimension has referred primarily to differences in the desired degree of government intervention in both society and economy.[3] Thus Laver and Hunt (1992, 12) write that

the left pole has in general become associated with policies designed to bring about the redistribution of resources from those with more to those with less, and with the promotion of social rights that apply to groups of individuals taken as a whole even at the expense of individual members of those groups. The right pole has become associated with the promotion of individual rights, including the right not to have personal resources expropriated for redistribution by the state, even at the expense of social inequality and of poverty among worse off social groups.

Scholars interested in social class issues in politics often adhere closely to the latter meaning. Thus Jansen, Evans, and De Graaf (2013, 54) say that "we construct a left-right party position based on economic and welfare policy issues," and they explicitly set aside broader definitions proposed by other scholars.

More loosely, other historical cleavages typical of Western societies (Lipset and Rokkan 1967) have sometimes been subsumed under the left-right rubric when they happened to line up with the views of left and right political parties. Thus debates over divorce laws, abortion, supranational integration, and many other issues are given "left" and "right" interpretations (Dalton 2012; Zechmeister 2006; Zechmeister and Corral 2013). As Inglehart (1990, 292) argues, "The Left-Right image is an oversimplification, but an almost inevitable one, which in the long run tends to assimilate all important issues." Hence the left-right dimension is sometimes described as a kind of "super-issue," especially in Europe.

Issues unrelated to governmental intervention in the market or in society have no persistent left-right meaning, however. There is nothing left or right about disputes among ethnic, racial, or religious groups, for instance. Similarly, neither the left nor the right has a monopoly on forceful assertions of nationalism. Across Europe, conservative and socialist parties are found on both sides of the debate over ceding some national sovereignty to the European Union.

Particular leftist parties may adopt certain social views in a particular historical period, of course, as may rightist parties. However, history demonstrates that the issue packages that seem so coherent and inevitable to partisans at the time have often varied dramatically in different times and places. In practice, major party platforms are strategic documents cobbled together to balance party factions and meet short-term electoral needs. They are not ideologically coherent statements of a political vision (see, for example, Bawn et al. 2012).

Thus we expect that when left-right language is extended beyond its central modern meaning, all sorts of jumbled statistical patterns will result. That is precisely what scholars have found (Fuchs and Klingemann 2009). Zechmeister (2010) even finds some reversed signs for the correlation between economic views and left-right self-descriptions in Latin American surveys because "left" and "right" are being used to mean something else in certain countries. "It is indeed a fact," Zechmeister (2015, 199) writes, "that the political significance of the left-right semantics varies across countries, across time, and even across subgroups of a population."

All these countries, however odd or broad the meaning they give to left and right, agree in one respect: in their party systems, "left" and "right" are meaningful political terms. The voters may understand them to a greater or lesser degree, but the words themselves are meaningful. What scholars have not discussed much at all, however, are countries in which those words are not used in electoral politics, so that the concepts "left" and "right" have no application to the party system. It is to such a case that we now turn.

Left and Right in Taiwan

Knowledgeable observers (Cheng and Hsu 1996; Rigger 2001, 39–41) are agreed that for good historical reasons, conventional left-right issues do not consistently differentiate the two main Taiwan parties, the Kuomintang and the Democratic Progressive Party. According to Sheng and Liao's longitudinal study (see chapter 5 of this volume), the DPP has often been seen as somewhat more favorable to "environmental protection," to "reform," and to "social welfare programs," leading some foreign observers to think of it as the left party. But in practice, across issues such as pensions and medical care programs, neither of the two parties has been consistently on the left or the right. Early in his term in office, DPP president Chen Shui-bian set aside many of his party's social welfare promises in favor of promoting economic growth, a typical right-wing choice. As Fell (2012, 199) remarks, "As with environmental issues, welfare is not a core ideological issue for the party, thus could be sacrificed."

Typically, the two main Taiwan parties are flexible, low intensity, and opportunistic on social welfare policies, differentiating themselves instead along national identity lines instead, as we have seen repeatedly in this book and as previous observers have noted (Cheng and Hsu 1996; Fell 2005b, chap. 4; Fell 2008, 69). Thus, elite politics in Taiwan is organized differently than in most Western countries, and the parties have little incentive to use left-right language in explaining themselves to voters.

Unsurprisingly, then, the left-right dimension does not predict voting in Taiwan. Norris (2004, 110–11) utilized the Comparative Study of Electoral Systems dataset to explore citizens' voting decisions in a variety of democra-

cies and found that respondents' left-right position was significantly correlated with their voting decision—with the exception of Taiwan and Belarus.
All this is quite different from most Western countries, where, in spite of
considerable noise and misunderstanding by many in the population, on
average the party placements make reasonable sense, and where individual
citizens' self-placements correlate at least fairly well with their voting decisions (for example, on France, see Converse 1966 and Fleury and Lewis-
Beck 1993; more generally, Norris 2004, 110–11).

Left-right semantics do not predict the vote in Taiwan because, as we
have seen, those words are not used in the political culture to describe party
differences. Survey respondents are forced to guess their meaning. Thus,
Chen (2003) found that only about half of Taiwan citizens were able to
specify their position on a left-right dimension, a much higher failure rate
than in most democracies. Moreover, even for those who did place themselves, Chen's study of their unconventional responses led him to question
whether respondents really understood what "left" and "right" meant. In
the same way, Jou (2010, 373) encountered very low left-right cognition in
his study of Taiwan citizens: fewer than 50% could place themselves on the
scale. Taiwan's left-right placement rate was the lowest among 35 countries
in CSES cases studied by Russell Dalton, and the only country under 50
percent (Dalton 2011, 107).

The evidence that Taiwan voters do not understand left and right language is strengthened when one looks at center self-placements by voters—a
5 on the 0–10 point scale. As Converse and Pierce (1986, 128–29) note,
respondents who choose the midpoint are often poorly informed and simply
trying to appear helpful to the interviewer: center placement "is an obvious
selection for a person who is neutral, uncommitted, and even thoroughly
indifferent to or ignorant about this generic axis of dispute." (Similarly, see
Lambert 1983 and Ogmundson 1979.) In two different studies, Jou (2010,
373) found very high center placement in Taiwan—among the minority of
voters who could place themselves at all, more than half chose the center position. Thus, altogether, more than three quarters of the Taiwan respondents
chose either the neutral position or no position at all. The same finding
appears in the 2012 TEDS survey: 78 percent of Taiwan respondents were
either neutral or uncomprehending when asked the left-right question.[4]

All these Taiwan anomalies raise several questions. Is there any sense of the
words "left" and "right," conventional or not, that has meaning for the voters?
What do ordinary Taiwan citizens mean when they are asked the meaning of
those words? And how do they place the parties on that dimension?

Taiwan Politics and the Cultural Connotations of "Left" and "Right"

As we have noted, a conventional left-right dimension seems to play little role in the vote choices of Taiwan's voters. In this respect, the citizenry simply reflect the nature of Taiwan politics. The voters see real differences between the parties on the national identity issue, but few on secondary issues like social welfare (Chu and Lin 1996, 92–95). As Sheng and Liao showed in chapter 5, since the beginning of democratization in the 1980s, citizen preferences on such issues as Taiwan independence vs. reunification with China, environmental protection vs. economic development, social welfare vs. low taxes, and reform vs. social stability have influenced party preferences and voting decisions to some degree (Hsieh, Niou, and Lin 1995; Sheng and Chen 2003; Tsai 2008; Wang 2001; Wang 2003). But the first of these—independence vs. reunification—is the most powerful issue, not only in locating the main two parties on the political spectrum, but also in determining voter choice. National identity concerns stemming from "the China factor" have been the main political cleavage to discriminate between the Pan-Blue camp and the Pan-Green camp (as chapter 4 reveals). However, national identity is not itself conventionally left-right in character, and those words are not used to describe the issue in Taiwan.[5]

Not only does left-right thinking fit Taiwan's current elite and electoral politics poorly, but in recent history that language was actively employed to characterize something else—Taiwan's foreign policy disagreements with mainland China. Before democratization in the late 1980s, the Kuomintang Party viewed the "leftist" Chinese Communist Party as the mortal enemy. With its monopoly on political communications, the KMT made every effort to suppress "left" views. Taiwan people were taught that the "left-side" was evil. Expressing sympathy for the left was a form of rebellion. The KMT emphasized that it was the "right" party. An element of negative evaluation still attaches to "left-side" political views in Taiwan.

These connotations of "left" and "right" are enhanced by the two Chinese dialects most used in Taiwan, Taiwanese (spoken by a majority of citizens) and Mandarin (the language of instruction in schools). Just as some respondents in English-speaking countries consider the political "right" to mean "correct" or "in the right," so also in the Taiwanese dialect the same word "right" is used to mean both "the opposite of left" and also "correct" or "true." "Left" in Taiwanese connotes "bad" in some way. The heritage from the authoritarian period enhances this identification.

An equally consequential factor for left-right usage in Taiwan is that, apart from all political overtones, "left" in the Mandarin dialect connotes deviousness, unorthodoxy, or heresy.[6] The inference extends even to left-handed people, who are often considered "alternative" or nonmainstream. In everyday Taiwan life, the right side when walking (or the right-hand seat when sitting) is reserved for elders, honored guests, or respected citizens.[7] The implication, then, is that one's favorite political party should be placed on the right and the disliked party on the left.

Thus we expect that placing Taiwan's parties on a conventional left-right scale will be difficult for ordinary citizens because that dimension is nearly irrelevant for party choice in Taiwan. When respondents are forced to place the parties or to define "left" and "right," they will often fall back on other meanings familiar from local culture, such as "Communist" vs. "anti-Communist," "bad" vs. "good," or "wrong" vs. "correct." To assess these propositions, we use both cognitive interviews and public opinion surveys. The cognitive interview data come from a project called "A Study of Major Political Identification Concepts of the Taiwan Public."[8] In this project, which was carried out in 2001, 50 respondents were asked to define the left-right dimension in politics, and then to place themselves and the major Taiwan political parties on the left-right spectrum. The interviewers gave no examples or cues of how this task was to be done. All the respondents had to define the concept and the positions according to their own understandings.[9]

We also employ opinion survey data collected by Taiwan's Election and Democratization Study after the 2001 legislative election and the 2008 presidential election (hereafter TEDS2001 and TEDS2008P). The sampling population is adult citizens in Taiwan. The number of successful interviews was 2,022 and 1,905, respectively. In TEDS, a 0–10 scale was utilized for the respondents' placement of themselves and the major parties, as well as for answers to issue questions.[10]

Citizens' Perceptions of "Left" and "Right"

We begin with a discussion of the cognitive interviews to give a sense of what Taiwan respondents mean by "left" and "right." In the end, all fifty respondents managed some sort of definition, but the task was not easy for most of them. When asked to give a definition, 18 respondents (36%) began by asking what the question meant. Another five respondents (10%) said that the left-right dimension was politically irrelevant in Taiwan. For example (our translations):

I don't think the concept of left-right exists in Taiwan. (No. 01)

I just don't get it . . . basically, I think the concept is meaningless in Taiwan. (No. 41)

Thus nearly half the respondents could not or did not use the left-right distinction in their thinking about Taiwan politics.

When pressed to a definition, respondents' answers varied widely, and most did not fit the customary meaning of left-right in Western democracies. We have attempted to catalog the respondents' answers into six different categories, with the "left" answer listed first: liberalism vs. conservatism (4%), doves vs. hawks (18%), Communism vs. democracy (18%), Taiwan independence vs. reunification with China (22%), bad vs. good (18%), and ruling party vs. opposition party (20%). Among the six different definitions, the first category clearly conforms to the definition of left-right in Western democracies, and the second might be generously interpreted to do so as well. But those two groups comprise fewer than 25 percent of the respondents. The remaining four categories reflect confusions of various kinds.

To convey a sense of how the interviewees in the nonstandard categories express themselves, we give a sample of their responses. We begin with the third category of respondents, those who regard all democracies as "right."

Communism vs. Democracy

Basically I think the left-wingers are closer to socialism, so socialists are counted as left. Closer to democracy and liberty are the right-wingers. From my point of view, in present-day Taiwan, no matter whether it's DDP, KMT, PFP, or TSU [abbreviations of the Taiwan parties], they are basically on the democracy side, so all the Taiwanese parties belong to the right. (No. 13)

The left reminds me of the Communist Party. . . . the left was referred to as the Communist Party . . . The right is the more democratic party. (No.29)

I always think Communism vs. democracy. . . . It seems to me that the right side is democracy and the left side is communism. I don't really get it. (No.42)

The fourth category reflects the main political cleavage in Taiwan, the orientation toward China's claim of ownership of Taiwan. As noted above, this policy dimension is not about economics or social class, but is rather a dispute between two versions of national identity. Thus it is not conventionally left-right.

Reunification vs. Independence

I don't have the concept of the left-right. . . . it is made by [other] people. . . . The left in politics is [Taiwan] independence, and the right is unification [with China]. (No. 06)

Generally speaking, the definition of the extreme right is strongly supporting unification, while the extreme left is strongly supporting independence. This is how I see it. (No. 34)

Finally, the last two categories, nearly 40 percent of the interviewees, completely misunderstand left-right categories. The first group takes their cue from the connotation in Mandarin and Taiwanese of "left" as deviant or subpar.

Good vs. Bad

I feel the left seems to be negative . . . and the right is more positive. . . . I feel it is good vs. bad. . . . Because I think the left means heresy in our old saying, that unorthodox ways are "left ways" [in Chinese]. . . . If I use "the left" to describe something bad, then I think the opposite side of it should be something better. (No. 07)

Left-right in politics means who does things right. Those who do the right things are the rights, while those who do the wrong things are the lefts. (No. 31)

The last group of respondents associates "right" with the ruling party, regardless of its ideology.

Ruling Party vs. Opposition Party

The left and the right? I think to say it in a simple way, it is the ruling party and the non-ruling party . . . I think the left is the non-ruling party and the right is the ruling party. (No. 33)

Ruling party is counted as the right, and generally speaking the left is the opposition party. (No.08)

Note that at the time of the interviews, the presidency was held by the pro-independence DPP. Categorizing them as "right," as these respondents do, contradicts the categorization given by those respondents who focused on reunification vs. independence and thereby called the DPP "left."

In summary, these cognitive interviews display the great range of interpretation of left and right among Taiwan's citizens. Only a few use European-derived interpretations to structure their dimensional thinking. Some impose idiosyncratic understandings. Many do not make use of the concept at all. Thus imposing Western left-right frameworks on Taiwan respondents violates their understanding of the island's politics and distorts the analysis of elections there.

Survey Evidence

These conclusions are strengthened when we turn to nationwide opinion survey data. We first explore how citizens locate themselves and the major parties on the left-right dimension and on a variety of policy issues, including Taiwan independence vs. reunification with China, environmental protection vs. economic development, promoting social welfare vs. keeping taxes down, and large-scale reform vs. social stability. The latter three items are conventionally left-right in character, especially the social welfare question, while the first issue concerns competing national identities and has no left-right ideological content, as we have discussed. In each case, the scale runs from 0–10 (question wordings are given in the appendix). These issues were discussed by Sheng and Liao in chapter 5 to validate the importance of Taiwan's principal political cleavage. Here our purpose is different: we explore the correlations between the left-right dimension and these four policy issue to verify that left-right is an inapplicable instrument for interpreting Taiwan politics. We begin with nonresponse rates.

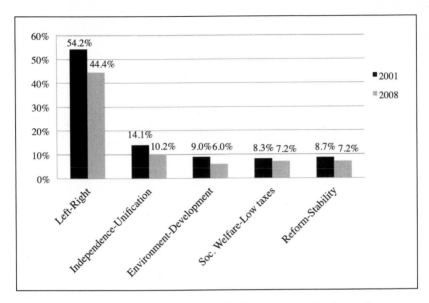

Fig. 9.1. Nonresponse rates for left-right self-placement and other issues. *Data Sources:* TEDS 2001 and TEDS 2008P.

Figure 9.1 reveals that across a variety of issues, the nonresponse rate for the left-right question is by far the highest. In 2001 and in 2008, about half the citizens could not respond when asked where they placed themselves on the left-right dimension. By comparison, only about 10 percent failed to provide their own opinions on standard Taiwan political issues. Many citizens give middle scores for their position on the ideological spectrum, probably because they are behaving cautiously in a task they did not fully understand, as discussed earlier.[11] Further investigation showed that, as expected, knowledgeable or highly partisan respondents were more often able to give an answer to the left-right question (as in Converse and Valen 1971, 131), while party preference made no difference. Nevertheless, even among those well-informed respondents who answered all five of the political knowledge questions or missed only one, almost 40 percent could not place themselves on a left-right scale in 2001. Failure rates were considerably higher among those with less understanding. Altogether, for half of all Taiwan citizens, there is no interpretation of left-right language that makes enough sense to allow them to place themselves on the scale, and, as we have already noted, the other half often manage the task only with idiosyncratic definitions of "left" and "right."

The conclusion is much the same when we examine placement of the

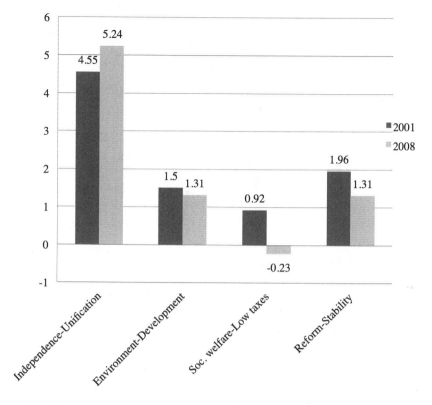

Fig. 9.2. Difference in average respondent placement of DPP vs. KMT (1–10 scale), *Data Sources:* TEDS 2001 and TEDS 2008P

two principal political parties on the same 0–10 scale. For each policy issue, figure 9.2 shows the difference of the mean DPP placement from the mean KMT placement, with positive numbers indicating that the DPP is closer to the first option in each issue choice. For example, on the issue of independence vs. reunification, a positive difference means that the DPP is seen (correctly) as closer to the independence position. As figure 9.1 demonstrated, some respondents could not place the parties on each issue. Hence the comparative placements in figure 9.2 are based solely on those respondents who did so.

As in Sheng and Liao's results in chapter 5, figure 9.2 shows that in both 2001 and 2008 the DPP is considered closer than the KMT to the positions of "independence," "environment," and "reform," with the party difference by far the largest on independence vs. reunification. Better informed and more partisan respondents perceived somewhat larger party differences (not shown but available from the authors on request). These findings are completely consistent with contemporary interpretations of party competition and elite political cleavages in Taiwan, as we noted above.

This optimistic view of the respondents is tempered by the one inconsistency between 2001 and 2008, however, which occurs on the clearest and most conventional left-right issue, social welfare vs. keeping taxes down. In 2001, the DPP was considered closer to "promoting social welfare" than the KMT, but this ordering was reversed in 2008. It may be that 2008 respondents were simply expressing their more pessimistic view of the Chen Shui-bian administration after its eight years in office, during which he deemphasized social welfare, as we have seen. In any event, the instability and vanishingly small party differences on this issue reinforce the point that Western notions of "left" and "right" do not distinguish the two principal Taiwan parties.

A second and more striking anomaly is that the respondents give their favorite party a more rightward (higher) score and their disliked party a more leftward (lower) score. Figures 9.3 and 9.4 show this effect for 2001 and 2008, respectively. The effect is visible in both figures, but is particularly dramatic in 2001. In that year, those respondents who liked the DPP (the proenvironment, "proreform" major party) moved its average placement so far to the right that it wound up to the right of the KMT. Here again is evidence that many Taiwan citizens consider their favorite party as "right" and their disliked party as "left," regardless of its actual policy views.

The argument that "left" and "right" do not have conventional meanings in Taiwan is further strengthened when left-right placement is correlated with issue positions on the four items mentioned above. If "left-right" in Taiwan captured standard Western notions about the role of government in society, the correlations should be strong and positive with the three domestic policy issues, particularly so for the social welfare vs. low taxes issue, but small or zero with the independence-reunification question. However, figure 9.5 reveals that in both survey years, all the correlations are very small—none larger than 0.130. Worse yet, in both years, left-right position is slightly *negatively* correlated with attitudes toward social welfare, just the reverse of what is required for conventional ideological meaningfulness.[12]

Part of the explanation for the reversed correlation may lie in the survey measurements. In conducting the TEDS questionnaire, interviewers show the respondents cards with a 0–10 scale. The "0" is located the left side, signifying "Taiwan independence," "environmental protection," "*lower taxes*," and "large-scale reform." On the other side, the "10" signifies "reunification with China," "economic development," "*promoting social welfare*," and

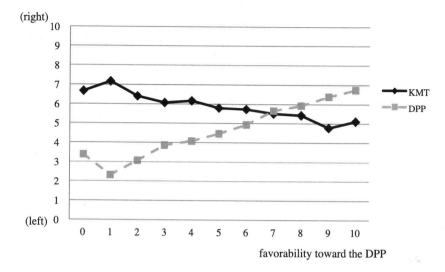

Fig. 9.3. Placement of the parties on left-right by favorability toward the DPP (2001). *Data Source:* TEDS 2001.

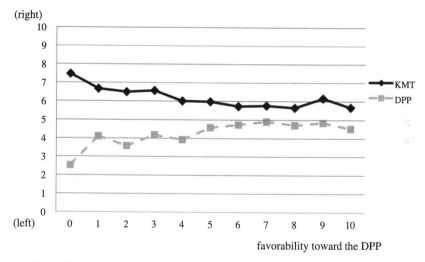

Fig. 9.4. Placement of the parties on left-right by favorability toward the DPP (2008). *Data Source:* TEDS 2008P.

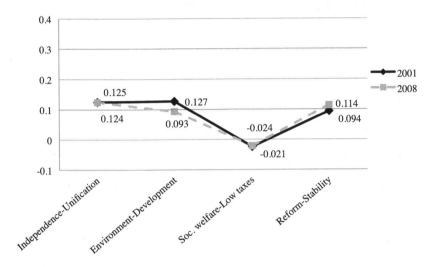

Fig. 9.5. Correlation of citizens' left-right position with issues. *Data Sources:* TEDS 2001 and TEDS 2008P.

"social stability." (See figure 9.6) Thus, some respondents who did not understand the meaning of left-right may simply have regarded all the issue positions on the left side of the card as "left," and all those on the right side as "right." Since among all four issues, only the "social welfare" question has the "left" answer on the right-hand side of the card and the "right" answer on the left (the bold-faced answers in the list above), this may account for the weak (and slightly negative) correlation between it and the respondent's left-right position. Once again, this suggests that the left-right dimension is little understood by Taiwan citizens and little related to their policy views.

Hard-core devotees of the conventional wisdom may yet have one final objection. "All right," they may say, "the left-right orientation is weak in Taiwan. Previous scholars have found that it does not predict voting. But perhaps by 2012, after several decades of democratization, the result is different. Doesn't everything in politics turn into left-right eventually?"

The answer, for the record, is no. As we have seen, a great many Taiwan respondents have to be discarded to assess the relationship of left-right position to the Pan-Blue vs. Pan-Green vote because they have no idea what the left-right question means. But even in that heavily truncated sample, no trace of causal importance appears. To give left-right orientation every chance, we did not load up the explanatory equations with many different noisy measures of related opinions, a tactic sure to reduce them all to statistical insignificance. Nor did we control for Michigan-style party identification questions, which have an overwhelmingly powerful impact in Taiwan (see

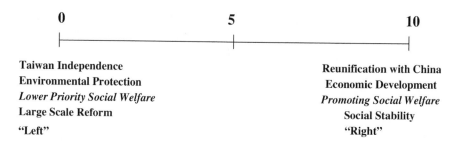

Fig. 9.6. Content and direction on TEDS show card

Chapter 12). But even with all these biases in its favor, the left-right position failed to show much sign of explanatory life. With the scale set to a range of 0–1 and controlling only for dummy variables indicating the respondent's party preference, the probit coefficient was just .1 and far from statistical significance. Taken at face value, that coefficient would imply at best a 3 percentage point impact on a little more than half the sample (the remaining group having zero impact because they do not recognize the terms "left" and "right"). But even a very modest effect of that size is far from reliable statistically.

Some indication of why the left-right variable fails is given by a close look at the party identifiers.[13] Just 17 percent of KMT supporters placed themselves on the far right (a score of 10). But fully 14 percent of supporters of the more radical DPP respondents placed themselves there. Indeed, 58 percent of the DPP sample placed themselves at one or another position on "the right" (scores 6–10). More dramatically, there were just three supporters of the strongly pro-independence TSU party in the sample, but they all placed themselves on the right. Overall, 77 percent of the sample placed themselves on the right.

As we have seen in Taiwan, "right" often means "correct." No wonder, then, that the left-right variable adds almost nothing to explaining vote choices once partisanship is controlled. Once we know which parties the respondents belong to, knowing that most of them also consider themselves "correct" adds no new information.

Conclusion

Some readers of early versions of this chapter felt that our central point was already well known, since many scholars have shown that the meanings of "left" and "right" differ across countries. Hence they felt that the Taiwan case brings nothing new. In the light of how the topic is treated in much previous literature, such a misconception is entirely understandable. But it misses our point entirely.

In the conventional view, the left-right dimension is a cultural near-universal. Whatever its meaning, every country should exhibit some form of left vs. right in politics. When a party system fails, scholars often blame the parties: too much clientelism, too little policy clarity, too little polarization, too little time for the voters to learn—all these are put forward as causes when left-right meanings are confused or impotent in voting decisions. (The European case is treated in van der Eijk et al. 2005, 177–80 and Berglund et al. 2005, 116–22; see Zechmeister 2015 for the Latin American counterpart.) If these party failures were corrected, the argument goes, a strong left-right effect would make an appearance. In Europe and Latin America and some other parts of the world where that argument has been made, it is probably accurate. But to suppose without close study that it applies everywhere would be reminiscent of those American tourists in the 1950s who imagined that if only they spoke English slowly and loudly enough, anyone around the world could understand them.

Our point is rather that research using left-right concepts may go seriously wrong if the left-right dimension essentially does not exist in some countries. For example, the idiosyncrasies of left-right language in Taiwan explain why Dalton and Tanaka (2007) measured low party polarization in Taiwan, a result that would surprise knowledgeable observers of Taiwan politics. As we have seen, in Taiwan a majority of citizens cannot place either themselves or the major parties on a left-right ideological spectrum. Even among those who can do so, many appear to be guessing or using idiosyncratic definitions of "left" and "right." As we have also seen, many Taiwan citizens identify their favorite party as "right" and consider the disliked party "left," corresponding to the Taiwanese or Mandarin connotations of "left" as "bad," "devious," or "heretical."

Now if many respondents favoring one major party put it on the right ("the right side") and the other party on the left ("the bad side"), while many respondents favoring the other party do the reverse, the rights and lefts will tend to average out in the mean placement of each party. Average party placements will be pushed toward the center, making a highly polarized party system appear convergent and consensual. But "low polarization" is simply mistaken. As we have seen repeatedly in this volume, cross-Strait relations help shape citizens' national identity (chapter 3), determine people's party identification (chapter 4), set the core political cleavage for party competition (chapter 5) and the party system (chapter 10), and thus are the critical factor for vote choice (chapters 7, 9, and 12). In particular, the issue of Taiwan independence has led to serious political conflicts and unusually bitter party divisions since Taiwan's democratization in the late 1980s and early 1990s, including fistfights on the floor of the national legislature.[14] Taiwan's parties are not ideologically similar, and polarization is not low. But the CSES survey imposes left-right language on countries that do not use it, and scholars thereby may be led astray.

National identity issues are often poorly assimilated to left-right categorizations. As Jou (2010, 371) insightfully phrased it, speaking of Taiwan, "One may . . . hypothesize that an entrenched national identity cleavage leads to the paradoxical scenario of greater polarization accompanied by lower left-right identification." It is precisely that sort of insight that is impossible to grasp unless one breaks out of the notion that some version of left-right applies everywhere.

The Taiwan voters' difficulties in understanding left-right political concepts are perfectly understandable. This volume's theme is that party competition in Taiwan is structured by the "China factor," especially on the "independence vs. reunification with China" issue, but this is clearly not a conventional left-right dimension. Hence even at the political elite level, left-right distinctions are generally irrelevant and a poor guide to sorting out the parties. Little wonder that the voters do not use it.

This finding has important implications, not just for understanding Taiwan, but for the study of other countries around the globe. The challenge of comparative political research is the great diversity of political life and culture in different countries. As electoral research becomes more truly international, some Western concepts and frameworks will inevitably come under challenge and be modified or set aside in many countries outside the West. We have argued that "left-right" is one such example—a framework to be used where it applies, but not elsewhere. Many countries, notably in Africa, have political systems primarily shaped by racial, ethnic, or linguistic divisions, not class conflict. Even in Western countries like Canada, with politics dominated by religious and linguistic divisions, voters struggle with the left-right concept, and some confuse "right" with "correct" (Ogmundson 1979, 800; Lambert 1983; Lambert et al. 1986). In Ireland, too, where divisions stemming from the Civil War have defined the party system for a century, the left-right concept has traditionally differentiated the main parties rather poorly, leaving the voters confused by it as well (Sinnott 1995, 24–33, 74–78, 162; Marsh et al. 2008, 42).[15] Left and right notions are rarely used in Africa either, apart from South Africa

(Jennifer Widner, personal communication). Taiwan provides an insightful example of how much difference the absence of left-right language may make in all these countries.

The "China factor" is central to understanding Taiwan politics. The parties and the voters divide over this question: How is Taiwan's nationhood to be understood in light of China's presence, its growing power, and its claims of sovereignty over Taiwan? It is that political dimension that shapes both Taiwan's party system and the voters' understanding of politics. Eurocentric notions of "left" and "right" simply do not apply.

To understand Taiwan, one must stop seeing it through a European lens. Conventional understandings of the importance of "left" and "right" in politics have no claim to universality. Many countries are well described in that way, but many others may not be, particularly in Asia and Africa. Here again, the study of Taiwan rewards the scholar with a deeper understanding of politics in many other places.

Appendix 9.A1.

Questionnaire Items and Operationalization of the Variables

Left-Right Ideology Question Wording:

In politics, sometimes people talk about the left and the right. This card lists eleven positions from the left (0) to the right (10). Which position do you occupy?

Taiwan Independence vs. Reunification with China Question Wording:

Sometimes people will talk about the question of Taiwan independence or reunification with China. Some people say that Taiwan should declare independence immediately. Other people say that Taiwan and China should unify immediately. Other people have opinions between these two positions. This card lists eleven positions from independence (0) to reunification (10). Which position do you occupy?

Environmental Protection vs. Economic Development Question Wording:

Regarding the question of economic development versus environmental protection, some people in society emphasize environmental protection while others emphasize economic development. On this card, the position that emphasizes environmental protection is at 0 on a scale from 0 to 10, and the position that emphasizes economic development is at 10. About where on this scale does your own view lie?

Promoting Social Welfare vs. Lower Priority for Social Welfare/Increasing Tax Question Wordings:

TEDS2001 On the question of social welfare, some people believe that people should take care of themselves and the government should not get involved while other people believe that the government should actively promote social welfare and take care of all the people. This card lists eleven positions from individuals should take care of themselves and the government should not get involved (0) to the government should actively promote social welfare (10). Which position do you occupy?

TEDS2008P Regarding the question of social welfare, some people believe that the government should merely maintain the current system in order not to increase people's taxes. Other people believe that the government should promote social welfare, even though it will lead to a tax increase. On this card, the position that maintaining the current system is the most important thing is at 0 on a scale from 0 to 10, and the position that promoting social welfare is most important is at 10. About where on this scale does your own view lie?

Large-Scale Reform vs. Social Stability Wording:

Looking at Taiwan's overall development, some people believe that large-scale reform is the most important thing, even if it means sacrificing some social stability. Other people believe that stability is most important and that reform should not be allowed to affect social stability. On this card, the position that large-scale reform is the most important thing is at 0 on a scale from 0 to 10, and the position that social stability is most important is at 10. About where on this scale does your own view lie?

Party Preference Question Wording:

Now we'd like to understand your opinions about each of the political parties. If 0 means you dislike a party very much, and 10 means you like that party very much, what number would you give the KMT? The DPP?

Notes

1. The cognitive interview data in this article come from a project entitled "A Study in Major Political Identification Concepts of the Taiwan Public" (NSC89–2414-H-004–022-SSS), whose principal investigator is Professor I-chou Liu of the Political Science Department of National Chengchi University. The survey data analyzed were collected by the Taiwan Election and Democratization Studies, 2001: The Legislative Election (TEDS2001) (NSC 90–2420-H-194–001) and 2008: The Presidential Election (TEDS2008P) (NSC 96–2420-H-004–017). The coordinator of the multiyear project TEDS is Professor Chi Huang (National Chengchi University). Further information is available on the TEDS website (http://www.tedsnet.org). T. J. Cheng gave us helpful comments. We also thank Charles Witke for timely advice about Latin meanings. The authors appreciate the assistance of each of these institutions and individuals. However, the authors alone are responsible for the views expressed here.

2. In the early years of the CSES, no exceptions were allowed. It is now possible to petition to be exempted if the question is meaningless in a particular country.

3. More generally, perhaps, conservatism (the "right") is the defense of the established order. Historically, this meant a defense of hierarchy and a preference for the status quo rather than for the untried and risky proposals of reformers (Huntington 1957; Beer 1966, chap. 9). By extension, "left" vs. "right" came to include divisions over change vs. custom, reason vs. tradition, and other issues raised by the revolutionary impulses of the eighteenth and nineteenth centuries. In practice, conservatives usually defended the interests of those who were successful and privileged within society. In the modern era of widespread democratization, acceptance of capitalism, and rapid scientific innovation, however, aristocratic views of society and defenses of stasis are out of fashion. Contemporary success and privilege in the West derive primarily from economic achievement within the capitalist order, and government intervention is their greatest threat. Hence modern conservatism opposes additional government intervention. Thus, in its central meaning, today's conservatism lacks the traditional emphasis on social hierarchy and reverence for the past, but it is nevertheless the legitimate descendent of its ideological ancestors.

4. Of course, some respondents may have had a legitimate thoughtful position at the midpoint of the scale. But as the next paragraph shows, many respondents at other scale positions were seriously confused. There is no simple escape from the central finding that the overwhelming majority of Taiwan respondents do not know what "left" and "right" mean in their politics, nor should they.

5. Of course, an outside observer can call any issue "left-right." Thus Fell (2005a, 112) accurately remarks that "[some] analysts talk of a left and right in Taiwan." How-

ever, this occurs almost exclusively among foreign scholars doing comparative work across many countries, using cross-national datasets like the CSES that impose the same left-right survey question on every country. It is quite rare for Taiwan scholars themselves to mention the left-right as a description of contemporary politics on the island, except to criticize it (Chen 2003).

6. English inherits a similar relationship from a now-dead language. In Latin, "dexter" means the right side, from which English takes the word "dexterous," meaning "skillful." The Latin word for "left" is "sinister," with overtones of bad omens from fortune tellers. The same word in English has come to mean "evil" or "portending evil."

7. One of us saw a Taiwan university official insist that a sign directing visitors to a set of university offices be placed on the right-hand wall, even though the offices were on the left side of the building. The reason given was that the right side was "greater."

8. The project is sponsored by National Science Council (Taiwan). The principal investigator is Professor I-chou Liu at the Political Science Department of National Chengchi University, who generously shared the data.

9. These respondents were chosen to represent both genders and a variety of ages and occupations. Their demographic profiles are available from Su-feng Cheng.

10. For the question wordings, see appendix 9.A1.

11. Respondents were somewhat more responsive in 2008, raising the possibility that experience with democracy is improving comprehension. Of course, a comparison of two time points can be no more than suggestive. However, similar gains in the coherence of political attitudes over time have been noted in other new democracies (for example, Arian and Shamir 1983, 150).

12. It is clear in figure 9.3 to figure 9.5 that Taiwan citizens locate party positions on the left-right scale mainly on the basis of their party preference, not the four traditional policy issues. This result also has been validated by a multivariable model, but the model cannot be included in the chapter due to space limitations. The model is available from Yi-ching Hsiao on request.

13. Just under 61% of the sample placed themselves at a neutral 5 on the 0–10 scale, yet another reminder of the weak understanding of this variable. Those respondents have been omitted in the percentage calculations that follow.

14. Dalton and Tanaka (2007) recognize that the main axis of Taiwan politics is the independence-reunification issue, not the European versions of "left" and "right," but they interpret their data as indicating only a little differentiation between the two main parties on the national identity issue.

15. Both Canada and Ireland have a social democratic party, so that conventional left-right language plays some role in party politics. However, both parties typically receive only modest proportions of the vote, finishing well behind the two principal parties. Even in the special circumstances of 2011, the best year ever for both, they finished in second place, well behind the top party.

References

Arian, Asher, and Michal Shamir. 1983. "The Primarily Political Functions of the Left-Right Continuum." *Comparative Politics* 15 (2): 139–58.

Barnes, Samuel H. 1971. "Left, Right, and the Italian Voter." *Comparative Political Studies* 4: 157–75.

Bartle, John. 1998. "Left-Right Position Matters, but Does Social Class? Causal Models of the 1992 British General Election." *British Journal of Political Science* 28 (3): 501–29.

Bawn, Kathleen, Martin Cohen, David Karol, Seth Masket, Hans Noel, and John Zaller. 2012. "A Theory of Political Parties: Groups, Policy Demands, and Nominations in American Politics." *Perspectives on Politics* 10 (3): 571–97.

Beer, Samuel H. 1966. *British Politics in the Collectivist Age.* New York: Knopf.

Berglund, Frode, Soren Holmberg, Hermann Schmitt, and Jacques Thomassen. 2005. "Party Identification and Party Choice." In *The European Voter: A Comparative Study of Modern Democracies*, ed. Jacques Thomassen, 106–24. Oxford: Oxford University Press.

Chen, Wen-chun. 2003. "The Blue and the Green: The Political Ideologies of the Mass Public in the 2000 Taiwan Presidential Election" [in Chinese]. *Journal of Electoral Studies* 10 (1): 41–80.

Cheng, Tun-jen, and Yung-ming Hsu. 1996. "Issue Structure, the DPP's Factionalism, and Party Realignment." In *Taiwan's Electoral Politics and Democratic Transition*, ed. Hung-mao Tien, 137–73. Armonk, NY: M. E. Sharpe.

Chu, Yun-han, and Tse-min Lin. 1996. "The Process of Democratic Consolidation in Taiwan: Social Cleavage, Electoral Competition, and the Emerging Party System." In *Taiwan's Electoral Politics and Democratic Transition*, ed. Hung-mao Tien, 79–104. Armonk, NY: M. E. Sharpe.

Converse, Philip E. 1964. "The Nature of Belief Systems in Mass Publics." In *Ideology and Discontent*, ed. David E. Apter, 206–61. Glencoe, IL: Free Press.

Converse, Philip E. 1966. "The Problem of Party Distances in Models of Voting Change." In *The Electoral Process*, ed. M. Kent Jennings and H. Zeigler, 175–207. Englewood Cliffs, New Jersey: Prentice-Hall.

Converse, Philip E., and Henry Valen. 1971. "Dimensions of Cleavage and Perceived Party Distances in Norwegian Voting." *Scandinavian Political Studies* 6 (6) : 107–52.

Converse, Philip E., and Roy Pierce. 1986. *Political Representation in France.* Cambridge: Belknap Press of Harvard University Press.

Dalton, Russell J. 2008. "The Quantity and the Quality of Party Systems: Party System Polarization, Its Measurement, and Its Consequences." *Comparative Political Studies* 4 (7): 899–920.

Dalton, Russell J. 2011. "Left-Right Orientations, Context, and Voting Choices." In *Citizens, Context, and Choice*, ed. Russell J. Dalton and Christopher J. Anderson, 103–25. Oxford: Oxford University Press.

Dalton, Russell J. 2012. "Parties and Representative Government." In *Political Parties and Democratic Linkage*, ed. Russell Dalton, David Farrell, and Ian McAllister. Oxford: Oxford University Press.

Dalton, Russell J., and Aiji Tanaka. 2007. "The Patterns of Party Polarization in East Asia." *Journal of East Asian Studies* 7 (2): 203–23.

Erikson, Robert S., Gerald C. Wright, and John P McIver. 1993. *Statehouse Democracy:*

Public Opinion and Policy in the American States. Cambridge: Cambridge University Press.

Fell, Dafydd. 2005a. "Measuring and Explaining Party Change in Taiwan: 1991–2004." *Journal of East Asian Studies* 5: 105–33.

Fell, Dafydd. 2005b. *Party Politics in Taiwan*. Oxford: Routledge.

Fell, Dafydd. 2008. "Inter-Party Competition in Taiwan: Toward a New Party System?" In *Presidential Politics in Taiwan*, ed. Steven M. Goldstein and Julian Chang, 49–84. Norwalk, Connecticut: EastBridge.

Fell, Dafydd. 2012. *Government and Politics in Taiwan*. Oxford: Routledge.

Fleury, Christopher J., and Michael S. Lewis-Beck. 1993. "Anchoring the French Voter: Ideology versus Party." *Journal of Politics* 55 (4): 1100–1109.

Fuchs, Dieter, and Hans-Dieter Klingemann. 1989. "The Left-Right Schema." In *Continuities in Political Action: A Longitudinal Study of Political Orientations in Three Western Democracies*, ed. M. Kent Jennings and Jan van Deth, 203–34. New York: Walter de Gruyter.

Hotelling, Harold. 1929. "Stability in Competition." *Economic Journal* 39 (153): 41–57.

Hsieh, John Fuh-sheng, Emerson M. S. Niou, and Huei-ping Lin. 1995. "Issue Voting in the 1994 Gubernatorial and Mayoral Elections: An Application of the Rational Choice Approach" [in Chinese]. *Journal of Electoral Studies* 2 (1): 77–92.

Huntington, Samuel P. 1957. "Conservatism as an Ideology." *American Political Science Review* 51 (2): 454–73.

Inglehart, Ronald. 1990. *Culture Shift in Advanced Industrial Society*. Princeton: Princeton University Press.

Jansen, Guido, Geoffrey Evans, and Nan Dirk De Graaf. 2013. "Class Voting and Left-Right Party Positions." In *Political Choice Matters*, ed. Geoffrey Evans and Nan Dirk De Graaf, 46–82. Oxford: Oxford University Press.

Jou, Willy. 2010. "The Heuristic Value of the Left-Right Schema in East Asia." *International Political Science Review* 31:366–94.

Lambert, Ronald D. 1983. "Question Design, Response Set and the Measurement of Left/Right Thinking in Survey Research." *Canadian Journal of Political Science* 16 (1): 135–44.

Lambert, Ronald D., James E. Curtis, Steven D. Brown, and Barry J. Kay. 1986. "In Search of Left/Right Beliefs in the Canadian Electorate." *Canadian Journal of Political Science* 19 (3): 541–63.

Laver, Michael, and W. Ben Hunt. 1992. *Policy and Party Competition*. New York: Routledge.

Lewis-Beck, Michael S., and Kevin Chlarson. 2002. "Party, Ideology, Institutions and the 1995 French Presidential Election." *British Journal of Political Science* 32 (3): 489–512.

Lipset, Seymour M., Paul F. Lazarsfeld, Allen H. Barton, and Juan Linz. 1954. "The Psychology of Voting." In *Handbook of Social Psychology*, vol. 2, ed. Gardner Lindzey. Reading, MA: Addison-Wesley.

Lipset, Seymour Martin, and Stein Rokkan. 1967. *Party Systems and Voter Alignments*. New York: Free Press.

Marsh, Michael, Richard Sinnott, John Garry, and Fiachra Kennedy. 2008. *The Irish Voter*. Manchester: Manchester University Press.

Norris, Pippa. 2004. *Electoral Engineering: Voting Rules and Political Behavior*. New York: Cambridge University Press.

Ogmundson, R. L. 1979. "A Note on the Ambiguous Meanings of Survey Research Measures Which Use the Words 'Left' and 'Right'." *Canadian Journal of Political Science* 12 (4): 799–805.

Potrafke, Niklas. 2009. "Does Government Ideology Influence Political Alignment with the U.S.? An Empirical Analysis of Voting in the UN General Assembly." *Review of International Organizations* 4 (3): 245–68.

Rigger, Shelley. 2001. *From Opposition to Power: Taiwan's Democratic Progressive Party*. Boulder: Lynne Rienner Publishers.

Sheng, Shing-yuan, and Yin-yan Chen. 2003. "Political Cleavage and Party Competition: An Analysis of the 2001 Legislative Yuan Election" [in Chinese]. *Journal of Electoral Studies* 10 (1): 7–40.

Sigelman, Lee, and Syng Nam Yough. 1978. "Left-Right Polarization in National Party Systems." *Comparative Political Studies* 11: 355–379.

Sinnott, Richard. 1995. *Irish Voters Decide*. Manchester: Manchester University Press.

Stokes, Donald E. 1962. "Spatial Models of Party Competition." *American Political Science Review* 57 (2): 368–77.

Tsai, Chia-hung. 2008. "Making Sense of Issue Position, Party Image, Party Preference, and Voting Choice: A Case Study of Taiwan's 2004 Legislative Election." *Journal of Social Science and Philosophy* 20 (1): 1–24.

van der Eijk, Cees, Hermann Schmitt, and Tanja Binder. 2005. "Left-Right Orientations and Party Choice." In *The European Voter: A Comparative Study of Modern Democracies*, ed. Jacques Thomassen, 167–91. Oxford: Oxford University Press.

Wang, Ding-ming. 2001. "The Impacts of Policy Issues on Voting Behavior in Taiwan: A Mixed Logit Approach" [in Chinese]. *Journal of Electoral Studies* 8 (2): 95–123.

Wang, Ding-ming. 2003. "Voting Utility and Choice Decision in 2001 Election: The Application of Spatial Voting Theory in Different Electoral Systems" [in Chinese]. *Journal of Electoral Studies* 10 (1): 171–206.

Zechmeister, Elizabeth J. 2006. "What's Left and Who's Right? A Q-Method Study of Individual and Contextual Influences on the Meaning of Ideological Labels." *Political Behavior* 28 (2): 151–73.

Zechmeister, Elizabeth J. 2010. "The Varying Economic Meaning of 'Left' and 'Right' in Latin America." *AmericasBarometer Insights* 38.

Zechmeister, Elizabeth J. 2015. "Left-Right Identifications and the Latin American Voter." In *The Latin American Voter*, ed. Ryan Carlin, Matthew M. Singer, and Elizabeth J. Zechmeister, 195–225. Ann Arbor: University of Michigan Press.

Zechmeister, Elizabeth J., and Margarita Corral. 2013. "Individual and Contextual Constraints on Ideological Labels in Latin America." *Comparative Political Studies* 46 (6): 675–701.

CHAPTER 10

Electoral System Change and Its Effects on the Party System in Taiwan

Chi Huang

On June 7, 2005, the ad hoc National Assembly of Taiwan ratified a constitutional amendment to change the electoral rules of the Legislative Yuan (the parliament) by halving the number of seats from 225 to 113, extending legislators' terms of office from three years to four, and adopting the mixed-member majoritarian (MMM) system[1] to replace the half-century-old single nontransferable vote (SNTV) system for legislative elections. The new mixed-member system in Taiwan consists of one tier of single-member districts (SMDs) of 73 seats and a party list tier of 34 seats. In addition, there are 6 seats reserved for highland and lowland aboriginals elected on the basis of the SNTV system (Huang 2007, 2008a).

This chapter examines the significant changes in the legislative electoral system in Taiwan and then evaluates their consequences to the political party system. Taiwan's electoral reform in 2005 is of great interest in itself because it illustrates how the cleavages, institutions, parties, and voters interact to produce election outcomes, both expected and unexpected. But more important, it constitutes a critical case to reexamine the popular seat-maximization approach to electoral reform (Benoit 2007), since in Taiwan it was the ruling-party legislators' own initiative to downsize the parliament, which ignited a raging controversy and then backfired. Curiously enough, the leaders of the two archrival parties, the Nationalist Party (Kuomintang) and the Democratic Progressive Party, appeared as if they were silent partners pushing through the same new MMM rule, although at the same time each was seeking its own goals. Furthermore, Taiwan's case fills a gap in the literature concerning the "redistributive" type of electoral reform (Renwick 2010) in new democracies and thus can be crucial for comparative studies of electoral engineering (Ahmed 2013; Colomer 2004; Norris 2004; Sartori 1994).

The chapter begins with a review of the theoretical literature on the party system followed by an outline of a comprehensive multilevel framework linking cleavages with electoral systems, after which is a discussion of party politics under the SNTV system. I then apply the framework to trace the process of events and interactions between agents that led to the critical junctures of the passage of the electoral reform proposal in August 2004 and its final ratification in June 2005. Last is a discussion of the impact of the new MMM system on Taiwan's party system at the national, district, and voter levels.

Theoretical Perspectives

There have been two main theories that explain the party system and voting behaviors in democracies: the cleavage structure and the electoral system. The former is represented by Lipset and Rokkan (1967), who explained changes to party systems, electoral realignments, and political mobilizations in Western European countries through cleavages along the lines of groups, regions, farmers, workers, laborers, and entrepreneurs. The Lipset-Rokkan "freezing hypothesis" claims that these preexisting cleavage structures were then "frozen" in the 1920s into party alignments through voter mobilization. That is, party systems basically stabilize only when they reflect the fundamental cleavages in societies. Once the party system is formed, it reinforces the cleavage system in order to perpetuate itself. The second school is represented by Duverger (1959), who believed it was the electoral system that principally shaped the party system. For many scholars, Duverger's "law" (that single-member districts favor a two-party system) and "hypothesis" (that proportional representation leads to a multiparty system; Riker 1982) still provide the foundation of how the electoral system affects the party system, while the relationship between district magnitude, M, and the effective number of parties has been extended into the "$M + 1$ rule," that is, voters will concentrate their votes on the top $M + 1$ candidates (Cox 1997).

In spite of debates in the literature, these two theories are not necessarily contradictory. While cleavage theory focuses more on the macro-level origins of the party system, Duverger's law focuses on the meso-level institutional structures. Indeed, later development of the literature witnesses greater appreciation of the interplay between social heterogeneity and electoral rules (Clark and Golder 2006; Cox 1997; Neto and Cox 1997; Ordeshook and Shvetsova 1994). In these interactive models, electoral systems set an upper limit to the number of parties and work like filters of social divisions. That is, within this upper limit, the more "permissive" an electoral system is (such as the proportional representation system), the easier it is for preexisting cleavages to manifest as political parties. The more "restrictive" electoral systems (such as the SMD system), on the other hand, tend to constrain the number of parties.

A Synthesized Framework

The literature on electoral rules is indeed impressive, and the area is often revered as one of the most advanced in political science. But previous studies of Taiwan's electoral reform only either examined legislative elections or looked at legislative and executive elections separately (e.g., Chang and Chang 2009). Yet legislative electoral systems, important as they are in translating votes into seats, do not operate in a vacuum. Their evolution and impact can be fully understood only when they are embedded within broader social and institutional contexts. Building upon the vast literature, Huang (2008a, 4–5) developed a three-level analytical framework that incorporates the macro perspective of social cleavages, the meso perspective of institutional structures and electoral systems, and the micro perspective of voting behaviors. Following Powell's (1982) insight that constitutional settings have a substantial impact on democratic performance, this general framework embeds the electoral systems within constitutional systems at the meso level. It assumes that political elites seek not only to maximize seats in the parliament but also to seize executive offices. It is the combination of the legislative electoral system and the constitutional setup that defines the payoffs of capturing executive offices and the degree of cross-district coordination required to win the executive offices. Hence "[t]o fully understand the effects of an electoral system, we must imbed it within the broader political contexts, especially the constitutional framework, of the country in question" (Huang 2016, 302).

In presidential and semipresidential systems, for example, the president exercises the executive authority. The ultimate goal of most political parties and their leaders is undoubtedly to control both the executive and legislative branches in order to form a unified government, although the appeal of and the competition for the presidency is often a higher priority (Batto and

Cox 2016; Curini and Hino 2012). This implies that presidential contests often spill over to the legislative elections (Huang and Wang 2009, 2014). Although parliamentary elections after a presidential one may allow the president to consolidate his or her honeymoon (Samuels and Shugart 2010; Shugart and Carey 1992), our general framework also reveals the possibility that the parliament becomes a second battlefield for blocking government policies or embarrassing the ruling party once a viable party loses the presidential contest, or both. In the latter case, the temporal proximity of presidential and legislative elections may well make campaigns appear to be never-ending tournaments that escalate the already-fierce competition and leave little room for party truces.

This synthesized framework, in contrast with the traditional legislature-centric perspective, broadens our theoretical landscape by taking into account the payoffs of holding executive office, the degree of coordination required to capture the executive office, and the sustainability of the executive office (term limit). Although Moser and Scheiner (2012) argue that strong presidentialism hinders party-system institutionalization, my framework does not exclude the possibility that the greater degree of national coordination required to win the executive offices may well motivate elites to form coalitions with or to join and stay in the major parties, or both (Hicken 2009; Hicken and Stoll 2008). I argue that the *joint* effects of the presidential and legislative electoral systems, as well as the temporal proximity of the two elections, exert pressure on elites and parties to engage in cross-district coordination. Furthermore, social diversity is more than a background condition waiting to be filtered by the electoral rules. I argue that deep-rooted sociopolitical cleavages can act as latent yet powerful forces structuring the speed and direction in which such coordination efforts move. Finally, the strategic actions of elites under these contexts shape the choice sets available to the electorate and its voting behavior at the micro level. Electoral consequences, both expected and unexpected, in turn affect the persistence of and change in the party system, institutional structure, and eventually the sociopolitical cleavages. The principal idea behind this comprehensive framework is simple: that is, social cleavage and constitutional structures are part and parcel of studying the evolution and effects of electoral systems.

Party Politics under the SNTV System in Taiwan

The evolution of the party system in Taiwan can be divided into three periods: the dominance of the single-party system under the KMT[2] before the late 1980s; the gradual emergence of small parties in the early 1990s that transitioned into a quite vigorous multiparty system after 2000 (Fell 2005); and the reversal of the latter system (as a result of changes to the electoral system) to a cleavage-based two-party system after 2008 (figure 10.1). In brief, competitive party politics emerged only after 1986, when opposition forces formed the DPP. The transition to full democracy was completed in the 1990s, when the national legislature was subject to regular reelection beginning in 1992 followed by the first presidential election in 1996. The first power shift occurred when the long-time opposition party, the DPP, won the presidency in 2000 followed by reelection in 2004. However, the KMT has retained continuous control of Taiwan's legislative branch, although the party went from a single-party majority to a majority in coalition and then back to a single-party majority. In the early part of the democratic era, the KMT retained a degree of dominance. After 2001, splinter parties forced the KMT into coalition arrangements, but the party returned to dominant status in the first postreform election of 2008 (see, for example, Stockton 2010).

Taiwan has employed the simple plurality system for presidential elections since 1996 (table 10.2), but the legislative electoral system is somewhat more complicated. Before its 2005 electoral reform, Taiwan employed an SNTV system for its national legislature (table 10.1).[3]

In the 1998, 2001, and 2004 legislative elections, for example, there were a total of 225 seats. Of these, 168 representatives were elected from 29 geographically defined multimember districts, and another 8 members were elected from 2 nationwide districts reserved for lowland and highland aborigines. The average district magnitude was 5.79 seats per district. Several districts had only 1 seat, while the largest district had 13 seats. In addition to the 176 SNTV seats, there were also 49 seats elected by closed proportional representation (PR) lists. The list designated for national party representatives had 41 seats, whereas the list designated for overseas representatives had 8 seats. There was no separate party list ballot for the PR seats. Instead, all the votes for the party nominees running in the SNTV districts were summed to obtain each party's national total. For all parties with at least 5 percent of the national vote, these totals were used to apportion seats on the two lists using a largest remainders formula (Farrell 2011; Wang 2012).

Under the SNTV system, Taiwan has developed from a single-dominant-party system in the early 1990s to a period of multiparty politics after the 2000 presidential election. Scholars have cited one-party dominance as the reason for the implementation of SNTV electoral rules. Under an SNTV system, political parties must coordinate their supporters' votes within

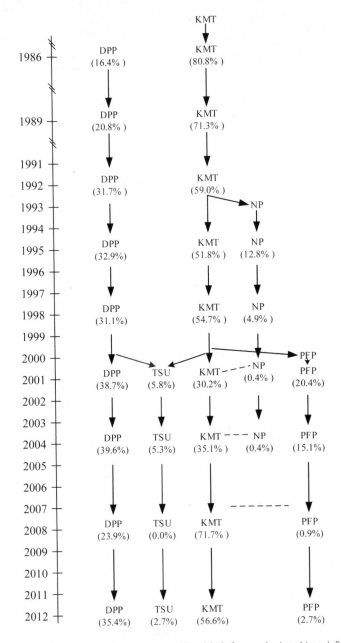

Fig. 10.1. Taiwan's political party system, 1986–2012. *Source:* Author. *Note:* 1. % in the parentheses denotes percentage of seats in the Legislative Yuan; the broken line denotes an alliance, loosely defined as some form of cooperation between parties. For example, many NP candidates ran under the KMT's umbrella in 2001 and 2004, and the PFP agreed not to run its own party list in 2008 in exchange for KMT's promise to nominate six former PFP legislators in six districts and also allowed the PFP to share four seats on the KMT's party list. Although formally there was no NP legislator in 2008 and 2012, NP continues to be active in some local elections.

TABLE 10.1 Features of the Legislative Electoral System in Taiwan since 1992

Term	Election year	Electoral system	Total seats	PR seats (%)	PR legal threshold %	Average district magnitude[1]	ENPP[2]	ENEP (SNTV)	ENEP (PR)	ENEP (SMD)
2nd	1992	SNTV	161	36(22.4)	5.0	4.41	2.46	2.52	—	—
3rd	1995	SNTV	164	36(22.0)	5.0	4.52	2.63	2.90	—	—
4th	1998	SNTV	225	49(21.8)	5.0	5.79	2.53	3.14	—	—
5th	2001	SNTV	225	49(21.8)	5.0	5.79	3.24	4.14	—	—
6th	2004	SNTV	225	49(21.8)	5.0	5.79	3.08	3.76	—	—
7th	2008	MMM	113	34(30.1)	5.0	1.00	1.47	—	2.49	2.29
8th	2012	MMM	113	34(30.1)	5.0	1.00	1.97	—	3.03	2.32

Source: Huang (2008b, 132) and Central Election Commission, ROC "Election Statistics: Legislative Elections." http://db.cec.gov.tw/ (accessed September 23, 2013).

1. (total number of seats elected from districts)/(total number of districts). 2. Effective number of parliamentary parties (ENPP) = , where P_i is the proportion of seats of the ith parties. Likewise, ENEP = , where Q_i is the vote shares of the ith parties.

TABLE 10.2 Presidential Election Results in Taiwan, 1996–2012

Year	Electoral system	KMT		DPP		NP		PFP (James Soong)		Others[1]	
		Vote	Vote %	Vote	Vote %	Vote	Vote %	Vote	Vote %	Vote	Vote %
1996	plurality	5,813,699	54.00	2,274,586	21.13	—	—	—	—	C: 1,074,044	9.98
										L: 1,603,790	14.90
2000	plurality	2,925,513	23.10	4,977,697	39.30	16,782	0.13	4,664,972	36.84	H: 79,429	0.63
2004	plurality	6,442,452	49.89	6,471,970	50.11	—	—	—	—	—	—
2008	plurality	7,659,014	58.44	5,444,949	41.55	—	—	—	—	—	—
2012	plurality	6,891,139	51.60	6,093,578	45.63	—	—	369,588	2.76	—	—

Source: Central Election Commission, ROC, "Election Statistics: Presidential Elections." http://db.cec.gov.tw/ (accessed September 23, 2013).

1. C refers to Chen Lu-an; L refers to Lin Yang-Kang; H refers to Hsu Hsin-liang.

constituencies in order to more evenly distribute votes across candidates. Without successful coordination, weaker candidates will get too few votes and stronger co-partisans will receive too many votes. If effective, intraparty coordination can result in political parties gaining an overrepresentation bonus. Governing parties have a tremendous advantage because they can use the resources of the state to overcome the coordination problems of nomination and division of votes (Cox 1997; Cox and Niou 1994; Cox and Rosenbluth 1993, 1996; Patterson and Stockton 2010; Rochon 1981). Meanwhile, small parties also face much smaller coordination problems since they often only nominate one candidate in any given district. With only one candidate, vote division is not a challenge (Taagepera and Shugart 1989, 28). Besides, the vote share necessary to win a seat decreases as the number of seats increases. Since candidates can win with support from a small minority of voters, they can appeal to highly personalized and niche voters (Flanagan et al. 1991). Under an SNTV system, there is electoral space for small parties, either newly formed or splintered from the existing big parties when antagonistic intraparty struggle cannot be resolved.

Electoral Reform: Tangles of Two Archrivals

Taiwan has experienced numerous institutional challenges, such as fractional politics, extremism, intraparty competition, money politics, party splintering, and an inefficient parliament, and many studies have attributed these disadvantages to the SNTV system (Cox and Rosenbluth 1993; Cox and Thies 1998; Richardson 1988; Wang 2012). Because of continual election scandals, the call for legislative electoral reform has often enjoyed widespread attention. However, it took the tension of stagnation and a stalemate caused by the divided government after the first power shift in 2000 to shake up the half-century-old SNTV system.

The hurdle of changing the legislative electoral system was unusually high in Taiwan when the DPP government took over power in 2000. The Legislative Yuan's organization and election are specified in Article 4 of the Additional Articles of Constitution of the Republic of China. Changing the electoral system therefore requires amending the constitution, the procedure for which is also specified by the constitution. As of June 2000,[4] a constitutional amendment required two stages: a proposal passed by the Legislative Yuan and then ratification by the National Assembly.[5] The proposal had to be initiated by at least one-fourth of the total seats of the Legislative Yuan and passed by at least three-fourths of the members present at a meeting attended by at least three-fourths of the total members of the Legislative Yuan. Once passed, the proposal had to be publicly announced for six months. Then 300 delegates had to be elected by proportional representation to the National Assembly to deliberate and vote on the Legislative Yuan proposal. Obviously, changing the legislative electoral rule was extremely difficult, not only because a constitutional amendment was called for but also because it took the incumbent Legislative Yuan, a beneficiary of the status quo, to initiate and pass the constitutional amendment proposal before sending it to the ad hoc National Assembly for ratification. Electoral engineering in Taiwan required Herculean efforts of both intra- and interparty coordination to achieve. Yet it did happen in 2005. Why?

Based on the comprehensive framework laid out previously, I argue that it was the introduction of popular presidential elections in 1996 and the subsequent power shift in 2000 due to the KMT's internal split that set the momentum of legislative electoral reform on track in order to "bring back order and end the parliamentary chaos." The power of the president in Taiwan, under its "president-parliamentary" semipresidential system (Shugart and Carey 1992, 24), makes the presidency a big enough prize to motivate political elites to cooperate in the electoral process in order to win by a plurality. Before 2012, Taiwan also had peculiar staggered electoral schedules for multiple political offices at different levels and branches of government (Huang and Lin 2013), as shown in figure 10.2. The temporal proximity of election schedules between the presidential and legislative elections in turn make the interparty competition for the former spill over into the latter like an endless election campaign.[6] Anxious to appeal to the electorate, the major parties campaigned on a reformist platform and each advanced its image as the true champion of electoral reform. Repeated promises as part of the continuing election campaigns not only suppressed opposing intraparty views but elevated the clamor for reform to such a point that party leaders resorted to party discipline to get legislators to pass the constitutional amendment act. The following paragraphs chronologically trace the trajectory of Taiwan's electoral reform so as to highlight the sequential interactions among cleavages, institutions, and agents that shaped reform politics in path-dependent ways.

In January 1994, the Japanese Diet passed electoral law reform bills that abolished the old SNTV system and adopted a new MMM system (Curtis 1999; Reed and Thies 2001). The 1994 electoral reform in Japan and its initial implementation in the 1996 House of Representatives election sent a shock wave through neighboring Taiwan, where the SNTV system had been blamed for intraparty competition and factionalism, as well as for money

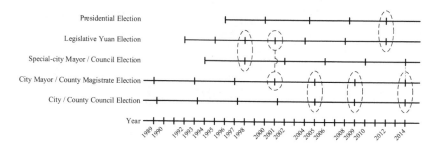

Fig. 10.2. Timing of Taiwan's major national and local elections. *Source:* Huang and Lin 2013. *Notes:* 1. Circles with dashed lines denote concurrent elections with the same set of ballots. 2. Dotted line in 2014 means special-city elections were held on the same day as other cities/counties but with a different set of ballots.

politics (see, for example, Cox 1996; Cox and Niou 1994). In late 1996, at the National Development Meeting summoned by President Lee Teng-hui of the KMT after his win in the March 1996 presidential election, a consensus was reached to replace the SNTV system with a mixed-member system. However, a proposed constitutional amendment about electoral reform failed in 1997 because the then-ruling KMT insisted on a Japanese-style MMM system, which favors big parties, while the then-opposition DPP and the New Party supported a more proportional, German-style mixed-member proportional system. Given that no consensus was reached on that point, the electoral reform proposal was dropped from the agenda. Instead, an amendment was ratified to increase the total number of seats in the Legislative Yuan from 164 seats in 1995 to 225 seats in 1998 so as to accommodate members of the then to-be-abolished Taiwan Provincial Council who might run for the legislature. As a result, the average district magnitude increased from 4.52 to 5.79 seats per district, and only 40,000 votes were usually sufficient to elect a district candidate. This 37 percent jump in the number of seats did defuse some resistance to the streamlining of the Taiwan Provincial Government, yet it unexpectedly increased the electoral opportunities for small parties and seeded the next-round initiatives of slimming the Legislative Yuan.

Three years later, the DPP won the March 2000 presidential election, while the Pan-Blue parties maintained control of the majority of seats in the Legislative Yuan and dragged their feet over the new DPP administration. The first power shift plus the first divided national government ever experienced in Taiwan intensified the fraught relationship between the executive and legislative branches and incited much mudslinging between the governing DPP and the opposition KMT and its allies. The opposition Pan-Blue parties were often portrayed as the source of chaos in the parliament. Frequent brawls that broke out on the floor further ruined the public's image of the Legislative Yuan as a whole.

On November 24, 2000, a year before the 2001 legislative election, a DPP legislator placed a campaign advertisement in the newspapers calling for halving the number of legislative seats.[7] This first call for such a reduction immediately caught the nation's attention and became a campaign slogan. It constituted a simple issue that could easily gain popular support and was difficult for opponents to disagree with in public. But it also motivated politicians to bundle their own political agenda with it. The effects went far beyond the December 2001 legislative election and extended to the March 2004 presidential election and then to the December 2004 legislative election. Among these three consecutive national elections within four years, the 2004 presidential election was the impetus for the final showdown on electoral reform. To a large extent, what happened in the May 2005 National Assembly election and with the assembly's ratification of the constitutional amendment in June was not so much a critical election, as Fell (2010) argued, but only the consequence of the long, harsh four-year election campaigns. The presidential hopefuls of the two major parties were betting that the new MMM electoral system would not only be favorable to their own party but also reduce the opportunities for the small parties. The two archrival parties, the DPP and the KMT, both dreamed of first winning the presidency and then a majority of seats and unwittingly appeared to act like silent partners in carrying out electoral reform.

In mid-April 2001, the DPP began openly advocating an MMM system, a reversal of the position it had held since 1997, when it was in opposition. In late October 2001, President Chen Shui-bian pledged that if the DPP became the largest party in the Legislative Yuan, he would advance bold and decisive parliamentary reforms, including replacing the SNTV system with an MMM system and downsizing the legislature. This was the first time that electoral system reform had been explicitly linked with the popular issue of assembly size. In mid-November, the KMT responded with a five-point parliamentary reform proposal that also included an MMM system and a reduction in the number of legislative seats. In late November 2001, President Chen Shui-bian accused the KMT and the NP of not supporting seat reduction and reiterated his pledge to reduce the total number of seats to 150 and replace the SNTV system with an MMM system, and, in addition, to synchronize legislators' three-year term with the president's four-year term. For fear of being labeled antireform, the KMT and NP responded that they had wholeheartedly supported the seat-reduction proposal from the very beginning. Under pressure from public opinion, the party caucuses promised to work on these proposals after the 2001 legislative election. The December 2001 election was a debacle for the KMT, whose seats decreased from 54.7 percent to only 30.2 percent. Meanwhile, the ruling DPP substantially increased its seats from 31.7 percent to 38.7 percent and became the largest party in the legislature. The election results definitely boosted the morale of the DPP.

Not long after the new legislature convened in 2002, the Taiwan Solidarity Union, which was formed months before the 2001 election and was considered to be an ally of the DPP, took the lead in proposing a constitutional amendment to reduce the assembly size by half. Other parties responded by proposing various versions of that proposal. In reality, however, the reform was unpopular with the rank-and-file legislators in both major parties, since they understandably were not happy about half of their seats in the legislature being eliminated. The two major parties paid lip service to the proposal, but the constitutional amendment committee did not even convene. The atmosphere began to change, however, after the KMT and the People First Party leaders, Lien Chan and James Soong, teamed up as running mates for the 2004 presidential election. While the KMT and PFP were still squabbling about their common platform, especially the PFP's objection to the MMM system, the Government Renovation Committee of the Presidential Office announced in early May a parliamentary reform plan that reiterated President Chen Shui-bian's campaign promises of the previous year. Soon the DPP party caucus and the DPP Standing Committee reached agreement on the reform plan and pledged to complete the constitutional amendment and put it into effect for the December 2004 legislative election. In June 2003, the KMT-PFP party caucuses dared the DPP to reduce the seats actually by half, that is, to 113 seats instead of 150, but they still criticized the MMM proposal as a campaign gimmick. In October, the KMT-PFP caucuses even began talking about reducing the number of seats to 100 but remained vague about whether they supported an MMM or mixed-member proportional system.

The tone of "reform bidding" turned acrimonious as the presidential election drew near. On November 13, Premier You Xi-Kun opened another battlefront by proposing to formulate a completely new Taiwan constitution via public referendum. This move touched upon the fundamental issue of Taiwan independence versus future unification with China (see Huang 2005, 2006). Caught by surprise and again worried about being labeled antireform by the DPP, the KMT chair, Lien Chan, countered by advocating a new Republic of China constitution. Lien, cajoled by the acquiescence of the PFP, vowed a sweeping reform based on 10 principles, the fifth principle of which concerned parliamentary reform: the MMM system; seat reduction to 100, 113, or 150; and synchronized terms. The content of this principle was suspiciously similar to the DPP's earlier proposal. Meanwhile, the KMT-PFP caucuses took the lead in late November to initiate a constitutional amendment based on Lien's pledge but with an explicit seat number of 113. While this initiative was still collecting the signatures of legislators, on December 30 the DPP's Central Standing Committee also reduced its original 150-seat proposal to 113 seats, partly at the strong urging of the DPP's former chair Lin Yi-Xiong. The two arch rivals now engaged in strange tangles.

On February 25, 2004, the Constitutional Amendment Committee of the Legislative Yuan convened and on March 10 passed a draft of the amendment proposal. It seemed that the major parties intended to rush the process, and they sent the bill to the floor right before the March 20 presidential election. Yet on March 15 the party caucus of the Nonpartisan Solidarity Union, a long-time opponent of the MMM system, motioned to send the bill for cross-party consultation, which would take four months according to the legislative procedure rule. This motion blocked the bill one step short of reaching the floor.

After winning reelection in 2004 by a thin margin, President Chen Shuibian vigorously pushed for electoral reform. In his inauguration speech on May 20, he vowed to fulfill his campaign promises by completing the constitutional renovation by the end of his second term in 2008. As before, electoral reform was unpopular with most rank-and-file legislators. Not surprisingly, the TSU and NPSU continued to oppose the MMM system. But even the KMT-PFP alliance began to weaken after losing the presidential election. The KMT chair, Lien Chan, again worried about public support in the upcoming December 2004 legislative election, threw his support behind the reform. Some PFP legislators, however, began to voice their objections to the MMM system for fear of a bleak future. The PFP chair, James Soong, who was also worried about being accused of breaking campaign promises, persuaded the PFP legislators to support the electoral reform bill so as to maintain a proreform image for the December legislative election. The pressure of the upcoming election was so great that eventually not only the DPP and the KMT-PFP caucuses went along with their party leaders but the TSU and NPSU legislators all voted unanimously, though reluctantly, on August 23, 2004, to send the constitutional amendment proposal to the National Assembly for ratification. The December 2004 legislative election outcome turned out to be a great disappointment to the PFP, for it lost a dozen seats (table 10.3).

TABLE 10.3 Legislative Yuan Election Results in Taiwan, 1992–2012

Year	Seats	Electoral system	KMT Vote %	KMT Seat (%)	DPP Vote %	DPP Seat (%)	NP Vote %	NP Seat (%)	PFP Vote %	PFP Seat (%)	TSU Vote %	TSU Seat (%)	OTHER Vote %	OTHER Seat (%)
1992	161	SNTV	52.7	95 (59.0)	31.4	51 (31.7)	—	—	—	—	—	—	15.9	15 (9.3)
1995	164	SNTV	46.1	85 (51.8)	33.2	54 (32.9)	13.0	21 (12.8)	—	—	—	—	7.8	4 (2.4)
1998	225	SNTV	46.4	123 (54.7)	29.6	70 (31.1)	7.1	11 (4.9)	—	—	—	—	16.9	21 (9.3)
2001	225	SNTV	28.3	68 (30.2)	33.8	87 (38.7)	2.7	1 (0.4)	18.4	46 (20.4)	7.8	13 (5.8)	9.1	10 (4.4)
2004	225	SNTV	32.8	79 (35.1)	35.7	89 (39.6)	0.1	1 (0.4)	13.9	34 (15.1)	7.8	12 (5.3)	9.6	10 (4.4)
2008	79	SMD	53.5	61 (77.2)	38.2	13 (16.5)	—	—	0.3	1 (1.3)	0.9	0 (0.0)	7.1	4 (5.1)
	34	PR	51.2	20 (58.8)	36.9	14 (41.2)	4.0	0 (0.0)	—	—	3.5	0 (0.0)	4.4	0 (0.0)
	113	(Total)	—	81 (71.7)	—	27 (23.9)	—	0 (0.0)	—	1 (0.9)	—	0 (0.0)	—	4 (3.5)
2012	79	SMD	48.2	48 (60.8)	43.8	27 (34.2)	0.1	0 (0.0)	1.3	1 (1.3)	—	—	6.6	3 (3.8)
	34	PR	44.6	16 (47.1)	34.6	13 (38.2)	1.5	0 (0.0)	5.5	2 (5.9)	9.0	3 (8.8)	4.9	0 (0.0)
	113	(Total)	—	64 (56.6)	—	40 (35.4)	—	0 (0.0)	—	3 (2.7)	—	3 (2.7)	—	3 (2.7)

Sources: Data from the Taiwan Provincial Election Commission of the Department of Civil Affairs and the Central Election Commission of the Ministry of the Interior, Republic of China.

Note: 1. In 2008 and 2012, SMDs included 6 SNTV seats for aboriginals.

As the election ended and campaign pressure subsided, political reality took over. In late March 2005, the PFP announced a change of position on the constitutional amendment bill that it had voted for the previous August. The TSU and NPSU soon followed suit. The election for the 300 National Assembly delegates held on May 14, 2005, was the only election in Taiwan based solely on the party list system. The record-low turnout rate of merely 23.4 percent signified not just the confusion about the PR rule but also the public's unfamiliarity with the debates on electoral rules (Huang, Wang, and Lin 2012, 2013; Huang and Yu 2011). The DPP earned 42.5 percent of the votes and the KMT garnered 38.9 percent. Not surprisingly, the smaller parties, including the TSU, PFP, NP, and NPSU, all opposed the bill, fearing a bleak future. But the minor parties did not have the clout to block the amendments since the two major parties, the DPP and the KMT, combined accounted for 244 (81.3%) of the 300 seats and exerted strict party discipline over their members. Eventually, the ad hoc National Assembly ratified the amendment in June 2005 with a vote of 249 for and 48 against with staunch support from the two big parties, which expected gains from forming a unified government under the new electoral rules.

The new MMM electoral system, specified by the new Article 4 of the amended Additional Articles of the ROC Constitution, has two tiers with a total of 113 seats. The tiers are not linked, so seats are determined independently in each tier. The nominal tier includes 73 seats (64.6%), which are elected by plurality in SMDs, and 6 seats (5.3%) are in two national SNTV districts for lowland and highland aboriginals. The remaining 34 seats (30.1%) comprise a single national list tier and are apportioned by a largest remainder rule. Note that the nominal tier seats far outnumber the list tier seats. Giving such heavy weight to the nominal tier is disadvantageous to smaller parties, since smaller parties often find winning a plurality in an SMD to be a daunting challenge and rely heavily on seats from the list tier for survival. With fewer list tier seats available, smaller parties find it harder to survive. Even worse, to win any of these seats, parties must win at least 5 percent of the national list tier vote. This 5 percent legal threshold also discriminates against smaller parties, since, without a legal threshold, parties winning at least 2.14 percent of the valid vote would be able to win a seat.[8]

Taiwan's electoral reform has important implications. Literature on electoral reform usually considers the costs and benefits to legislators. As might be expected, legislators, especially from small parties, were generally against reform. However, the critical players were actually the national party leaders/presidential contenders who effectively sold out their legislators in order to play to public opinion in hopes of advancing their own careers. We cannot understand the electoral reform without reference to the semipresidential system. Additionally, these key presidential contenders represented the two camps of the identity cleavage. That is, the identity cleavage was hidden at the very root of Taiwan's electoral reform.

Effects of Electoral System Change on the Party System

Preludes to the Postreform Legislative Election

Most studies evaluating the impact of the new MMM system in Taiwan focus on the January 2008 legislative election (Hsieh 2009; Jou 2009; O'Neill 2013; Shyu 2011; Stockton 2010). My comprehensive framework clearly points out that the new electoral system directly affects politicians' strategic entry and exit decisions as well as the formation and dissolution of intraparty and interparty coalitions. Interactions among political elites, in turn, determine the voters' choice sets on ballots in elections.

Indeed, the impact of the MMM system had been felt almost immediately after the ratification of the constitutional amendment. The effects were particularly acute for legislators of small parties. They were squeezed from both ends: by a 50 percent decrease in total seats, as well as by a plurality rule in the newly drawn SMDs. Small-party incumbents intending to run for reelection were fighting an uphill battle. But of course this had been part of the plan of the two big parties pushing for the MMM system. As a result, the first and immediate impact of MMM on the party system manifested itself among the political elites, including large-scale party switching during 2006 and 2007 as well as interparty negotiations inside the Pan-Blue and Pan-Green camps. In the two years after the 2005 electoral reform, as many as 22 incumbent PFP legislators switched to the KMT while 5 TSU legislators switched to the DPP. Therefore, party realignment started long before the first postreform legislative election held in January 2008. More important, the multiparty system began to converge toward a two-party system split along the preexisting fundamental cleavage, that is, independence versus unification.

However, interparty coordination proves to be not as easy as party switching on the part of individuals. Two years before the 2008 legislative election, the KMT reached out to and eventually negotiated successfully with the PFP to nominate six former PFP legislators in six districts and also allowed the PFP to share four seats on the KMT's party list. The

KMT also made way to NPSU candidates in three SMDs, and promised not to nominate a candidate in the first district in Pingtung so as to allow an independent candidate, also affiliated with the NPSU, to compete against the DPP candidate. Apparently, the then-opposition KMT, after losing the 2000 and 2004 presidential elections, was anxious to form a Pan-Blue coalition aimed at the presidential election in March 2008 and thus was more willing to make compromises with its allies. In contrast to the coordination in the Pan-Blue camp, the DPP and the TSU squabbled with each other and eventually failed to reach any substantive agreement. The DPP seemed to believe that the TSU would simply back down and follow its lead. Yet the TSU eventually fielded 13 candidates in districts to fight its battle for survival. The effects of such differences in the interparty coordination within each camp were further magnified by the new electoral system, since the mechanical effect of the SMD tier favors the party capturing the majority of popular votes.

Effects at the National Level

As discussed in the previous section, the reform of the legislative electoral system was initiated by the then-ruling DPP to win an absolute majority in the Legislative Yuan and gain full control of both the executive and legislative branch. However, the lame-duck president, Chen, was unable to reach an agreement with the TSU. Even worse, a series of scandals involving the president and his family broke out in 2006 and tarnished the clean image of the DPP. As a result, the outcome of the 2008 legislative election starkly demonstrated the new MMM system's disproportionality effect on the losing party. Actually, the DPP received 38.2 percent of total district votes but only 13 (16.5%) out of 79 SMD/SNTV seats. For the PR ballot, the DPP received 36.9 percent of the total votes and 14 (41.2%) of 34 party seats. On the other hand, the KMT garnered 53.5 percent of the total district votes and 61 (77.2%) out of the 79 SMD/SNTV seats, as well as 51.2 percent of the total at-large votes and 20 (58.8%) of the 34 party seats (Huang and Hsiao 2009). If we count the 3 seats won by the NPSU, the Pan-Blue, indeed, secured an overwhelming victory over the DPP in the 2008 legislative election, which also paved the way for the landslide victory of the KMT presidential candidate, Ma Yin-jeou, in March 2008. In 2008, 12 parties filed lists on the PR ballot, but only the two big parties, the KMT and the DPP, surpassed the 5 percent threshold. Although the two small parties, the NP and TSU, did receive 4 percent and 3.5 percent for the PR votes, respectively, neither of them managed to reach the 5 percent threshold required for parties to be allocated PR seats.

The presidential and legislative elections became synchronized on January 14, 2012, when Taiwan held its first-ever concurrent presidential and legislative elections. The elections also served as a test of the tenacity of the new two-party system under Taiwan's MMM rules embedded within the semipresidential system. The PFP chair, James Soong, lamenting being cheated by the KMT, ran as an independent presidential candidate and also nominated 10 legislative-district candidates in order to file the party list.[9] The TSU, on the other hand, ran on the party list only, without nominating any district candidates. So each party essentially ran on its own in 2012, with the exception of a tacit alliance between the KMT and NPSU. In this three-way presidential race, the incumbent president, Ma Ying-jeou of the KMT, defeated his main challenger, Tsai Ing-wen of the DPP, by a substantial margin. The third candidate, James Soong, received only 2.8 percent of the popular vote (Huang and Wang 2014). Meanwhile, the two major political parties took the lion's share in the legislative election (table 10.3). The ruling KMT received 48.2 percent of the total district votes and 48 (60.8%) SMD/SNTV seats, as well as 44.6 percent of the total party list votes and 16 (47.1%) party seats. The DPP, on the other hand, performed much better than it did in 2008 by garnering 43.8 percent of the total district votes and 27 (34.2%) SMD/SNTV seats. For the PR ballot, the DPP received 34.6 percent of the total votes and 13 (38.2%) party seats. Three PFP candidates were elected: one through the aboriginal SNTV district and two through the list tier with 5.5 percent PR votes. The TSU also won three seats from its 9.0 percent list votes. Besides PFP and TSU, none of other seven parties that filed lists got as much as 2.9 percent. Notably, the outcome of the 2012 election indicated the consolidation of the two-party system without coalitions.

The last four columns of table 10.1 present the Laakso-Taagepera effective number of parliamentary parties (ENPP) and the effective number of electoral parties (ENEP) in moving from an SNTV to an MMM system (Laakso and Taagepera 1979; Taagepera and Shugart 1989). According to Duverger's law, the number of parties in SMDs would shift toward two, due to mechanical effects and strategic voting owing to psychological effects. But Duverger's hypothesis predicts that multiple parties remain in the PR tier of the system because voters have stronger incentives to vote sincerely. Figure 10.3 clearly indicates that there was an immediate sharp drop in the ENPP from 3.08 to 1.47, which is almost one-party dominance in parliament. With a much stronger performance by the DPP, and after the PFP split from the Pan-Blue coalition and ran its own candidates in the 2012

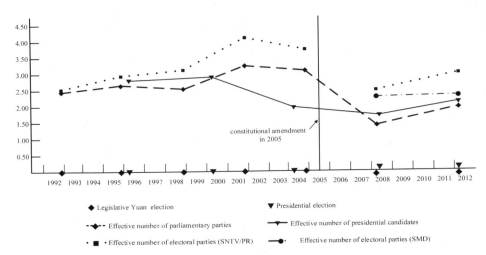

Fig. 10.3. Effective numbers of parliamentary parties and presidential candidates. *Source:* Huang 2013.

legislative election, the ENPP rose to 1.97, which is much closer to 2.00. ENEP indexes are not directly comparable between single-ballot SNTV and two-ballot MMM systems. Still it is not difficult to see that the growing trend of ENEP under SNTV was interrupted after the change of electoral system. Furthermore, as Duverger's law and hypothesis expect, the ENEP in the SMD tier hovers around 2.30 while its PR counterpart is slightly higher. Actually, the ENEP in the PR tier rose from 2.49 in 2008 to 3.03 in 2012 because both the PFP and TSU's party votes exceed the 5 percent legal threshold.

Effects at the District Level

The national-level indexes were further checked and tested at the district level. It can be shown that the changes at the district level are also congruent with the electoral-system theories. Specifically, I exploit the SF ratio (the ratio of the second to the first loser's vote total) patterns over time and across two tiers. Cox (1997, 85) used the SF ratio to test the $M + 1$ rule, a generalization of Duverger's law. The $M + 1$ rule holds that, at the district level, the effective number of candidates will decline toward the district magnitude (M) plus one. SF ratios demonstrate the extent to which the number of votes cast for less competitive candidates trail behind $M + 1$. Cox reasoned that in Duvergerian equilibria, when strategic voting by voters occurs, the $(M + 2)$th candidate will be deserted and thus the SF ratio will be near zero. In non-Duvergerian equilibria, however, the first and second losers receive nearly the same number of votes, and thus the SF ratio will be near one. When M is small, such as in SMDs, where $M = 1$, strategic voting is more likely to occur in closely contested districts. As M grows larger, such as in an SNTV system with multiple seats in each district, strategic voting becomes more difficult due to the lack of clear information for voters. In other words, we should expect a greater number of districts concentrated at the lower end (closer to zero) in the nominal tier under an MMM system than in an SNTV system. If we plot the histogram of SF ratios of all the districts, the $M + 1$ rule predicts a right-skewed distribution with most districts having near-zero values concentrated on the left side and only a small number of exceptions on the right.

The SF ratios of Taiwan's seven legislative elections at the district level were computed and then classified into 10 intervals, as shown in figures 10.4 and 10.5. An examination of these figures reveals a dramatic reversal of district distributions after the electoral system switched from SNTV (figure 10.4) to MMM (figure 10.5). During the SNTV period from 1992 to 2004, many of the multimember districts fell at the higher end of SF ratio (i.e., closer to 1.00). In the last two legislative elections of 2008 and 2012 under MMM, however, most single-member districts' SF ratios indeed had values close to 0.00 and thus concentrated at the lower end. This means that two-party competition has become the norm at the district as well as at the national level.

Effects at the Voter Level

As mentioned earlier, Duverger (1959, 205) asserted that single-member district plurality would tend to generate two-party competition, and he also proposed that PR systems would encourage multiparty competition. Besides the mechanical factor of SMD that leads to the underrepresentation of the weaker parties, the psychological factor that supporters of the third party tend to "transfer their voter to the less evil of its two adversaries" (Duverger 1959, 226) also causes strategic voting. A mixed-member electoral system is characterized by the hybrid of both SMD and PR tiers. If identifiers with small parties indeed vote strategically on the SMD ballot and sincerely on the PR ballot, this ticket-splitting pattern becomes a micro-level evidence of electoral system effects.

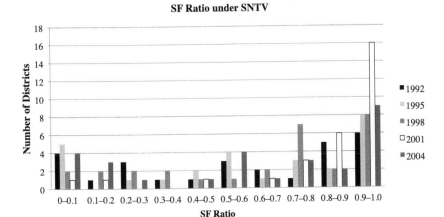

Fig. 10.4. SF ratio of Taiwan's Legislative Yuan elections, 1992–2004. *Source:* Huang 2013.

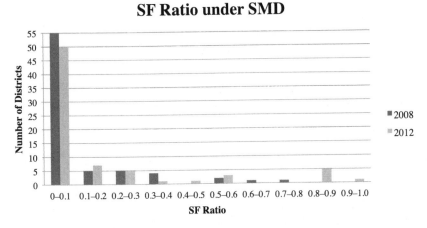

Fig. 10.5. SF ratio of Taiwan's Legislative Yuan elections, 2008–2012. *Source:* Huang 2013.

There is an abundant extant literature on voting choices and ticket-splitting under the MMM system at the voter level based on survey data, especially the TEDS 2008L and TEDS 2012-T surveys (Huang 2008b; Huang and Chou 2013; Huang and Hsiao 2009; Huang and Lin 2009; Huang, Wang and Kuo 2008; Wang, Lin and Hsiao 2016). It emphasizes that partisan voting is dominant for either of the two major party identifiers on both SMD and PR ballots. Yet certain supporters of the smaller parties indeed tend to vote strategically for the major party candidates of their own "color" camp, but vote sincerely for their most preferred party on the PR ballot. Besides partisanship, ethnic identity and attitude toward Taiwan independence vs. unification with China remain important explanatory variables of voting choices. For example, compared to those who identify themselves as Taiwanese, those who identify themselves as Chinese or as both Taiwanese/Chinese are more likely to vote for KMT candidates in districts and vote for the Pan-Blue camp on the party ballot.

In spite of the tendency of strategic voting from minor parties' supporters, however, the MMM electoral system still squeezes smaller parties from two ends. That is, PR portion in Taiwan accounts for only 30.1 percent of the total 113 seats plus its relatively high 5 percent legal threshold causes the MMM electoral system to exert heavy pressure on small parties and thus push down the number of parties. Meanwhile, the force of gravity of the SMD portion in Taiwan's MMM electoral system tends to favor any major party that can garner near 50 percent vote share in legislative elections.

Conclusions

This chapter has employed a comprehensive framework with which to study the evolution and effects of electoral systems embedded within social and institutional contexts. It has examined the change in legislative electoral system in Taiwan and evaluated its consequences on political party systems from the perspective of this broad framework. It is interesting to note that after switching from an SNTV system to an MMM in 1994, Japan experienced only a gradual evolution from a multiparty to a two-party system, taking five House of Representatives election cycles, whereas the party system in Taiwan changed immediately and dramatically in the first postreform election (Huang 2011; Huang, Kuo, and Stockton 2016). Taiwan's fast convergence toward two-party competition can be partly attributed to institutional factors. That is, the powerful presidency of Taiwan's semipresidential system motivates party leaders to synchronize the legislative electoral system to make it easier to form a unified government.

However, institutions alone do not explain the direction in which multiple parties converge. This chapter argued that the fundamental cleavage in Taiwan, that is, independence versus unification, has played a hidden yet significant role in three ways. First, it directed the centripetal force of the plurality system of presidential election toward the two camps. Although the old SNTV system left room for splinter parties within camps, the cleavage motivated elites to push for a new electoral system that was more compatible with the enduring social division. Second, it accelerated the speed of convergence toward the two-party system along the borderline of the preexisting cleavage by skipping time-consuming trial and error in coalition permutations. Last, but certainly not least, it crystallized a relatively stable two-party competition with regular power shifts under the semipresidential system.

Notes

1. In Chinese, the new MMM rule is literally called "single-member district, two-ballot system." This chapter adopts the classification and terminologies of two subtypes of mixed-member systems used by Shugart and Wattenberg (2001, 13–14). In the MMM systems, there is no link between nominal and list tiers in the allocation of seats to parties. The plurality formula used in the nominal tier can lead to significant disproportionality, and the list tier merely mitigates rather than erases this disproportionality. In contrast, the mixed-member proportional systems prioritize the list tier, that is, the second ballot, and each party's total seat share is proportional to the list tier vote share.

2. The KMT, which was founded on the mainland, was the ruling party of the Republic of China on the mainland. It moved to Taiwan in 1949 after losing the civil war with the Chinese Communist Party.

3. As explained below, the prereform system was technically a mixed system since it had a nominal tier, with voters choosing specific candidates in the SNTV tier, as well as a list tier (see Farrell 2011). However, for the purpose of clarity, this chapter will refer to the prereform system as an SNTV system. In an SNTV system, each district has one or more seats and each voter can cast only one ballot for one specific candidate. There is no provision for preference rankings, so if a voter supports a candidate who does not win, the vote cannot be transferred to a second-favorite candidate.

4. Before 2000, the constitution could be amended by the National Assembly alone upon the proposal of one-fifth of the total delegates and by a resolution of three-fourths of the delegates present at a meeting having a quorum of two-thirds of the entire Assembly. The KMT government took advantage of its overwhelming majority in the National Assembly to pass six constitutional amendments during the 1990s.

5. The second stage was changed into a national referendum when the 2005 constitutional amendment abolished the National Assembly.

6. Both the learning effect of the 2000 presidential election and the centripetal effect of the plurality rule pushed the effective number of presidential candidates toward two in the ensuing presidential elections, as shown in figure 10.3. This downward trend may well affect the effective number of parties in legislative elections.

7. The DPP legislator Zhang Xue-shun used a sensational approach, pointing to the majority KMT as the "source of chaos and disorder" in the Legislative Yuan and argued that halving the seats would bring back order. See *Commercial Times*, November 24, 2000.

8. According to Lijphart (1997, 74), given the district magnitude M, the effective threshold is $0.75/(M + 1)$.

9. Article 24 of the Election and Recall Act provides that unless a party has attained 2.0% and more of the total valid votes in the recent presidential election or has won at least 2.0% of the votes in the previous three legislative elections or has five seats or more in the Legislative Yuan, it has to nominate at least 10 candidates in SMDs or indigenous districts in order to qualify for a party list.

References

Ahmed, Amel. 2013. *Democracy and the Politics of Electoral System Choice: Engineering Electoral Dominance.* Cambridge: Cambridge University Press.

Batto, Nathan F., and Gary W. Cox. 2016. "Introduction: Legislature-Centric and Executive-Centric Theories of Party Systems and Faction Systems." In *Mixed-Member Electoral Systems in Constitutional Context: Taiwan, Japan, and Beyond*, ed. Nathan F. Batto, Chi Huang, Alexander C. Tan, and Gary W. Cox. Ann Arbor: University of Michigan Press.

Benoit, Kenneth. 2007. "Electoral Laws as Political Consequences: Explaining the Origins and Change of Electoral Institutions." *Annual Review of Political Science* 10: 363–90.

Chang, Alex Chuan-Hsien, and Yu-Tzung Chang. 2009. "Rational Choices and Irrational Results: The DPP's Institutional Choice in Taiwan's Electoral Reform." *Issues & Studies* 45 (2): 23–60.

Clark, William Roberts, and Matt Golder. 2006. "Rehabilitating Duverger's Theory: Testing the Mechanical and Strategic Modifying Effects of Electoral Laws." *Comparative Political Studies* 39 (6): 679–708.

Colomer, Josep M. 2004. "The Strategy and History of Electoral System Choice." In *Handbook of Electoral System Choice*, ed. Josep M. Colomer, 3–78. Hampshire, UK: Palgrave Macmillan.

Cox, Gary W. 1996. "Is the Single Nontransferable Vote Superproportional? Evidence from Japan and Taiwan." American Journal of Political Science 40(3): 740–55.

Cox, Gary W. 1997. *Making Votes Count: Strategic Coordination in the World's Electoral Systems.* Cambridge: Cambridge University Press.

Cox, Gary W., and Emerson Niou. 1994. "Seat Bonuses under the Single Non-Transferable Vote System: Evidence from Japan and Taiwan." *Comparative Politics* 26 (2): 221–36.

Cox, Gary W., and Frances Rosenbluth. 1993. "The Electoral Fortunes of Legislative Factions in Japan." *American Political Science Review* 87 (3): 577–89.

Cox, Gary W., and Frances Rosenbluth. 1996. "Factional Competition for the Party Endorsement." *British Journal of Political Science* 26 (2): 259–69.

Cox, Gary W., and Michael F. Thies. 1998. "The Cost of Intraparty Competition: The Single, Non-Transferable Vote and Money Politics in Japan." *Comparative Political Studies* 31 (3): 267–91.

Curini, Luigi, and Airo Hino. 2012. "Missing Links in Party-System Polarization: How Institutions and Voters Matter." *Journal of Politics* 74 (2): 460–73.

Curtis, Gerald L. 1999. *The Logic of Japanese Politics*. New York: Columbia University Press.

Duverger, Maurice. 1959. *Political Parties: Their Organization and Activity in the Modern State*. 2nd English ed. New York: John Wiley and Sons.

Farrell, David M. 2011. *Electoral Systems: A Comparative Introduction*. 2nd ed. New York: Palgrave Macmillan.

Fell, Dafydd. 2005. *Party Politics in Taiwan: Party Change and Democratic Evolution of Taiwan, 1991–2004*. London: Routledge.

Fell, Dafydd. 2010. "Was 2005 a Critical Election in Taiwan? Locating the Start of a New Political Era." *Asian Survey* 50 (5): 927–45.

Flanagan, Scott C., Shinsaku Kohei, Ichiro Miyake, Bradley M. Richardson, and Joji Watanuki. 1991. *The Japanese Voter*. New Haven: Yale University Press.

Hicken, Allen. 2009. *Building Party Systems in Developing Democracies*. New York: Cambridge University Press.

Hicken, Allen, and Heather Stoll. 2008. "Electoral Rules and the Size of the Prize: How Political Institutions Shape Presidential Party Systems." *Journal of Politics* 70 (4): 1109–27.

Hsieh, John Fuh-sheng. 2009. "The Origins and Consequences of Electoral Reform in Taiwan." *Issues & Studies* 45 (2): 1–22.

Huang, Chi. 2005. "Dimensions of Taiwanese/Chinese Identity and National Identity in Taiwan: A Latent Class Analysis." *Journal of Asian and African Studies* 40 (1–2): 51–70.

Huang, Chi. 2006. "The Evolution of Taiwanese Identity: A Pseudo Panel Analysis." Presented at the 102nd Annual Meeting of the American Political Science Association, Philadelphia, August 31–September 3.

Huang, Chi. 2007. "Assessing the Impact of Mixed Electoral System in Taiwan: Methodological Challenges of Testing Interaction Effects." Presented at the International Symposium on Mixed Electoral Systems in East Asia, National Chengchi University, Taipei, May 26.

Huang, Chi. 2008a. "Contexts and Consequences of Electoral Systems: An Introduction" [in Chinese]. In *Ruhe Pinggu Xuanzhi Bianqian: Fangfalun de Tantao* [The consequences of electoral system change: Methodological perspectives], ed. Chi Huang and Chin-hsing Yu, 1–17. Taipei: Wu-nan Publications.

Huang, Chi. 2008b. "Voting Choices under the Mixed-Member Majoritarian System: A Multilevel Mixed Logit Model" [in Chinese]. In *Ruhe Pinggu Xuanzhi Bianqian: Fangfalun de Tantao* [The consequences of electoral system change: Methodological perspectives], ed. Chi Huang and Chin-hsing Yu, 129–50. Taipei: Wu-nan Press.

Huang, Chi. 2011. "Political Consequences of the MMM Electoral Systems in Taiwan and Japan." Presented at the 2011 Annual Meeting of the American Political Science Association, Seattle, September 1–4.

Huang, Chi. 2013. "Taiwan's Political Geography Information System (TPGIS)." http://tpgis.nccu.edu.tw/nccu/. Accessed September 30, 2013.

Huang, Chi. 2016. "Mixed-Member Systems Embedded within Constitutional Systems." In *Mixed-Member Electoral Systems in Constitutional Context: Taiwan, Japan, and Beyond*, ed. Nathan F. Batto, Chi Huang, Alexander C. Tan, and Gary W. Cox. Ann Arbor: University of Michigan Press.

Huang, Chi, and Chang-chi Lin. 2009. "Vote Choices under the SNTV and MMM Electoral Systems: A Panel Study of Taiwan's 2004 and 2008 Legislative Elections." Presented at the 2009 Annual Meeting of the American Political Science Association, Toronto, Canada, September 3–6.

Huang, Chi, and Chang-chi Lin. 2013. "The Effects of Concurrent Elections on Voter Turnout: A Causal Analysis" [in Chinese]. In *2012 Nian Zongtong yu Lifa Weiyuan Xuanju: Bianqian yu Yanxu* [Continuity and change in Taiwan's 2012 presidential and legislative elections], ed. Lu-huei Chen, 47–83. Taipei: Wu-nan Publications.

Huang, Chi, and Ching-hsin Yu. 2011. "Political Cycle of Voters' Understanding of the New Electoral System: The Case of Taiwan." *Japanese Journal of Electoral Studies* 27 (2): 60–76.

Huang, Chi, and T. Y. Wang. 2009. "The Effect of the 2008 Legislative Yuan Election on the 2008 Presidential Election in Taiwan: Pendulum or Bandwagoning?" [in Chinese]. In *2008 Nian Zongtong Xuanju: Lun Erci Zhengdang Lunti zhi Guanjian Xuanju* [The 2008 presidential election in Taiwan], ed. Lu-huei Chen, Ching-hsin Yu, and Chi Huang, 31–56. Taipei: Wu-nan Publications.

Huang, Chi, and T. Y. Wang. 2014. "Presidential Coattails in Taiwan: An Analysis of Voter- and Candidate-Specific Data." *Electoral Studies* 33:175–85.

Huang, Chi, and Yi-ching Hsiao. 2009. "Vote Choices under the Mixed-Member Majoritarian System in Taiwan's 2008 Legislative Election." Presented at the 2009 Asian Election Studies International Conference, "Elections in Taiwan, Japan, and Korea under the Mixed-Member Majoritarian Systems," Election Study Center, National Chengchi University, Taipei, Taiwan, May 24.

Huang, Chi, and Ying-Lung Chou. 2013. "Split-Ticketing in Taiwan's 2012 Concurrent Presidential and Legislative Elections" [in Chinese]. In *2012 Nian Zongtong yu Lifa Weiyuan Xuanju: Bianqian yu Yanxu* [Continuity and change in Taiwan's 2012 presidential and legislative elections], ed. Lu-huei Chen, 85–124. Taipei: Wu-nan Publications.

Huang, Chi, Ding-ming Wang, and Ming-feng Kuo. 2008. "Straight- and Split-Ticket Voting in a Mixed-Member Majoritarian System: An Analysis of the 1996 House Election in Japan" [in Chinese]. *Xuanju Yanjiu* [Journal of Electoral Studies] 15 (2): 1–35.

Huang, Chi, Hung-chung Wang, and Chang-chih Lin. 2012. "Knowledge of the Electoral System and Voter Turnout." *Taiwan Zhengzhi Xuekan* [Taiwanese Political Science Review] 16 (1): 239–79.

Huang, Chi, Hung-chung Wang, and Chang-chih Lin. 2013. "Knowledge of the Electoral System and Voting: The Case of Taiwan's 2012 Legislative Election." *Issues & Studies* 49 (4): 1–45.

Huang, Chi, Ming-feng Kuo, and Hans Stockton. 2016. "The Consequences of MMM on Party Systems." In *Mixed-Member Electoral Systems in Constitutional Context: Taiwan, Japan, and Beyond*, ed. Nathan F. Batto, Chi Huang, Alexander C. Tan, and Gary W. Cox. Ann Arbor: University of Michigan Press.

Jou, Willy. 2009. "Electoral Reform and Party System Development in Japan and Taiwan: A Comparative Study." *Asian Survey* 49 (5): 759–85.

Laakso, Markku, and Rein Taagepera. 1979. "Effective Number of Parties: A Measure with Application to West Europe." *Comparative Political Studies* 12 (1): 3–27.

Lijphart, Arend. 1994. *Electoral Systems and Party Systems: A Study of Twenty-Seven Democracies 1945–1990*. Oxford: Oxford University Press.

Lijphart, Arend. 1997. "The Difficult Science of Electoral Systems: A Commentary on the Critique by Alberto Penadés." *Electoral Studies* 16 (1): 73–77.

Lin, Jih-wen. 2016. "The Consequences of Constitutional Systems on Party Systems." In *Mixed-Member Electoral Systems in Constitutional Context: Taiwan, Japan, and Beyond*, ed. Nathan F. Batto, Chi Huang, Alexander C. Tan, and Gary W. Cox. Ann Arbor: University of Michigan Press.

Lin, Tsong-Jyi. 2011. "Institutionalization of Party System in Taiwan: An Analysis on the Mass Political Attitudes" [in Chinese]. *Taiwan Minzhu Jikan* [Taiwan Democracy Quarterly] 8 (4): 141–66.

Lipset, Seymour M., and Stein Rokkan. 1967. "Cleavage Structure, Party Systems, and Voter Alignments: An Introduction." In *Party Systems and Voter Alignments: Cross-National Perspectives*. ed. Seymour M. Lipset and Stein Rokkan. New York: Free Press.

Moser, Robert G., and Ethan Scheiner. 2012. *Electoral Systems and Political Context: How the Effects of Rules Vary Across New and Established Democracies*. Cambridge: Cambridge University Press.

Neto, Octavio Amorim, and Gary W. Cox. 1997. "Electoral Institutions, Cleavage Structures, and the Number of Parties." *American Journal of Political Science* 41 (1): 149–74.

Norris, Pippa. 2004. *Electoral Engineering: Voting Rules and Political Behavior*. Cambridge: Cambridge University Press.

O'Neill, Daniel C. 2013. "Electoral Rules and the Democratic Progressive Party's Performance in the 2004 and 2008 Legislative Elections in Taiwan." *Journal of Asian and African Studies* 48 (2): 161–79.

Ordeshook, Peter C., and Olga V. Shvetsova. 1994. "Ethnic Heterogeneity, District Magnitude, and the Number of Parties." *American Journal of Political Science* 38 (1): 100–123.

Patterson, Dennis P., and Hans Stockton. 2010. "Strategies, Institutions, and Outcomes under SNTV in Taiwan, 1992–2004." *Journal of East Asian Studies* 10 (1): 31–59.

Powell, G. Bingham, Jr. 1982. *Contemporary Democracies: Participation, Stability, and Violence*. Cambridge: Harvard University Press.

Reed, Steven R., and Michael F. Thies. 2001. "The Causes of Electoral Reform in Japan." In *Mixed-Member Electoral Systems: The Best of Both Worlds?*, ed. Matthew Soberg Shugart and Martin P. Wattenberg, 152–72. Oxford: Oxford University Press.

Renwick, Alan. 2010. *The Politics of Electoral Reform: Changing the Rules of Democracy*. Cambridge: Cambridge University Press.

Richardson, Bradley M. 1988. "Constituency Candidates versus Parties in Japanese Voting Behavior." *American Political Science Review* 82 (3): 695–718.

Riker, William H. 1982. "The Two-Party System and Duverger's Law: An Essay on the History of Political Science." *American Political Science Review* 76 (3): 753–66.

Rochon, Thomas. 1981. "Electoral Systems and the Basis for the Vote: The Case of Japan." In *Parties, Candidates and Voters in Japan: Six Quantitative Studies*, ed. J.

C. Campbell, 1–28. Michigan Papers in Japanese Studies, No. 2. Ann Arbor: University of Michigan Center for Japanese Studies.

Samuels, David J., and Matthew S. Shugart. 2010. *Presidents, Parties, and Prime Ministers: How the Separation of Powers Affects Party Organization and Behavior.* Cambridge: Cambridge University Press.

Sartori, Giovanni. 1994. *Comparative Constitutional Engineering: An Inquiry into Structures, Incentives and Outcomes.* New York: New York University Press.

Shugart, Matthew S., and John S. Carey. 1992. *Presidents and Assemblies: Constitutional Design and Electoral Dynamics.* New York: Cambridge University Press.

Shugart, Matthew Søberg, and Martin P. Wattenberg. 2001. "Mixed-Member Electoral Systems: A Definition and Typology." In *Mixed-Member Electoral Systems: The Best of Both Worlds?*, ed. Matthew Søberg Shugart and Martin P. Wattenberg, 7–24. Oxford: Oxford University Press.

Shyu, Huo-yan. 2011. "Taiwan's Democratization and the Freezing of the Party System." In *Political Parties, Party Systems, and Democratization in East Asia*, ed. Liang Fook Lye and Wilhelm Hofmeister. Singapore: World Scientific.

Stockton, Hans. 2010. "How Rules Matter: Electoral Reform in Taiwan." *Social Science Quarterly* 91 (1): 21–41.

Taagepera, Rein, and Matthew Søberg Shugart. 1989. *Seats and Votes: The Effects and Determinants of Electoral Systems.* New Haven: Yale University Press.

Wang, T. Y., Chang-chih Lin, and Yi-ching Hsiao. 2016. "Split-Ticket Voting under MMM." In *Mixed-Member Electoral Systems in Constitutional Context: Taiwan, Japan, and Beyond*, ed. Nathan F. Batto, Chi Huang, Alexander C. Tan, and Gary W. Cox. Ann Arbor: University of Michigan Press.

Wang, Yeh-Lih. 2012. *Bijiao Xuanju Zhidu* [Comparative electoral systems]. 6th ed. Taipei: Wu-nan Publications.

CHAPTER 11

Political Participation in Taiwan

Chung-li Wu with Tzu-Ping Liu

Political participation by ordinary citizens is the essence of democracy. Verba and Nie (1972, 3–4) stress that political participation is at the heart of democratic theory and has "a particularly crucial relationship to all other social and political goals." Dahl (1971, 1) also posits a strong link between the two: "A key characteristic of a democracy is the continuing responsiveness of the government to the preferences of its citizens, considered as political equals." To this end, a democracy must provide its citizens with equal opportunities to formulate preferences, to signify those preferences, and to have their preferences influence the formation of the government. Therefore, higher levels of participation by citizens in political activities can be viewed as a norm that supports a democratic political regime.

Political participation comes in many forms, including contacting public officials, participating in political demonstrations, and many others. To an ordinary citizen, however, voting is the commonest, simplest, and least costly form of participation in electoral politics, although it has profound implications for the political system. Under a system of voluntary suffrage, voter turnout not only indicates how much interest the electorate has in the election but it also reveals the electorate's degree of psychological attachment to political affairs (Milbrath and Goel 1977, 46–47; Rosenstone and Hansen 2003, 245–48). Likewise, voting is the key mechanism for responsiveness in democratic society. Citizens cast ballots to choose among candidates from competing political parties, and their choices are important in the selection of political leaders and public policies. The desire for office certainly makes political elites modify or even totally change policies to meet the expectations of voters (Almond and Powell 1988, 49; Nie and Verba 1975, 9–10).

Thus electoral participation in general, and voter turnout in particular, are important elements in the maintenance of democracy. Both have been widely studied in Western countries; however, they have received comparatively little attention elsewhere. This chapter explores political participation in Taiwan since the early 1990s, with a particular focus on electoral participation and voter turnout from 2001 through 2012. Our main purpose is, first, to describe trends in voter turnout since democratization, and second, to analyze the personal attributes of Taiwan citizens that have led them to become involved in politics over the past decade.

Voter turnout in Taiwan has been relatively high compared to other democracies, with an average of about 70 percent; however, it has declined substantially since 2000. To understand this pattern, we will use individual-level survey data to explore the question of who votes in Taiwan, comparing people of different ages and ethnicities. We will also examine party identification and political knowledge to learn their effects on the decision to vote. Finally, we will discuss how each of these demographic and cognitive factors influences other forms of political participation. The survey data used originate from the multiyear Taiwan Election and Democratization Study conducted by the National Chengchi University Election Study Center.[1]

The Framework of This Chapter

The term *political participation* encompasses many different activities. This chapter adopts Rosenstone and Hansen's (2003, 4–5) definition, so our research is focused on voting, persuading others, campaigning, giving money, contacting others, attending meetings or rallies, and signing petitions. To explain these activities, we focus first on two sociodemographic variables—age and ethnicity.

Demographic factors are important for understanding political participation because individuals' social backgrounds are central to the development of their political attitudes and behaviors. It is a generally accepted proposition that age is a predictive variable where political attitudes and participation are concerned. According to the life-cycle effects theory, political information and experience rise steadily with age, a phenomenon confirmed by previous empirical studies in the United States (Campbell et al. 1960, 485–87; Conway 2000, 19–24; Milbrath and Goel 1977, 114–16). Political participation increases through a person's thirties, forties, and fifties, and is at its height in Taiwan when individuals are in their late fifties and early sixties. Participation among those older than sixty-five declines primarily because these people are in poorer health and are less physically mobile. Thus a person's ability to participate in political activities will be closely related to age.

Among the socioeconomic variables used to explain political participation, race/ethnicity is probably the most thoroughly researched factor (Rosenstone and Hansen 2003; Tate 1991; Verba and Nie 1972). Ethnicity has been a critical issue in Taiwan's political life, especially in relation to the ethnic differences between Minnan and mainlanders (Wang 1994, 1998).[2] In the light of Taiwan's unique historical background and sociopolitical environment, ethnicity and its related issues (e.g., ethnic consciousness, national identity, and disputes over unification with or independence from the mainland) may all be regarded as social cleavages.[3] Mainlanders have political attitudes and voting behavior that are distinct from those of other ethnic groups, mainly Minnan and Hakka (Hsiau 2000; Hughes 1997; Wu 2008; Wu and Hsiao 2006).

In addition to individual characteristics, we consider the effects of cognitive variables as well. Previous studies have demonstrated that these subjective psychological determinants could be more important than the sociodemographic factors noted above. Party identification, which refers to how closely a person identifies with one of the major political parties, is in theory closely related to political involvement (Abramson, Aldrich, and Rohde 1995, 72–75; Campbell et al. 1960, 121–23; Miller and Shanks 1996, 154–56). It is a key part of an individual's belief system and is characterized by long-term stability. Previous studies have demonstrated that party identifiers have a greater degree of political interest than those without any party preference (Conway 2000, 52–55; Milbrath and Goel 1977, 54). In Taiwan, many voters think of themselves as Pan-Blue supporters, others consider themselves Pan-Green.[4] The rest—with the exception of the few who identify with a minor party—are labeled independents.

Research has shown that independents tend to be less concerned about politics, have less political information, are less interested in political activities, and tend to vote less often. Partisans, in contrast, are more involved and informed and more likely to register and vote, to talk about politics, to evaluate the outcomes of elections, to discuss candidates' campaign promises, to try to influence others, to engage in campaign activities, and so on (Wu and Hsu 2003; Wu and Huang 2007). Partisans are also treated as the object of mobilization efforts by political parties, so they tend to participate more actively in the political process.

Intimately connected with ethnicity and party identification is the issue of national identity, or what is sometimes termed "ethnic consciousness," which is widely regarded as an important issue that attracts the most attention in Taiwan's politics, and is also considered to be a key variable in research on political behavior (Fell 2005; Hsiau 2000; Hsieh 2005; Wachman 1994). National identity comprises individuals' attitudes and beliefs toward their own nationality—Taiwanese, Chinese, or both Taiwanese and Chinese. Over the decades when Taiwan was ruled by a Kuomintang-controlled, mainlander-dominated authoritarian regime, a China-centered political ideology was the mainstream value. However, since the beginning of the democratization process in the mid-1980s, a Taiwan-centered consciousness has gradually risen to prominence. This is confirmed by there being a greater number of respondents who identified themselves as "Taiwanese only" compared to those who chose "Chinese only."

It is necessary to explain that although ethnicity and national identity should be closely related, the former is an objective characteristic, while the latter is based on a subjective psychological sense of belonging. Regarding the direction of political participation, it is hypothesized that an individual having a more intense ideological identification (i.e., those who identified themselves as "Taiwanese only" and "Chinese only") is predisposed to participate in politics more actively.

In addition to party identification and national identity, political knowledge is another subjective cognitive factor related to political participation. In theory, participation is strongly linked to information about government and politics. The available empirical evidence on this point indicates that individuals who have more information about what the government is doing tend to be more active politically (Delli Carpini and Keeter 1996, 62–104; Stone and Schaffner 1988, 204–5). Actually, there is a positive-feedback relationship between participation and information: as individual citizens gain more political information, they participate more, thereby acquiring more experience and skills, thus further increasing their political knowledge. Previous studies on Taiwan politics have confirmed that a person's political knowledge is directly related to sociopolitical involvement (Liao 2006; Tsai 2001; Yang 2003). In the data collected for this chapter, political knowledge is self-reported by the respondents in surveys. In other words, it reflects the respondents' confidence about their own level of political knowledge, which may contain some degree of bias.

The Historical Trend in Voter Turnout in Taiwan

In 1949 the KMT government retreated to Taiwan after the civil war in mainland China. From the early 1950s through the mid-1980s, the KMT regime, in view of its comprehensive domination over the government's ruling apparatus, bore the characteristics of an authoritarian one-party state with elements of totalitarianism (Tien 1989; Winckler 1984). The control seized by the KMT was comparable to that of the ruling party in a Leninist-style state, with two exceptions. Those exceptions were the existence of private ownership and, more significantly, the institutionalization of local elections (Cheng 1989, 477–78).

The first local elections for executive posts were held in two stages in 1950 and 1951. Over the next five decades, voting was gradually expanded from local to national elections. From 1950 to 1968, electoral competition was limited to the chief executives and representative bodies at the city, sub-county, and county levels and to the provincial assembly. In these elections, no organized political opposition was permitted to compete with the governing KMT. In 1969, the authorities initiated limited electoral competition for supplementary representative seats at the national level. With the lifting of martial law and the end of the Period of Mobilization for the Suppression of Communist Rebellion, all members of the National Assembly and the Legislative Yuan were subject to direct election in 1991 and 1992. The most important development was the first popular presidential election, which took place in 1996. At present, all representative bodies and major executive officials—except the premier, who is appointed by the president—are elected by popular vote.

After the lifting of martial law in 1987, voting participation in Taiwan's national elections, at an average of approximately 70 percent, was relatively high in comparison with that of other democratic countries. Nevertheless, Taiwan's aggregate-level turnout rate for presidential and parliamentary elections has exhibited a downward trend similar to that in many developed countries (Powell 1986). Generally speaking, the rates of voter turnout in presidential elections are somewhat higher than those in parliamentary elections, as shown in table 11.1. For presidential races, turnout increased from 76 percent in 1996 to 83 percent in 2000, and then slipped to 80 percent in 2004, 76 percent in 2008, and 74 percent in 2012.

The turnout rates for legislative elections exhibit an obviously declining trend. The turnout in the 1992 Legislative Yuan elections was about 72 percent, which was high compared to the elections that followed. In 1995, 1998, and 2001, the average was approximately 67 percent. The level of voter turnout then plunged to 59 percent in the 2004 year-end legislative election. Save for 2012, which was the first occasion upon which a presidential election coincided with a legislative vote, and when, as might be expected, there was a higher turnout rate (Fornos, Power, and Garand 2004; Nikolenyi 2010), the turnout rate for legislative elections has consistently decreased, reaching its lowest point in 2008 at about 58 percent. Overall, Taiwan's voter turnout has declined for both presidential and legislative elections at the aggregate level. This drop in citizen engagement raises worrisome questions for the health of Taiwan's democracy to which we will return at the end of this chapter.

Explaining Voter Turnout in Taiwan

To understand who votes in Taiwan, we examine the TEDS multiyear survey data mentioned above. These data allow us to trace the pattern of changes in the turnout rate in recent elections. In each election year, the survey data constitute a nationally representative, multistage probability sample of adults living throughout Taiwan.[5]

The respondents were asked whether they had cast ballots, but in Taiwan, as in other countries, people sometimes report that they voted when in fact they did not.[6] The actual turnout of individual citizens is known to the Taiwan Election Commission, but their records are secret. Unlike in some other democracies, researchers are not given access to these records, even on a confidential basis. Thus turnout reports in Taiwan cannot be "validated," that is, checked against official records. The result is that turnout in Taiwan as reported in surveys is higher than the official records, as may be seen in

TABLE 11.1. Voter Turnout in Taiwan's National Elections, 1989–2012

Year	Type of election	Turnout (%)
1989	Supplementary representatives of the Legislative Yuan	75.2
1991	2nd session representatives of the National Assembly	68.3
1992	2nd session representatives of the Legislative Yuan	72.0
1995	3rd session representatives of the Legislative Yuan	67.7
1996	9th presidential election	76.0
	3rd session representatives of the National Assembly	76.2
1998	4th session representatives of the Legislative Yuan	68.1
2000	10th presidential election	82.7
2001	5th session representatives of the Legislative Yuan	66.2
2004 March	11th presidential election	80.3
2004 December	6th session representatives of the Legislative Yuan	59.2
2008 January	7th session representatives of the Legislative Yuan	58.5
2008 March	12th presidential election	76.3
2012 January	13th presidential election	74.4
2012 January	8th session representatives of the Legislative Yuan	74.7

Source: Election Study Center, National Chengchi University, http://www.esc.nccu.edu.tw/.

the charts below.[7] Thus surveys are not very good at estimating absolute levels of turnout. Fortunately, however, turnout comparisons across groups are less affected by this problem, and that is our focus in this chapter. In order to provide clearer ideas, we present the results in figures (11.1–11.5) and tables (11.2–11.6).

Figure 11.1 shows the differences in voter turnout rates by age group. The first thing to note is that the reported turnout rate in presidential elections is higher than that in legislative elections, which is as expected. Moreover, in both types of elections, the turnout rate increases with age. However, with the exception of voters in their fifties and older, the reported turnout rate has gradually decreased with time. Thus the problem of declining interest in voting is concentrated among younger voters. Their turnout has declined faster than the average seen in figure 1. This raises special concerns for Taiwan's democratic health as Taiwan's older and more reliable voters inevitably reach the age at which they can no longer participate actively.

Ethnicity has long been a politically sensitive issue in Taiwan, especially the cleavage between the majority Taiwanese and the minority mainlanders (Moody 1992; Wachman 1994). Mainlanders are often thought to participate more. Contrary to expectations, however, the results in figure 11.2 reveal that mainlanders do not have a significantly higher turnout rate than Minnan and Hakka. Thus subethnic differences in Taiwan have very little impact on turnout. As we will see, however, differences reappear when we look at electoral participation more broadly.

Next, we explore the relationship between an individual's party identification and turnout rate, as displayed in figure 11.3. Party identification, in theory, is closely related to political involvement. As expected, an individual with a preference for a specific political party, either a Pan-Blue or a Pan-Green supporter, is more likely to vote in both presidential and legislative elections. The differences are typically not large (5 to 10 percentage points), but they have existed in all elections after the 2001 Legislative Yuan contest.

Contrary to expectations, the results in figure 11.4 indicate that there is no specific relationship between voter turnout and national identity. Individuals who have a clear national identity (either Taiwanese only or Chinese only) have relatively high turnout rates; however, the differences are weak and insignificant. More specifically, those who identify themselves as Chinese are more likely to vote. Overall, the findings are consistent with the results displayed in figures 11.2, 11.3, and 11.4—that individuals who have a distinct idea of their ethnicity, party affiliation, and national identity are more likely to vote, although these variables merely exert conditional effects on voting participation.

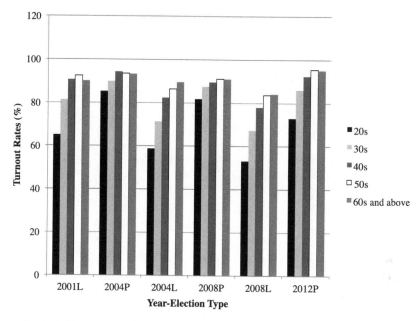

Fig. 11.1. Voter turnout by age group. *Note:* From left to right in each year, bars represent voters in one of five age groups: 20s, 30s, 40s, 50s, and 60s and above. Numbers on the bars represent the percentage turnout for each age group. L: legislative; P: presidential.

Also as hypothesized, the turnout rate in presidential elections increases with the level of (self-reported) political knowledge (see figure 11.5). The turnout rate for individuals with a low level of political knowledge is around 84–86 percent. The rate for those with either a moderate or high level of political knowledge is generally higher than 90 percent. However, in the elections to the Legislative Yuan, the relationship between turnout and knowledge is more erratic. Not until the 2008 election does a legislative election exhibit the expected pattern, with more knowledgeable individuals voting at a higher rate. It may be that the parties formerly mobilized voters differently in the two kinds of elections but no longer do so; this is a topic that deserves further investigation.

In summary, an individual's age (up to 65), party identification, national identity, and level of political knowledge are all positively correlated with turnout rates, just as they are in most democracies. Essentially, the more experienced and more engaged citizens are more likely to vote, as one would expect. However, we did not find strong differences between Taiwan's sub-ethnic groups.

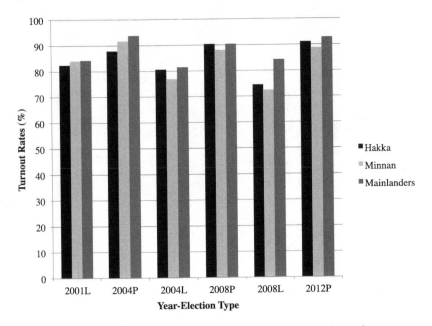

Fig. 11.2. Voter turnout by ethnicity. *Note:* From left to right in each year, bars represent Hakka, Minnan, and Mainlanders. L: legislative; P: presidential.

Explaining Other Kinds of Political Participation in Taiwan

Voter turnout is just one aspect of democratic participation. Citizens may influence their representatives in many different ways, and all of those pathways matter for democratic responsiveness. Thus we now proceed to examine other types of participation, using the same explanatory factors we used to study voter turnout. Due to the different types of participation being recorded in our multiyear datasets, we divided respondents into two groups, participants and nonparticipants, for analytical convenience. Participants are defined as those who took part in at least one form of political activity in the surveyed time period, while nonparticipants are those who indicated an abstention from all such activities.[8]

Differences in electoral participation by age group, by an individual's ethnicity, by party identification, national identity, and by level of political knowledge are displayed in figures 11.6–11.10.

Age, ethnicity, party identification, national identity, and political knowledge are all more or less positively correlated with the level of an individual's electoral participation, as was the case with turnout rates. However,

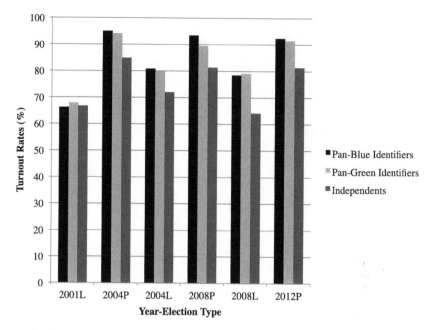

Fig. 11.3. Voter turnout by party identification. *Note:* From left to right in each year, bars represent Pan-Blue identifiers, Pan-Green identifiers, and independents. L: legislative; P: presidential.

all these explanatory factors make a bigger difference to electoral participation broadly defined than they do to turnout. Age matters more; mainlanders participate more, at least in recent elections; and partisanship, political knowledge, and national identity matter much more significantly than they did for turnout. Thus substantial inequality in political participation persists in Taiwan, with older, more engaged mainlanders participating more.

If this trend of inequality in participation continues, it will have a negative impact on the future development of democracy in Taiwan. If younger people drop out of the politically active population, the nation's political agenda will be dominated by the interests of older, possibly more conservative, voters in the future. Economically, this might result in more government resources spent on welfare programs geared toward the elderly as well as protection of inefficient traditional industries at the expense of financing future-oriented policies, such as improving education and providing incentives for starting new businesses. Politically, it might cause young people to become disillusioned with the democratic establishment, pushing them toward ever more radical methods of promoting their own interests. The

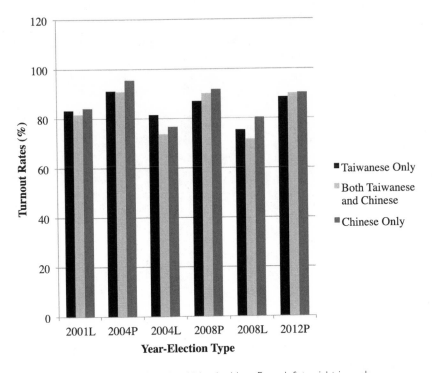

Fig. 11.4. Voter turnout by national identity. *Note:* From left to right in each year, bars represent voters who identify themselves as: Taiwanese only, both Taiwanese and Chinese, and Chinese only. L: legislative; P: presidential.

recent Sunflower Student Movement is an illustration of youth's lack of confidence in a political system led by an older generation with apparently little concern for the needs of the young.

Conclusion

This chapter covers the development of voter turnout and electoral participation in Taiwan. Both voting and participation in electoral activities are essential elements in the formation and maintenance of democracy. Elections, especially, are the most important way of promoting political participation among ordinary citizens. Through elections, citizens select political leaders and shape public affairs, while the government uses them to guarantee its legitimacy (Jackman 1987, 405–6). According to Lipset (1981, 27), "democracy is a complex society . . . which supplies regular constitutional

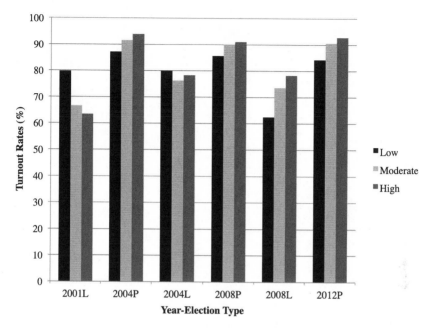

Fig. 11.5. Voter turnout by self-assessed political knowledge. *Note:* From left to right in each year, bars represent low, moderate, and high levels of political knowledge. Because different survey questions on political knowledge were used, varying scoring scales were adopted. For data from TEDS 2001, TEDS 2004L, TEDS 2004P, and TEDS 2008L, we recoded political knowledge by level: low (score 0–1), moderate (2–3), and high (score 4–5); for data from TEDS 2008P, scoring was recoded to low (score 0–1), moderate (score 2), and high (score 3); for data from TEDS 2012, scoring was recoded to low (score 0–2), moderate (score 3–4), and high (score 5–7). L: legislative; P: presidential.

opportunities for changing the governing officials, and a social mechanism which permits the largest possible part of the population to influence major decisions by choosing among contenders for political office." In a democracy, political participation affects the distribution of social values, and one way of judging its effectiveness is to see who plays an active role in the political process, and how much they participate in it.

Despite the importance of political participation to democracy, we find that empirical research on this topic has been limited primarily to Western countries, and that systematic analysis of electoral participation in developing democracies such as Taiwan remains scarce. Research into the level of political participation among Taiwan citizens is therefore likely to have implications for government authorities and civic groups, as they seek to sta-

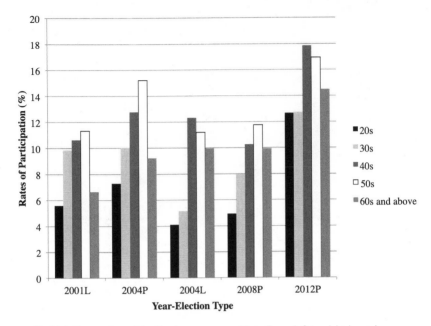

Fig. 11.6. Electoral participation by age group. *Note:* From left to right in each year, bars represent the percentage of voters in one of five age groups: 20s, 30s, 40s, 50s, and 60s and above. L: legislative; P: presidential.

bilize and strengthen the island's fledgling democratic institutions. The need to deduce what drives political participation in Taiwan is even more pressing due to a significant downward trend in turnout for both presidential and legislative elections in recent years.

We end this chapter as we began it, by highlighting that political participation can be affected by sociodemographic characteristics and subjective cognition, as well as people's personal attitudes and life experiences. Political socialization is a continuing process. Reviewing the similarities and differences displayed above, we note in particular that voters in their fifties and sixties, those who identify with a particular party, those who perceive themselves to be Chinese, those who have high levels of political knowledge, and those who are mainlanders are more likely to vote and engage in political activities. This more engaged group can be seen as the established higher social class within Taiwan society. They tend to be an economically well off sector whose interests are at least in part opposed to those of younger voters.

In this sense, social and economic factors are fundamental to political participation. The findings of this chapter confirm the proposition that the

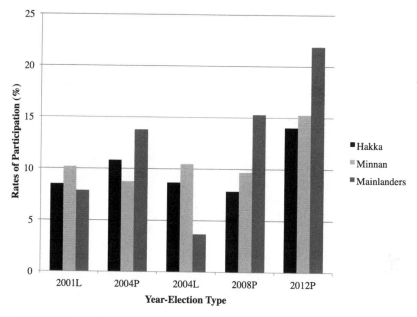

Fig. 11.7. Electoral participation by ethnicity. *Note:* From left to right in each year, bars represent Hakka, Minnan, and Mainlanders. L: legislative; P: presidential.

higher a person's social status, the more likely they are to be an active participant in political life. People in the upper and middle classes tend to be more interested and involved in public affairs than lower class individuals. The unequal distribution of political participation may have the effect of driving Taiwan toward an "elite regime" in which the established upper class will be able to use its financial resources and political knowledge to dictate the policy agendas of elected politicians, gradually creating an environment more favorable to corporate and business interests at the expense of labor. Such a development would not only further strengthen the dichotomy between the young and the old but also create an insurmountable gap in power between the urban and the rural populations, the rich and the poor, as well as between the politically connected and unconnected members of the public. Socioeconomic disparity between groups and regions would be accompanied by political unfairness, and the democratic system would no longer guarantee an equal voice for all voters as it was originally meant to do.

The potentially divisive nature of unequal political participation means that it is necessary for Taiwan to reengage those groups of voters who are un-

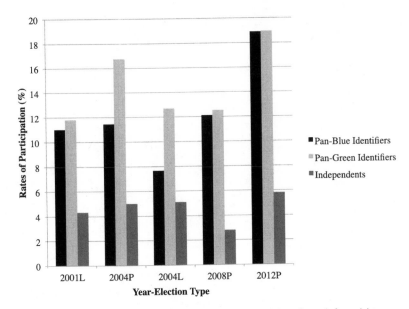

Fig. 11.8. Electoral participation by party identification. *Note:* From left to right in each year, bars represent Pan-Blue identifiers, Pan-Green identifiers, and independents. L: legislative; P: presidential.

derrepresented in the electorate. To be fundamentally and sustainably effective, this process of reengagement must emphasize cooperation between the higher levels of society and the grassroots. On the one hand, populist civic groups must be established to educate people about the long-term harm caused by political indifference. These groups should not only be encouraged but also financed, if necessary, by the government. On the other hand, the government must be tolerant of dissent. Negotiations with the Sunflower Student Movement and even partial incorporation of their platform into official policy, for instance, may trigger renewed interest among those young people who have become disillusioned with politics.

What is most important, however, is the need to continue monitoring the levels of political participation by different groups, as has been done in the research presented in this chapter. The ability to identify which groups have become estranged from the mainstream political establishment allows measures to be taken to rectify this state of affairs before the drifting away of certain voters creates systemic problems for policymakers and for Taiwan society.

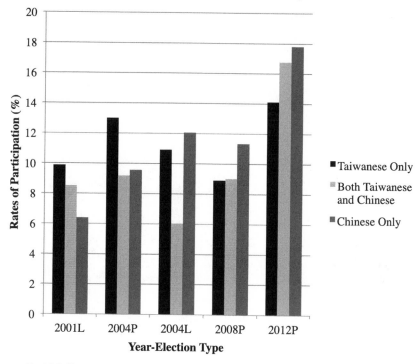

Fig. 11.9. Electoral participation by national identity. *Note:* From left to right in each year, bars represent voters who identify themselves as: Taiwanese only, both Taiwanese and Chinese, and Chinese only. L: legislative; P: presidential.

Appendix 11.A1. Survey Questions and Coding of Variables

Voter Turnout. "Did you vote for the Legislative Yuan Election?" (1 = *yes*; 2 = *no*) (TEDS 2001L) (TEDS 2004L) (TEDS 2008L)
  "In this presidential election many people went to vote, while others, for various reasons, did not go to vote. Did you vote?" (1 = *yes*; 2 = *no*) (TEDS 2004P) (TEDS 2008P) (TEDS 2012)
Electoral Participation. "Respondents' total amount of political activities listed below: did volunteer campaign work for either a candidate or a party; attended an election-related gathering or banquet; joined a candidate's support organization; reminded friends to watch candidate debates or campaign; persuaded others to vote for a particular candidate or party; gave money to a political party or candidate; purchased a candidate's souvenirs; attended a candidate's rally) (1 = *none*; 2 = *at least one of them*) (TEDS 2001L) (TEDS 2004P) (TEDS 2004L) (TEDS 2008P) (TEDS 2012)

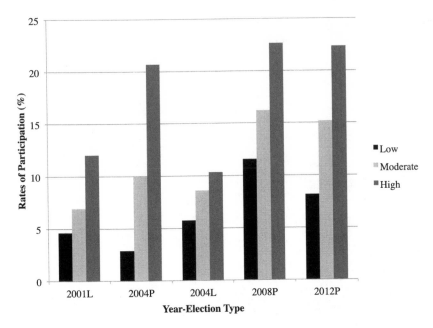

Fig. 11.10. Electoral participation by self-assessed political knowledge. *Note:* From left to right in each year, bars represent low, moderate, and high level of political knowledge. L: legislative; P: presidential.

Age. Respondent's age measured in years. (1 = *20 to 29*; 2 = *30 to 29*; 3 = *40 to 49*; 4 = *50 to 59*; 5 = *above 60*)

Ethnicity. Ethnic background of respondent's father. (1 = *Hakka*; 2 = *Minnan*; 3 = *Mainlander*; aborigines coded as missing)

Party identification. "Among the main political parties in our country, including the KMT, DPP, PFP, NP, and TSU, do you think of yourself as leaning toward any particular party?" "Which party is that?" (1 = *Pan-Blue supporter* [KMT, NP, and PFP]; 2 = *Pan-Green supporter* [DPP and TSU])

National identity. "In Taiwan, some people think they are Taiwanese. There are also some people who think that they are Chinese. Do you consider yourself as Taiwanese, Chinese, or both?" (1 = *Taiwanese*; 2 = *both*; 3 = *Chinese*)

Political knowledge. Respondents' total amount of correct answers to the following questions: "Who is the current Vice President of our country?"; "Who is the President of the PRC?"; "Who is the current President of the United States?"; "How many years are a legislator's term?"; and, "Which institution has the power to interpret the Constitution?" (1 = *low* [total correct answers are 0–1]; 2 = *moderate* [total correct answers are 2–3]; 3 = *high* [total correct answers are 4–5]) (TEDS 2001L)

"Who is the President of the PRC?"; "Who is the current President of the United States?"; "How many years are a legislator's term?"; "Which institution has the power to interpret the Constitution?"; and, "Who is the current Vice President of our country?" (1 = *low* [total correct answers are 0–1]; 2 = *moderate* [total correct answers are 2–3]; 3 = *high* [total correct answers are 4–5]) (TEDS 2004P)

"Who is the current Vice President of our country?"; "Who is the President of the PRC?"; "Who is the current President of the United States?"; "How many years are a legislator's term?"; and, "Which institution has the power to interpret the Constitution?" (1 = *low* [total correct answers are 0–1]; 2 = *moderate* [total correct answers are 2–3]; 3 = *high* [total correct answers are 4–5]) (TEDS 2004L)

"Who is the current President of the United States?"; "Who is the current premier of our country?"; "Which institution has the power to interpret the Constitution?" (1 = *low* [total correct answers are 0–1]; 2 = *moderate* [total correct answers are 2]; 3 = *high* [total correct answers are 3]) (TEDS 2008P)

"Who is the current Vice President of our country?"; "Who is the current President of the United States?"; "Who is the President of the PRC?"; "Which institution has the power to interpret the Constitution?"; and, "How many years are a legislator's term?" (1 = *low* [total correct answers are 0–1]; 2 = *moderate* [total correct answers are 2–3]; 3 = *high* [total correct answers are 4–5]) (TEDS 2008L)

"Who is the current President of the United States?"; "Who is the current premier of our country?"; "Which institution has the power to interpret the Constitution?"; "Which of these persons was the finance minister before the recent election?"; "What was the current unemployment rate in Taiwan as of the end of last year"; "Which party came in second in seats in the Legislative Yuan?"; and, "Who is the current Secretary-General of the United Nations, Kofi Annan, Kurt Waldheim, Ban Ki-moon, or Boutros-Ghali?" (1 = *low* [total correct answers are 0–2]; 2 = *moderate* [total correct answers are 3–4]; 3 = *high* [total correct answers are 5–7]) (TEDS 2012)

Notes

1. Data analyzed in this chapter were collected as part of the research project entitled "Taiwan's Election and Democratization Study, 2012: Presidential and Legislative Elections" (TEDS 2012) (NSC 100–2420-H002–030). The coordinator of the multiyear TEDS project is Chi Huang of the Department of Political Science at National Chengchi University. The principal investigator is Professor Yun-han Chu of the Institute of Political Science at Academia Sinica. More information is on the TEDS website (http://www.tedsnet.org). The following were responsible for distributing the date: the Department of Political Science, National Taiwan University; the Department of Political Science, Soochow University; the Graduate Institute of Political Science, National Sun Yat-Sen University; the Department of Political Science and Graduate Institute of Political Economy, National Cheng Kung University; the Department of Political Science, Tunghai University; and the Election Study Center, National Chengchi University. The authors appreciate the assistance of the institutes and individuals aforementioned in providing data. This research is partially supported by National Chengchi University's Top University Project. The views expressed in this chapter are those of the authors alone.

2. For a discussion of ethnic and subethnic differences in Taiwan, see chapter 1.

3. Although Minnan and mainlanders have different attitudes and characteristics, in reality politics is the main factor generating the ethnic consciousness of both groups. See chapters 1 and 3.

4. As a reminder for readers, the Taiwan party system is generally divided into the Pan-Blue camp, which espouses eventual political unification with China, and the Pan-Green camp, which consists of supporters of Taiwan independence. The major parties of the Pan-Blue camp are the Kuomintang, the People First Party, and the New Party, while the Pan-Green parties are the Democratic Progressive Party, the Taiwan Solidarity Union, and the Green Party.

5. The TEDS data are weighted by gender, age, and education to achieve national representativeness. The population statistics are based on census data reported in the official documents, *Taiwan-Fukien Demographic Statistics, Republic of China*, released by the Ministry of the Interior, Republic of China.

6. The topic of vote misreporting is important both theoretically and practically (Wu 2006, 224). Research on both electoral turnout and vote choice depends heavily on self-reported behavior, but it is generally found that a number of respondents do not accurately report their electoral behavior. One cause of errors in survey research is that more respondents claim to have voted in postelection interviews than have actually cast ballots. A possible consequence is that misreporting does indeed produce some misleading conclusions, since much of the scholarly work tests models of electoral behavior based on survey measurements containing a relatively large amount of error.

7. In figure 11.2, for example, all but the small, youngest group reported turnout rates exceeding 80% for the 2001 Legislative Yuan election, but as figure 11.1 shows, the actual turnout rate in that election was only 67%.

8. The 13 electoral activities in the TEDS are as follows: read the official election notice; read candidates' leaflets, newsletter, or newspaper ads; watched candidate

debates or campaign speeches on TV; did volunteer campaign work for either a candidate or a party; attended an election-related gathering or banquet; joined a candidate's support organization; reminded friends to watch candidate debates or campaign; persuaded others to vote for a particular candidate or party; gave money to a political party or candidate; purchased a candidate's souvenirs; invited to participate in a candidate's rally; attended a candidate's rally; and visited a candidate's website.

References

Abramson, Paul R., John H. Aldrich, and David W. Rohde. 1995. *Change and Continuity in the 1992 Elections.* Washington, DC: Congressional Quarterly Press.

Almond, Gabriel A., and G. Bingham Powell, Jr. 1988. "Political Socialization and Political Culture." In *Comparative Politics Today: A World View*, 4th ed., ed. Gabriel A. Almond and G. Bingham Powell, Jr., 34–48. Glenview, IL: Scott, Foresman and Company.

Campbell, Angus, Philip E. Converse, Warren E. Miller, and Donald E. Stokes. 1960. *The American Voter.* New York: John Wiley and Sons.

Cheng, Tun-jen. 1989. "Democratizing the Quasi-Leninist Regime in Taiwan." *World Politics* 41 (4): 471–99.

Conway, M. Margaret. 2000. *Political Participation in the United States.* 3rd ed. Washington, DC: Congressional Quarterly Press.

Dahl, Robert A. 1971. *Polyarchy: Participation and Opposition.* New Haven: Yale University Press.

Delli Carpini, Michael X., and Scott Keeter. 1996. *What Americans Know about Politics and Why It Matters.* New Haven: Yale University Press.

Fell, Dafydd. 2005. *Party Politics in Taiwan.* London: Routledge.

Fornos, Carolina A., Timothy J. Power, and James C. Garand. 2004. "Explaining Voter Turnout in Latin America, 1980 to 2000." *Comparative Political Studies* 37 (8): 909–40.

Hsiau, A-chin. 2000. *Contemporary Taiwanese Cultural Nationalism.* London: Routledge.

Hsieh, John F. 2005. "Ethnicity, National Identity, and Domestic Politics in Taiwan." *Journal of Asian and African Studies* 40 (1–2): 13–28.

Hughes, Christopher. 1997. *Taiwan and Chinese Nationalism.* London: Routledge.

Jackman, Robert W. 1987. "Political Institutions and Voter Turnout in the Industrial Democracies." *American Political Science Review* 81 (2): 405–24.

Liao, Yih-Hsing. 2006. "The Research of Voter Turnout: Case Study of Taiwan." *Journal of Chinese Public Administration* 3: 185–202.

Lipset, Seymour M. 1981. *Political Man: The Social Bases of Politics.* Baltimore: Johns Hopkins University Press.

Milbrath, Lester, and M. L. Goel. 1977. *Political Participation.* Chicago: Rand McNally.

Miller, Warren E., and J. Merrill Shanks. 1996. *The New American Voter.* Cambridge: Harvard University Press.

Moody, Peter R., Jr. 1992. *Political Change in Taiwan.* New York: Praeger.

Nie, Norman H., and Sidney Verba. 1975. "Political Participation." In *Handbook of Political Science: Volume 4, Nongovernmental Politics*, ed. Fred I. Greenstein and Nelson W. Polsby, 1–74. Reading, MA: Addison-Wesley.

Nikolenyi, Csaba. 2010. "Concurrent Elections and Voter Turnout: The Effect of the De-Linking of State Elections on Electoral Participation in India's Parliamentary Polls, 1971–2004." *Political Studies* 58 (1): 214–33.

Powell, G. Bingham, Jr. 1986. "American Voter Turnout in Comparative Perspective." *American Political Science Review* 80 (1): 17–43.

Rosenstone, Steven J., and John Mark Hansen. 2003. *Mobilization, Participation, and Democracy in America*. New York: Longman.

Stone, William F., and Paul E. Schaffner. 1988. *The Psychology of Politics*. 2nd ed. New York: Springer-Verlag.

Tate, Katherine. 1991. "Black Political Participation in the 1984 and 1988 Presidential Elections." *American Political Science Review* 85 (4): 1159–76.

Tien, Hung-mao. 1989. *The Great Transition: Political and Social Change in the Republic of China*. Stanford, CA: Hoover Institution Press.

Tsai, Chia-Hung. 2001. "Why Do Taiwanese Vote?" *Journal of Electoral Studies* 8 (2): 125–58.

Verba, Sidney, and Norman H. Nie. 1972. *Participation in America: Political Democracy and Social Equality*. New York: Harper and Row.

Wachman, Alan M. 1994. *Taiwan: National Identity and Democratization*. Armonk, NY: M. E. Sharpe.

Wang, Fu-chang. 1994. "Ethnic Assimilation and Mobilization: An Analysis of Party Support in Taiwan" [in Chinese]. *Bulletin of the Institute of Ethnology Academia Sinica* 77 (Spring): 1–34.

Wang, Fu-chang. 1998. "Ethnic Consciousness, Nationalism, and Party Support: Taiwan's Ethnic Politics in the 1990s" [in Chinese]. *Studies on Taiwan's Sociology* 2 (July): 1–45.

Winckler, Edwin A. 1984. "Institutionalization and Participation on Taiwan." *China Quarterly* 99: 481–99.

Wu, Chung-li. 2006. "Vote Misreporting and Survey Context: The Taiwan Case." *Issues & Studies* 42 (4): 223–39.

Wu, Chung-li. 2008. "Ethnicity, Empowerment, and Political Trust: The 2005 Local Elections in Taiwan." *Issues & Studies* 44 (1): 105–32.

Wu, Chung-li, and Cheng-tai Hsiao. 2006. "Empowerment Theory and Ethnic Politics in Taiwan." *Issues & Studies* 42 (1): 103–36.

Wu, Chung-li, and Wen-pin Hsu. 2003. "Who Are Partisans and Independents? Determinants of Party Identification of Taiwan's Voters in 2001" [in Chinese]. *Political Science Review* 18: 101–40.

Wu, Chung-li, and Chi Huang. 2007. "Divided Government in Taiwan's Local Politics: Public Evaluations of City/County Government Performance." *Party Politics* 13 (6): 741–60.

Yang, Meng-Li. 2003. "Voter Turnout and Economic Adversity in Taiwan." *Journal of Electoral Studies* 10 (2): 159–91.

CHAPTER 12

Conclusion

The Power of Identity in Taiwan

Christopher H. Achen and T. Y. Wang

Most countries are politically divided along lines that reflect their internal cleavages. Those cleavages may be religious, linguistic, ethnic/racial, regional, or class-based. Most countries contain several politically relevant divisions. In multiparty systems, particularly those with proportional representation and a low threshold for gaining parliamentary seats, some minor cleavages (farmers, small ethnic or linguistic minorities) may have their own party in the legislature. Larger parties usually represent coalitions. In two-party systems, both parties are large, and in consequence each party will represent a broad combination of groups. Large parties frequently reflect many entirely distinct and unrelated cleavages in the society, sometimes in ways that make common sense, and sometimes not. In the United States, for example, liquor distributors and conservative evangelical Christians, once bitter enemies in the Prohibition era, now find themselves side by side in the Republican Party.

Thus, in most countries the major parties embody many different identities. The voters, too, are often a jumble of identities, some more strongly felt than others, but all of them subject to activation and mobilization under the right circumstances. Studying the role of social identities in politics is typically quite difficult. Different voters will identify with a particular party for very different reasons. Many voters themselves will have more than one identity that drives them toward a particular party, and perhaps some other identities that are in conflict with that party.

As the parties adopt new positions, some voters will feel conflicted. Most will stay with their partisanship, simply living with the tensions or tuning them out. Others will move toward political independence, perhaps eventually switching to another party with which, again, they are in imperfect agreement. But the result is that at any given time, there is no simple relationship between identity, partisanship, and issue positions. All three are tangled up in not wholly consistent ways.

In consequence, the study of how identities relate to partisanship and political attitudes is very complex in most countries. A small proportion of voters, often discriminated-against minorities, may have one main identity driving their political stances. But for most voters, too many things are affecting too many other things. Voters have too many identities. Even when identities are the main factor driving party choices and issue positions, the catch-all nature of the parties and the complexity of the voters' own political lives create a vortex of causal arrows, making it extremely difficult to discern why the voters are thinking and choosing as they do. Any attractive theoretical account comes up against mixed empirical support and plausible counterarguments. Put another way, most countries are not very good places to study how social identities connect to political identities, issue preferences, and vote choices.

Taiwan, however, is a happy exception, as this book has demonstrated. Social cleavages are few. Apart from a tiny minority, Taiwan voters do not differ racially. The great majority adhere to a low-intensity, syncretist religious tradition with a mixture of Buddhist, Taoist, and Confucian elements, which has never been a source of political divisions. In the absence of an exploitative industrial revolution and without the associated development of strong employee unions, social class has not been central to Taiwan politics. (Compare the heavy emphasis on class in treatments of European politics—a recent example is Evans and De Graaf 2013.) In Taiwan, the principal division is linguistic and ethnic—whether the language one speaks at home is Mandarin, Hakka, Hokkien (Fujianese), or one of the aboriginal languages. In turn, this cleavage relates to the historical time of arrival on Taiwan from elsewhere, and the associated history and culture of each group.

As we discussed in chapter 1, events of the past 70 years have reinforced those linguistic and cultural divisions and made them politically salient. Other divisions are much weaker. That means that Taiwan has just one central cleavage—a gift to scholars trying to understand how identity operates in politics. Of course, as we have seen, that cleavage has evolved. Once tied more strictly to ethnicity, with a Mandarin-speaking ruling elite enforcing their culture on everyone else, the issue is now more closely related to differing conceptions of national identity.

Ethnicity still matters: only a minority of mainlanders identify as strictly Taiwanese, and extremely few Minnan identify as purely Chinese. But with a more open society, intermarriage, and the passage of time, the categories have blurred. Some Hakka and aboriginal citizens, with their own historical grievances against the Minnan, feel free to line up politically with mainlanders, for example. What matters less and less are the divisions of the 1950s. What matters more and more, regardless of ethnicity, is where one stands on the status of Taiwan. Is China the ancestral homeland of which Taiwan is an integral part, even if currently administered separately? Or is China a different country from Taiwan, home to a fundamentally different people? Debates of this kind are familiar from the history of many countries.[1]

In this book, we have addressed the question of how Taiwan voters make their decisions when they go to the polls. We have found that the central political cleavage and its associated social and political identities are central to voters' thinking. Candidates' personal traits, the domestic issues of the day, cross-Strait relations, and Taiwan's institutional arrangements all play a modest role as well. But what shapes politics on the island much more than anything else is "the China factor," the central dispute over Taiwan's national identity. Over and over again in this book, we have found that it dominates voters' decisions. And because left-right language is used to describe that division by almost no one in Taiwan, the conventional Western view that "left" and "right" apply everywhere in one form or another among knowledgeable citizens simply collapses when applied to Taiwan, as chapter 9 showed.

Because the two main parties are perceived to take opposite sides on the fundamental cleavage, partisanship embodies the same electoral division. Thus, whether the national identity issue directly shapes some policy dispute, or whether partisanship structures it instead, the result is the same: the dispute will be molded by the underlying cleavage over Taiwan's national identity. Nothing else matters to the same degree, and certainly not the conventional left-right dimension that gives form to politics in most Western countries.

Repeatedly, therefore, the analyses in the various chapters have identified partisan identification as the most important factor in Taiwan voters' electoral calculus.[2] That is, the island citizens' self-declared partisan affiliations with the Pan-Blue Alliance and the Pan-Green Alliance exert the most significant effects on how and why they support specific candidates. As figure 12.1 shows, partisanship has an extremely powerful effect in Taiwan.[3] In the 2012 presidential election, knowing the voter's partisanship was tantamount to knowing how he or she voted in the vast majority of the cases. Only independents fell toward the middle: everyone else was polarized. In contem-

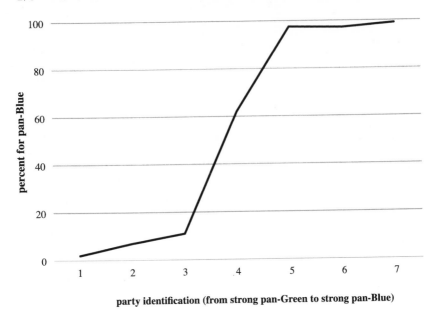

Fig. 12.1. Pan-Blue vote in 2012 Taiwan presidential election

porary Taiwan, there simply is not much about the vote left to explain once partisanship is accounted for.

The finding that partisan identification plays an important role in understanding citizens' political behavior in democratic polities is not new, of course. More than half a century ago, the authors of *The American Voter* convincingly demonstrated "the role of enduring partisan commitments in shaping attitudes toward political objects" (Campbell et al. 1960, 135). They concluded that "the strength and direction of party identification are facts of central importance in accounting for attitude and behavior" (121).

What Taiwan voters add to this familiar story is that their partisan identifications largely embody the single most important political cleavage on the island—Taiwan's future relationship with China, generally characterized as the issue of unification vs. independence. Because this key political cleavage is also intertwined with the island citizens' psychological attachment to China (or detachment from it), partisan identification mirrors Taiwan voters' conception of Taiwan's national identity. The Pan-Green Alliance sees Taiwan's de jure independence and its permanent separation from China as the ultimate objective, whereas the Pan-Blue Alliance does not preclude the island's eventual unification as a possible outcome.

In the public's view, the Pan-Green Alliance is pro-independence while the Pan-Blue Alliance is pro-unification. As these are two diametrically different positions, the Taiwan voters' decision to adopt a partisan identification is easier than in many other countries—the choice is clear and unmistakable. Cross-Strait relations and Taiwanese/Chinese identity have always been key campaign issues in presidential elections. All other issues are secondary, as Sheng and Liao's chapter demonstrates. Subjects related to Taiwan's relationship with China have been main instruments employed by the two political alliances to energize their supporters. Also, because Taiwan's party structure reflects the key political cleavage in the society, all other issues, even essentially administrative policy issues such as absentee voting or the adoption of an English translation system, can be formulated as aspects of the main cleavage and debated in partisan terms, as we saw in chapter 1. Of course, the impact of partisanship varies across countries, as hundreds of studies have shown. (The case of Latin America, for example, is discussed in Lupu 2015.) The clarity of choice and the polarization provided by the party system are often thought to enhance the development of partisanship. (The European case is treated in Berglund et al. 2005 and van der Eijk, Schmitt, and Binder 2005, 177–80; see Zechmeister 2015 for the Latin American counterpart.) Both clarity and polarization apply to Taiwan, and the strength of partisanship there confirms the usual comparative logic of how citizens become partisans. These Taiwan findings handsomely coincide both with Western studies and with Bartels's conclusion in the American political setting that partisanship is "a pervasive dynamic force shaping citizens' perceptions of, and reactions to, the political world" (Bartels 2002, 138).

Thus, partisan identification plays a central role in the Taiwan voter's electoral calculus, as it does elsewhere. Yet other countries' voters often give weight to the character of the candidates and the state of economy in making their vote choices. Is that true in Taiwan? The chapter by Wang and Chen (chapter 8) clearly shows that the notion of candidate issue ownership is applicable in Taiwan. That is, voters' perceptions of candidate traits are closely connected with party labels. In general, the Pan-Blue candidates, or more precisely the KMT candidates, are perceived as more capable of handling issues related to economic development and cross-Strait relations, whereas the Pan-Green, or the DPP, candidates are associated with eliminating corruption and initiating political reforms. Yet the perception of personal traits does not provide substantial advantages or disadvantages to candidates during elections. Citizens' electoral decisions continue to be conditioned by their partisan affiliations.

As Lewis-Beck (1988) and Paldam (1991) demonstrated, and as many subsequent studies have confirmed, the strength of economic voting varies dramatically from one country to the next. Powell and Whitten (1993) and Anderson (2007) each argued that context matters: if clarity of responsibility is unclear, for example, or if no credible alternative government exists, economic voting may diminish or disappear. (Gelineau and Singer 2015 review the literature and discuss the Latin American case.) In the case of Taiwan's essentially two-party system, the president's responsibility is clear and the opposition is credible. Economic voting should occur. Indeed, the Taiwan public's assessment of the economy does appear to have an effect on their voting decisions. However, Taiwan voters appear to be rather tolerant of incumbents' past economic performance. Rather than punishing sitting presidents for a bad economy, they apparently have a tendency to reward candidates that offer a promising economic future. That is, prospective economic voting is more prevalent in Taiwan than retrospective voting, as both the postelection survey data and the aggregate cross-county economic evidence suggest. Nevertheless, as Tsai concludes in chapter 8, Taiwan voters' "partisanship is a better predictor" of electoral outcomes than their assessment of the state of the economy.

Comparative Strength of the Factors Influencing Vote Choice

In this book, we have reviewed a variety of factors that influence vote choice—ethnicity, national identity, issues, and economic evaluations—and we have compared each with partisanship. Repeatedly, we have found that partisanship was the controlling factor, with an impact much stronger than any of the other single forces at work. However, we have not yet assessed these competing factors jointly. We have seen only that partisanship is dominant, but not which of the remaining influences on the vote are also somewhat consequential. It is to that task that we now turn.

We begin by using all available explanatory variables to account for the presidential vote in 2012. The small vote (2.8%) for James Soong is grouped with that for Ma Ying-jeou to form the Pan-Blue vote; the vote for Tsai Ing-wen is the Pan-Green vote. Logit analysis is employed to model this dichotomous variable. In addition to party identification, the explanatory variables include the three principal ethnicities (with Hakka as the excluded category), and the three types of national identification ("Taiwanese," "Chinese," and "Dual"), with "Dual" (i.e., "both Chinese and Taiwanese") as the excluded identity. We also create a category ("No ethnic identity") for the small but distinctive group who replied "other," "don't know," or who refused to answer the question. This group is more senior (a large majority older than 49) and less educated (a majority with junior high school or less).

More than 70 percent have no partisanship, but they often retain the one-party KMT voting loyalties of their youth.

Other variables included were measures of opinion on unification/independence, on social welfare expenditures, and on the cross-Strait economic agreement (ECFA). Economic evaluations were also included—first, the county-level change in disposable income per capita, and then also the respondent's prospective and retrospective evaluations of the national economy. (See chapter 6 for the definitions of these variables.) Preliminary exploration of the data indicated that the only category of occupation with a possible substantial effect on vote choice was being a postsecondary student. Similarly, having a junior high school education or less was the only possibly influential category of education. Dummy variables for each were included in the explanatory model, along with two variables for demographic factors—gender and age. All variables were scaled to 0–1 for easy comparison.[4]

The first column of table 12.1 displays the result of this initial exploratory model.[5] Partisanship is by far the most powerful factor, as expected. The other variables generally take on their expected sign, although not all are statistically significant. Retrospective evaluations in particular fail to be influential, just as one would expect from the results in chapter 8. Age is also neither powerful nor significant, and in most alternate specifications it looked even less influential than it does here. And of course, that is to be expected, especially because the age distribution of ethnicities and identities does not differ in Taiwan: there are young and old in all groups.

The second column of table 12.1 therefore drops retrospections and age, and reestimates the model. As expected, very little changes. Thus, if retrospections or age somehow have small effects, we can be comfortable that their exclusion is not distorting the impact of other factors.

The issue that arises next concerns the prospective evaluations. The TEDS survey is conducted after the election. Thus, when voters are asked whether "the state of the economy of Taiwan will get better, stay about the same, or get worse," they already know who won the election. We have known since *The American Voter* (Campbell et al. 1960, 397–400) that economic outlooks are powerfully influenced by partisanship: winners are optimistic, losers are pessimistic. Thus, as chapter 8 discussed, some scholars have expressed the concern that the TEDS prospective economic evaluations appear influential only because they are caused by the dependent variable, and not because they have genuine explanatory power on their own. Thus, the impact of prospective evaluations may be substantially inflated in column 2. There is no way to know for certain with the data available.

TABLE 12.1: The Pan-Blue Presidential Vote in 2012

	(1)	(2)	(3)	(4)
Party identification	9.72***	9.71***	9.68***	9.59***
	(.702)	(.687)	(.626)	(.620)
Minnan	−.464	−.492	−.150	−.138
	(.326)	(.324)	(.287)	(.286)
Mainlander	1.68***	1.65***	2.19***	2.16***
	(.603)	(.604)	(.571)	(.567)
Taiwanese ID only	−.414*	−.392	−.424	−.472**
	(.252)	(.250)	(.228)	(.226)
Chinese ID only	.084	.045	−.128	−.166
	(.772)	(.777)	(.651)	(.648)
No ethnic ID	1.23	1.39	.200	.080
	(1.11)	(1.06)	(.598)	(.589)
Unification/independence	1.54**	1.54**	1.79***	1.80***
	(.705)	(.701)	(.596)	(.593)
Social welfare	.603	.634*	.410	
	(.379)	(.379)	(.322)	
ECFA	1.85***	1.79***	1.95***	1.89***
	(.409)	(.392)	(.356)	(.354)
2011 change in county	.773*	.808*	.407	
disposable income	(.459)	(.457)	(.400)	
Prospective evaluation	1.11***	1.08***		
	(.388)	(.355)		
Retrospective evaluation	−.222			
	(.395)			
Postsecondary education	−.926	−.840	−.511	
only	(.616)	(.592)	(.535)	
Primary education only	.935**	.839***	.913***	.987***
	(.394)	(.312)	(.248)	(.244)
Female	.326	.327	.436**	.435**
	(.229)	(.227)	(.201)	(.200)
Age	−.484			
	(.797)			
Intercept	−6.61	−6.78	−6.69	−6.42
	(.733)	(.705)	(.622)	(.587)
Pseudo-R^2	.67	.67	.64	.64
N	1,190	1,203	1,393	1,393

Note: * significant at .10.   ** significant at .05.   *** significant at .01. Dependent variable is 1 if the respondent voted for pan-Blue (Ma or Soong); 0 if for DPP (Tsai). Logit parameter estimates (with standard errors in parentheses).

To allow for this possibility, column 3 of table 12.1 drops prospective evaluations from the statistical model. Partisanship remains as powerful as ever, as do most of the other variables, but the impact of social welfare attitudes drops, and the estimated effects of changes in county disposable income and postsecondary education are cut in half. None of the latter three coefficients is large and none is even close to statistical significance: they may have a modest effect, but there is not enough evidence to support keeping them as explanatory factors.[6]

Column 4 of table 12.1 then drops these three variables with unprovable effects. The remaining coefficients change little, letting us assess the ethnicity and national identification effects. Column 4 shows that being a mainlander has an important positive impact on voting pan-blue, as expected, but being Minnan has only a small and statistically insignificant effect. That is, the Minnan are not distinguishable from the excluded category (Hakka). And second, being a Taiwanese identifier has a substantial and significant negative effect on voting pan-Blue, again as expected, but the other categories of ethnic identity ("Chinese" and none) have small and statistically insignificant effects; that is, they are indistinguishable from the excluded category ("dual identity"). Thus, within the limits of the available data, there are actually just two dichotomies where ethnicity and national identification are concerned: mainlanders vs. everyone else, and "Taiwanese" identification vs. everything else.[7]

Table 12.2 uses these two dichotomies to replace the more elaborate coding of table 12.1. All the other remaining variables are retained, generating our final, preferred model. Every variable is now comfortably statistically significant and most coefficients are quite large. Partisanship retains its overwhelming effect, and apart from the demographic factors of being female or having little education, all the other explanatory factors are closely related to the central political cleavage on the island. Being a mainlander and identifying as "Taiwanese" make a difference even after partisanship is controlled, as do opinions on unification/independence and on the cross-Strait economic agreement, ECFA.

Thus again we find that partisanship, ethnicity, national identity, and the main political dimension are more tightly linked in Taiwan than elsewhere. Ethnicity is fixed, but the other three can be chosen. We find that they are causally joined with each other, so that for most politically knowledgeable Taiwan citizens, conceptions of national identity, partisan identification, and position on issues related to China are strongly connected. Other political issues tend to be swept up into this complex of interrelationships: the clarity of that relationship on the island suggests strongly that politics elsewhere works the same way, even if the researcher cannot otherwise penetrate the murkiness of most countries' multiple identities, issues, and parties. In that sense, the bright clarity of Taiwan's political life helps us see into the shrouded complexity of other countries' polities. That is what we have tried to help the reader accomplish in this volume.

A New Cleavage?

Recent political developments in Taiwan have led some scholars to speculate that "class politics based on wealth gap has become a new driving force of Taiwan's party politics" (Wu 2014, 1). That is, the dominant political cleavage has shifted away from the unification-independence issue to the widening gap of economic distribution. Indeed, beginning in the early 2000s, Taiwan's economy experienced a gradual slowdown, economic inequality worsened, and the rate of unemployment rose as well.

TABLE 12.2: The Pan-Blue Presidential Vote in 2012

	(1)
Party identification	9.46***
	(.600)
Mainlander	2.24***
	(.506)
Taiwanese ID only	–.470**
	(.210)
Unification/independence	1.71***
	(.580)
ECFA	1.92***
	(.349)
Female	.423**
	(.195)
Primary education only	1.00***
	(.238)
Intercept	–6.42
	(.516)
Pseudo-R^2	.63
N	1,428

Note: * significant at .10.   ** significant at .05.
*** significant at .01. Dependent variable is 1 if the respondent voted for Pan-Blue (Ma or Soong); 0 if for DPP (Tsai). Logit parameter estimates (with standard errors in parentheses).

As a remedy for Taiwan's economic misfortunes, leaders of the Pan-Blue Alliance see the Chinese mainland as an economic opportunity, and they argue that an economic liberalization policy is the means to the island's economic revival. Access to China's vast market, however, is contingent on an improved cross-Strait political relationship. Thus, after taking office in 2008 the Ma administration of the KMT implemented a policy of rapprochement toward Beijing. As was explained in chapter 1, cross-Strait tension attenuated after a series of accords were signed between the two governments, including the landmark trade deal known as the Economic Cooperation Framework Agreement. Unfortunately, the expansion of cross-Strait economic exchanges did not improve Taiwan economic fortunes in the short term, and the island's unemployment rate and economic inequality continued to worsen. Leaders of the Pan-Green Alliance therefore criticized Ma's liberalization policy as only allowing the import of cheap Chinese goods, thereby hurting the island's own industries, widening the gap between haves and have-nots, and worsening the job prospects of the younger generation. Pan-Green leaders also argued that Ma's rapprochement policy of advancing cross-Strait relationship on the basis of the "1992 Consensus"—or "one China with different interpretations"—is tantamount to surrendering Taiwan's sovereignty to the Beijing government.[8] These concerns were a prominent feature of the 2012 presidential election, and they constituted the underlying appeal of the 2014 protest known as the Sunflower Movement, led by a group of young people.[9]

But do the recent economic concerns and the disputes over ECFA herald the arrival of a new central dimension in Taiwan political life (Wu 2014)? Or is ECFA just another issue being swept up into the usual partisan cleavage? We have argued throughout this book that on Taiwan, issues are primarily consequences of partisanship and national identity, not causes. Disagreements over ECFA certainly involve differences over trade liberalization vs. autarky, and thus they might represent purely economic disagreements—a new dimension, perhaps even a partisan realignment. But ECFA also requires closer integration with China, and that aspect of the policy might be dominant in people's thinking in the way that we have seen repeatedly in this volume.

Fortunately, the 2012 TEDS survey permits a test of these alternate explanations. The survey contains a question about conventional left-right attitudes, which we have called the "social welfare" issue:

> Regarding the question of social welfare, some people believe that
> the government should merely maintain the current system in order

not to increase people's tax. Other people believe that the government should promote social welfare, even though it will lead to a tax increase.

As Wu (2014, 16) notes, this question is not directly about redistribution. However, it is certainly related to it: maintaining the status quo is precisely the means to avoid tax increases of all kinds, including those for reducing inequality through redistribution. Laissez-faire domestic attitudes should predict laissez-faire international trade policy attitudes, at least to some degree, if a new economic dimension is really emerging. Thus, if arguments about ECFA are truly economic arguments, answers to this social welfare question will inevitably be related to attitudes toward ECFA. On the other hand, if ECFA is just another aspect of the main cleavage, then partisanship and attitudes toward unification/independence should be far better predictors of what people think about ECFA.

Table 12.3 shows the result of an ordered logit analysis of ECFA opinions on partisanship, unification/independence, and the social welfare question. As the table shows, the first two factors are powerful and statistically significant predictors of ECFA attitudes. The coefficient on the social welfare item, on the other hand, is not only small and highly statistically insignificant, but

TABLE 12.3. Attitudes toward ECFA in 2012

	(1)
Party identification	3.50***
	(.201)
Unification/independence	1.57***
	(.283)
Social welfare	−.129
	(.152)
cut 1	.089
	(.150)
cut 2	3.25
	(.174)
Pseudo-R^2	.14
N	1,826

Note: * significant at .10.   ** significant at .05.
*** significant at .01. Dependent variable is 1 if the respondent believes that ECFA will make his family better off; 0 if worse off, and .5 if the same or not sure. Ordered logit parameter estimates (with standard errors in parentheses).

it actually has the wrong sign. Net of partisanship and unification attitudes, laissez-faire attitudes toward social goals have zero effect on what people think about the laissez-faire policies embodied in ECFA. The obvious conclusion is that in the voters' minds, ECFA was about China, not about economics. Like postal voting, ECFA is yet another policy pulled into the main Taiwan cleavage. Indeed, a survey conducted after the Sunflower Movement confirms the above observation (Yen, Kay, and Chen 2015). Their results indicate that the perceived economic interests of Taiwan citizens do affect their positions on trade policies, but that Taiwanese nationalism and security concerns play a more paramount role in their positions.

If Taiwan's democracy survives its external threats long enough, then some day, undoubtedly, Taiwan's internal political divisions will represent something other than disputes over national identity. That day may arrive quickly, or it may not. But as of 2012, the date of the most recent presidential survey data available, such additional considerations had at best only a small impact on the presidential election. We find no credible evidence that the beginnings of a new dimension had emerged in voters' minds.

Looking to the Future

Now if partisanship in Taiwan is strong and other issues matter relatively little, how stable is Taiwan voters' electoral behavior? What are the implications of our findings for Taiwan's future elections? Taiwan's party system has consolidated into what is effectively a two-party system, as chapter 10 explains. The resulting stability corroborates Lipset and Rokkan's (1967) "freezing hypothesis": a party system reflecting key political cleavages in the society is expected to be fairly stable. In fact, a 2012 TEDS panel study reinterviewed the 2008 respondents, finding that among those who voted KMT in the 2008 presidential election, 89 percent voted for the KMT again in 2012. The corresponding number for the DPP was precisely the same—89 percent. These stability rates are similar to those in other two-party democracies, such as the United States, and they indicate that Taiwan's democracy is consolidating its party system and the loyalty of partisans. Whether this stability is due to American-style psychological identification with the parties or to the steady force of other attitudes and identities makes no difference for our purposes.

The analysis in chapter 2 has shown that the Pan-Blue Alliance has enjoyed on average a 5–10 percentage point electoral advantage at the national level since 2000, and yet the DPP has won three of the six presidential elections since democratization. How is that possible? First of all, as past experience has shown, the Pan-Blue Alliance is notoriously susceptible to internal division. As was discussed in chapter 2, the KMT was severely divided in the 1996, 2000, and 2012 presidential elections. When a number of party members failed to secure the party nomination for the presidency, they ran as independents or became party switchers. Indeed, it was Pan-Blue candidates, Soong and Lien, who divided nearly 60 percent of the electoral support and thereby delivered the victory to the DPP-affiliated Chen in the 2000 presidential election, who won the election with only 39.3 percent of the votes. Even in the absence of Pan-Blue divisions, a properly engineered campaign strategy by the Pan-Green Alliance may secure a win, especially when economic prospects look weak under Pan-Blue control.

Furthermore, even if Taiwan voters' electoral behavior is largely determined by their partisan affiliations, the vision for the country that a candidate presents continues to play an important role in citizens' electoral calculus. As chapter 3 shows, the majority of the island citizens consider Taiwan an independent state separate from China, but they are risk-averse and pragmatic on cross-Strait relations. The majority of them are not willing to sacrifice their hard-won democratic way of life and economic prosperity for such radical political changes as declaring de jure independence or unification. Precisely because the island's future relation with China is the key political cleavage of the society, any presidential hopeful will need to present a realistic and workable vision to the electorate or suffer the consequence of losing the election.

The 2012 presidential election best illustrates this logic.[10] Indeed, observers generally believe that the loss of Tsai Ing-wen, the DPP nominee, in Taiwan's 2012 presidential election was related to her ambiguous stand on cross-Strait policy. Tsai's campaign strategy was to deemphasize cross-Strait issues, a strong suit for the KMT but a major DPP weakness, and to focus more on social issues such as economic growth and inequality. While Ma's policy had a proven record of engaging China and had been praised by Washington, Tsai's "Taiwan Consensus" was necessarily short on specifics due to the internal politics of the DPP. On the one hand, the DPP needed to court the backing of its core supporters, who were generally in favor of Taiwan's de jure independence from China. On the other hand, the DPP also needed to win the support of moderate partisan identifiers from both alliances who did not support unification but wanted to avoid inflammatory rhetoric and policies that could lead to cross-Strait tension. Tsai was thus trapped in the dilemma of needing to mobilize the party's core supporters by appealing to their political identity, while not alienating the more moderate centrists. The ambiguity and lack of specificity provided the KMT with ammunition for an attack. It also raised uncertainty about cross-Strait relations should she win the election, with a potential to destabilize Taiwan's uneasy but carefully managed relationship with the mainland. Ultimately, the election came down to a choice between "1992 Consensus/stability" vs. "Taiwan Consensus/potential instability," which was a manifestation of Taiwan's key political cleavage. The incumbent Ma was a vulnerable candidate with many weaknesses, but he managed to win a second term.

Interestingly, during the 2016 presidential election held on the island, the cross-Strait relationship appeared to be a mute issue. If the China factor heats up Taiwan's dominant political cleavage, as we have argued, why were there no sparks thrown off during the campaign? In our view, this is due to a divided KMT and a moderate stance adopted by the DPP presidential nominee, Tsai Ing-wen. As we noted earlier, the Pan-Blue Alliance is notoriously susceptible to internal division. The 2016 election was no exception. Immediately after Hung Hsiu-chu became the party's presidential nominee, many KMT elites and local leaders contemplated replacing her with someone else (Peng and Chin 2015). They eventually succeeded, making Eric Chu the KMT nominee. James Soong, formerly of the KMT, also ran as the candidate of the PFP. Meanwhile, realizing that cross-Strait policy is her Achilles' heel, Tsai moderated her stance by claiming that she would maintain the cross-Strait status quo if elected. Although Tsai's vague China policy presented the KMT with an opportunity for attack, as it did in the 2012 election, the divided KMT could not launch an effective offensive against Tsai's stance on cross-Strait relations (Lowther 2015). The unpopularity of the Ma administration and the relatively stagnant economy probably also helped Tsai. In the end, she won easily. Thus the China factor may have played a less explicit role in the 2016 campaign than in past years. But does that mean that the traditional Taiwan political cleavage will be any less influential in voters' decisions or in the near term?

As the old Danish proverb has it (sometimes attributed to the Danish physicist Niels Bohr or to the American baseball player Yogi Berra), "Prediction is very difficult, especially about the future." We know no reliable fortune teller who could tell us how Taiwan's politics and international status will evolve. For the medium term, however, we see no prospect that a de facto independent Taiwan will develop another cleavage to replace the powerful role of "the China factor." China is too near, too antagonistic, and too strong. Each of the two parties may trim, modify, and deemphasize, but inevitably one will represent faster progress toward independence and the other will want to go slow, engage with China, and avoid irreversible declarations that would likely lead to war. Those differences, tied to deep social cleavages, will not evaporate any time soon.

Chinese-American relations may have much to do with the outcome that prevails. Taiwan is a small country, and its fate is not entirely in its hands. But so long as it persists as a democracy, it can talk about the future it wants for itself, and it can use elections to put alternate teams in place, teams that differ on the right national identity for the island country. As we have shown in this book, that is what politics in Taiwan is fundamentally about.

There are many lessons to be taken from the study of Taiwan, and we conclude with just one that seems to us the most important. Taiwan illustrates in great detail the power of identity in politics. In every country that we know, the choice of partisanship is not primarily about issues; it is about identity. Election campaigns are not centrally about proper positioning in some ideological space; they are primarily about mobilizing identity groups. Candidate personalities and the state of the economy matter at the margin, but the major effects shaping democratic elections are determined well in advance by the balance of partisanship in the electorate. And that balance is determined by the complex, interconnected histories of the relevant identity groups and their resulting affinities and antagonisms.

Yet there is dispute about these claims among scholars. Some believe that an understanding of politics has to begin from preferences, and that preferences are about self-interest, often material self-interest and social class. Indeed, in most countries, it can be hard to tell the difference between self-interest and identity explanations in the welter of competing identities and interests. But Taiwan is a place where one can see those forces in undiluted form and without the multiple cleavages and countervailing effects present in larger countries. Because identity effects are not being obscured in the cross-section by equally large and opposite identity effects, as they often are elsewhere, Taiwan lets us see just how strong those identity effects are. And the answer from Taiwan is: very strong indeed. Just as the Galapagos Islands showed Darwin how evolution worked everywhere, but in a clear and indisputable way, so also the island of Taiwan demonstrates in a clear and indisputable way that identities are where to start in thinking about electoral politics.

In turn, that suggests that the first questions to ask about another country's party system are not: What are the main political issues? Or: How are the parties positioned from left to right? Both questions may matter for governmental policy but have little resonance in the public mind. For the average citizen, perceptions of issues and ideologies are primarily derivative rather than causal, as this book has repeatedly shown and as other scholars have demonstrated for other countries (Campbell et al. 1960, chaps. 6, 7; Lenz 2012; Achen and Bartels 2016, chaps. 9, 10).

Thus an implication of this book is that the key questions for understanding voting are not issues and party positions, as so many comparative studies assume. Instead, scholars should ask: What are the principal identity groups? And how are they connected to the political parties? Those are questions that need to be posed everywhere. But we hope that we have convinced the reader that nowhere is their value and power more obvious scientifically than in Taiwan. For that reason, the study of Taiwan, valuable for its own sake, is even more valuable for what it has to teach us about how elections should be understood around the world.

Notes

1. Citizens of Britain and the United States may recall a similar dispute from the 1770s.

2. In Taiwan's TEDS survey, party identification is measured in the usual international manner, as "leaning to" a political party. That language is quite different from the original American survey item, and it also differs from the wordings in use in some other democracies. Question wording matters substantially where party identification is concerned (for example, Sinnott 1998), and a better understanding of what wording is best for Taiwan now that the party system has consolidated is an important topic for future research. For our purposes, however, it makes no difference whether Taiwan's partisanship is a meaningful psychological identity or simply a habituated behavioral partisanship. The point is that, either way, it organizes attitudes and votes.

3. Throughout this chapter, partisanship is coded on a seven-point scale, ranging from "very strongly" lean to the DPP to "very strongly" lean to the KMT. The middle category represents those who do not lean to either party.

4. The opinion items and the prospective and retrospective economic evaluations all have three response categories, and they are coded 0, .5, and 1, with upper values indicating more pan-Blue/proincumbent attitudes. Age is coded so that age 20 = 0 and age 100 = 1. Percentage disposable income changes are divided by 20, so that they range approximately from -.5 to +.5. All other explanatory factors are dummy variables coded either 0 or 1. We have not included candidate traits because the list of such factors is very long, and because chapter 8 demonstrated that such evaluations are driven primarily by partisanship. We also excluded left-right orientation because, as chapter 9 showed, that variable is meaningless in Taiwan, and thus the variable was dropped from the 2012 TEDS presidential study. Previous work on the 2008 presidential election showed that left-right positions had only a small, statistically insignificant effect on the vote (Hsiao and Lin, 2013).

5. We found repeatedly that the survey weights made no meaningful difference, and so we have chosen to present unweighted results throughout this chapter.

6. The county-level disposable income figures are quite variable from one year to

the next, especially for the smaller counties, which are difficult to survey adequately in every country. Thus the available measures may represent actual disposable income changes with substantial error. In addition, there have been too few presidential elections to run regressions with national-level data. Our provisional conclusion in this book is that retrospective economic voting is not very consequential in Taiwan, but the topic cries out for additional research.

7. We also tested the coefficients for Chinese identity and no identity to see whether they were jointly significant. However, the Wald test in each of the four columns of table 12.1 was very far from statistical significance, meaning that deleting both variables was justified.

8. The "1992 Consensus" maintains that the notion of "one China" should serve as the basis for cross-Strait interactions. However, the two governments had different interpretations of what "one China" was. This is the tacit understanding presumably reached by Beijing and Taipei in November 1992. See Su and Cheng (2002).

9. The "Sunflower Movement" was a protest against a proposed cross-Strait trade-in-service agreement. It lasted more than 20 days between March 18 and April 10, 2014, during which time student demonstrators occupied the Legislative Yuan and damaged the main government buildings of the Executive Yuan. The movement reflects the public's concern about Taiwan's increasingly close economic ties with China. It also led to a massive demonstration against the Ma administration's cross-Strait policies in front of the presidential office on March 30 (J. R. 2014).

10. For further discussion of the 2012 presidential election, see Romberg (2011) and Paal (2012).

References

Achen, Christopher H., and Larry M. Bartels. 2016. *Democracy for Realists*. Princeton: Princeton University Press.

Anderson, Christopher J. 2007. "The End of Economic Voting? Contingency Dilemmas and the Limits of Democratic Accountability." *Annual Review of Political Science* 10: 271–96.

Bartels, Larry M. 2002. "Beyond the Running Tally: Partisan Bias in Political Perceptions." *Political Behavior* 24 (2): 117–50.

Berglund, Frode, Soren Holmberg, Hermann Schmitt, and Jacques Thomassen. 2005. "Party Identification and Party Choice." In *The European Voter*, ed. Jacques Thomassen, 106–24. Oxford: Oxford University Press.

Campbell, Angus, Philip E. Converse, Warren E. Miller, and Donald E. Stokes. 1960. *The American Voter*. New York: John Wiley and Sons.

Evans, Geoffrey, and Nan Dirk De Graaf, eds. 2013. *Political Choice Matters*. Oxford: Oxford University Press.

Gelineau, Francois, and Matthew M. Singer. 2015. "The Economy and Incumbent Support in Latin America." In *The Latin American Voter*, ed. Ryan E. Carlin, Matthew M. Singer, and Elizabeth J. Zechmeister, 281–99. Ann Arbor: University of Michigan Press.

Hsiao, Yi-ching, and Tsong-Jyi Lin. 2013. "Exploration of Political Polarization in Taiwan: Measurement and Analysis" (in Chinese). In Chi Huang, ed. *Methodology of Taiwan's Election and Democratization Study (TEDS): Retrospection and Prospection.* Taipei: Wu-nan.

J. R. 2014. "Politics in Taiwan: Sunflower Sutra." *Economist*, April 8. http://www.economist.com/blogs/banyan/2014/04/politics-taiwan. Accessed January 20, 2015.

Lenz, Gabriel S. 2012. *Follow the Leader? How Voters Respond to Politicians' Policies and Performance.* Chicago: University of Chicago Press.

Lewis-Beck, Michael. 1988. *Economics and Elections.* Ann Arbor: University of Michigan Press.

Lipset, Seymour M., and Stein Rokkan. 1967. "Cleavage Structure, Party Systems, and Voter Alignments: An Introduction." In *Party Systems and Voter Alignments: Cross-National Perspectives*, ed. Seymour M. Lipset and Stein Rokkan, 1–64. New York: Free Press.

Lowther, William. 2015. "Tsai Vows 'Consistent' Cross-Strait Ties." *Taipei Times*, June 5. http://www.taipeitimes.com/News/front/archives/2015/06/05/2003619951. Accessed October 10, 2015.

Lupu, Noam. 2015. "Partisanship in Latin America." In *The Latin American Voter*, ed. Ryan Carlin, Matthew M. Singer, and Elizabeth J. Zechmeister, 226–45. Ann Arbor: University of Michigan Press.

Paal, Douglas. 2012. "Taiwan Election Has the United States and China on Edge." Carnegie Endowment for International Peace, January 11. carnegieendowment.org/publications/index.cfm?fa=view&id=46441. Accessed October 10, 2015.

Paldam, Martin. 1991. "How Robust Is the Vote Function?" In *Economics and Politics*, ed. Helmut Norpoth, Michael S. Lewis-Beck, and Jean-Dominique Lafay, 9–31. Ann Arbor: University of Michigan Press.

Peng, Hsien-chun, and Jonathan Chin. 2015. "KMT Politician Demands Review of Hung's Selection." *Taipei Times*, October 4. http://www.taipeitimes.com/News/front/archives/2015/10/04/2003629216. Accessed January 12, 2012.

Powell, G. Bingham, Jr., and Guy Whitten. 1993. "A Cross-National Analysis of Economic Voting: Taking Account of the Political Context." *American Journal of Political Science* 37: 391–414.

Romberg, Alan D. 2011. "The 2012 Taiwan Election: Off and Running." *China Leadership Monitor*, no. 35 (Summer). http://media.hoover.org/sites/default/files/documents/CLM35AR.pdf. Accessed December 31, 2011.

Su, Chi and Cheng An-guo (eds.). 2002. Yige Zhongguo, gezi biaoshu' gongshi de shishi (One China, Different Interpretations: An Account of the Consensus). Taipei: Guojia zhengce yanjiu jijinhui.

Sinnott, Richard. 1998. "Party Attachment in Europe: Methodological Critique and Substantive Implications." *British Journal of Political Science* 28 (4): 627–50.

Van der Eijk, Cees, Hermann Schmitt, and Tanja Binder. 2005. "Left-Right Orientations and Party Choice." In *The European Voter*, ed. Jacques Thomassen, 167–91. Oxford: Oxford University Press.

Wu, Yu-Shan. 2014. "Paradigm Shift in Taiwan's Politics: From Identity to Distribution." Presented at the Conference on Democratic Governance, Cross-Strait Security and Prosperity, Taiwan and Asia Program, College of William and Mary, October 13.

Yen, Wei-ting, Kristine Kay and Fang-Yu Chen. 2015. "Unpacking Support for Free Trade: Experimental Evidence from Taiwan." Paper presented at the 2015 Midwest Political Science annual meeting, Chicago, April 16-19, 2015.

Zechmeister, Elizabeth J. 2015. "Left-Right Identifications and the Latin American Voter." In *The Latin American Voter*, ed. Ryan Carlin, Matthew M. Singer, and Elizabeth J. Zechmeister, 195–225. Ann Arbor: University of Michigan Press.

Contributors

Christopher H. Achen is a professor in the Politics Department at Princeton University, where he holds the Roger Williams Straus Chair of Social Sciences. His primary research interests are public opinion, elections, and the realities of democratic politics, along with the statistical challenges that arise from those fields. He is the author or coauthor of five books, including *Democracy for Realists* (with Larry Bartels), published by Princeton University Press in 2016. He has also published many articles. He has been a member of the American Academy of Arts and Sciences since 1995, and has received fellowships from the Center for Advanced Study in the Behavioral Sciences, the National Science Foundation, and Princeton's Center for the Study of Democratic Politics. He was the founding president of the Political Methodology Society, and he received the first career achievement award from the Political Methodology Section of the American Political Science Association in 2007. He has served on the top social science board at the National Science Foundation, and he was the chair of the national Council for the Inter-University Consortium for Political and Social Research (ICPSR) from 2013 to 2015. He is also the recipient of awards from the University of Michigan for lifetime achievement in training graduate students and from Princeton University for graduate student mentoring.

Lu-huei Chen is Distinguished Research Fellow at the Election Study Center and is a Professor in the Political Science Department, National Chengchi University in Taiwan. He holds a PhD degree from Michigan State University. His research focuses on Taiwanese political behavior, political socialization, research methods, and cross-Strait relations. He has published articles in such scholarly journals as *Issues and Studies*, the *Journal of Electoral Studies* (in Chinese), *Social Science Quarterly*, and *Taiwan Political Science Review* (in Chinese). His edited volumes include books on the 2012 presidential election in Taiwan (in Chinese) and public opinion (in Chinese).

Su-feng Cheng is a Research Fellow at the Election Study Center, National Chengchi University, in Taiwan. Her research interests include voting behavior, public opinion, and survey methods. She has published articles in many journals, including *Electoral Studies, Issues and Studies, Journal of East Asian Studies, Journal of Electoral Studies, Taiwanese Political Science Review*, and *Taiwan Democracy Quarterly*. Her edited volumes include books on electoral studies and survey methodology.

Karl Ho is Clinical Associate Professor of Public Policy, Political Economy, and Political Science and Director of Academic Computing at the School of Economic, Political and Policy Sciences, University of Texas at Dallas. His research focuses on political behavior in new democracies and state behaviors in response to challenges to democratic development. He is also interested in public policy and the political economy of Taiwan, Hong Kong, and China. His recent research examines civic engagement, political attitudes, and electoral behavior in Taiwan and Hong Kong. He has published on elections in East Asia, global women's rights, and political research and technological advances. He serves as the co-investigator of the Hong Kong Election Study and a member of the *Electoral Studies* editorial board. His works have appeared in *Electoral Studies, Human Rights Quarterly, Journal of African and Asian Studies*, and the *Journal of Information Technology and Politics*.

Yi-ching Hsiao is an Associate Professor in the Department of Public Administration at Tamkang University, Taipei, Taiwan. He received his PhD in political science from National Chengchi University in 2009. He is interested in voting behavior, electoral systems, public opinion surveys, and congressional politics. His articles have appeared in such journals as the *Asian Journal for Public Opinion Research, Election Studies* (Korea), *Issues & Studies: A Journal of Asian Pacific Studies* (in Japanese), and the following journals in Chinese: *Taiwanese Political Science Review, Journal of Electoral Studies, Taiwan Democracy Quarterly, Political Science Review, Soochow Journal of Political Science*, and *Chinese Political Science Review*.

Chi Huang is a University Chair Professor of Political Science and Research Fellow of the Election Study Center at National Chengchi University, Taiwan. His research interests focus on survey research, quantitative methodology, electoral systems, and voting behavior. He has coauthored or coedited seven books and published many articles in leading international and Taiwanese journals, including the *American Political Science Review, American Journal of Political Science, Journal of Politics, Comparative Political Studies*,

Electoral Studies, Party Politics, Political Research Quarterly, Japanese Journal of Electoral Studies, Issues & Studies, and *Taiwanese Political Science Review.* He served as president of the Taiwanese Political Science Association (2003–05), founded Taiwan's Election and Democratization Study (TEDS) inter-university survey project in 2000 and has been the Coordinator since its inception.

Hsiao-chuan (Mandy) Liao is an Assistant Professor in the Department of Political Science at National Taiwan University, Taiwan. She received her PhD in the Department of Political Science from University of South Carolina. Her current teaching field is international relations and China's external relations in particular. Her research interests include international conflict, international relations theory, foreign policy and decision making, and Northeast Asian studies. Her research has appeared in such refereed journals as *Asian Politics and Policy, Taiwan Political Science Review,* and the *Journal of International and Public Affairs.*

Tzu-Ping Liu is a PhD student in the Department of Political Science, the University of California at Davis. His articles have been published in the *Japanese Journal of Political Science, Journal of Electoral Studies,* and *East Asia.*

Shing-Yuan Sheng is a professor in the Department of Political Science at National Chengchi University, Taiwan. She also serves as a member of the Planning Committee of the Taiwan's Election and Democratization Study (TEDS). Her research interests include legislatures and legislative behavior, election and voting behavior, as well as party and democracy. Her current research includes "Party Institutionalization of the Legislative Yuan" and "How the Taiwan Public Perceives Party in Legislature." Her scholarly work has appeared in the *Taiwanese Political Science Review, Soochow Journal of Political Science,* and the *Journal of Electoral Studies.* She holds degrees from National Chengchi University (BA and MA) and the University of Michigan (PhD).

Alexander C. Tan is Professor of Political Science at the University of Canterbury in Christchurch, New Zealand, and University Chair Professor of Political Science at National Chengchi University in Taipei, Taiwan. He has published works in the areas of East Asian politics, comparative political economy, and political parties, and his articles have appeared in such journals as the *Journal of Politics, Political Research Quarterly, Comparative Political Studies, Comparative Politics, European Journal of Political Research, Elec-*

toral Studies, Party Politics, and the *Journal of Asian Security and International Affairs*. His most recent books include a coedited volume, *Mixed-Member Electoral Systems in Constitutional Context: Taiwan, Japan, and Beyond* (University of Michigan Press, 2016), and a coauthored book, *Taiwan's Political Economy: Meeting Challenges, Pursuing Progress* (Lynne Rienner, 2012).

Chia-hung Tsai is Director and Research Fellow at the Election Study Center, National Chengchi University, Taiwan, and holds a joint appointment with the Graduate Institute of East Asian Studies. Tsai received his PhD. from the Ohio State University in 2003. His fields of specialization include public opinion, methodology, and comparative politics. He was a visiting scholar at the Department of Political Science, MIT. He has published research in such journals as *Party Politics, International Political Science Review, Journal of Asian and African Studies*, and *PLOS ONE*.

Hung-chung Wang is a research fellow of the Taiwan Foundation for Democracy (TFD). He had served as associate managing editor of the *Taiwan Journal of Democracy* and the *Taiwan Democracy Quarterly*. Wang received his PhD from the Department of Political Science at the University of New Orleans in 2010 and was a postdoctoral researcher at the Election Study Center (ESC), National Chengchi University, from 2011 to 2013. His primary research interests include political behavior, public opinion, legislative behavior, local politics, and American politics. Wang has published articles in *Issues & Studies, Taiwan Democracy Quarterly, Journal of Electoral Studies*, and the *Taiwanese Political Science Review*.

T. Y. Wang is Professor of Politics and Government at Illinois State University and currently serves as the coeditor of the *Journal of Asian and African Studies*. He was the Coordinator of the Conference Group of Taiwan Studies (CGOTS) of the American Political Science Association. His primary research interests are national identity, East Asian politics, electoral behavior, U.S. policy toward China and Taiwan, and research methodology. He has authored/coauthored and edited/coedited seven books and special issues of journals and published more than 40 articles/book chapters in such scholarly journals as the *American Political Science Review, Asian Survey, International Studies Quarterly, Issues and Studies, Journal of Peace Research, Political Research Quarterly*, and *Social Science Quarterly*.

Chung-li Wu, PhD in Political Science, University of New Orleans (1997), is Research Fellow of the Institute of Political Science at Academia Sinica in Taipei, Taiwan. His research interests are American politics (political institutions), comparative politics, urban and minority politics, comparative politics, and electoral studies. He is the author of articles published in *Party Politics, China Quarterly, Parliamentary Affairs, Journal of Black Studies, Asian Survey, International Relations of the Asia-Pacific, Japanese Journal of Political Science,* and several others. Among the academic awards he has received are Outstanding Researcher Award (Ministry of Science and Technology and National Science Council) in 2016 and 2009, the Investigator Award (Academia Sinica) in 2014, Outstanding Research Award (College of Social Sciences, National Chung Cheng University) in 2005, Outstanding Research Award (National Chung Cheng University) in 2003, and Young Scholar Award (National Chung Cheng University) in 2002.

Ching-hsin Yu is a Research Fellow at the Election Study Center at National Chengchi University, Taiwan. He earned a PhD in political science from Pennsylvania State University and specializes in election and party competition in Taiwan. He has served on the editorial board and as a reviewer for academic journals. He has also published widely in refereed journals on such topics as identity, political knowledge, political accountability, and party system change. He is currently studying the development of the new party system in Taiwan.

Index

Page numbers in italics indicate tables and figures.

power of identity in, 289

relationship with candidate evaluation, 174, 188–89, *189*, *190*, 191–92

relationship with partisanship, 88–90, *89*, *90*

See also economic voting; *specific issues*

voter identity, 45–70, 273–290

Chinese/Taiwanese consciousness boundary, 51–58, *53*, *55*, *57*, 64–65

comparative strength of factors influencing vote choice, 278–82, *280*, *282*, 289n4

complexity of, 273–74

economic voting and, 277–78

ethnicity boundary, 48–51, *50*, 64

evolution from ethnic to national, 274–75

implications for future elections, 285–89

importance in electoral decision-making, 2

national identity boundary, 58–62, *60*, *61*, 65

overlap of national identity and partisan identification, 275–77, *276*

overview, 45–46

role of ECFA attitudes in central cleavage, 282–85

theoretical frameworks, 46–48, 64

unification/independence issue effects on, 62–64, *63*, 65

See also ethnic identity; national identity

voter level changes, postreform, 243–45

voter turnout

explanations of, 257–59, *259–63*

historical trends in, 255–57, *257*

importance to democracy, 252–53

misreporting of, 257, 270nn6–7

relationship with partisanship, 87, *88*, *89*

Wattenberg, Martin, 172, 246n1

wealth distribution

evolution of issue, 100, 101, 106–11, *109*, 129–130, 282–85, *284*

importance in electoral decision-making, 17

questionnaire wording and results, 130, *132*

status as most important problem facing Taiwan, *124*, *125*, 126

wealth inequality

economic development effects, 155n1

increase in, 107, 110–11, 129, 282–85, *284*

unequal political participation and, 265–66

Western democracies, left-right political spectrum, 198, 199–201, 215

Whitten, Guy, 278

Wilson, J. Matthew, 141

Wong Chung-chun, 134n9

Wu, Chin-en, 142, 146

Wu, Yu-Shan, 284

xin-Taiwanren (new Taiwanese), 50, 52

xin-xing-min-zu (rising new nation), 50

Yough, Syng Nam, 198

You Xi-Kun, 235

Zaller, John, 152

Zechmeister, Elizabeth, 3, 200–201

Zhang Xue-shun, 246n7

zheng-ming-yung-dong (Rectification Movement), 52